TOKENS OF AFFECTION

Southern Voices from the Past

Women's Letters, Diaries, and Writings

Carol Bleser, General Editor

This series makes available to scholars, students, and general readers collections of letters, diaries, and other writings by women in the southern United States from the colonial era into the twentieth century. Documenting the experiences of women from across the region's economic, cultural, and ethnic spectrums, the writings enrich our understanding of such aspects of daily life as courtship and marriage, domestic life and motherhood, social events and travels, and religion and education.

TOKENS OF AFFECTION

The Letters of a Planter's Daughter in the Old South

EDITED BY CAROL BLESER

The University of Georgia Press
Athens and London

© 1996 by the University of Georgia Press

Athens, Georgia 30602

All rights reserved

Designed by Sandra Strother Hudson

Set in 11 on 14 Fournier

by Tseng Information Systems, Inc.

Printed and bound by Maple-Vail

The paper in this book meets the guidelines

for permanence and durability of the Committee on

Production Guidelines for Book Longevity

of the Council on Library Resources.

Printed in the United States of America

00   99   98   97   96   C   5   4   3   2   1

Library of Congress Cataloging in Publication Data

Tokens of affection : the letters of a planter's daughter

in the Old South / edited by Carol Bleser.

p.   cm. — (Southern voices from the past)

Includes bibliographical references and index.

ISBN 0-8203-1727-6

1. Plantation life — Georgia — History — 19th century.

2. Georgia — Social life and customs.   3. Georgia —

History — 1775–1865.   4. Bryan, Maria —

Correspondence.   5. Cumming, Julia Bryan, d. 1879

— Correspondence.   I. Bleser, Carol K. Rothrock.

II. Series.

F290.T65   1996

975.8'03'092 — dc20   94-40961

British Library Cataloging in Publication Data available

To Caroline Johnson Rothrock

her book

CONTENTS

PREFACE

John Shaw Billings II was a gifted journalist who became the first managing editor of *Life* magazine in 1936 and the second in command of Henry Luce's Time-Life-Fortune empire in the 1950s. He was a big, heavyset man in his mid-fifties with cool blue eyes and sandy colored hair who ran Luce's magazine publications with icy detachment, efficiency, and tough-minded precision. At corporate headquarters in Rockefeller Center, he selected the issues to be highlighted in the Luce journals. He made the final decisions as well on all copy, photographs, and text. The headline news of the early 1950s included the Korean War; the Kefauver Commission; Whittaker Chambers; the Eisenhower presidential campaign, including Richard Nixon's Checkers speech; the death of Stalin; Senator Joseph McCarthy; and the French war in Indochina, in addition to the usual stories on entertainment, murder, and disasters. Yet, through all the late-breaking news, Billings secluded himself, night after night, in the study of his Fifth Avenue penthouse apartment reading the beautifully written letters of Maria Bryan. On one occasion, he recorded in his private diary that he had been at work at his office on stories of Harry Truman and Chiang Kai-shek but had looked forward to getting home to read Maria Bryan's letters, "which were so much more interesting."[1]

Billings presumably fell under the spell of the exquisite Maria Bryan sometime after 1935, when he came into possession of his family's plantation home, Redcliffe, at Beech Island, South Carolina, where he had been born in 1898. Redcliffe had been built in the 1850s by James Henry Hammond, a pre–Civil War governor, a United States senator, and one of the richest planters in the

---

1. John Shaw Billings diary, March 13, 1953, John Shaw Billings Diaries, 1910–1972. South Caroliniana Library, University of South Carolina, Columbia, S.C.

antebellum South. Billings, although named for his distinguished paternal grandfather from New York City, took great pride in his mother's southern heritage. John Billings, having been drawn to Redcliffe again and again over the years, recorded in his diary on March 21, 1935, how happy and excited he was at "having that wonderful old place" for his own. He was "about to become a Southern landowner in the grand sense." Immediately, he and his wife, in the midst of the worst economic depression in American history, set about spending money to restore Redcliffe until the formerly dilapidated South Carolina plantation home looked "like a great white frosted wedding cake or a spectacular movie set." [2]

With the house had come several hundred acres of land, all that remained of the more than fourteen-thousand-acre estate owned by great-grandfather Hammond. Stored in the attic of the house among the jumble of old clothes and broken furniture were cartons of family correspondence, including the letters written by Maria Bryan to her sister Julia Bryan Cumming of Augusta, Georgia. Julia, Billings's great-grandmother, saved many of her sister's letters, and after Maria's unexpected death at the age of thirty-six in January 1844, she put them away in neat bundles, sentimental tokens of affection of her sister's brief life. Julia also, in memory of her sister, named her eighth and final child, born just weeks after Maria's death, Maria Bryan Cumming. When Julia Cumming died in 1879, her daughter Emily Cumming Hammond, the daughter-in-law of James Henry Hammond, came into possession of many of her mother's personal belongings, including her mother's private correspondence. Emily transferred Maria's letters, along with other Cumming possessions, to her home at Redcliffe, where they were stored in the attic and forgotten.

Years later, Billings found them along with a voluminous collection of old family correspondence spanning nearly two centuries of letter writing. After the restoration of Redcliffe, Billings began the systematic reading of these family letters, carrying boxes of them with him back to New York. He noted in his diary that "they were like a narcotic." In reading them he was "transported . . . into the past." [3] The letters he apparently found most addictive were those of his great-great-aunt Maria Bryan. He paid a secretary to type many

2. Billings diary, April 28, 1938.
3. Billings diary, December 2, 1947.

of them out and then spent endless hours at night and on weekends seeking to understand the complex network of family and friends she described. He wrote of Maria's life, "[I] was crazy to know more." [4] Even on the landmark date in his life, April 14, 1953, when Henry Luce made John Shaw Billings editor in chief of all Time-Life-Fortune publications, Billings hurried home from the office and immersed himself in Maria's letters.

Why had John Shaw Billings become so fixated on the letters of a woman who had died more than a century before? On one level, Billings, as one of the most noted journalists of his age, recognized in Maria a good storyteller. Maria was a lively and humorous letter writer who had a special talent for writing interesting narrative prose. On a much more personal level, Billings had confessed often enough in his diary to being in a rut. A moody man, disenchanted with his career, and probably bored by his personal life, Billings became enchanted with the elusive, beautiful Maria. Her intelligent letters became, at one time in his life, his constant companions, yet he could never bring himself to publish them, even though at one time he stated he intended to do just that. [5]

Billings retired from Time, Inc., to Redcliffe in 1954, and for almost two decades he continued to collect and put together the history of four generations of his Hammond-Bryan-Cumming ancestors. That work was still incomplete when his health began to fail in the late 1960s. In 1973, he donated all his books and family papers to the University of South Carolina in Columbia. Redcliffe he deeded to the Palmetto State. When John Shaw Billings died in 1975, at the age of seventy-seven, he was buried in the cemetery at Redcliffe. The pleasure of editing and publishing Maria's remarkable letters has now been given to me.

Many Victorians exchanged painted miniatures as tokens of affection. [6] For as long as I can remember, I have been interested in the art of miniature

---

4. Billings diary, December 19 and 28, 1952. See also the entries of January 12 and 19, 1953; March 3, 7, 8, and 23, 1953; and April 12, 1953.

5. Billings diary, March 6, 1953.

6. Robin Bolton Smith and Dale T. Johnson, *Tokens of Affection: The Portrait Miniature in America* (Washington, D.C.: National Museum of American Art, 1990). This exhibit was coorganized by the Metropolitan Museum of Art and the National Museum of American Art,

portraiture. So far I own only two painted miniatures. One is of a handsome nineteenth-century South Carolina planter painted on ivory. The other depicts a late-eighteenth-century woman, delicate in looks, fashionably dressed, and also painted on ivory. Whenever I wear the portrait miniature of this unknown woman, which has been fashioned into a locket, people are drawn to her likeness and are curious to know who she is. Much as I am drawn to these painted miniatures, I am also drawn to the letters of Maria Bryan. Like the talented miniaturists, the tools and materials she used in her art were portable and small—a goose-quill pen and plain paper. The results, however, were quite extraordinary.

Maria Bryan successfully captured in her correspondence a vanished civilization in miniature exactness. For more than two decades, from the mid-1820s to the mid-1840s, Maria produced a picture of the life of a planter family of a middling sort residing on a plantation in Mt. Zion, Georgia, a small southern frontier community seventy-five miles from Augusta. In Maria's letters we encounter a woman of remarkable education and taste. She recounts to her married sister, Julia, who is living in Augusta, at that time the third largest city in Georgia, the myriad of details of life in rural Georgia.

Maria's letters are also a testament to the falseness of our standard portrait of the "typical" plantation daughter in the antebellum South. Although supported by the labor of her family's slaves and comfortable by virtue of her rank and privilege, Maria is not like Scarlett, the pampered pet of a southern patriarch. In her early letters to Julia, Maria discusses her life, which is much like that of the majority of planters' daughters: she keeps house, tends the sick at home and in the neighborhood, and cuts out and sews clothing for the family's slaves. She also tutors her younger siblings; grades papers for the teachers at the local academy; entertains a continuous procession of visiting ministers, teachers, relatives, and friends; regularly attends church and revivals; makes countless social calls to friends and acquaintances in nearby towns; and still finds time to devour copious novels, biographies, and autobiographies.

The private and personal lives of nineteenth-century southern women had

Smithsonian Institution, Washington, D.C. It appeared in 1990 at the Metropolitan Museum of Art, the National Museum of American Art, and the Art Institute of Chicago.

long been neglected as legitimate subjects of inquiry for historians. However, fortunately for us, Julia Bryan Cumming failed to comply with her sister Maria Bryan's repeated instructions to "burn [her] letters." These letters now provide an irresistibly rich opportunity to explore this developing field.

For instance, there is a historiographical return of interest as to whether southern white plantation women were eager supporters or vehement opponents of the institution of slavery. Maria's letters contain some fascinating references to individual slaves, household workers, the courtship of a black slave woman, slave marriages and families, and the death of some favorite servants. In only one letter, however, written when Maria was nineteen years old, did she reveal her feelings at that time on the institution of slavery. In January 1827, Maria wrote Julia that their overseer had punished Maria's personal slave, Jenny, because she had not done her full quota of spinning. "It would have distressed you to see her face bloody and swelled," she wrote Julia. "Oh how great an evil is slavery."

Of additional historical interest, Maria comes of age in the 1820s—before slavery and secession became inseparably entwined as the all-consuming issues in the South. This is an era when the nation is not yet on trial and the South is flourishing as the Cotton Kingdom. We have few firsthand published accounts, especially by women, of this period in southern history, the period that is the prelude to the Civil War. The winds of change that led to the great national tragedy began to be especially felt around the time of the annexation of Texas in January 1845, a year after Maria's death. Many of the characters in her letters were ultimately deeply affected by the cataclysm, as is summarized in the epilogue.

The memory of Maria's life, which could have been only a faded name on a moldy tombstone in the Mt. Zion cemetery, is preserved because of the fortunate retention of her letters, their substance, and Maria's storytelling ability. In a continuous flow of letters to her sister Julia, Maria unself-consciously describes the culture of the Old South, including her nineteenth-century views on slaves, romance, courtship, marriage, childbirth, family life, child rearing, friendship, religion, sickness and home remedies, death, books, fashion, travel, education, politics, and social events. In style and sensibility, Maria's letters remind me of the novels of Jane Austen, Edith Wharton, and Barbara Pym. However, Maria's fascinating story is true.

ACKNOWLEDGMENTS

Hancock County in middle Georgia was once the heart of the greatest cotton-growing region in the world. It is not hard today to find signs of the old cotton prosperity in Sparta, the county seat. The town boasts of several streets of fine Greek Revival antebellum houses and an elaborate Victorian gingerbread county courthouse crowned with a high clock tower. In 1825, the town of Sparta hosted a gala ball in honor of the Marquis de Lafayette during his triumphal tour of America.

Hancock County is now much poorer, and seven miles from Sparta the village of Mt. Zion, once prosperous and bustling, where Maria Bryan lived almost all of her life, has vanished almost without a trace. The houses, farm buildings, and even the famous Mt. Zion Academy are all gone; the Mt. Zion Presbyterian Church stands abandoned. On a visit to Mt. Zion in October 1992, I stared out across a vacant field that had once been the home place of the Bryan family. Only a huge tree, which Maria must have seen daily, remains. It stands next to an unpaved country road, probably the same dirt road that served the Bryans and their neighbors more than 150 years ago.

My greatest debt is to John Shaw Billings for preserving Maria Bryan's letters, which appear to be the sole source for documenting her life and much of plantation life in middle Georgia during the heyday of the Cotton Kingdom. Billings not only preserved Maria's letters to her sister Julia but also called special attention to their importance by plucking them out of a vast collection of family correspondence spanning almost two centuries. As noted in the preface, Billings had many of Maria's letters transcribed. It was an enormous help in preparing this book for publication to have available his copy.

It is my pleasure also to thank Allen Stokes, the director of the South Caro-

xvii

liniana Library of the University of South Carolina, for his continued interest and invaluable research assistance over the years, as well as for his enduring friendship. I should like to express appreciation also for the help given me by Laura Costello, Henry Fulmer, Charles Gay, Tom Johnson, and all the rest of the courteous staff of the South Caroliniana Library. I am deeply grateful to the library staffs of the University of Georgia, Augusta College, Augusta Public Library, Clemson University, the University of South Carolina, the Mary Willis Library (Washington, Georgia), the Milford (Connecticut) Library, and on Long Island, New York, the South Country (Bellport) Library and the Patchogue-Medford Library.

My gratitude goes especially to Doreen Heimlich and Robert Barrett, who have assisted me from beginning to end in shaping this manuscript for publication, always with good grace and good humor.

I owe a very special acknowledgment to Nancy and Hugh Connolly of Augusta, Georgia, whom I have known since 1981. Nancy Cumming Connolly, the great-great-great niece of Maria Bryan, has provided me with family information of inestimable value and family photographs that appear in this book.

Adele Logan Alexander, author of *Ambiguous Lives: Free Women of Color in Rural Georgia, 1789–1879,* published by the University of Arkansas Press, was most gracious in allowing me to adapt her map of nineteenth-century middle Georgia. Many of the places described by Maria appear on this map.

I am grateful for a sabbatical leave from Clemson University and especially for the continuing support of Mrs. Calhoun Lemon of Barnwell, South Carolina. My colleagues and friends at Clemson University have been an unfailing source of support and collegiality. I wish especially to thank President Max Lennon, Provost Charles Jennett, Vice President Gary Ransdell, Vice-Provost Jerome V. Reel Jr., Dean James Barker, and Professors N. Jane Hurt, Donald McKale, Charles Lippy, Donald Nieman, and Alan Schaffer.

My friends Catherine Clinton, Mollie Davis, Mary Giunta, Ann Knapp, Linda Nieman, Wylma Wates, and C. Vann Woodward deserve special thanks for their interest and encouragement of my work in women's and family history.

I am enormously indebted for the first-rate work of the entire staff of the University of Georgia Press. Most particularly, I would like to thank Malcolm

Call, director, and Madelaine Cooke, managing editor, for their commitment to fostering the progress of this manuscript in every way. Photographs are provided through the courtesy of the South Caroliniana Library and Nancy Cumming Connolly of Augusta, Georgia.

Lastly, I wish to thank members of my family. Eileen Powers Feeney has been a cheerful, supportive, and loving aunt throughout my life in ways I will appreciate and remember always. To my in-laws, who celebrate their eighty-seventh birthdays this year, I express my heartfelt thanks and wish them continued good health. To Elizabeth and Gerald I am profoundly grateful for their love and for their bringing Caroline into my life. Finally, and ever important, there is my husband, Edward, who will always be the central inspiration in my life.

Bellport, N.Y.
May 1995

EDITORIAL PRACTICES

One hundred and fifty years after Maria Bryan Harford Connell wrote her last letter to her sister Julia, her correspondence has been chronologically arranged, transcribed, annotated, and made ready for publication. The world-view of a young woman raised in a slaveholding family on the Georgia frontier in the early nineteenth century reflects both the place and the time. It is, of course, very different from that of the modern reader. Thus, to enable the reader to understand the past and its peoples, the editor has in all cases left the original language of these letters intact. It is hoped that the reader will rise above the occasional intolerant views of Maria and appreciate how, through her generosity of spirit, she usually transcends the common customs of her place and time.

Since none of Maria's letters I deemed repetitious, the collection, which consists of 167 letters, is published in its entirety. One hundred fifty-five of these letters were from Maria to Julia, ten of them were from other family members to Julia and enclosed by Maria in her letters to her sister, and two letters were from Maria to other members of the family. Many of these letters were originally transcribed under the direction of John Shaw Billings as noted in the acknowledgments. These transcriptions have been fully scanned and corrected by the editor against the original letters in the Hammond-Bryan-Cumming Family Papers on deposit at the South Caroliniana Library. The editor also transcribed those letters that were not included in the Billings work and deciphered almost every word written by Maria. Occasional quotations from the letters of Henry Cumming to his wife Julia are also from this same collection.

As editor, my two major objectives in the publication of Maria's letters were to maintain for the scholar the textual integrity of her correspondence and, just as important, to make the letters readily accessible to the general reader. To those ends, I have let Maria's letters and their occasionally irregular spellings of words, family names, and place-names stand much as they are. I have, however, in some instances, adjusted the punctuation to modern usage. I have also standardized the heading of each letter. In addition, paragraphing within the letters, chapter divisions, and chapter titles are of my own choosing. Ellipsis points are seldom necessary. In the interest of the general reader and of the scholar, both of whom can appreciate how closely knit and intelligible this family story is, I have used, instead of footnotes, editorial interventions within the letters to identify for the reader the people, places, and events mentioned by Maria; such interventions are enclosed in the text in brackets ([   ]). In some instances, however, no matter how hard I tried to find the answer to a matter or an event described by Maria, it remained a mystery.

In editing these letters I have also added headnotes for most of them to provide a tight, cohesive, unfolding narrative. It is hoped that they will advance the story and guide the reader in such a way as to be informative and yet not too intrusive or too revealing.

INTRODUCTION

Mt. Zion lay in Hancock County, seven miles northwest of Sparta, the county seat. When Maria Bryan's father migrated there in the mid-1790s, the county was newly opened virgin land. The county had been founded in 1793, coincident with the invention of the cotton gin, which promptly led to the rapid spread of cotton as the major crop throughout Hancock County, as throughout much of the South. The prospering cotton farmers were soon able to replace their simply built frontier cabins with comfortable large houses, and even some grand mansions. The small yeoman farmers were unable to compete with the newly wealthy, slave-based planters, resulting in a dramatic decrease in the white population of the county and an equally dramatic increase in the slave population. By 1820, Hancock County reportedly produced more cotton than any other county in Georgia. Mt. Zion was a small but affluent region, the home of numerous large plantations, several churches, and, most important, both a male and an adjunct female academy.

Joseph Bryan, the "Pa" of Maria's letters, had been attracted to Georgia as his personal land of opportunity. He had been born in Milford, Connecticut, on Long Island Sound between New Haven and Bridgeport in 1768, but left home (which probably still stands as the Thomas Buckingham house in Milford) at eighteen, when his mother, over his strong objections, remarried. He settled first in Savannah, but when Hancock County opened up, he moved to Mt. Zion, which was to be his home for the remainder of his long life.

Joseph married Anne Goode, originally of Virginia, in 1796. Together, Ma and Pa Bryan made a substantial living for their family, acquiring holdings amounting to approximately eighteen hundred acres and one hundred slaves. In the 1830s, Pa also sought to expand his holdings by seeking out new land in Alabama. Although he held many slaves, Bryan, a member of the American Colonization Society, was considered by some of his neighbors to have abolitionist leanings, as attested to in Maria's letters. The Bryans had eight children, of whom five reached maturity.

Joseph Bryan, the eldest son, was born in Mt. Zion in 1801 and appears in Maria's letters as "Brother." Julia Ann Bryan, the recipient of Maria's letters, was born in 1803 at home and was educated for a time in New Haven, Connecticut. She made an excellent match in her marriage in 1824 to wealthy Henry Harford Cumming of Augusta, Georgia. Maria Bryan, the writer of these letters, was born on New Year's Day in 1808. She received an excellent education, most likely at the Mt. Zion Academy, of which her father was a trustee. Her brother, George Goode Bryan, born in 1812, also attended Mt. Zion Academy before his appointment to West Point in 1829. Maria tutored at home her youngest sister, Sophia Bryan, born in Mt. Zion in 1815. These five children who had been born in the Georgia Piedmont came to know their Connecticut grandmother, Juliana Smith Bryan Buckingham, late in her life, after she had become a widow for the second time. Patching up her differences with her son Joseph, Mrs. Buckingham, at the age of seventy-five, left her New England home in Milford, Connecticut, and went to live with Joseph Bryan and his family in Mt. Zion. She lived with her son for almost two years until her death in 1818. When she died, three of her children were close by — Joseph, Isaac, and Julia.

Isaac Bryan, born in Milford in 1780, had followed his brother Joseph to the South and settled in Augusta. He remained a bachelor. Isaac Bryan appears frequently in Maria's letters as "Uncle," a miserly character who torments his brother Joseph, who owes him money. Maria's letters indicate that her father probably borrowed money from Isaac to buy land during the flush times of the early 1830s, and now Pa was haunted by debt following the serious financial depression of 1837. Julia Bryan Wales, born in Milford in 1776, was the "Aunt Wales" of Maria's letters. She was the second wife of Isaac Miles Wales of New Haven. By his first marriage, Wales had a son, Sam, and a daughter, Catherine. After Wales married Julia Bryan, they moved to Mt. Zion to be near her brother Joseph. Isaac Wales, in partnership with two others, began the publication of the *Missionary* in 1819, a weekly newspaper that campaigned tirelessly for temperance and the strict observance of the Sabbath, as well as resolutely opposing horse racing, the theater, and dancing. Wales died in 1825. His daughter Catherine, though no blood relative of the Bryans, was almost like a sister to Julia and Maria, her stepmother's nieces. Aunt Wales, when widowed, kept a boardinghouse in Mt. Zion and was a gossipy busybody according to Maria. Her namesake, Julia, seventy-five miles away, was more tolerant of her Aunt Wales. Catherine Wales, a year younger than Maria, figures prominently in Maria's correspondence. In 1838, at age twenty-nine, Catherine married Alexander Erwin. They moved to Clarkesville and had four children. Aunt Wales visited her stepdaughter and grandchildren off and on at Clarkesville, but at her death she was buried in the Mt. Zion cemetery near the Bryan family.

Nothing much is known of Maria's childhood, except that she grew up in a piously Presbyterian household, comfortably fixed and surrounded, in general, by people of education and taste. It is assumed that Maria attended Nathan Beman's Mt. Zion Academy, one of the most celebrated educational institutions in the early history of Georgia. Pa Bryan, descended from Alexander Bryan, an original settler in 1639 of Milford, Connecticut, carried a bit of his six generations of New England heritage with him when he arrived among the first settlers in Mt. Zion. Although Joseph Bryan never became one of the most prosperous planters in Georgia, it was he who persuaded Nathan Beman to come to Mt. Zion in 1812 to open the school and to become pastor of the newly organized Presbyterian Church. Originally, the academy accepted only male students, but within the year a department for young women was added. Nathan Beman and his younger brother Carlisle, graduates of Middlebury College in Vermont, made the school famous in the South. Nathan eventually declined, for personal reasons, the presidency of the University of Georgia and returned north to Troy, New York, becoming a leading abolitionist and president of Rensselaer Polytechnic Institute. Carlisle went on to become the first president of Oglethorpe University.

In this stimulating, intellectual environment, Maria most likely received an extraordinarily rich classical education, especially for a young woman growing up in a small Georgia town. At the age of sixteen, she was able to write graceful and apposite references to Newtonian astrophysics. Her letters are testimonials to the quality of the learning dispensed. Undoubtedly, her parents, especially her father, were, along with the Bemans, major forces in

Maria's intellectual development. In Maria's letters to Julia, her grammar is almost perfect, her spelling generally good, despite some phonetic variations. She was a rapid and retentive reader who continuously requested books and journals of opinion to sustain her mental appetite. For the most part, Maria had a fondness for romantic novels, but her range of interests was eclectic, including her reading of a multivolume biography of William Wilberforce, the leading English abolitionist of her day.

Maria's religious nature sometimes verged on fervor, but her faith also provided her upon occasion with an admirable equanimity, especially in times of trouble. She was not, however, above preaching pious resignation and "God's will" to others in trouble. Throughout the nineteenth century and on into the twentieth, religious institutions and religious activity more thoroughly shaped and dominated southern life than that of other regions in the United States. The very pervasiveness of southern religion differentiates the South even today from the rest of the nation. Maria Bryan's faith as reflected in her letters was that of an orthodox Presbyterian who did not doubt the state of her soul, and throughout her life she reaffirmed her theological ties with John Calvin, his emphasis upon God's sovereign power, stern justice, and saving grace. As a member of the Elect she regarded herself, noted John Shaw Billings, as "a footsore pilgrim . . . on her way to the eternal mansions of her heavenly Father." Sermons interested her, yet she was discriminating about the ministers who delivered them and commented critically on their various intellectual abilities. Although she was a Presbyterian, the daughter of one of the principal founders of the Mt. Zion Presbyterian Church, she seemed to retain a lifelong fascination with the Evangelical Baptists in her community. When Maria called someone a good Christian, she paid that person the highest compliment in her vocabulary. Similarly, she worried over those in her circle whose souls she knew were destined for Hell.

A woman of deep feelings, Maria at the beginning of her correspondence was the caretaker of an ailing mother and a cantankerous father, as well as nursemaid to her younger siblings. Her letters to Julia reveal some resentment that she was expected always to defer to the men in her life — her father, uncle, brothers, brother-in-law, suitors, and male friends who may or may not have been her equal, especially in the matters of the mind. In one letter to her sister, written after her second marriage, she wrote in exasperation of the plight of women in the plantation South who, like herself, sought to escape the narrow confines of their lives. "How much of a slave a woman finds herself when she comes to act out of her usual routine." Her affectionate admiration for her older sister Julia, however, was boundless, and in her letters to Julia she passed on as an echo of her own sentiments every compliment to Julia that she heard. Maria had a remarkably good sense of humor and was amused by the vagaries and absurdities of the human condition, which she also passed on to Julia in her letters.

An attractive dark-haired woman, Maria also had considerable social charm and conversational ability. She married twice but bore no children. Her child-lessness apparently did not disappoint Maria or either of her husbands, despite her contemporaries' belief that wives without children were incomplete, as has been noted by Mary Boykin Chesnut, the famous Civil War diarist. Maria wrote Julia on one occasion after seeing a pregnant friend that she regretted "that the happiness of the conjugal relation was obliged to be bought at so dear a price." The two men she married remain, in her letters to her sister, relatively dim, faceless characters. Her love for her first husband, William Harford, can best be determined by her impulsive actions, not her words. She married Harford in 1831, despite the strong opposition of her patriarchal father and her gentle but sickly mother, and she left her unforgiving family behind in Georgia, moving with her new husband to New Orleans. She remained in the Crescent City through several seasons of cholera and yellow fever, epidemics that she described to her sister in much detail but with much detachment, an observer on location at that exotic and deadly seaport. She did, however, worry aloud in her letters to Julia over her husband's health as he struggled as an engineer to help construct the Pontchartrain Canal. Maria suffered severe pangs of homesickness that lasted unabated until she returned, a widow, to Mt. Zion in 1836.

Presumably left quite well off at Harford's death, Maria, in the summer of 1839, set off on a five-month tour of the North, including a stay at the fashionable United States Hotel in Saratoga Springs, New York. In her letters to Julia, the thirty-one-year-old widow described at length her stay in Saratoga and bragged of meeting President Martin Van Buren, Secretary of State of John Forsyth, Henry Clay, Winfield Scott, "the Rutledges, Heywards, and Draytons of [South] Carolina, the Livingstons of New York and all the elite of the land." She recounted to Julia the budding romance of their brother Joseph, her traveling companion, and a southern belle whom they met at the resort. The flirtation ended abruptly when Brother was accused by a friend of the young woman's family of having overstepped the bounds of social propriety. They quickly parted. Although Maria had been dazzled by this small, privileged corner of the world, she returned home apparently even more convinced of the superiority of the southern way of life. After her return to Mt. Zion, the restless Maria at age thirty-three married a local doctor on April 11, 1841. Her father again objected to her marriage.

When Maria's letters begin, on March 7, 1824, she is just sixteen years old; two weeks before, her sister Julia had married Henry Harford Cumming. The bridegroom was the son of Ann Clay and Thomas Cumming of Augusta. By the time of Henry's birth in 1799, his father was Augusta's first mayor, following the city's incorporation in 1798. Thomas Cumming was a prosperous merchant and president of the Bank of Augusta from 1810 until his death in 1834, at the age of sixty-nine. Henry's two older brothers attended Princeton University, but since Henry's health had never been robust, his parents chose to send him on the cure-all Grand Tour of Europe. The nineteen-year-old became so infatuated with French culture and politics that he traveled mostly around France. He visited dutifully and more briefly in Italy and Switzerland. Soon after he returned to Augusta, he met Julia Bryan at a ball in 1822, and after almost two years of courtship, Henry and Julia were married at her Mt. Zion home. At the age of twenty-one, Julia left Mt. Zion to live near her new family in Augusta, where Henry would go on to become one of the ablest lawyers in Georgia.

In reading Maria's letters we can easily imagine the loneliness felt by the teenager at her sister's departure for Augusta and a new life. The emotional links between the Bryan and Cumming households were to be Maria's letters; the more practical bond was to be cemented by Uncle Jacob, a Cumming slave, mentioned frequently in Maria's letters, who regularly drove a wagon between Augusta and Mt. Zion, delivering both news and parcels. Augusta, too, as time went by brought bright lights and more social opportunities to the young Bryan women isolated in Mt. Zion. Maria and her younger sister, Sophia, found husbands while staying in Augusta with Julia and Henry, and Catherine Wales, Maria wrote, "did not care about returning to the humdrum sort of life" in Mt. Zion after "quaffing so largely of the sweets of fashionable life in Augusta." Henry appears in Maria's letters as "Brother Henry" and later as "Mr. Cumming." The relationship between sister-in-law and brother-in-law was sometimes strained. In Maria's first letter to Julia after her marriage, she confessed to wishing that Julia had remained single, so that they could have been "nice snug old maids living always together." Two months after her marriage to Henry, Julia returned to Mt. Zion on a three-week visit. Henry wrote longingly to his bride on April 27, 1824, that he missed her. "I am," he said, "now more completely *Julia sick* than you have ever been *homesick* in the whole course of your life." On the surface, Henry appeared kindly and affectionate toward Maria, but behind her back he wrote his wife that Maria played the role of a belle, was frivolous and vain, and seemed addicted to pursuing male attention.

Maria wrote on May 13, 1824, that Julia would "by degrees become far more attached to other objects, and estranged from *me*." Maria, of course, was right. Over time, Julia's visits home diminished. In the early years of her union, Julia spent the long summer months in Mt. Zion, and Henry came out from Augusta whenever he could. Julia also went home for most of her confinements until Ma Bryan's death in 1837. Her fifth child and second daughter, Emily Harford Cumming, born on November 16, 1834, and named for both her husband and her brother-in-law, was the last of Julia's children born in Mt. Zion. Her children's stays in Mt. Zion, however, became more frequent under the supervision of their Aunt Maria, who, though childless, seemingly was astute in the raising of her sister's children.

For almost twenty years, Maria filled her lively letters to Julia with the story of her life and the people who, with all their strengths and frailties, inhabited the world in which she lived. When Maria begins her first letter, on March 7, 1824, four Bryan brothers and sisters are still at home in Mt. Zion.

FAMILY MEMBERS AND OTHER PRINCIPALS

Hundreds of people, white and black, move across the pages of Maria's letters. Those who are still identifiable are usually cited when they make their first appearance in the correspondence. Printed here as a guide to the reader is a listing of the people—family, neighbors, friends, and household servants—who are most frequently mentioned and are most important to Maria's life.

Maria Bryan's Immediate Family

Joseph Bryan ("Pa") (1768–1861) married (1796)
Anne Goode ("Ma") (1775–1837)

Their children:

Joseph Jr. ("Brother")	(1801–63)
Julia Ann	(1803–79)
Maria Martha	(1808–44)
(George) Goode	(1812–85)
Sophia	(1815–84)

William Harford (1807–36), married Maria Bryan (1831)
　　No issue
Dr. Alva Connell, married Maria Bryan (1841)
　　No issue

Henry Harford Cumming (1799–1866), married Julia Ann Bryan (1824)

Children of Henry Harford and Julia Bryan Cumming:
　　Anne Maria (Hall)　　　　　　(1826–55)

Alfred	(1829–1910)
Julien	(1830–64)
Thomas William	(1831–89)
Emily Harford (Hammond)	(1834–1911)
Joseph Bryan	(1836–1922)
Harford Montgomery	(1838–72)
Maria Bryan (Lamar)	(1844–73)

Close Family Relatives

Juliana (Julia) Bryan (Wales) ("Aunt Wales") (1776–1846), sister of Joseph
Bryan ("Pa")

Isaac Bryan ("Uncle") (1780–1853), brother of Joseph Bryan ("Pa")

Anne Eliza Cumming (1805–83), Henry Harford Cumming's sister

Sarah Wallace Cumming (1807–95), Henry Harford Cumming's sister

Catherine Wales (Erwin) (1809–84), stepdaughter of Juliana Bryan Wales

Caroline Goode Holt (Iverson) (?–1830), niece of Anne Bryan ("Ma"), named
her daughter Julia Maria for the Bryan sisters. Julia Maria Iverson lived
with the Bryans and the Cummings for several years as a schoolgirl after
her mother's death. Alfred Iverson, Caroline's husband, a lawyer in Clinton, Georgia, after his wife's death became a United States senator from
Georgia and married Julia Forsyth, daughter of John Forsyth, secretary
of state during Andrew Jackson and Martin Van Buren's administration
(1834–40).

Friends and Neighbors

The Alston family was from Sparta, Georgia.

Jane Armour, of Savannah, Georgia, the second wife of Joseph Bryan Sr., was
thirty years his junior. Over the years Jane had been a visitor at Mt. Zion
and a friend of the family.

Margaret Bailey, of Mt. Zion, daughter of the widow Bailey and close friend
of Maria and Julia, married Dr. Cosmos P. Richardsone of Savannah, Georgia. She died of "brain fever" in 1838. In 1839, Dr. Richardsone married
Elizabeth Bailey, the twenty-four-year-old sister of his first wife, Margaret.

Carlisle P. Beman (1797–1875), younger brother of Nathan S. S. Beman, the well-known Presbyterian minister, educator, and abolitionist, ran the Mt. Zion Academy (established by his brother in 1812) after his brother Nathan's departure in 1823 for Troy, New York. In 1823 Carlisle Beman married Avis De Witt, and they had three sons and one daughter. Eventually, Carlisle became the first president of Oglethorpe University. He died at Mt. Zion in 1875 and was buried there beside his wife, who had died in 1863.

Dr. Brown was a longtime minister of the Mt. Zion Presbyterian Church.

Carrington, a local merchant in Mt. Zion, was considered by Maria to be mean and heartless to his debtors. He lost all his money and left his family destitute when he died in 1829.

Thomas Flournoy Foster (1790–1848), a lawyer from Greensboro, Georgia, served in the United States House of Representatives (1829–35 and 1841–43), was an admirer of Julia, and proposed marriage to Maria.

Mr. Little taught at Mt. Zion Academy and conducted a Sabbath School class at the Presbyterian Church. He was the father of three daughters, Eliza, Sarah, and Margaret. Margaret Little married Carlisle Martin, who took over Mt. Zion Academy upon Carlisle Beman's departure in 1835.

Dimas Ponce and his wife, Isabella, a Savannah couple, owned Pleasant Valley Plantation near Mt. Zion. Ponce, along with a number of Hancock County planters, formed the Hancock Planters Club, which sought to control soil erosion and promote progressive farming methods in the cotton belt.

Mrs. Richardson, who lived nearby, was the mother of a Mrs. Skinner, whose daughter, Jane, Maria described as a "prim stiff Yankee girl." Mrs. Richardson apparently disliked all the Bryans and did not attempt to conceal her feelings. However, her daughter, Lavinia Richardson, married Pulaski Holt, a nephew of "Ma" Bryan and brother of Caroline Goode Holt Iverson. Lavinia died from a miscarriage in 1836.

Deborah and Timothy Rossiter, an elderly couple, and probably childless, were close neighbors of the Bryans.

Satterlee was a Sparta friend of Maria's brother, Joseph. Nothing much is known of him. He turned up in Maria's letters from New Orleans where Maria's husband, Harford, provided him with a job on the canal construction. Much later, when he was dying of tuberculosis, Maria and her second husband, Dr. Alva Connell, took Satterlee into their home at Mt. Zion.

Nathan Sayre, a lawyer and a family friend, lived as a bachelor at his large house, "Pomegranate Hall," in Sparta. His secret family is discussed in Adele Logan Alexander's *Ambiguous Lives*.

William Terrell (1778–1855) was born in Virginia, studied medicine at the University of Pennsylvania, and opened a practice in Sparta, Georgia. He served two terms in Congress (1817–21). From Maria's letters we learn that he attended "Ma" Bryan, and that Maria visited frequently with Dr. Terrell and his wife, Eliza, at their home in Sparta.

Richard Henry Wilde (1789–1847), a poet, lawyer, and a congressman from Augusta, Georgia, was a close personal friend of the Bryans and Cummings. As a member of the United States House of Representatives (1815–17; 1825; 1827–35), Wilde secured in 1829 Goode Bryan's appointment to West Point.

Bryan and Cumming Household Slaves

Uncle Jacob (Cumming) operated a freight wagon between Augusta and Mt. Zion.

Patty (Bryan) was an excellent seamstress who also helped "Ma" Bryan around the house. She was the wife of the slave George (Bryan).

George (Bryan), husband of Patty (Bryan), appears in Maria's letters as a drunk. Patty and George lost two of their children within four months, in November 1829 and March 1830. Patty died in 1837, the same year as "Ma" Bryan.

Henny (Bryan) was the wife of Uncle Ned (Bryan). Their children included: Jenny (Bryan), Maria's personal maid; Rachel and Cynthia (Cumming). Henny and her daughter Jenny accompanied Maria to New Orleans. Maria's husband, Harford, disliked Henny.

Creasy, the Bryan cook at Mt. Zion.

Celia, Julia Cumming's nurse, the "Mammy" to whom the Cumming children sent fond greetings when they sent letters to Augusta from Mt. Zion.

Daphne, a Bryan house servant on loan to the Cummings.

Tom, the Bryan butler.

Robert, the Bryan houseman, gardener, and companion to Goode Bryan.

TOKENS OF AFFECTION

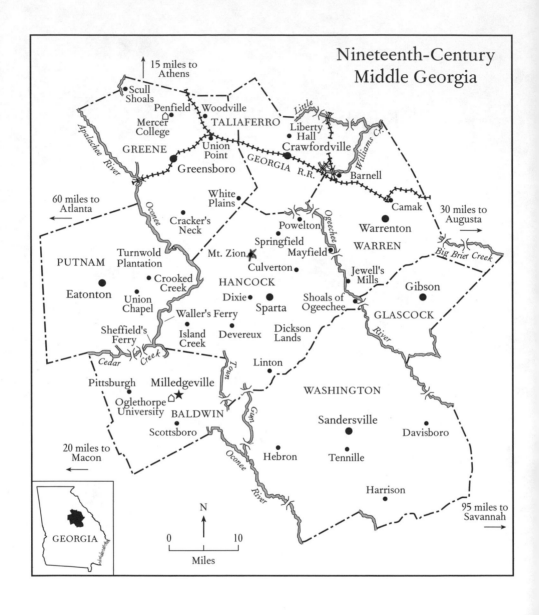

Nineteenth-Century
Middle Georgia

15 miles to
Athens

Scull
Shoals

Penfield Woodville

Mercer
College

TALIAFERRO

Little

Liberty
Hall

GREENE

Union
Point

Crawfordville

GEORGIA R.R.

Williams Cr.

Greensboro

Barnell

White
Plains

60 miles to
Atlanta

Apalachee River

Oconee

Camak

30 miles to
Augusta

Cracker's
Neck

Powelton

Warrenton

Big Brier Creek

Turnwold
Plantation

Springfield
Mayfield

WARREN

PUTNAM

Mt. Zion

Culverton

Ogeechee

Jewell's
Mills

Gibson

Crooked
Creek

HANCOCK

Eatonton

Dixie

Sparta

Shoals of
Ogeechee

GLASCOCK

Union
Chapel

Waller's Ferry

Devereux

Dickson
Lands

River

Sheffield's
Ferry

Island
Creek

Cedar

Creek

Linton

Pittsburgh

Milledgeville

WASHINGTON

Oglethorpe
University

BALDWIN

Sandersville

Davisboro

Scottsboro

Town

Hebron

Tennille

20 miles to
Macon

Oconee

Harrison

River

N

95 miles to
Savannah

GEORGIA

0   10

Miles

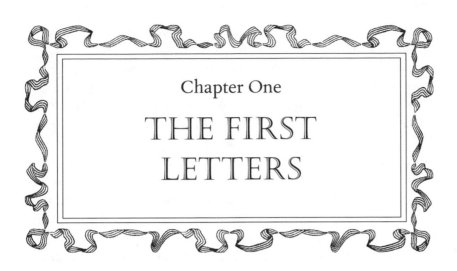

Chapter One

THE FIRST LETTERS

"We ought to be a very grateful family."

Julia Ann Bryan married Henry H. Cumming on February 24, 1824, in Mt. Zion, Georgia, and moved to Augusta, seventy-five miles away, to make her new home. This is sixteen-year-old Maria's first letter to her sister Julia after that event. The other Bryan children appear at once in the first communication: Joseph Bryan Jr. ("Brother"), the older brother who rarely does what he says, and Sophia and Goode, the younger children. The "Miss Mary and Anne" are Henry Cumming's sisters in Augusta. Caroline, who is reading Clarissa Harlowe *and nibbling a cocoa nut slip, probably is Cousin Caroline Goode Holt. Adelaide, who is sewing pantalets, cannot be positively identified.*

Maria Bryan to Julia Ann Bryan Cumming

Rotherwood
March 7, 1824 (Sunday)

I fully intended, my dear Julia, to have written you by the last mail but Brother told me (and to my infinite surprise) that *he* had written you a long letter. I then concluded to defer writing until you had had time to digest his epistle, but I cannot wait any longer lest you should lay the sin of neglect to my charge, a crime which would in the present instance be very heinous.

I don't know whether to tell you we were glad or sorry at your departure. Your strange way of thinking has often made me suppress a warm protestation when it was perched on my tongue and just ready to hop out. I doubt not you have often in your heart accused me of coldness and indifference; yet, my dear sister, I have not a doubt in the world but you were the cause of such an appearance. Just consider how often (feeling a very loving mood come athwart me) I have gone up and announced my intention of kissing you and as a preliminary step threw my arms around you, when "get out" and "blarney" or "deceit" has sent all these warm emotions scampering back to my heart. You may have thought it beneath your dignity to meet my advances but don't you know that the earth goes as far, in proportion, to meet a body impelled towards it by attraction as the body does?

But in deed and in truth, my dear Anne [Julia's middle name] we are most truly, *truly* sorry to give you up, and there was a day or two since delivered of a little dead-born wish that you might never have married but we two have been nice snug old maids living always together as "happy as the day is long." But this wish was too selfish to live. And I have only to be very glad that you have not, as I told you before, married some "poor drunken criter" who would bring you to want. (That is the very place for encomiums on my brother Henry, but I make it a point never to tell a woman that which I do not want her husband to know.) Sophia takes it upon herself to be very much grieved on the occasion and expresses her sorrow so often that it makes me suspicious she feels it *necessary* in order to be believed. But Goode's lamentations are, I doubt not, real and unaffected.

Were I a stranger, I should imagine you had been a most important personage in the family since you are named on every pretence, all your deeds and sayings are scraped up and related and "the sable pall of oblivion" seems to have covered my actions since you are made to be the heroine where you were before only a subordinate agent and I am allowed only the second place in adventures of which I was perhaps the ringleader.

By the bye, Julia, why could you not have written me a line or two by Dick, for really you have undergone so great a change in my imagination that it would require your own hand and seal to convince me you are the same person that wrote to me while at Eatonton. Do let me entreat you, write me as soon and as often as possible, for what greater comfort can I have in my present widowed state.

Caroline is at present very deep in *Clarissa Harlowe* [a sentimental romance by Samuel Richardson set in early-eighteenth-century England and made up entirely of letters written by the various characters to each other]. She thinks and speaks of hardly anything else and so often reiterates that "Lovelack certainly is the greatest villain that ever lived" that I am seriously apprehensive her head will never work again on anything but villainy. I wish you could see her with *Clarissa,* so interested that eyes, nose and mouth seem to sympathize in all the poor girl's distresses, and with a little slip of cocoa nut in her hand which she occasionally nibbles, but all its flavour and juice is, I am sure, entirely lost upon her unattending palate. Adelaide is occupied in the very important avocations of learning some tune or other "with variations" and working a pair of pantalets and it's so the face of busy concern she increasingly wears might make one suppose she is hatching vast events. She has promised to make Ma a cap and when she is plying her needle with unrivalled assiduity, the thought of the cap every now and then strikes her, as you may discover from the renewed energy and an "Oh dear, I guess I've got work *enough* before me."

They all join in love to yourself and the family. Give my love to Miss Mary and Anne and tell Henry I am very much obliged to him for writing, it was so kind and brotherly. The flagellet arrived safe and for that I thank him and you too. It was very good of you to remember my unhoping wish.

Pray, my dear sister, write soon and beg Anne to write me. Caroline speaks of sending you a line this week but lest you should calculate on it with too much certainty, I must forewarn you that there are four volumes of *Clarissa* yet to come. In great haste, I remain your

Affectionate Sister Maria

I must lay down a few conditions of writing to you often. In the first place no living mortal must see one of my letters. In the second place they must not [be] thrown about from pillar to post as has been the case with the letters of some of your correspondents in days of yore. Thirdly they must be immediately answered and fourthly I request you as a particular favour to burn them as soon as they are read.

Yours ever

Maria

Most miserable pen, you know our situation about pens. I have wanted so much to know your opinion of my last Arethusa. Do, *do* burn this letter.

M.

Julia Cumming has just returned to Augusta and to her new husband after a three-week visit with her family at their home, "Rotherwood," in Mt. Zion. It burned a few years later, and when they built a new house, it remained nameless. In this letter appear for the first time "Aunt Wales" and her stepdaughter, Catherine Wales. By way of entertainment Maria reproduces a conversation between Thomas Flournoy Foster, an admirer of Julia's, and a Miss Brooking. A lawyer from Greensboro, Georgia, Foster was serving in the Georgia House of Representatives (1822–25).

Maria Bryan to Julia Ann Bryan Cumming

Rotherwood

May 13, 1824 (Thursday)

My dear Julia,

The first thing you ought to do on the reception of this letter is to present your thanks to a kind providence for bestowing on you such a *sister* as you have; who seized the first moment of leisure to devote to your amusement and gratification. I have a great mind to tell you how I lamented and deplored your departure; but I believe I will not, since the communication would no doubt be received with incredulity.

I think however, my ire against your [husband] was never stronger than at the present moment, when I look around at those scenes you once animated now lone and deserted, turn in vain for a companion with whom I may hold sweet converse. I verily believe that he, with all his *fine, soft* speeches, would be unable to mollify my bitter feelings. I have never been without you to be with me, and regard [you] as an elder sister, and dear friend and director, and when I think over the subject in all its bearings that you are now never, *never* more to be with me, that you will by degrees become far more attached to other objects, and estranged from *me,* I cannot tell you half my unhappiness. Julia, you never could have loved me with one quarter of the affection that I have felt towards you, or you would never have given me up with so much willingness. But I do not say this to reproach you. I well know that I am not formed to inspire very ardent attachments, as you are. I say it because I never could speak so freely face to face. I never did speak in this manner before, and I doubt not but you will excuse me when I promise you I will not again trouble you with my distresses.

Colonel Foster came here the Tuesday after you left home, and in the course of his visit he related the conversation he had with Miss Brooking about you, and as it may amuse you I will report what I can recollect of it.

(Colonel) "Are you acquainted with Mrs. Cumming, Miss B.?"

(Miss B.) "I have been in her company several times, but were I to be with her a hundred years, I could never get acquainted with her, and I must candidly say I do not like her."

(Colonel F.) "I have always found Mrs. Cumming affable and friendly, and I believe, Miss B., you have an aunt who is very intimate with her?"

(Miss B.) "Oh yes, Aunt Eliza is very fond of her, and I have often, since I saw Mrs. Cumming, wondered how there could be so warm a friendship between characters so different, for my aunt is one of the sweetest creatures in the world. Valeria likes her too, very much — but I don't know what it's for. It has been remarked that we are too much alike ever to become acquainted." Miss Brooking then observed that she thought there was not the slightest resemblance between Mrs. Cumming and herself.

(Miss B.) "Ha ha, I should hope not."

(Colonel F.) "I think I have never known any lady who possessed all the qualities that constitute a finished woman, in as high a degree as Mrs. Cumming, and for beauty, intelligence, grace and elegance of person and manner, I think she excels any person of her age I ever saw."

I leave you to make your own comments. I write this because I have nothing else to write; if it does not interest you I have nothing more entertaining to relate.

There has been one letter from Mr. Cumming, taken out of the office since you left here, and it lies on the chimney piece with the seal unbroken awaiting your orders. It looks quite lengthy and moreover very pithy and interesting, and I should like to take a cursory survey of its contents very much, as I dearly love to read *love* letters. Yet I hardly allow myself to touch it, and when I come in contact with it turn my head. This precaution serves the same purpose that Ulysses effected, by stopping his ears with wax to resist the fascination of the syrens, and I am in hopes I shall be able to disregard the temptation of "the charmer, charm it never so wisely."

Mr. Ringold spent last night with us and he charged me over and over to present you his compliments and tell you he was very much disappointed in not seeing you. He talked so incessantly of you that I threatened absolutely to tell Brother Henry, but he valiantly declared he will fight him at ten paces.

Ma's health is worse since you left home. She has lain down the principal part of this time since Tuesday. She says I must tell you to take care of yourself and drink no wine. Catherine and Aunt Wales join me in love to you. Goode is at present in perfect good humour with you, and I believe likes you better for the temporary intermission of his favour. Do, my dear Julia, write soon, and write a long letter.

Excuse this bad writing and mistakes, for I write in haste and with a bad pen. Pray what has become of Brother? Burn this immediately for I would not have it by any accident fall into other hands for any consideration. Your affectionate sister and friend.

M.

Maria Bryan visited her sister Julia in Augusta probably in December 1824 and has been back in Mt. Zion long enough to have written her sister five letters. In this letter she had been to visit Mrs. Deborah Rossiter, wife of Dr. Timothy Rossiter, and that sixty-year-old Mt. Zion neighbor plied Maria with questions about Julia. Another neighbor named her newborn twins George Washington and Lafayette. In 1825, the marquis de Lafayette visited Sparta on his triumphal tour of America.

Maria Bryan to Julia Ann Bryan Cumming

January 27, 1824 [1825] (Thursday)

I believe this is not the first time, my dear Julia, that I have been reproached for neglecting you, when I have given frequent proofs to the contrary. I have written to you, this will be the fifth time since I returned home, and should have written even oftener, had I not heard that such an unceasing repetition of letters would have been troublesome. One of my letters, which I hope you have by this time received, was written solely with the view to persuade you to pay us a visit. Should it have miscarried, let me re-urge you to consent to come up, for Pa says he is still willing, and indeed anxious, to go down for you.

Ma has been very unwell for some days, and is quite low-spirited, I think. More so than she was before she was so much better, for she had begun to feel very much encouraged about getting well, and she now says it is useless to cherish much hope of that kind. Pa has been looking very anxiously for an answer to his last epistle, for a week or two. I am sure, Julia, your heart would melt could you witness how uncomplaining and resigned he bears his repeated disappointments, though he looks forward from one mail to another, in the full assurance of hearing from you. He is very much pleased that the cow and calf arrived safe as both himself and Ma were apprehensive that the bad weather would be very injurious to them.

I suppose you are at present surrounded with bustle and gaiety. By the bye, I am very much obliged to you for thinking of my *predilection*. Did I not know that you must have some one or other to tease me about, I would tell you I would not crook my finger to see Colonel, or General Heard; though I will not deprive you of the pleasure of mentioning *his* name to me, now and then, but I should be in truth a predicament, as the fox in the fable, who as soon as one swarm of fleas was driven away was tormented by another, still more hungry and voracious.

I have lately been to see Mrs. Rossiter and the number and strangeness of her questions concerning you and Henry puts my patience and memory somewhat to the test. Such as "How does Julia *look* keeping house, and how did you *feel* in Julia's house?" "Do, Maria," said she, "tell me *all*, how and about it." Ma was quite amused and a little pleased, I believe, at your hint to send a little more butter. She has today been making arrangements to furnish you more plentifully, such for instance, as ordering large dishes of gravy, "for Goode and Joseph love gravy quite as well as they do butter."

Mary Sunday has been quite sick this week, but is now better. Her little daughter she calls Mary Watkins. They say that during her illness her husband was dreadfully distressed. He walked the fields and cried, in the utmost agony. Mrs. Harris calls her twins, one George Washington and the other LaFayette Harris at their birth.

Sarah Little and her husband [an instructor at Mt. Zion Academy] have been down, for a day or two past. She looks very much pleased with her new situation in the character of *wife,* though she is quite anxious to come to this place to live. I am told that when she makes this remark her husband gallantly observes that "he *has* all he *wants* of Mount Zion." They say her sapient brother-in-law, in order to evince his cordiality towards her and his knowledge of gentility and etiquette, uniformly calls her "Sister Gregory." I was at a quilting at Mrs. Norton's the other day, and the girls began to plague Nancy Robertson about Butch Lyons whom it is said has actually popped the question to her. She was very much vexed and said she'd "let people know that she felt herself above him, and that she accounted herself too good to keep company with such a fellow." P. Gilbert said that "Someone had told her, he intended trying his fortune with her but she wanted none of Nancy's discarded suitors."

I believe, to use your expression, I have nearly "emptied my budget of news," and if you throw aside the letter in anger and disgust, I shall not be at all surprised. Yet I must have written such stuff as this or sent you blank paper, an alternative I certainly should have chosen, in preference to the first, were it not for your strict charge to write long letters.

Brother went to Sandersville court Monday, and we have since heard that he has gone to Augusta. If he is there, Julia, I would thank you to send by him Cecil's *Remains,* if you can find them, and a *cuff* I made while with you. I hope you like the pantalets I sent you. I did not send the bonnet to *you,* because I knew it would have given you considerable trouble and more perplexity, to have given the directions to the milliner. Julia, will you be so good as to send us *Tales of a Traveller* [the 1824 publication by Washington Irving], I omitted to read it; I will see that it shall be returned. Do, my dear Sister, write often;

excuse this shocking production, and please burn it. I have been to meeting tonight and am very much fatigued and withal low-spirited. Farewell.

[January 28, 1825]

I have blotted my paper and am almost ashamed to send it, but besides that this is not worth the trouble of copying. I shall not have time to do so before the mail leaves. Today is Friday, and I wish very much that I could send my letter by this mail, but I much fear it will have to remain until Monday. You know, Julia, how remiss they are at this office, and how difficult it is to have letters conveyed to Sparta; let me entreat you then, when you fail of hearing from us at an expected time, to believe that it is owing to something of that kind, and not to my negligence or forgetfulness. I would write you as often as you wish me to, for when addressing you in this manner, I almost forget my bad pens and aversion to writing. Pa and Ma join me in love to Henry and yourself, to Mrs. Davis [Mary Cumming, Henry Cumming's sister had married the Reverend Samuel Davis], Anne and Sarah. Tell Anne I could not have believed she would have neglected me so. I wrote to her soon after I arrived, and have not received one line in answer. Once more, adieu, my dear Sister.

Love to Henry.

The comings and goings of the Bryan family can be followed in Maria's letters. Here "Ma" Bryan is visiting her daughter Julia in Augusta, and "Pa" is missing his wife greatly but not quite enough to break his custom of not writing letters. Julia Cumming herself is very soon coming up to Mt. Zion for a visit from June until late October. These long summer visits to the country were thought to be medically necessary to escape "the sickly season" that enveloped southern cities in a miasma of fevers — yellow, typhoid, malaria — which lasted until the first real frost.

Maria Bryan to Julia Ann Bryan Cumming

May 30, 1825 (Monday)

My dear Julia,

It is almost useless to write, as you will be up so soon, but as you seem to think I neglect you, I must convince you to the contrary. There has been great joy diffused abroad at the news of your coming. Indeed if we may judge from appearances, you must have some very affectionate friends. Like Sampson who slew more after his death than during his whole life, you seemed to have gained more friends since your marriage, in this place at least, than you ever had before.

I do not think you have reason to say a word with regard to my want of punctuality in writing for positively, Julia, you have neglected me most shamefully. Particularly when you know I am almost entirely alone, you might have consented to solace me with an epistle now and then for Pa is usually about all day, and here I sit with not a creature in the house to speak to.

Tell Ma we have had Doctor Burton quartered upon us for several days. She can tell you something of him, a man who dresses in the costume of the days of Sir Charles Grandison, with short clothes and a cue halfway down his back, with other things corresponding. I was sitting upstairs with my room door open and I heard a grave solemn voice say, "Who keeps house?" Eliza who was in the next room, and it would seem went for consistency, did not rise from her seat to open the door, but said in answer, "Come in." The Doctor marched in with great pomp, a man about six feet two inches in height. She ran upstairs to call me, and he after her. Fortunately I met him on the stairs, and turned his course. I told him I had sent for my father. He bowed with a grave and dignified air as a tragic hero, and said, "I thank you, *truly* thank you." I could fill pages with the recital of his sober nonsense, but really should consider it as a most unprofitable business to record it.

It is getting late, my dear Julia, so I will conclude. Tell Caroline I would write her by this mail, but have not time for a long letter, which I propose sending her. Remember me affectionately to Henry and all inquiring friends. Farewell.

Your Sister

Mrs. Alston and Henrietta called here the other day. [The Norton Alston family resided in nearby Sparta. Joseph Bryan Jr. was a close friend of the

Alston sons and for a time was supposed to be in love with the Alstons' daughter, Henrietta.] The latter spent a day and night, and rode home with Mr. Satterlee [a Sparta friend of Joseph Bryan Jr.'s]. She seems to hold you in grateful and affectionate remembrance.

Yours ever

Catherine [Wales] will be down Wednesday evening.

Tell Ma that her *spouse* is extremely anxious to behold her sweet face again. When we are sitting at the table sometimes he says, "Well, Maria, I hope by such a time there will be someone else to occupy that seat. Well *really*, I miss your Mother very much." Goode undertakes now and then to rally him for liking her so much, and he [Pa] says, "You must remember me as an old acquaintance. Your Mother and I have known each other a long time." He has been strongly tempted to overcome his reluctance to writing so far as to write Ma an epistle but, I believe, thinks we would smile.

I have begged Catherine to accept of your invitation by going immediately to your house but she will not consent. Her mother tells her that she might just as well put up at one of the hotels when she arrives in New York, and send word to her Aunt Staples [a sister of Isaac Wales, Catherine's father, who married a well-to-do New Yorker named Staples] that she is in town.

Tell Ma I wish she would not forget the cambric I want, and I believe Pa intends sending her word to procure some fine linen.

Adieu my dear Julia until I see you.

Eighteen months elapse between Maria's fourth and fifth extant letter — a blank certainly due to letters lost, not letters unwritten. Julia appears to have been at her parents' home from June to October 1825, and again in 1826 she spent the summer in Mt. Zion. Henry Cumming also spent most of the summer with his wife. He promised to be by her side until "I leave you with something to remind you of me." On September 21, 1826, Julia gave birth to their first child, Anne Maria Cumming, the "little beloved" of this letter. In December 1826, Henry Cumming returned to Mt. Zion to take his wife and daughter home to Augusta, where he had just built them a large new house about three miles from the center of the city.

They left early Monday morning, December 11, and that evening Maria wrote her sister this somber description of the Bryan family circle in their absence. On November 29, 1826, the Bryan home — Rotherwood — had burned to the ground.

*Maria here refers to their "unfortunate house burning" and "that beloved house of
ours" where she was "never lonely and seldom sad."*

Maria Bryan to Julia Anne Bryan Cumming

December 11, 1826
(Monday Evening)

Could you send your spirit in, my dear Julia, this evening without your
body, and take a view of us, you would be almost surprised to find what a
difference is produced by your absence. Goode is still at the store selling his
"articles," I suppose. Sophia is gone to bed complaining dreadfully of pains
in her bones, and Pa and Ma and myself are now the only ones around the
fireside that was so lately enlivened by your presence and Mr. Cumming's,
and last not least, that little beloved's.

Ma has escaped her chill today and seems as well as usual. Pa, I think, has
been more complaining and tonight at supper, in spite of good counsel, he
ate some sausage which has made him more unwell. After you left us this
morning he came in and, drawing a long sigh, said, "Well, this parting is very
disagreeable but she's got so good a home to go to."

"Yes," said Ma, "and such a husband, too."

Brother stood by and to use Celia's phrase "said nothing," and as for me, I
fell into a fit of musing, to which I have been addicted since our unfortunate
house burning, which threatened to be interminable.

You had not been gone more than five minutes before Mary came up with
a basket for you. I took a peep into it, it was covered over with a nice white
towel, and saw some fine light nut cakes not yet cold, sausages, and something
else which was so enveloped in the mystery of brown paper that I did not
attempt to find out what it was. Mary carried them off with a most aggrieved
and disappointed look, and said that her mistress would feel very bad.

You know I made a kind of promise that I would write a letter every day; it
may be the means of your hearing from us more frequently, and writing part
of a letter will not seem so large a task as writing a whole one, but I'll warrant
you it will entail upon you the reading of a great deal of unimportant matter.
However you must blame yourself. You know you tell me that is my way to
shift all the blame off my own shoulders.

Ma has been remonstrating with her lord all the evening, but in vain, for sitting in his stocking feet, and walking about, and indeed he has once or twice been out of the door without his shoes. She tells him, "Mr. Bryan, if I was as imprudent as you, I should expect to have the ague all my life be it long or short."

They also were speaking of you today, and their voices faultered. It was not from sorrow, though, it was in pride and pleasure that they spoke of you. I believe I have been sometimes thought of a jealous disposition, but if I know my own heart, Julia, I feel none of it towards you. It rejoices me to find how dear you are to our parents. I might have wished to be loved as well as you, but never that you might be loved *less*.

Oh, that beloved house of ours! In it I was never lonely and seldom sad. I think of it now more than ever. I know I ought to feel resigned, as you say we ought not to stop there, we have reason to feel grateful — and I do sometimes comfort myself with the words of Scripture — "Afflictions spring not from the ground neither do troubles come by chance." I would have had my first journalizing written in a somewhat neater hand but there is not a knife nor a good pen in the establishment. Good night.

December 12, 1826 (Tuesday Evening)

I have just found out that I shall have an opportunity of sending to Sparta in the morning, and though we have company, I have determined to finish my letter. Sophia has had a very high fever all day, and is quite unwell. She walked to the hill yesterday, and the ague has again assailed her. Pa and Ma are both better, but continue to miss you exceedingly.

Mrs. Rossiter has been with us, and moreover we had Mr. Bailey [who had come to teach at Mt. Zion Academy] to dine with us. I am very much disappointed with him indeed. He is very good looking in face and person, really handsome at times, but he is so much a coxcomb in his manners that it does away all the agreeable impression he makes. He came with prejudices against the place, which I presume were acquired at Powelton where he staid last night, such as that it was very sickly, and that there would be few scholars. He intimated that he was perfectly indifferent whether he took a school or not, or whether he engaged in any business. He said it was his design to remain in

Georgia, and he wished to ascertain if the climate would agree with him. But [he] told Dr. Brown and Pa that he certainly could not engage himself unless the trustees would pledge themselves to compensate him for what might be failing in tuition. This they would not do, and he took his leave, and has gone back to Powelton. He brought us some very kind messages from Mr. Stewart. Do you remember him? He came home with us from the Hill once, and you promised to ask him to your wedding. Mr. Bailey said he felt acquainted with the family almost by hearing him speak of them.

Hamilton [Goode, 1801–67, eldest son of Ma Bryan's brother Samuel Watkins Goode of Alabama and Maria's first cousin] arrived that morning, and met with rather a cold reception. He made a great many apologies and indeed I am surprised to find Pa so much mollified as he appears to be. Mrs. Staples had been spending the day at the other house. I did not see her, but Aunt Wales says she is very much out of health, and extremely low spirited. By the way she is very low spirited herself, and is more unwell today. She seems alarmed about herself, and says she don't know what is to come of her yet.

Pa and Ma are just now talking about you. The former says he should like very much to peep in tonight and see how you are all employing yourself. I have a good mind to continue the conversation as they carry it out. Pa says to Margaret, who is sitting by, "How strange it is that one with such kind friends and so good a home should be so loth to leave us."

"Ah," says Ma, "she had rather be living here by me than to be with all the friends in the world."

"She was, I presume," says Hamilton, "almost compelled to return." Ma had just related the true story about your crying because she would not prescribe for it.

Pa is going to Prayers so I must finish. Hamilton asked, when he took the Bible just now, if he got that in Washington. "In Washington! No" says Pa. "I doubt if there ever was such a one in the place." And he is telling the history of it.

Do write to me very soon and tell me everything. You must really excuse this miserable writing for my pen is shocking. If you can put up with the trifles of this letter I shall be contented to furnish you with the like, and often as possible.

Do remember me affectionately to my Brother Henry, and tell him to think of me *tenderly* enough to admit that I may need overshoes to wear to church. Give the little beloved as many kisses as I should if I were there, even at the risque of waking her. Give my love to Catherine and ask her if I may not expect a letter now and then.

Goode says Dr. G. [Gilbert?] says that Mr. Cumming is the smartest man he ever saw in his life, and he loves him like a Brother. My love to Anne, Sarah and the family. In haste your affectionate Sister.

As strict Presbyterians, the Bryans did not celebrate Christmas as a feast day. But, as this letter indicates, there is some exchange of presents among family and friends.

Maria Bryan to Julia Ann Bryan Cumming

December 21, 1826 (Thursday Evening)

Two letters a day, my dear Julia — but Brother is going to Sparta in the morning and as my last letter will cost you no postage, I do not hesitate so much in making you pay for some more trash. It is not affected humility which makes me call it so. I really have nothing important to speak about, in the way of news. Sentiment I know you hate, and I am beginning to think that worse trash than anything else. I want too to thank you, for the pains you took to try and please me. Pa gives us a lively idea of your constant exertion — going from one store to another, in spite of Annie's bawling and your own fatigue. I must tell you I am very well pleased with all, everything, you sent — curls, gloves, frocks — and accept my extra thanks for the belt, which is beautiful.

We have all been sitting round the fire very happy, talking of you all — Pa, Ma, Brother, Uncle [Isaac Bryan, Pa's bachelor brother in Augusta] and I. We ought to be a very grateful family. Some of the members of it, I have no doubt, are so — but for me, much as I shrink from trouble and pine under it, I cannot be grateful as I ought. Did I tell you that Hugh Love and Colonel Foster were at the wedding? The latter expressed the most sincere and heartfelt sympathy for our misfortune [the burning of the Bryan house] of anyone I have met with. Hugh says he thinks just as much of you as ever, and that he is very sorry you have gone away so far from him.

By the way, it was a very lucky thought which prompted you to send Miss Sarah Louisa a pair of long gloves, for she had on a pair of dirty white ones which her Mother and herself seemed equally proud of; the former was showing them to her acquaintances as something very remarkable. Tell Catherine [Wales] I really think she might have written to me before now, and pray how came she to send her frock up when it was ready basted, to her sick Mother, who has her hands full of work? The latter has had Patty over there for two days to help her sew — much as we have to do. I can't bear such things. Goode is very much delighted with his crackers which he has lined up till Christmas Eve. Ma tells me to give her love to you, and thank you for the gown. Sophia did not have a present of any kind, which disappointed her very much, but she bears it with more philosophy than expected.

Good night my dear Sister.

December 22, 1826 (Friday Evening)

Brother is going soon, so I must finish my letter. I have never in my life known Uncle appear so well as he does now. He speaks very freely of the unpleasantness of his prospects of old age — and it really makes me feel more interest for him than I ever did. He begs me, to use his expression, to make hay while the sun shines, and says if I can only do as well as Julia he shall be more than satisfied. "I don't believe," he continues, "that you have had as good offers as she, for she had the first in the whole country — and it used to keep me constantly uneasy to see her refuse such men as she did." "Oh," said he, "I did used to think a great deal of Julia, no one knew how well I liked her."

I cannot understand by Miss Filley's pattern or description, how I must trim my dress — and do tell me if they wear capes. The full frock makes me look shockingly. Was there no belt at Bigelow's like it? I have like to have forgotten to tell you how much Mrs. Alston liked her cap. It was universally admired and Henrietta says she must have it herself, or at least have the first wearing of it. I am glad to find by Catherine's letter to her Ma that she is very much pleased, and sincerely hope she may continue to feel gratified. Aunt Wales speaks some of moving back to her house, as Mr. Carrington asks one hundred and twenty dollars for his house. I hope you will write just as often

as you can, and do excuse my miserable writing and worse still the dullness
of my letters, for my pens are so bad always that it impedes my ideas. I do
think I must give up writing until some of us can get a knife. [Maria's letters
were written with goose quills, which needed constant sharpening.] I am very
sorry to hear that Annie is so cross. Ma says you must let her learn to eat
or she will quite break you down. Give my love to Mr. Cumming, Catherine
and Sarah.

Ever your affectionate Sister.

P.S. Don't forget to answer my questions about the fashions. Ma says you
have forgot Aunt's table cloth.

*A cold December—Ma and Pa have gone to bed to keep warm. The Bryan house,
which had recently burned, was still being discussed by neighbors.*

Maria Bryan to Julia Ann Bryan Cumming

December 27, 1826
(Wednesday Evening)

No letter from you today, my dear Julia, and Pa and Ma are quite uneasy
about you. The former was riding out today and met Mrs. Skinner and her
daughter, who told him she had seen you, and that you were not well.

What weather it is! We have done nothing today but shiver. Pa and Ma
could not keep warm by the fire, so they have gone to bed, though it is not
nine o'clock—and it was some time before I could muster resolution enough
to get the paper and pen and ink to write to you. Last night when I left
Mrs. Rossiter she complained of feeling unwell—and we have lately heard
that they thought she would die. She was taken with the colera morbus and
puking violently. She is considerably relieved, we understand, but we knew
nothing of her indisposition until late in the evening or some of us would
have gone down.

Pa was walking over to the old place (as we call it) since dinner and met
little George as drunk as he could be. He was so provoked at finding him in
such a state that he said if anyone would give what he had paid for him, he
would sell him. George immediately answered that he knew folks that would

buy him at that price. "Well then," said Pa, "I will give you a pass, and you may go and look out a master." In a short time he came staggering in, and asked Pa if he had the paper ready, for he wanted to start. Pa told him to go to bed for if he went out tonight he would freeze to death, but when he got sober he might set off as quick as he pleased. Patty is very angry with him, and scolded him severely. "You are the biggest fool," said she, "in the world when you get a little liquor in your head, and give you the smallest chance and you'll get drunk."

Goode said (a little while ago) "David is mighty in love with Catherine." "How do you know?" I asked. "Why," said he, "I jokes him about her, and he blushed like a *dog*."

I wrote you last night, and sent the letter to Cooper, who meant to have gone to Sparta today. He did not go, however, and I do not know when you will get it now. While I was at the Dr.'s [Rossiter's] Pa gave to Brother a letter I had written to Anne [Cumming] to be put in the mail at Warrenton. I don't know that he will do it — or that she will receive it at all. Good night.

December 28, 1826 (Thursday Evening)

Mrs. Skinner sent for me today to go and dine there, and accordingly Pa and I went. I cannot say I am pleased with [her daughter] Jane — and yet I was prepared to like her. She is a real Yankee girl, has all the precision and primness of a northern fine lady, erect and stiff without anything like gracefulness. She says you are one of the handsomest ladies she ever saw and the very image of her Cousin Susan. Mrs. Richardson seems very much delighted. She was condoling with us on the loss of our house, and expressed her gratitude that hers had been preserved. "I really," said she, "humbled myself in the lowest value of humiliation that I have a roof over my head."

We are very sorry to hear you have been unwell. Ma frequently sighs since she heard it, and says, "Poor thing, I'm afraid she is never to have any health." Aunt Wales is nearly well, and has concluded to stay here — she gives Mr. Carrington one hundred dollars [rent].

I have been quite anxious lately to go to Scottsborough, but I have but little idea of doing so, as I have no way of going, nor no one to go with me. Brother prefers waiting on any other person to me, and will leave all his business to go to any place where his whim may incline him, but he always pleads pressing business when I ask him to accompany me. I really feel hurt sometimes when I think of it.

Do write to me as soon as you are well enough. You must not expect to hear from me as often henceforth as hitherto, for I have a great deal of work to do and really nothing of sufficient importance to communicate in a letter. I am often ashamed of the trifling and insipid epistles I am obliged to send. Fulton [the overseer] is here, and his bed is on the floor, so I must give up the room. My love to Mr. Cumming.

Yours sincerely,

Here Maria Bryan reveals that January 1 is her birthday. She is now nineteen years old.

Maria Bryan to Julia Ann Bryan Cumming

January 1, 1827 (Monday Evening)

At last, my dear Julia, I have received a letter from you. Mr. B. brought it to me yesterday. I really had begun to think you did not mean to write to me. This is my birthday and 'tis always a serious anniversary with me, for the double reason that it is so, and that I have taken my last farewell of the past, and have entered on a new year, and I know not what events it may bring forth.

We have just returned from prayer meeting. Carlisle [Beman] is wonderfully stirred up—he is hardly like the same man—he really thundered—tells us to awake from our slumbers and declared in plain terms that it is our own fault that we are in such a state of lukewarmness. Yesterday Mr. [Joseph] Stiles [a first cousin to Henry Cumming] preached, and in the afternoon there was a meeting here, and they both spoke. They spent the evening here, and Mr. Stiles, as he is wont to do of late, burst out into an invective (I think I may call it) against the Methodists. He seemed almost to forget himself, stomped across the floor, and sitting for a minute or two, and then jumping up and walking again. Pa seemed very uneasy, looked aggrieved and disturbed. At last said he, "I am really sorry to see that you feel so, and to hear you talk in such a manner." "You are," continued he, "injuring yourself and carving out work for future repentence. Leave them alone," said he, "the weapons of *your* warfare are not carnal."

This reproof was lengthy, almost severe. I trembled, expecting every moment to see the other turn in his wrath upon Pa. So far from this, however, it seemed to calm him immediately. I never saw him appear so well as while in the act of conquering his spirit. He was standing up by the fire, and he bowed, really with considerable gracefulness, and said, "I thank you, Sir. I thank you. I shall think of what you have said, and God grant that it may do me good."

What do you think he said to Pa today? They went into Sparta together. Speaking of his brother Sam [Stiles] he said he was a man of remarkably fine talents. "Sam," says he, "does not like Cousin Henry. He thinks he is very proud, and that he does not treat him well." Pa, you may be sure, entered into a very warm defense of his son [-in-law] — wondered to hear him called proud, he had seen nothing of the kind in him. Do not mention this to your husband, not that he would mind it, but I do much hate the occupation of telling, "*but to you*" — is my salvo frequently.

Anne Goode has joined the Baptist church, and Dr. Pope believes he has experienced a change. Mr. Stiles thinks the work there is retarded greatly, within a short time, owing to the dissentions between the different denominations. Robert said to me just now, "Are you writing to Julia?" "Yes." "It seems to me you write to her very often." I do indeed, and if I could hear from you oftener, I should not mind it. I saw Margaret and delivered your message. It is her intention to come see you, and I believe she is very anxious to do so — and her mother even more so than herself. Jane Erwin is there now. She came over yesterday to go to Savannah with Mrs. Ponce, and seemed to be greatly disappointed to find her gone. Says she has heard from her lawyer there, who urges her to come immediately. I think, from what I can learn indirectly, that Mrs. Norton would prefer the northern homespun and Ma thinks the unbleached much the best, and would prefer it for herself.

Pa has entered into a kind of contract with Jerry Miles the other day to build the [new] house. I was very much amused with their conversation. Pa grew tired of his spouting at last, and said, "Miles, you remind me of the copy I used to write at school: 'A man of words and not of deeds is like a garden full of weeds.'"

"Ah, Squire," says Jerry, "a body must talk with you so as to be *sartin* of a thing. You are such a *sharper*. You are as keen as a two edged sword and you can get round any one in a *mity little* time."

"It takes you to go around," quoth Pa. "You can go around me two or three times before I get ready to start."

"Squire," said he, "it stands me in hand to arn [earn] all I can. I've got a power of money to send on to the North, and look at the orphan children I've got to labour for. Now there's Jim and Jack. They are no account. Jim would never have got to the North in the world if it had not been for me. I let him have the money," and so he went on.

Brother returned to Sparta today, and told Pa he should be out tomorrow. Ma is not so well, and continues low spirited. She likes her calico as well as could be expected. Did you not receive the letter in which I informed you of my entire satisfaction with all my "articles"? Jane Skinner is going to stay some time at her grandmother's, as the whooping cough is in Sparta and she has never had it. Our opinions of her seem not to agree. I shall most gladly acknowledge mine to be erroneous if I can.

Sophia told me to tell you to kiss "Nanny" [Annie Cumming] fifty times for her. "She is sick," said I, "and therefore it is imposing too hard a task upon her." "Well then," said she, "Brother Henry must do it for me." She says she knows if all our clothes had been burnt up, Miss Filley would have given her a frock. My pen is miserable again, and with it and the cold together I take no comfort in writing. I am glad to hear of some good ones for there is nothing to make or mend with. My love to Mr. Cumming and Catherine [Wales]. Tell her to write to me.

Ever yours sincerely

Maria composes a long gossipy letter to Julia that is mostly free of problems.

Maria Bryan to Julia Ann Bryan Cumming

January 14, 1827 (Sunday Night)
9 o'clock

My dear Julia,

I felt very much gratified to hear from you at last. I really began to think you did not mean to write at all. I should have sat down earlier to this employment, but in the afternoon Mrs. Bailey came in, and as you know how given she is to travelling after night, she and Margaret stayed until a few moments ago. Soon after supper Dr. and Mrs. Brown [a longtime minister at Mt. Zion] stepped in, and then Dr. Gilbert [a local physician] who, with Mr. Foote, made up quite a party. The latter intends taking the school [at Mt. Zion] should there be any scholars, but there has been so much uncertainty about the arrangements, that almost everybody that was expected here has gone off to [the academy at] Powelton. Mr. Foote, should he conclude to *come*, wishes to board with his wife at Aunt Wales's. [After Aunt Wales's husband Isaac died in September 1825, she has begun to take boarders.] I have not heard what the latter says to the plan. Indeed I do not know that it has yet been proposed to her.

Dr. Gildersleeve and his wife are in the neighbourhood, staying at the Doctor's. She is a pretty, pleasant little woman, and I feel extremely sorry for her. She had been living in the hope of visiting her Mother in the Spring, and the day before her school broke she found greatly to her surprise, by some symptoms which she could not misunderstand, that she was considerably advanced in pregnancy. The disappointment was so great that it actually made her sick and she was obliged to go to bed, and she expects to be confined in April. I expect, notwithstanding this, you will pronounce her a very happy woman, to be so perfectly well as to be ignorant of her situation.

Mrs. Rossiter is extremely unwell, is confined to bed several days, almost every week, and when she is up she appears unable to be anywhere but in bed. I am seriously uneasy about her, and cannot but fear sometimes that she is not long for this world. Last Tuesday night again they thought she would die, her extremities were cold, and she almost senseless. For days she has been confined to her bed.

Eliza and Arianora Bird [daughters of Colonel William Bird of the "Aviary" at the Shoals of Ogeechee] were at Church, the latter more friendly than I have known her before of late. Pa wishes to be attentive to her, and she said she would come out and stay a day or two in the neighbourhood if I would go in for her. Accordingly, Tuesday was the day fixed upon, and Eliza is coming out too.

Jane Skinner is exciting considerable commotion in town now, of one sort or another. Innumerable remarks are made of her and her speeches, or what is

attributed to her is frequently reported. It is told in Sparta that when she was
with you [in Augusta], she enquired who *that* Mr. Davis was, saying she did
not like him, and if she had known how he preached she would not have gone
to hear him. "Who is he?" said she. "A Brother-in-law of mine," responded
Mr. Cumming. Soon after, as the story goes, she asked, "Who is this wonderful Mr. Stiles, that is turning all Georgia upside down?" "A Cousin of mine,"
again answered Mr. Cumming. Satterlee was my informant. I know not how
he heard the story.

There is a piece of news I am going to tell you, which has been whispered
about through a circle of some half a dozen under a strict charge of secrecy,
which thing has marvellously delighted the good, and the old folks, in our
community. I must enjoin it upon you, however, not to mention it particularly
to Catherine. You remember John Walker, a relation of Colonel Carter's who
used to board at Dr. Rossiter's. Well, he has been up to see Emily Brown
[the daughter of Dr. Brown], and they say has actually courted her. He is
sanguine of success, and they who calculate on the expediency of such things,
say it is the best thing Emily can do for herself. He is a remarkably steady
young man, quite intelligent and well read I know, is now studying law in
Milledgeville and will be admitted in April. He has, moreover, about twenty
negroes, and a tract of land. He told some friend here that he knew that her
mind was inferior to many other girls and but little cultivated, but he could
not help loving her notwithstanding, he always had loved her and though he
had often endeavoured to draw off his affections from her, "twas in vain."
We may wonder in what consisted the *je ne sais quois* which captivated him.
However, she is certainly improved of late, and I am heartily rejoiced with
her good prospects.

Prithee, Julia (between you and I), what is the prospect for your protegee
[Catherine Wales]? I cannot but hope she has made an impression, which may
obtain her a better situation and secure her a good home. I know of nothing
which would gratify me more than to see her well settled.

I am delighted with your account of Mr. Douglas [a minister]. Nothing
I have heard of him has raised him so in my estimation, for I can depend
on your opinion, as I know you are rather fastidious. Aunt Wales is making
considerable preparations to entertain him, and is very anxious that Catherine
should be home at that time.

Everybody gives us so fine an account of little Annie [Julia's infant] that we are inclined to think her a wonderful child. I do feel extremely desirous to see her.

Ma tells me to say to you she cannot go to see you unless she gets much better. Indeed, Julia, I have seldom seen Ma so very unwell as she is now. She is not comfortable a moment, and has fevers, and then severe sweats, almost every night. I was never more discouraged about her than I am now. I never saw one more earnestly long for anything than she does to go to the North. It is the only subject almost on which she converses with any interest. I sometimes wish that you or Mr. Cumming would say something to Pa about it, or propose some plans. I know you both have more influence with him than anyone else — and in spite of the great inconvenience which might result from his going, her health and comfort ought surely to stand prior to every other earthly consideration.

Mr. Lancaster brought his son Joseph Bryan the other day. He is a good looking child but is very awkward and, I am afraid, dull. Did you hear that Dr. Park who married Sarah Gaither had killed himself a short time since? The cause is not known or suspected.

Do you mean to pay your Brother and Sister a visit this winter? I have nearly given up the idea of going to Scottsborough, for I cannot feel easy to leave Ma, or think it is my duty to do so. Adelaide is certainly married. Mr. Warner and, I believe, Mrs. intend coming down before long, we understand. Have you noticed a piece in the Avertian of poetry? Folks whisper that it was written by J.B. to M. But if I talk much more in this style you will begin to think I have grown to be the veriest gossip in the whole country. Where is Mr. Wilde, you never mention him nor Mr. & Mrs. Crawford. Pa saw Dr. Battle today, who told him of you. Write soon. Love to Mr. Cumming. Pa says he will write soon.

Your affectionate Sister —

January 17, 1827 (Wednesday)
[Postmark: January 18]

I have had no chance to send this before and I do not know what you will think of me. I asked Pa to write to you. He says he has not time now for he means to write a long letter. Ma has had a *dream* of you and Mr. Cumming and is quite uneasy about you. Do write soon.

Preacher Douglas, highly recommended by Julia Cumming, arrives at the Bryan home in Mt. Zion with dusty clothes and muddy boots.

Maria Bryan to Julia Ann Bryan Cumming

January 19, 1827 (Friday Evening)

My dear Julia,

I sent a letter to you to the office this afternoon, and I think it quite probable that this will reach you by same mail. Yet, as Pa intends going into Sparta in the morning, I must improve the opportunity as of late I find it extremely difficult to get a conveyance to the office.

Yesterday about twelve, Ma had lain down, and Pa had gone out, and Miss Arianora, Eliza and myself were sitting together by the fire. I heard a gentle knock at the door. I arose and opened it, and found a young man standing. We looked each other in the face about a half second. "Miss Bryan," said he. "Mr. Douglas." I gave him, as Catherine prophesied, a hearty shake of the hand, for your liking to him secured him a kind reception, and then introduced him to the ladies. He was quite in travellers plight, muddy boots, long beard and dusty clothes; he had walked from Powelton. He was unable to hire a carriage, and did not wish to borrow a horse, or go on to Sparta; and what was more than all, lost his way, and says he is sure walked in all at least fifteen miles.

Notwithstanding appearances, though, I soon found out that I should like *him*—and I really do like him exceedingly, and so does Pa and Ma. He is so frank, and amiable, and I feel as if I had known him always. When he laughs he looks like Mr. Iverson, I think. He says to me this morning, "I like your sister very much." "What a mixture," he continued, "of frankness and reserve there is about her. The second time I called she came to the door and met me, and was very cold in her manners, and I told her of it afterwards," says he. "I'll give you an instance of her frankness. The night before I came away, she said, 'I wish you were going to stay longer.' I asked why? 'Why,' said she, 'if I must be candid with you, I really do like you.' "

Pa assured that he need not doubt your word for you never made professions, if you could not speak from the heart. He went to Sparta this afternoon, for he said he did not know what they all would say to him for coming here first. You must tell Catherine [Wales] that he says she and I speak precisely alike, voice, tone and emphasis.

Ma, I hope, is better—much more cheerful. Mrs. Rossiter has again been very sick. I saw her this evening. Mrs. Brown says she saw Colonel Taylor in [South] Carolina and he enquired very particularly of you, and with a great deal of affection.

I hope you will write to me as frequently as you can. Your letters do us all so much good. Sophia speaks frequently of going to see you, and wishes to do so very much. Her health is still very bad, she has chills still—and you have seldom seen her look worse. 'Tis very late, my dear Julia, so I must bid you good night.

Ever your affectionate Sister—

Ma has just commanded me to come to bed. Adieu.

January 20, 1827 (Saturday Morning)
[Postmark: January 20]

While I was writing to you last night I heard a loud scream suddenly at Aunt Wales's, and soon after she came to the porch and asked for Pa to go over. It seems it was Henry Edwards with a mask going from window to door to frighten them. He made his escape, however, without being seen afterwards.

Have you heard of the death of Mrs. Winder? Eliza Long attended her funeral, she says, just before she left Washington. I find from Anne's letter that Caroline [Goode Holt Iverson] must have stayed some time in Augusta.

Pa got a letter from Mr. Burritt in Milledgeville yesterday and I could not but smile to see how ridicule will affect our opinion in spite of ourselves. 'Twas to tell him how much he was pleased with Mr. Williams. It began in this way, "Thank you, thank you, Sir, for introducing to our acquaintance our little friend Mr. Williams." I saw Pa was very much pleased with the attention it implied, and more so that his favourite Mr. Williams, whom he had been the means of sending there, had been so well received. But really, it struck me so ludicrously that the man should make Pa pay postage just to know that he (Mr. Burritt) was very much pleased with their little friend Mr. Williams that I laughed immoderately. I saw Pa did not like it, but still it caused him to look upon the letter a little differently, and "At least," said he, "he might have paid the postage." But to conclude all, Mr. Burritt says, "If I thought you were not assured how much we all like him, I would come to Mt. Zion just to convince you."

Ever yours

The building of the new Bryan house, on the same site as the one destroyed by fire, is distressingly slow in starting. News about "Brother" and the household slaves is of interest in this letter of Maria's.

Maria Bryan to Julia Ann Bryan Cumming

January 22, 1827 (Monday Evening)

My dear Julia,

I am beginning to grow a little impatient to hear from you, and I do hope that tomorrow's mail will bring us a letter. Ma continues quite unwell. Last night, after she went to bed, she had a chill which was succeeded by a fever, which lasted during the greater part of the night. She was wild, and was frequently starting and singing, as you may remember to have heard her. Today she is more weak than usual, and even more low spirited and persists in saying, whenever she speaks on the subject, that she knows she cannot live long.

I think, Julia, you would be distressed to witness the dilatory movements with regard to the house. It is not yet begun, and the lumber not even engaged, and Pa draws so many long sighs about the trouble and expense of the undertaking that I sometimes fear we are never again to be restored to that much loved spot. Indeed, Pa and Ma both seem most of the time so filled with perplexity and trouble about one thing or another, and principally about Brother, that it really saddens me.

I have spoken of him to you but seldom of late, and yet I know you take great interest in all that concerns him, but the reason is that I have had nothing very important or satisfactory to write. In various ways of late, Pa has heard complaints of him, sometimes that he would not settle with persons with whom he had accounts, at others that he has not paid those for whom he had collected money, and so forth and so forth. You know how much such things torture Pa. They wound his pride as well as disturb his bitter feelings. Indeed he was miserable.

At last he collected resolution to speak to Brother on the subject, and you know how illy he can stand reproof. The conversation was a private one. Pa remarked that he wished Brother to inform him of the state of his affairs, and if he was unable to pay his debts, he would cheerfully assist him. Entreated him, if he could obtain his own consent, to give up the practise of *law*, and offering to settle him as well as his means would in any manner justify. Brother the next day appeared vexed, and said to Ma and I that he was determined never to take another new case in Sparta. Said that Pa would not settle him in case he did not marry, and he was fully determined not to do that. Oh, when I think of how Brother conducts himself towards the best of parents who are constantly solicitous concerning his welfare, it makes me tremble for him.

Julia, I am convinced in my own mind that he loves H—— A—— [Henrietta Alston] and that his mind is soured because he knows he cannot obtain the consent of his family to marry her. I do believe moreover that at the time of the camp meeting there was an understanding between them, and that it was my decided conduct that was considered as the expression of the feelings of the family, which put an end to it. I cannot tell you why I think this, for my opinion is not founded on one circumstance alone, but on a succession of little things which has left this impression most forcibly. I must beg you though not to mention this to a soul (you know who I mean by a soul) for I have not said it to Pa or Ma, and after all it may *not* be so.

Mr. Douglas preached twice yesterday, and I believe was considerably admired. He came home with Pa on Saturday, and went to Sparta again this morning. I like him much, he is most agreeable as a domestic fireside companion, acts as if he was at home, perfectly free from restraint himself—and restrains no other. I think Aunt Wales is considerably hurt [that Mr. Douglas did not stay with her], and I don't know but a little vexed with us. Catherine had written to her to invite him, to make that his home, and she had made her arrangements accordingly. So when he came here, she seemed disappointed, but she came over, and invited him to go there, and take a room, or at any rate to stay with her as much as he could. The day after he came he called there, and staid about an hour, and last night after supper he asked me if I would not go over with him there. I did not for I was afraid she would think we kept a very strict watch over him, but in a very little while he came back. I have been induced to believe he does not like to be with her, because she talks to him constantly almost about Mr. Staples' family. Yesterday as we were coming home from church, she said to him that we had often heard from him before we saw him, indeed she continued, smiling very meaningly, "I've long heard of you by *letter*, as well as in other ways."

I must not forget, my dear Julia, which I do most sincerely, to thank you for my pens. I hope I shall not again soon be so dreadfully at a loss for a good one. Mrs. Rossiter, we heard today, is very sick. Did you forget to send her spectacles? She speaks of wanting them very often. Uncle Jacob [a slave of Henry Cumming who serves as a courier between Augusta and Mt. Zion] talks a great deal of Annie, in the most rapturous terms for him. Says, "Bless her little heart, she does *cackle* fairly when he speaks to her." "Mistress," said he, "Miss Julia showed me her legs, and you never see such great fat dumpy hard little things in your life. But thar's my way. Mas Henry says to me, 'Uncle Jacob, you are a fool about your Master's children.' "

By the bye, Julia, I must justify myself in that Daphne is sent instead of Henny. I know that my character throughout the family is one of extreme selfishness, but I must in this case shake the blame off my own shoulders. I was willing, nay even anxious, that Henny should go, after I heard you wanted her, though I have again taken her in hand, and I urged Ma to let her go, but she said that Daphne would do as well as Henny for you, and that Henny had got to be a great help to her, by mending Ma's clothes, and doing little things about the house.

Pa received a letter from Mr. Burroughs the other day directing him to sell the P[leasant] Valley plantation [near Mt. Zion], negroes and stock, thereby intimating that Mr. & Mrs. Ponce are not coming back to live. Pa is anxious that Brother should buy it, and says if he will sell the river plantation he will assist him to do so.

Let me beg you to burn this letter. You perceive that there are some things in it which ought not to be seen.

January 23, 1827 (Tuesday Morning)

Old Mrs. [Elisabeth] Reid died last night [at the age of eighty-eight]. She had been a little indisposed for a day or two, and old Chloe was placed in the room with her. On waking up, towards day, she found her mistress stiff and cold. What an immense change . . . "Let us not be weary in well doing for we shall reap if we faint not."

I must again beg you to write as often as you can. You certainly cannot complain of me now. I had like to have forgotten to tell you that Mr. Douglas desired me to remember him kindly to you when I write. My love to Mr. Cumming and Catherine.

Ever your affectionate Sister

Maria, in this letter, continues to paint in the dark side of her brother, Joseph Bryan Jr., his debts and his sulking behavior.

Maria Bryan to Julia Ann Bryan Cumming

January 24, 1827 (Wednesday Evening)

My dear Julia,

You don't know how very much I was disappointed that I did not receive a letter from you by this day's mail. I have written so often of late, and I thought certainly I should hear either from you or Catherine. I have just returned from the interment of old Mr. Wiley. It is somewhat remarkable that him and Mrs. Reid should both have died on the same day. Sayre was there and he came up and spoke to me, and stood conversing in his usual light way. I do dislike very much to laugh or talk at such a place, and I remembered hearing you speak of his making you laugh at Squire Bailey's funeral.

Mr. & Mrs. Foote have come and are boarding at Aunt Wales's house — the school is yet very small.

Pa wrote to you (a short letter) today by Uncle Jacob & he wishes me to say to you that he forgot to say anything about some cravats he wishes you to get for him—four, and he says "Tell her I do not want them remarkably fine, nor remarkably large."

Daphne was delighted at the idea of going to Augusta, since she knew Miss July would dress her in nice calico, and black *funnel* shoes. Aunt Wales was in here spending the evening. She says I must ask you to tell Catherine that she is very anxious for her to come home, but she knows not how she is to come. I think Ma is a little better today, at least I hope so.

I received a letter from Cousin Caroline [Goode Holt Iverson, the daughter of Ma's sister, Martha Goode Holt] the other day. She says that little Julia Maria [her daughter named for the Bryan sisters] has been very sick, and Christmas week they were afraid she would die. Says that she is extremely anxious to go and see you, but she is growing very clumsy (is her expression), but she thinks you might write to her, particularly as you promised to do so. Tabitha was married about a fortnight since. I could not make out the name of the man. He is, however, a young lawyer of the place. She says Pulaski [Holt, the brother of "Cousin Caroline"] was there a short time ago, and said that [his mother-in-law] Mrs. Richardson was very much vexed with her for having written to me that Lavinia [Richardson Holt, Pulaski's wife] was in the family way, and said that she did wish we could all let her family alone, and many other things. Cousin Caroline never wrote me such a thing in her life, and I never heard it said that that was Lavinia's situation.

January 25, 1827 (Thursday Evening)

We have just got home from meeting, and as I shall have an opportunity to send this to town tomorrow, I determined to fill it up without delay. I do wish you could be where you could always hear Dr. Brown. He particularly excels in those exhortations which he delivers at night, and seems to point out so plainly the path of duty, saying "This is the way. Walk ye in it." He remarked that the best and surest way to prepare ourselves for every evil in life, in whatever shape it may come upon us, is to aim constantly to do the whole will of God. Not, says he, to fix the attention on some one Christian duty, and seek with the whole energy of the mind to do that, but to lay ourselves out completely for the service of our Saviour. "Provoke one another," said he, "to love and to good works, endeavour constantly to benefit your fellow creatures, your brethren, and be assured that in proportion as you benefit others, will you be in the way of receiving benefit from them. Oh! what a blessed thing," he continued, "is religion! The blessings it confers upon us even in this life are rich and great but how altogether larger are those it will confer in the life to come, those blessings which are unspeakable, and full of glory, which are reserved in Heaven for those who patiently continue in well doing."

Pa intends to set off to Milledgeville tomorrow morning, and will probably be gone until Monday. I have seldom seen Ma more vexed than she was today. Pa was going by the gate this morning and Aunt Wales called him, and told him she feared from what she had heard, that Brother's affairs were in a dreadful situation, that she understood he was to be *ruled* at the next court for a very large amount. "And I wish," she added, "that three thousand dollars may cover his debts. I told Isaac [Bryan, the brother of Pa and Aunt Wales] some time ago that I feared Joseph's business was greatly perplexed, and that he might prepare himself to aid him, for he would have it to do." I could not persuade Ma that it might possibly be that her motive was kindness to Brother. Pa was considerably offended but gossip has made him more uneasy than ever. Brother's conduct, and the effect it has upon Pa and Ma, half crazes me sometimes, but there is no help for it. He has not been here for nearly a fortnight, and appears to be doing nothing at all in Sparta. Pa is so grieved at his want of attention, and says he should think he might come home now and then and assist him about arrangements for the [new] house.

Mrs. Rossiter is very unwell indeed. I saw her this evening; she keeps to her bed most of the time. I wish you would try and persuade Anne or Sarah [Cumming] to come up and see us. The latter, I suppose, would not be willing to come.

Do write soon. Ma begs me to say to you that the Dr. has directed her to drink black tea, and she wishes you would please send her about a half pound that she may make an experiment of it.

Ever yours.

Chapter Two

THE BELLE

"Maria," said she, "is a very good girl—but I think she courts attention rather too much."

Maria describes to Julia how an overseer named Duncan Fulton had pummeled a slave girl named Jenny (later Maria's personal maid) until her face was bloody and swollen. Seeing Jenny in that condition, Maria exclaimed to Julia, "Oh how great an evil is slavery." She does not confront the overseer, but she does confront her Aunt Wales for gossiping about her brother Joseph.

Maria Bryan to Julia Ann Bryan Cumming

January 27, 1827 (Saturday Night)

My Dear Julia,

We are alone tonight, as Pa has gone, but though I have leisure to write a few lines, I am almost too much *piqued* to do so; for again and again have I been disappointed in my reasonable expectation of receiving a letter from you. Ma has been very unwell today, though during the latter part of the week she has thought herself better. I am anxious for her to take a short journey, as I think it might be serviceable, but she thinks she is unable to travel.

Pa has been considerably disappointed by finding that Duncan Fulton is not coming. He has been compelled to join the party who has gone out against the Indians. Today Jenny came in crying very much, her face bloody and swelled. She said that Fulton had beat her with his fist, because she had not spun a sufficient quantity. It would have distressed you to have seen her. Oh! how great an evil is slavery. She may have been to blame, but we have imagined that Fulton is altered of late. He is so constantly with Kelly, and evil communications will corrupt the purest manners. We hear that Satterlee is with you, sick.

January 29, 1827 (Monday Morning)

I am anxious to finish this, and send it to the mail but I am so thoroughly vexed that I am not in a state of mind to write or do anything else. This morning I went to Aunt Wales's, and in the course of conversation, I asked her what was the reports that she had heard of Brother. She turned as pale as death and said they were the common topics of conversation. I asked her who had told her. She said a great many persons, whose names she did not like to mention. Indeed, she had known of the disorder of his affairs for more than two years and had wished to let us know of them, but Catherine and Sam [Wales] would not suffer her to say anything to us on the subject. I asked her who he owed. She said he owed for his board, he owed Marshall, and Mansfield, and many others, and that he would be ruled at the next court, either compelled to pay the money or else put in jail.

I remarked that it was very strange that people should go to her and talk of us, and that it had hurt our feelings very much to know that she should talk to others of our misfortunes, that we had heard she had made it a topic of conversation with Mr. Foote, David Smith, Carrington, Cooper, and Charlotte Beman. She said she had never mentioned the subject to Mr. Foote but that she had to the others, but she could not be blamed for listening. I said that no one would come to us and speak aught against her, without being silenced. She said she had acted conscientiously by telling Pa, because she thought so much of Joseph that she wanted him relieved from difficulty. A very great deal more was said on both sides which I dare say you do not wish recapitulated. Suffice it to say I have been crying ever since, and am crying while I write this. How difficult a thing to do our duty towards those who are dependent on us, when we think we have been injured by them. But it would distress you, Julia, as I have before said, to see how Pa and Ma feel, and as for me I do not know whether I am more vexed with or sorry for Brother.

To increase the general perplexity and trouble, Fulton has got in a pet, without anyone's saying a word to him, and threatens to go off. I think I do wrong to tell you of all this, since you are away from the scene of vexations, but right that you should [not] remain ignorant of what disturbs us.

Do write to me soon. It has been nearly a fortnight since I have received a line from you, and I am sure I have written nearly half a dozen letters to you within that time. I think Ma is a little better. Mrs. Rossiter is more unwell.

In haste, your affectionate Sister.

P.S. Ma and, for that matter, all of us are very anxious to have you come up [even] if you can only stay a week. She says she will send for you if you will come.

The whole Bryan family is "overjoyed" at the prospect of a visit from Julia. She stayed in Mt. Zion from February 28 to March 7, 1827. Maria, in Sparta on a round of social calls prior to Julia's visit, saw Mrs. Wilson Bird (Frances Pamela Casey, 1791–1855), the mother of Edgeworth Bird of the book The Granite Farm Letters, *edited by John Roʒier. She dropped in also on Dr. Terrell, his wife, and her sister, Sarah Ruffin Rhodes Crawford.*

Maria Bryan to Julia Ann Bryan Cumming

February 7, 1827 (Wednesday Evening)

My dear Julia,

I was extremely gratified to receive a letter from you this morning; if I had not then, I would hardly have known what to think.

We are really overjoyed to find that you are willing to come. Pa speaks of sending down the carriage the last of next week, and I have not seen Ma in so good spirits as she has been today for a long time. Yesterday it would have distressed you to see her. She kept to her bed nearly all day, and so gloomy and desponding. She said that she was going to die, and set Sophia to crying, and you may imagine what a scene I had, particularly as Pa was not at home.

She has desired to see you more, I think, than anything in the world. She would frequently be silent for an hour, and then, as if she had been all that time thinking of you, would say, "What would I give to see Julia!"

I believe, indeed, that the thought of you is the principal thing that supports them against the misconduct of Brother. They often converse to this effect, that they have no right to complain, for they have at least one truly dutiful and affectionate child. Today they were speaking of you and Ma actually wept, and the tears stood in his eyes, when they recalled your affection and recited your good qualities; but Mr. Cumming, I can assure you, occupies a rank but little inferior to your own in their estimation.

Monday, Pa and I went to Sparta. I had promised to spend a day with Mrs. Watkins and Miss Potter. When I got in they were out, and I went down to Dr. Bird's. I found there Mrs. Wilson Bird. I really do admire and like her extremely, and her twins are the sweetest children I almost ever saw. She sent a very pressing invitation to Ma, to go and spend some time with her at the Shoals [in Warren County, Georgia], said she knew the change of air would do her good, and she could promise her as much *solitude* as she could desire. She said to me, "Maria, I understand you are to have a *stile*ish wedding before long. Is it a fact?"

By the way, this reminds me of a very singular report that is current in Milledgeville and those parts, as I am told. It is that Mr. Smith and I are to be married (the missionary) or that such a thing is on the tapis. Did you ever hear of anything so foolish? But Mrs. Bird said, "You are obliged to have a *Minithter,* there ith no help for it."

We dined at Mr. Watkins's, and after dinner Mr. Douglas came in. He always enquires very kindly after your health and welfare, and asked me if I had heard from you since he had seen me. He is nearly as much caressed and admired as ever Mr. Stiles was.

I must tell you of how I committed myself or rather how badly I behaved. You know how deaf Mrs. Watkins is. I was sitting across the room from her, and had been conversing for some time with Douglas, when Mrs. Watkins who was sitting alone began to speak with me. I answered her in as loud a tone as was necessary, and she continued talking. I had heard herself and Miss Potter say something of Daniel's little son (I did not know before that he had one, or was in the State), and as there were a number present, I asked no questions. But at this time she was speaking of the family, and I screamed out the question, "How old is Daniel's little son?" "Why really," said Mrs. Watkins, "I do not recollect. I *ought* to know too," and she looked down and knit her brow, and appeared to be making a calculation. At last said she, "I think about twenty four years old." I was so utterly surprised at the answer, which I expected would be "about two or three months," that when she immediately went on to speak of Mrs. John Watkins' death, and of the great loss her family had sustained, I had burst out a-laughing and to have saved my life I could not resume a countenance of gravity notwithstanding what she was speaking about.

I saw Martha Carnes for a few moments. She is better but very low. Her father is likewise better. As we were coming out of town, we stopped a few minutes at Dr. Terrill's, and when I stepped in the room to my surprise found Mr. Douglas there, and Mrs. Crawford. [William Terrell, born in Virginia, was brought to Georgia at an early age. A physician and planter, he served in the Georgia House and was elected to two terms in Congress (1817–21). Maria persistently misspelled his name "Terrill."] Mrs. Terrill appeared to be playing off her greatest attractions of smiles and manner, and you know when she does that she is obliged to be interesting. She tells me that she is not going to Augusta, for the Dr. has put it off so long that she is not willing to go so late. Mrs. Crawford said she was afraid if she went so late Sarah Louisa would be taken sick. [Joel, Sarah Crawford's husband and Terrell's brother-in-law, served in Congress with Terrell and practiced law in Sparta after the expiration of his second term.] Speaking of them — reminds me that Nathan Warner is positively to be married to Miss Rembert very soon.

The other night Ely staid here. Pa and Ma laugh very much at me, and say that they know he means to ask me to go to Augusta, but seriously, you have no idea of the airs of consequence that the little fellow put on. He did not seem to remember that we were at all interested in the Cummings, from the manner in which he spoke. Then Pa did stare when he said that "It was a great pity that the Presbyterian ministers now settled in the church were not men of talents. But," said he, "I think they will call Stiles next year. They will certainly not settle either of those who are now there." He had a great deal to say of Colonel C. [William Cumming, older brother of Henry Cumming] — that "it *had* been said he would take off Mrs. Young, but that idea was pretty much given out." He had a great many anecdotes to relate of him, and whenever he spoke of him invariably called him *"Cummins"* (without his title) said he "I think for a man of talents, and one who has had such opportunities, *Cummins,* does as little *give* to society as any man in it." Indeed next day, he seemed determined to stick it out here and I never was more heartily tired of a person and I am certain he would not have moved perhaps till now had not Pa about literally ordered him off. "I" said Pa "am going to ride, and if you are going to Sparta, I shall have your company part of the way." I really would have showed my contempt very openly had I not remembered that the command to "Do to others as we would they should do to us" extended to coxcombs as well as to other people. Mr. and Mrs. Alston seem very anxious to know if he stays with you. I do not know any thing I have heard lately which pleases me so much as that you are taking music lessons. I hope you will be diligent in practicing. Do you not want some of my music books, or are you learning new pieces, if you do I will send any of them that you would like to learn by Uncle Jacob. Poor Mrs. G. looks like dejection itself—a very sick child and worse than all such a husband . . . I think if you could see her and understand her situation it would cause you to know how to value yours. Do give my love to all and kiss that "beautiful" child for me. Ma feels anxious to know how you like Daphne and how she behaves. It is getting late so I must stop, after begging you to write soon.

Ever yours affectionately.

Maria writes a "gossipping letter" and describes a teasing match between her younger brother Goode and her sister Sophia.

Maria Bryan to Julia Ann Bryan Cumming

February 14, 1827 (Wednesday Evening)

My dear Julia,

I can't tell you how much we were disappointed in not receiving a letter from you by Monday's mail. Ma was uneasy for fear you were sick, and Pa *"wondered,"* and I was greatly surprised, as well as sorry.

I hope Annie has got well before this time. I have delighted Catherine

[Wales] beyond measure in recounting her tricks of various kinds, and when I told her of your making her "*wipe up*," she seemed as if she would have gone beside herself.

I carried Aunt Wales her gown Monday morning and she fell to making it forthwith, herself and Catherine both admired it very much, and she desired me to say to you that she was very much obliged to you and that nothing could have been more acceptable. Their box of goods which was committed to the care of Mr. Floyd of S—— they have not yet heard of. Martha Carnes was here when I gave Catherine her gloves, and she went home with her, and Aunt Wales said she had hardly got in the house before she said, "Well, Mrs. Cumming has sent you a bottle of snuff and Catherine a pair of gloves." "Yes," said Aunt Wales, "and she has sent me a gown too." "She has? Why, I did not hear anything of that," said she, "did you, Catherine?" and Aunt Wales says she really looked disappointed that she could not be the first to tell her. She had said to me, "I never saw such a person as Mrs. Cumming. She is always giving somebody something. I heard that she had given Anne Alston a beautiful veil."

By the way, speaking of the latter, you did come very near having the young ladies a month longer or just as long as you pleased. Mr. & Mrs. Alston, and Henrietta, dined here Sunday and spent several hours. Mrs. Alston said, "Anne was delighted with her visit, and she loves *July* very much." She said they gave her a severe scolding for coming home, and Mr. Alston said he had no notion of her coming home when she did. "I wanted her to stay a month longer." Miss Sperry, who was with them, asked me in a laughing way how Jane had liked her visit. I told her I did not know, but I believed she was very much pleased. "But why do you laugh?" I enquired. "Nothing," said she, still laughing, "only I believe that Anne told me everything Jane said or did while she was gone." Henrietta asked me if it was possible Mrs. Terrill had staid with you, and how she enjoyed herself, and if there was much attention paid to her.

Goode and Sophia [age fifteen and twelve respectively] have been *by* nearly all the time since I have been writing, talking very loudly. They do amuse me extremely sometimes, their teasing ways to each other, and the contempt they pretend to throw on each other, while they mutually have a high respect for one another. Sophia has lately taken it into her head to study after supper, and she sometimes goes into the room where the boys have a fire. Goode does not like to have her, and says, "*Soph,* you love boys too well for my use."

Just now, says she to him, "Brother Goode, I heard a compliment paid you by a young lady while I was gone. Mary Gardner said, 'Sophia, is that your younger brother's portrait?' and I told her, 'Yes,' and she said, 'He is very handsome. Does he look like it now?' and, said she, I told her 'Not much now, for you was much coarser.'" "I'll be bound," says she, "she was a little upstart like you, one of your dropshot sort." "Sister," said he, turning to me, "what sized gal is she?" I told him she was not quite as large as Julia Sheldon. "Well, she's not large enough for me. If ever I marry Julia Sheldon," he said, pulling up his new black cravat with a very mannish air, "I want her to be a great deal larger than she is now."

Brother left home yesterday for Clarke and does not expect to be at home until Friday. I wish, Julia, you would consent to come up, whether Brother goes down or not. I think you would enjoy a fortnight at home very much, just fix the time in your next. Pa is more than willing to send the carriage if Mr. Cumming can spare you. [Julia visited her family for a fortnight in March.]

Ma is, I think, a great deal better than she was, and infinitely more cheerful since she came home.

Mr. Stiles is probably with you now. He spoke to me very affectionately of you and the pleasant times he had while he staid with you. "I really became attached to her," said he, and as he had frequently remarked to me before, "I never knew her until then." We had a very interesting meeting. No one united with the Church, but Mrs. Suc—— [under seal] professes to have experienced a change of heart, and Amanda Morse and Margaret Little wished to come forward but were advised to wait until another opportunity.

Do write very soon. Tell Sarah [Cumming, Henry's youngest sister] I hope she will continue in the mind to come up with you. This is emphatically a *gossiping* letter, but I supposed you would like to know all that has transpired — of importance I was going to say, but little of importance ever occurs in this peaceful region. Do write by Monday's mail, for I like to have a letter for the stage Tuesday which is the only certain way we have of sending one. Kiss Annie, and remember me to Mr. Cumming.

Yours affectionately.

The Bryan house is going up at last. Julia's sister-in-law is visiting the Bryans. In Maria's letters neighbors and friends come and go for dinner—often no more than an unidentifiable name and a snatch of conversation. But Julia Cumming evidently knew them all and appreciated news about them. Although Joseph Bryan had been away from Milford, Connecticut, for nearly forty years, the place of his birth still had a sentimental interest for his children, and the small doings of the "Milford people" are briefly recounted here by Maria.

Maria Bryan to Julia Ann Bryan Cumming

March 27, 1827 (Tuesday Morning)

My dear Julia,

I felt very much disappointed that I did not receive a letter from you by either of the two last mails. Mr. Douglas who arrived late Saturday night informed us that you were much better. He dwells with much seeming delight on his last visit, and is very warmly attached to you. Henry, he seems to love as a brother. He said to me the other day that you two were the only couple he ever had known, which he could like equally and feel no drawback from one or the other. "The Colonel [William Cumming]," he says, "treated me just as I like to be in one's house. He did not make a fuss with his hospitality. 'Twas as if he took it for granted that I was at *home,* and he did not seem to think it necessary to be any more from his office, or seat himself down to talk with and entertain me."

Yesterday morning, we received a visit from Mrs. Richardson and her granddaughter Jane spent the day with us, and, though my wits were sorely stretched to entertain her, on the whole I like her a great deal better than I have before. She came with a very pressing invitation from her mother to Anne [Cumming, a particular friend of Maria's], to spend either Wednesday or Thursday with her, and the latter has promised to go.

Mrs. John Berrian and her daughter Mrs. John Whitehead [Julia Maria Berrien] were at church on Sabbath, and came home and dined with us. They came to Sparta to see Mrs. W.'s little daughter, and Miss Douse. Mrs. Berrian enquired very particularly and kindly of you, and expressed a wish to see your child, and likewise that you might see Eliza's. I did not expect to see her as composed. She appears not only resigned but even cheerful.

Pa is still hard at work on the house. He says he wishes us to move before he goes to Macon, though it seems, to look at the place, as if it would take a month to clean it. Ma now and then speaks as if she would like to accompany him to the Presbytery, or at least go as far as to Cousin Caroline's, but I do not know what she will determine on.

Mr. Foote and his wife intend going on to the North, in a month or two. What is to be done with the school if they do go we cannot tell. He is informed that the Milford people have dismissed Mr. Clarke, their minister, and he wishes to succeed him if he should be pleased with the place. Don't you think it will be a shame for him to leave Georgia when he was educated by the people of this State? Carlisle [Beman] has concluded not to go on himself to the North but has written for his wife to come out with her brother Garret.

I believe I have told you all the news, and really this rainy dull day makes me feel so stupid that I cannot write anything else. I disliked, however, to allow another mail to pass without something from us to you. Ma is not so well today, although on the whole I think she is better since she returned. Give my love to Mr. Cumming and Sarah and all who will care for my remembrance.

Ever your affectionate Sister.

Do write soon.

The Bryans have not yet moved into the new house. In the family circle Goode is "thoughtful," Sophia "sulky," Ma "low spirited," and Maria's twenty-five-year-old brother Joseph "unhappy."

Maria Bryan to Julia Ann Bryan Cumming

April 6, 1827 (Thursday Evening—9 o'clock)
[Thursday was April 5]

My dear Julia,

We are quite alone tonight, the house which so lately was a scene of bustle and confusion, is now quiet as can be. Joe, you know, never speaks unless, like a ghost, he is first spoken to. Goode seems very thoughtful. Robert, in a temporary fit of pique, has gone to tarry with Aunt Wales. Sophia is sulky because I told her the talents of the little Alstons were as good as hers, and

Ma, as is usually the case, when Pa is gone and she is alone, seems to be very low spirited. But what adds very much to her depression is the thought of Brother.

Julia, I think he is one of the most unhappy young men I know. He staid with us until late in the afternoon and, as Ma says, if Pa could have seen his conduct and heard his expressions, it would almost have broken his heart. His temper is more irritable than ever I knew it. He speaks in bitterness of everything and almost everybody. [He] said today he wishes he had been taught a trade, and never had known a letter in the book. As to his being religious, he said that was a thing entirely out of the question — and as for being sent to Hell, he thought that place "was no greater a place of torment than this world." Oh, it makes my heart ache to see him. I feel almost unkind to speak thus, both for his sake and yours, but I trust I have not a spirit of harshness towards him, and I know you have a right, and wish to be informed of all our family concerns, griefs as well as joys. All we can do for him is to pity and pray for him. Let us pray for him, my dear Julia. He is the same Brother whom we once loved beyond everyone but our parents, whom we once knew so *kind,* and so *amiable,* him on whom for twenty five years the anxious hope and care and expectation of his Father, and the doting affection of his Mother has been placed. If evil, worse evil befall him, truly we may fear that the heads of his parents will be brought with sorrow to the grave.

I hope you will not be much disappointed that I did not go down with Anne [Cumming] as I hope to be able to come before very long. 'Tis growing late so farewell for tonight.

April 7, 1827
(Saturday Night — 10 o'clock)
[Postmark: April 10]

I have been very sorry that I have not had an opportunity of sending this to the mail. I shall have to wait until Monday morning and by that time it will be considerably out of date.

Margaret Bailey [Maria's close friend] is quite sick with the fever. I saw her yesterday morning and she was confined to her bed having just had a chill, and Sophia who came from there this evening says she is worse, and that her mother is very much depressed. I do not know of anyone for whom I feel so sorry. Mr. Norton it is said (entre nous) drinks a great deal, and though not unkind, is far from being the devoted husband he once was. But what is certain, is that instead of soothing and consoling his wife and family in their misfortunes, he yields not only to gloom, but indulges harsh repinings whose profanity is absolutely shocking. The other day he came in and one of the children had had a chill. He fretted and stormed, and said, "Well, I do think God Almighty treats me worse than anybody in the world." "Oh husband," said Mrs. Norton, and turned pale as death. It reminds me much of Alice and Walter Syndbay.

Today I was there and while I stayed Mrs. Smith and Mrs. Lacee came in, and I was quite amused at the little conversation which took place which, by the way, is hardly proper to put on paper. "*Natheless.*" Little John needed some office to be performed about his person not of the most delicate kind and Mrs. Smith took him in her lap to do it. While thus engaged, she laughed and said, "Maria, I wonder how you would like to do this if you had a child."

"Oh very well," said I. "Julia often does it for *her* child."

"She *does?* Well now, it was only the other day that Nancy Carrington and I were talking of it, and wondering if she had ever done it in her life for her child."

Mr. and Mrs. Lancaster came this afternoon, and I have never before seen Joe so much moved to any passion as to joy in seeing them. We have likewise Dr. Hanes with us tonight. He is, as usual, extremely civil and sociable, and really is quite entertaining and agreeable in his conversation. He certainly is not so much of an egotist as he once was, but he reminded me of a half cured [drunkard] who, when now & then overcome by the force of strong temptation, takes such large draughts as amply to remunerate him for his temporary abstinence. Mr. Satterlee [a Sparta friend of her brother Joseph's], who was here this afternoon, proffered his services in a very earnest manner to carry me to Augusta. I am far from intending to take him at his word, however. I trust, though, that some means of conveyance more to my liking will occur before very long as I wish to go as soon as we move, for I had rather be there before it grows so very warm. Do write very soon. Ma has been quite unwell, but seems a little cheered up this evening.

In haste, yours affectionately.

Love to my Brother Henry.

Mrs. Rossiter has been begging me for some time to ask you if you have forgotten to send up the cotton to knit Mr. Cumming's socks. She says she cannot finish those she has begun until she can get more.

Maria Bryan to Julia Ann Bryan Cumming

[April 11, 1827] (Wednesday Evening)

I was very much gratified to hear from you today, my dear Julia, for I had made up my mind to get a letter from you and should have been dreadfully disappointed if I had not received one. I am glad you feel satisfied with my excuse. Pa says, "Oh, Julia is far from being unreasonable." I did mean to write you a long letter but have not time now. Mr. Smith says he will call and deliver this and he is going immediately after breakfast. He preached last night, and I have not heard a better sermon in three years.

Pa has returned from Macon very much delighted with his visit. He says you must request Uncle Jacob to call at Mr. Ponce's and get some things Mr. Burroughs has sent. We wished very much to get into the house this week if we could, but I think we shall be obliged to defer it until the beginning of next. I will endeavour to write a long letter as soon as I get time as you seem to think I am very brief. Sophia tells me to say to you that as soon as Annie wears out her feathers she will send her some more.

Give my love to Mr. Cumming, and kiss Annie. Do excuse the shortness of this letter but Mr. Smith is going. Ma is pretty well.

Ever yours.

The Bryans have now moved into their new house, and it being springtime, Maria begins to ask Julia when she is coming home for a visit.

Maria Bryan to Julia Ann Bryan Cumming

April 17, 1827 (Tuesday Morning)

My dear Julia,

I was very agreeably surprised in receiving a letter from you yesterday, but it certainly was short and sweet as Pa says. I intended to have answered it last night and wrote a long letter, but I felt so sick that I was obliged to go to bed.

Ma has been considerably better since we came here — indeed the excitement of scrubbing and "putting to rights" seems to animate her very much. Pa is quite unwell although he keeps constantly at work. He has a very bad cough and looks pale.

Mac Goode [1803–42, the second son of Ma Bryan's brother Samuel Watkins Goode] spent the night with us. He has just returned from Philadelphia, and when he entered I had not the slightest recollection of him, so much is he altered. He walked directly up to me and called me cousin, and even then, to save my life, I could not remember him. He is very much grown, about the size of Casey, and very much improved. He is really a very genteel young man. You would meet him in the street and be very apt to take him for Mr. Ringold, or at least for his twin brother, and he is altogether more interesting than [his older brother] Hamilton. He says he was a day or two in Augusta, and would certainly have gone to see you, but (very complimentary) he entirely forgot that you lived there, until he got here and they asked him if he had "seen his Cousin Julia."

We heard this morning that Henrietta Alston professed to be converted. She went last week with Mr. Howard to Milledgeville where there was a meeting, and arrived home yesterday or the day before. Mr. Howard seems at present to exercise great influence over the whole family. He goes home with them from church and has family worship, and Mr. Alston says he made the first prayer that was ever heard in that house.

When do you mean to come home? You never say anything about it. I am very often asked if you are going to spend the summer with us, and when you will be here. Mr. Douglas says when he went to Mrs. Richardson's that she asked him a great many questions about us all, and at last asked him how he liked me. "Maria," said she, "is a very good girl — but I think she courts attention rather too much."

Daniel Richardson is making preparations, it is said, to go to Macon and court Catherine McDonald. I have no doubt of it for my part. You would hardly know him he is so much improved in dress and appearance. I heard that he says he never was happy but when his Mary smiled on him.

You must have been dreadfully *hurt,* it made my blood *crawl* as they say, to hear the recital—but poor Mr. Davis, I expect, suffered even worse, for, as Mr. Douglas says, laudanum could not cure him.

I still live in the hope of being able to go and see you this Spring, but when or how, I am unable to say. From Anne [Cumming] I account our little niece is more lovely than ever. I think Thomas is on the wane in her affections. She says Annie's eyes look like "lakes—so deep and blue and calm."

Have you heard that David Smith and Carrington have sold their store in Barefield. David and Turner are going into partnership, and settle in Walton. I have heard several whispered suspicions of late that he and Catherine would yet be married but I cannot be sure.

I really am rejoiced that we are so far from Aunt Wales and Catherine for they have so little kindness to us that I do not like to be compelled to see them whether we will or no, and I firmly believe they hate me.

Do write soon, and frequently. Pa and Ma send their love to Mr. Cumming and yourself. Sophia says, "Give my love to Sister and Brother Henry and tell them to kiss Annie twenty times for me."

In haste, yours affectionately.

Following Julia's brief spring visit, Maria writes that at her parents' request she is taking lessons from a man who cuts men's garments on "mathematical principles." She hates it.

Maria Bryan to Julia Ann Bryan Cumming

June 4, 1827 (Monday Morning, Evening Rather)
Oh, I am so glad, my dear Julia, that you have concluded to come. [Julia Cumming would return to Mt. Zion from June 10 to November 15.] Pa says he will dispatch the horses Friday morning. I do not think there has been as long a time since you left here that proper time prevented us from hearing from

you until this morning which makes it a fortnight. Ma has been dreadfully uneasy and has had all sorts of fancies about you — and it was only yesterday evening when Uncle Jacob brought your note that she could be persuaded you might be well.

I am very much obliged to you for the collars and so forth that you sent — nothing could be more acceptable. My bonnet I like a great deal better than I did before, and it is a great deal more becoming than it was. I write in absolute pain, for there is a couple of Kentuckyians sitting by and talking very loud. One of them giving an account to Pa and Ma of "Ulisious Lewis" who, he says, collected three hundred dollars for him and has never paid him. We have had Ben Franklin with us a day or two past; he brought a letter from Catherine M. in which she inquires about you, and seems anxious to visit you. Franklin says she does not expect to go to Augusta, for she has no way, but he expresses a willingness to carry her, and indeed I think would like to do so very much. He is a very smart young man, and very agreeable, and I think is extremely amiable.

I hope Brother is enjoying himself. I believe he anticipated a great deal of pleasure in this visit. Uncle Jacob was giving Pa a long account of the trouble he had with his horse, when he met him. "I did not know before," said he, "that Mas Joe ever cursed. Maybe he did not curse his horse!" "Hut-tut-tut," said Pa, "I am astonished at Joseph," and he seemed really grieved. I thought Uncle Jacob might have had a little more discretion.

Margaret says that Mrs. Terrill intends going to Elbert before long, but says she will certainly come and see you before you go home. Ma says she asked her if *I* did not think *you* were smarter than any other person in the world. Margaret, says she, told her she believed I thought you were a non pareil in some things. She enquired if I had not told her how Anne had treated Jane. "No," said Margaret, "she had not." "You have not seen her, have you?" "Yes," said Margaret, "I staid with her the Sunday after the Sacrament." "Ah, that was the reason," said she. "When you see her again I'll be bound she tells you." Margaret said she became acquainted with Miss Sherrill and she seems very much attached to you. She told her how very kindly and politely she was treated at the house — though when she remembered, as she frequently did, in what manner she had gotten to the house she could not help from feeling a little mortified.

There is a man in the neighbourhood who is teaching school to learn to cut *men's* garments, coat, vest, pantaloons, on mathematical principles. I am going to him to please Pa and Ma, though I never did hate to engage in anything more in my life. Today while I was occupied there, Pa came and said Lavinia wanted to see me. I ran out and found her and Pulaski sitting in the gig. They would not be persuaded to call. I spoke to them as kindly as I could though *they,* particularly *Lavinia,* seemed confused. She urged me very much to go and see her and said she would send Milton for me. I do not feel disposed to, for Mrs. B. [Bailey] says Mrs. Richardson, tells, "You see how the Bryans want to make up the breach. Mrs. Cumming and Maria came into the funeral."

Ben Franklin says Dr. Rogers is on the point of laying himself and his possessions at the feet of Miss Julia Forsythe [daughter of Senator John Forsyth of Augusta, Georgia]. You know him, don't you? that long fellow in the yellow breeches that we saw at Mrs. Alston's party; and that Mr. Everett Pierce is suspected of entertaining a similar intention with regard to the lady. I think she will have taken her pigs to a poor market if she accepts either of these gentlemen, and I know Cousin Goode is far superior to either, and I cannot but hope that he will be pleased with her.

Will you do me the favour to ask at Mr. Gates's for the notes of "Allen & Dale."

Yours affectionately.

Julia Cumming and her fifteen-month-old daughter, Anne, have returned to Augusta after a five-month visit in Mt. Zion. During their time away Henry Cumming visited them. He wrote from Mt. Zion to his father in Augusta that Annie is a fine child; she has a tooth and creeps. His wife, however, has not been in fine health since their marriage.

Maria gives Julia the local social news and reports on the rivalry of Hamilton Goode and Joseph Bryan Jr., first cousins and both twenty-six years old, for the attentions of a Miss Blair.

Maria Bryan to Julia Ann Bryan Cumming

December 16, 1827 (Sabbath Evening)
[Postmark: December 18]

My dear Julia,

Your letter was really quite refreshing. I am glad you took the trouble of telling me how my niece [Annie] was received in her *debut* into the society of her relations, and she certainly deserves my warmest approbation. Surely *then*, Celia's emphatic remark was true—"hit knows." I felt disappointed when I learnt that you did not receive my letter on Wednesday. I sent it to town by Hamilton [Goode]. I hope, however, that you have before this found out how faithful I have been.

We are all much obliged to you for the good things you sent. Sophia had eat herself into an ague, and Goode if he was not ague-proof, must certainly have done the same. *I,* like a more knowing and skillful epicure, feed with more moderation, but not, I presume, with less relish. For the frock likewise, receive my hearty thanks. I really have no choice in the silk—and indeed I had much rather you would choose for me. I must observe by the way however, that those at the lowest price are an object in these hard times of ours.

I received an invitation to Kitty's wedding last night, written I suppose by Mr. King—in which he informed me that "Mr. John Lucas and Lady send their compliments" to me and desire to see me the nineteenth. I feel no anxiety whatever to go, but Ma insists upon it and says she will go to Mrs. Rossiter's and stay, and the latter urges me with all imaginable earnestness, as she will thereby obtain Ma's company which she could not expect on any other conditions. The news of the neighbourhood at present is that "Squire Reeves has a daughter" and that there is great joy and rejoicing in consequence, and that Daniel Richardson has returned with his mother-in-law.

I am very glad to hear that there is some hope of a revival in Augusta. If Sarah [Cumming] were indeed to become pious, it would be an event equally astonishing and gladdening. I told Brother that Anne [Cumming] had joined the Church, and he seemed considerably startled at first. After a pause of some minutes, "Now," said he, "she will marry a minister." Ma wishes me to say to you that her health is very much as usual.

Give my love to Mr. Cumming and the baby. Tell Anne I expected a letter from her by George. Remember me to Catherine [Wales] and tell her she must not forget her promise to write me. I hope she is pleased with her new acquaintances and will be pleased with her visit. I am very much afraid I shall not be able to send this by tomorrow's mail but do not blame *me*. Excuse the shortness of this letter. I will write again soon and write more. Do let me hear from you often.

Your affectionate Sister.

P.S. Ma has begged me every time I have written to ask you to send her word whether you have left anything you need. We entirely forgot to send the epaulette box. H. [Hamilton Goode] intimated to Brother (so he tells us) that he has little doubt of succeeding with Miss Blair—and strongly recommended Miss H. to his notice. Brother told him he need not say a word, for he was determined to see Miss B. and he should have a poor opinion of himself if he thought he could not cut him [Hamilton] out. At this remark, Brother says, he seemed but little pleased. Aunt Wales is much better.

Yours in haste.

Maria seldom reveals even to Julia any personal interest in young men. Here, however, Mr. Douglas, the preacher, engages her attention and admiration, and she writes, "I am half crazy to see him."

Maria Bryan to Julia Ann Bryan Cumming

January 31, 1828 (Thursday Evening)

My dear Julia,

Oh! how earnestly I still hope to receive a letter from you by yesterday's mail, but alas, as usual, not a word from you. It is after nine o'clock, and Robert has to sleep on the floor with Goode, so as I got my writing materials ready Pa said to me I must go away, for Robert would not go to bed while I staid. But still reasoning as Horace did about the timber, I bethought me whether the self-denial of Robert would be so great as the advantage gained, and of the result. *Ecce Signum!*

Your friend Mr. Chamberlain came tonight, and of course Pa asked him to go to prayers. Among his petitions for the family, he prayed that "She who was to all human appearance on the confines of the grave," might be supported. Such things of late have quite an unhappy influence on Ma, and I dreaded that this would, but, serious as was the subject, I could not refrain from laughing at the manner of the man and the little discretion that he manifested. After Ma went in her room to go to bed I followed her, and said smiling, "Ma, Mr. Chamberlain seemed determined to bury you without delay." She laughed and said, "He seemed to be so convinced that my fate was fixed that he did not even pray for me to be restored."

Mr. Williams and Mr. Douglas have been staying with us for a day or two, but they have now both gone, the one to Milledgeville, the other to Sparta. They are very fine young men and we are all highly pleased with them. I really cannot tell you how much I like Douglas. He is really an admirable character, so entirely free from the slightest affectation. Margaret [Bailey] came here last night and has been staying with me ever since. She expresses almost an extravagant wish to go to see you, and has a trembling hope that she may be able to do so, as her brother has partly promised to take her. She has just this moment turned round and begged me to give her love to you, and say that she does long to go and see you.

Pa and Ma went to Sparta today, the former principally to see Brother, and enquire definitely into the state of his affairs. Ma says he appeared very much affected. She put in at Mr. Wilcox's whilst Pa and he were conversing, and the former remarked to him that his mother felt dreadfully about him, and that now she could not stand very much. Ma says when he came in to the shop he did not look at her, and appeared as if he hardly could speak to her. They however seemed considerably more composed about him, and he told Pa that he would come out tomorrow, for he wanted to have a long conversation with him.

Mr. Jones and Martha Carnes are both extremely low with the pleurisy. Ma says she would not be surprised at all to hear of Martha's death. Yesterday her poor little suffering boy was buried. It was not sicker than common. They laid it down in its cradle to sleep and when they looked at it some time after, the little creature was lifeless. Only a faint quivering of the skin was discernible, and it breathed no more.

February 1, 1828 (Friday Evening)

We received your notes and presents by Uncle Jacob today, and thank you for remembering us so kindly. Ma says she does think there never was a better child than you in the world. A few hours after your note came Margaret had gone home, and her mother came in. I read her what you said of Margaret's going to see you. She desired me to give her love to you, and thank you for your kind invitation, and say that she had never her heart more set on anything, and that nothing should be lacking on her part to enable her to go. If her brother could make it convenient to carry her you might depend on a visitor. Alexander has been, and still is, very sick with the yellow jaundice; he looks dreadfully.

Mrs. Rossiter continues quite as unwell; today we heard that she was more so. She has not been out of her house, not even to church, in several weeks. I think you would be very much pleased with Mrs. Gildersleeve, as well as induced to pity her very much; she is a woman of very considerable refinement, as well as intelligence, and I cannot but feel sorry that she has not a husband more of her own stamp of character. By the bye, speaking of this family, Mr. Williams told us of Mr. Gildersleeve's disappointment with Urania. It seems when he went down to Milledgeville with Mr. Smith & Wilson, that that was his business but contrary to his hopes and my fears, she gave him a most decided negative. I really was considerably surprised, for I was impressed with the notion, which I communicated to you, that she was *softened* towards him. I believe I quite shocked Mr. Williams who, in the kindness of his heart, was pitying him very much by expressing most unequivocally my sincere gratification. It has been generally supposed that Mrs. Rossiter was an advocate for him, but she was exchanging sentiments with me on the subject some time ago, and intimated plainly that she did not approve of the thing. She said (as I understood her, in reference to him), that *love* was a very restless, uneasy passion and had but lately seen one affected by it in its greatest height, and she surely had her sympathy and even pity very much excited. *Entre nous,* if you please.

We are all very anxious to see the trio which compose your family. That blessed little creature I verily think I could devour. Will you not pay us at least a flying visit? Pa says he will send for you with all his heart if you will consent to come. Ma, I think, is better within a day or two, and her spirits are certainly much better. I think the two young Timothys have been of great service to her. They have been so vastly attentive to her, talking with her, and seeking to cheer her up. She likes them as much as I ever knew her to like strangers, particularly Douglas, whom, she says, "really is an exception."

By the way, as I never omit telling of a compliment, Douglas flatters me very much by calling me like Mary Gardner. Satterlee calls "Capitano Ramathic" *ugly*. Nevertheless I am half crazy to see him. I do wish he would come back this way. How many hearts do you think he will carry away with him? Anne & Sarah, I am inclined to suspect, have been captivated. You ought to be thankful that your daughter is not grown, as you might have trouble with her. Just to think of her falling in love. But it makes me distracted to see her just to talk, or think of her. Catherine McDonald speaks of coming up before long to stay a day or two. If she does, I think I shall return with her.

Do, my dear Julia, try and write oftener—your letters are so infrequent. You said something of adopting my plan of writing a little every day. I shall be tempted to doubt your "gratitude" for mine, if you do not give greater proof of it. Indeed I sometimes fancy that their number is oppressive. Henceforth, I think I shall confine myself to answering yours, in order that the correspondence may be more proportionate. My love to Mr. Cumming.

Your affectionate Sister.

For all its fresh air and sunshine Mt. Zion was afflicted with its full share of ill health, and Maria's letters report these details. Maria's account of Mt. Zion's interest in establishing churches and schools, however, was unusual for such a semifrontier community in the Old South. Carlisle Beman was to remain on and off at Mt. Zion Academy until 1859. At this writing he had more than fifty pupils at the academy.

Maria Bryan to Julia Ann Bryan Cumming

February 18, 1828 (Monday Evening)

My dear Julia,

I have such a dreadful headache, and altogether feel so badly that if tomorrow was not mail day, I should certainly put off writing until another time. It makes me so stupid, too, that I feel as if I had not a single clear idea.

Pa and Ma have both been quite unwell, since I wrote last. I do not know but the latter is as much indisposed as she was before she left home. They talk of paying a short visit to Uncle Sam [Goode, of Montgomery, Alabama] principally for the sake of traveling. I think if you were to come up with Annie and stay awhile, it would be the best medicine she could have. Do come, Julia. I do not know anything that would cheer *me* so much. It seems almost an age since you were here.

Brother does not say whether he means to pay you a visit or not, though I have several times asked him. His health is very bad. He has a chill and high fever now every night, and when it is on him he talks constantly and most eloquently. He was from home the other night and, I am told, in his delirium gave a long discourse on the truths of Christianity.

Ma is at present very much engaged in planting and building. Brother brought her upwards of forty different kinds of flower seed from Greene, and Achilles is constructing a most splendid summer house, that is, he thinks so.

You say that I might write two letters to your one, but if you knew how much I have to do you would not think so. Sophia confines me very closely, and takes up a good deal of my time, for she has a number of studies, and recites long lessons, and I am now serving for Ma for she has an abundance of work. You know how very slow Patty is, and her child being constantly sick takes her off from her work frequently. And Ma has to make Brother's shirts, and clothes for Goode & Robert & Joe, and Pa insists on having Dr. Brown's clothes made here, for he says if they are given to them, they will be ruined.

We were very sorry to lose the box, and with regard to myself, as Ma says, the want of my articles is more than the worth of them. There is nothing I regret more than my little shawls, but I was much relieved to find my blue cap saved. Pa intimated that he could have borne the loss of that with peculiar fortitude. I will thank you to send my bonnet by Uncle Jacob as I shall need it soon.

Pa returned last night from South Liberty where himself, Dr. Brown and Mr. Beman were Sunday, and the Dr. remained to organize a church today. Pa says he staid at Leroy's [Leroy Holt, Ma Bryan's nephew] who lives in the neighbourhood, and himself and his wife both appear to be serious. There is considerable religious feeling in the neighbourhood, and they intend inviting Mr. [Carlisle] Beman to preach for them part of the time. The latter has a very good school, about fifty three scholars, and Mr. Gregory is assisting him.

Eliza Little, it is said, is looking with quite a favourable eye upon our cousin John—who, with a broad black streamer upon his hat, is gallanting all the young ladies who are willing to receive his attentions. She has been for a long time, I believe, compelled to sing the mournful ditty, "Each has a love but me," but I think when she becomes Mrs. Childers she will strike up a strain still more in the Adagio.

I cannot tell you how very greatly Goode was disappointed when I told him what you have written about the prospect of obtaining a situation for him at West Point. Ever since he heard that Mr. Cumming had actually written on to Washington to engage Mr. Wilde's [Congressman Richard Henry Wilde from Augusta, Georgia] exertions, he has believed certainly that he should go, has studied considerably, and endeavoured to improve himself in writing and arithmetic, and it was really a great shock to him that the case was doubtful, and even unfavourable. He says, now, "Oh I know I shan't go, and I don't care how soon Pa puts me to the plough, for if I can't go to West Point I do not want to go anywhere else."

I was sorry to hear of Mr. Stiles's unhappiness, although when he was here, he seemed very wretched. He did not eat enough to sustain life scarcely, and one day Ma was urging him to take something more, he said to her, "I have meat to eat that ye know not of." Ma said she frequently accounted for his abstinence by assigning that reason. "Not holy thoughts either," said he. "What then," I asked him, "trouble?" "Yes," he answered. Pa told him just before he left here that if he did not live so far off, he would invite himself to his wedding. "Ah," said he, "I don't know; all my concerns are uncertain, and though I know nothing, yet I have been so unfortunate that I dread something constantly, and I sometimes think that Providence never intends that I shall enjoy the comforts of domestic life."

I am very much obliged to you for thinking of my necessity and contributing to relieve it. You seem to possess that kind of imagination which some moralist has said is the foundation of benevolence, "putting oneself in the place of another, and fancying what may be their feelings, and their wants, and their troubles."

Pa requests that you would get Sophia a comb suitable for keeping up her hair behind. If you cannot get it at either of the two places where he deals, send him the bill from some other place and he will pay it. Ma wishes you to get her a couple of the same kind of dresses as those she lost, either at Field's or Kyle's, and get at the former's two swan's down (she calls it) vest patterns, for Goode, and a yard of jacconet to ruffle night caps. Pa who is sitting by, says, "Tell Julia the carriage can go for her at any time when she chooses to come up." Do write soon.

Affectionately yours.

Julia and her young daughter Annie visited Mt. Zion for three weeks in March 1828, and Julia took Ma and Pa back with her for a visit to Augusta. Now the Mt. Zion house has an air of desertion.

Maria Bryan to Julia Ann Bryan Cumming

March 31, 1828 (Monday Night)

My dear Julia,

So many things may occur between now and Friday to prevent my having a letter ready that to be certain I will begin the promised one tonight. Perhaps, too, I am induced by the craving of some intercourse with you, occasioned by a three weeks' luxury of that kind. I am almost sick tonight, too. I feel just as I did that Spring when I had the Influenza at your house. My bones and my head ache, and I have some fever but I am going to bathe my feet and hope I shall be well in the morning.

Brother has been in the house nearly all day, writing. This evening he has been conversing very fully of Henrietta [Alston] and the family, and protests that he has nothing serious in view with regard to the former, and says he does not think he could get her if he wanted her. I accused him of being in love with her. He denies it, but very faintly, I thought.

Sophia came to me this evening and said Harriet did want her to ask her to stay all night with her very much. This I understood to be a hint, and as I thought she must be lonely I told her to ask H., so that she has been spending quite a jolly evening. They are in quiet possession of your room, and as I pass by, Sophy said she did feel so bad, that room made her "think so much of Sister and Annie." We do indeed miss you very much, the house hardly looks like the same place, and you can hardly imagine the appearance of desertion it has.

Today Creasy sent Daphne down to Dr. Rossiter's for something, and when she came back I was sitting on the sofa sewing and Sophia came running to me. "Sister," [said Sophia,] "Aunt Rossiter is speechless, and Mrs. Brown says we must go down there directly." I threw my work down in an instant and was running to get ready, thinking I might find Mrs. R. in the agonies of death. I stopped a moment and reflected that it was only Daphne's tale, and I knew that she [Mrs. Rossiter] could not speak during a paroxysm of her violent headaches. Just then she [Daphne] came up, stuttering in her haste to relieve herself of the news. "Miss Rossiter had got a very bad headache. Miss Brown says she can't say nothing at all and she say she wants you to go there." Sophia saw the latter this evening, and she confirmed the report that Mrs. Rossiter had had a very sick day. I suppose from coming out and driving herself yesterday, but I do not know when I have been more alarmed than at Sophia's sudden intelligence.

April 3, 1828 (Thursday Night)

Emily Walker has come. After receiving repeated messages during the day to go and see her, Sophia and I walked up late in the evening. She is very cheerful, and steps about with as light and active a movement as if she weighed no more than she did the *nineteenth* of last June [when Emily Brown married John Walker]. She looks a little strange, to be sure, and I could hardly prevent an undue excitement of my *risibles,* but on the whole she does not look badly. Her person [Emily is pregnant] was very decorously covered with a shawl (*a la* Mrs. Cumming, "as Maria would say"), and though not quite as lovely an object as a field of green wheat, upon the whole she appears tolerably interesting as a young wife. To confess the truth, however, as I was walking homeward I could not but regret that the happiness of the conjugal relation was obliged to be bought at so dear a price. I went likewise this afternoon to see Mrs. Norton and Aunt Wales.

Tell Sarah [Cumming] Mrs. N. was very easily pacified and regretted that she had not been to see her, not because she felt herself slighted, but she was "anxious to know Miss Sarah for every one who had become acquainted with her was so much delighted and spoke in such high terms of her." You may tell her moreover that I hear her praises and regrets that she is gone reiterated by all I see.

"Catherine is fled like a dream —
So vanishes pleasure, alas,
But has left a regret and esteem
That will not so speedily pass."

I found Catherine [Wales] gone on a fishing expedition with Cornelia DeWitt, Mrs. Kelsey, and such beaus as the neighbourhood could muster. Though I did not desire particularly to have gone, yet I felt slightly neglected at not being invited to join them, more especially as Catherine had formed one in every party of pleasure in which I have lately been engaged.

No one has been to stay with me yet, though I have been so hard at work since you left that I have not felt oppressively lonely. Sophia and Goode were standing together near me, looking very gloomy, and I said to them, "If Ma can only get better by her journey we ought not to regret being left alone." "*No*" — they both heartily exclaimed.

By the way, we heard from her this morning by Jemmy Lundy, and were very much pleased and I hope thankful to know that she was doing very well. Brother came in smiling in a very joyful manner, and said, "Ri, Jemmy Lundy says he staid with Mother last night, and she said she was better than when she left home." I do hope she will be much improved, and do let us hear from you all as often as possible.

Will you say to Mr. Williams, Julia, that I regret very much that I forgot to give him his pen knife which I borrowed. If I could find any way I would send it down before he leaves Augusta. The article I wished to have put on my memorandum was some hooks and eyes of various sizes. Tell Ma not to forget *tape*. I saw Carlisle [Beman] this evening, and he says, "Julia's admiration of my boy flatters me very much." He is engaged might and main against the Baptists, and was going, when I met him, to have the bell rung, for he said, "Old Daddy *Battle* [a Baptist minister] had come again," and he was determined to have the meeting in the usual way. See how these Christians love one another.

Do write to me very soon. Present me very affectionately to your Colonel.

Give my love to Pa and Ma. Tell the latter if good wishes will do her any good, she has them from everybody for her restoration. I am almost ashamed to ask you not to forget to send my old green veil, for it is almost one of my indispensables. My love to Anne & Sarah.

Yours truly.

A late spring frost has killed crops and flowers. Pa will probably have to cut his Augusta visit short and return to Mt. Zion to replant.

Maria Bryan to Julia Ann Bryan Cumming

April 7, 1828

My dear Julia,

I was very much alarmed this morning for an instant after receiving your and Anne's letter. I observed that they were both but *partly* filled and I imagined that you had written in haste to inform me of Ma's increased indisposition, or something worse, and I involuntarily turned and looked at the seal. Travelling does indeed seem to have a magical effect upon her, and I cannot but hope her improved health will be permanent.

I am afraid that Pa will feel obliged to hurry home on account of Brother's information, with regard to the frost. There is great lamentation in the neighbourhood on account of the destruction it has caused. Mr. Richardson and Robert in particular are distressed, the one for his corn and wheat, the other for his garden. We have endeavoured to take good care of Ma's flowers, but the "nipping frost" has destroyed many a "fair young bud." Robert says he wishes I would write to Pa to get some more garden seed for everything is killed. Tell Ma I have taken special care of her *baby,* and have taken her with me everywhere I have gone.

This afternoon we spent at Mr. Little's. They certainly do appear better in their own house than anywhere else. They regretted not having seen you, and Sarah and Eliza said that every day they had wished to come and see you but always heard that the house was full of company. I was amused at a remark at Mr. Little's. Eliza said that her Mother and Sarah thought she *talked* too much. I observed to the former that if she complained of Eliza, I did not know what she would think of *me*. "You? Why you are a very silent girl, everybody gives you that character. Whenever I hear people speak of you they say you are very silent. You don't say harm of anybody, and that you are a very *harmless good creature*." I was aware that many of the neighbours had this opinion of me, Catherine [Wales] passes for the wit among them, but I did not expect to be told to my face that my highest encomium was simply that I was a "harmless good creature."

I hope by this time you have seen more of your *Beloved*. If not, I think you might as well come back to us at once. Brother has been at home most of the time since you left here, except two or three times he has been to Sparta. He is there tonight so that we have to keep house alone.

Tell Pa that Mr. Craft has again lost his wife. He had carried her to Carolina to her father's to be confined, promising to be with her at the time that the event was expected to take place. He went, and in two or three miles of the place he met some person who told him his wife had given birth to a child. He rode on in fine spirits, alighted at the house, and met the family with the utmost cheerfulness. After going through with the customary greetings, he enquired how his wife was doing, and to his consternation learned that she had been dead four days.

Nathan Warner is likewise dead. Though he was a man who never interested me much except for his personal beauty yet I have felt very melancholy since hearing of his death, for it does afford so striking a proof of the vanity of earthly things. He had so much to make life desirable, doing remarkably well in his profession, rising to wealth and eminence, married to a fine woman, but lately a father, and cut off in the midst of all.

Mrs. Rossiter is much better since I wrote last. Mrs. Russell is much more unwell. Saturday her mother thought she was dying. I saw her this evening. She was sitting up, though she appeared to be extremely feeble.

Do write soon. I shall hope to get a letter by Wednesday's mail. Goode was very much pleased at getting yours this morning though it seems he is unable to bring his mind to the mighty task of answering it. Give my love to Pa and Ma if they are still with you, and Mr. Cumming. Tell Sarah I find she passes for a beauty, in the neighbourhood. Mrs. Little and Eliza said she was so handsome and looked so modest that they liked her looks very much.

Yours very affectionately.

Maria recommends a book to Julia, Anna Maria Porter's novel Honor O'Hara, *published in 1826. She describes the book's hero, Lord Francis Fitzjames, in highly romantic terms and says, "There are no such men in these parts, or I should fall in love."*

Maria Bryan to Julia Ann Bryan Cumming

April 14, 1828 (Monday Evening)

My dear Julia,

I sent Henny upstairs a moment ago for the inkstand and letter paper, and she came down with a small piece about the fifth of a sheet. I concluded you would be but little satisfied at having only that filled, so after giving her a scold at her stupidity, I have at last got seated and address myself to my employment of writing to you.

Ma came home very unexpectedly to me. She was much better, and has continued to be so. Pa and herself have gone tonight to Mrs. Brown's, so we are alone again, for Brother is from home. Goode and Frank just now put in a humble petition, praying that I would allow them to go a-fishing. I offended them not a little by intimating that they chose purposely a night in which Pa was from home, but Goode says it is no such thing. He asked because the creek is in good order for fishing after the rain.

Henrietta Alston came out (Brother brought her) Saturday evening to attend the Baptist meeting and to witness the immersion, which took place yesterday. I suppose you knew the Baptists were to have had a two days meeting about this time. They were so offended with us that they refused to make use of the [Presbyterian] church though it was tendered to them, and cleared the grove where they intend to build their house, and placed benches there, and Saturday they preached there, but yesterday it rained so heavily that they were obliged to use the church.

I did not intend going to the baptizing but Henrietta was so anxious to see the ordinance performed that I accompanied her. There were five persons "immarsed," as Robert says, by the gentleman who is in the habit of promising his audience a "*little somhin.*" The two first I could sympathize with, Mrs. Ina Allen and Mrs. Plunkett. The former, who is a very good woman, appeared as if she acted from a sense of duty, and if [so] still it was a trial to her, and Mrs. Plunkett seemed to me like a victim, for they say she left this church against her will to please her husband. But there was so much of the ludicrous about Rowena that I could not refrain from laughing. They had tied up their heads just in the way that I do when I have no night cap, and you know that this is trying to the good looks of the handsomest woman. What effect then would you imagine it to have had on persons who, in a crowd, would be remarked for their plainness? What made it still more (ridiculous, I had like to have said) the banks were very steep opposite the place where they were baptized, and they had to go in at a sloping place twenty feet below and walk up the stream until it was sufficiently deep. The females whose feet were trammelled by having the bottom of their dresses tied, were obliged to walk very slow and make extremely short steps.

Before Mr. Battle put Nathan under the water as he was holding him, he said aloud, "I have seen this young man's father" (who was a preacher) "baptize many a one, and now I have the pleasure of baptizing him." He had said the day before, "I knew this good man, and was like a ripe watermelon, everybody loved him."

There was an old negro man went in (Jack's daddy-in-law) and as he was marching up, he laughed as you have seen persons when they were shouting.

"Don't laugh so, old man," said Mr. Battle in a low tone.

"I can't help it, Sir," said the other.

"Is it because you think you are following Christ in that ordinance makes you laugh?"

"Yes, Sir," was the reply.

As the old man was lifted up from the water there was a gush of tobacco spittle from his mouth, and altogether he was such a sight as is seldom seen. Moreover he was dressed in white hummums (or something of that kind) pantaloons with nothing under them, so that it stuck fast to his skin, and colour and form were distinctly visible through them. John Brown told me today that Phebe Thomas was very angry with me for laughing. I was surprised for I thought I had been so careful that, jealous as they are, the Baptists could see nothing to be offended at in my demeanor.

I was at Mrs. Bailey's today. John Bailey was there, and is quite a pleasant agreeable man, not unlike John Wilde in his appearance. He spoke of going to Augusta the first of next week, and Margaret asked him if he could not take *her.* He very readily consented, so that I should not be surprised if she paid you a visit of two or three days.

Julia, do if you can either buy, beg or borrow *Honor O'Hara,* Miss Porter's last novel. I have just read it, and was highly interested, not by the variety of adventures, hairbreadth escapes, or deep suspence which Cooper makes use of to wind up the excitement to the highest pitch, but just by the detail of domestic scenes, and making her characters so interesting to us that the slightest event connected with them draws our attention.

By the way, I was amused yesterday. Speaking of the book reminds me. "Henrietta," said I, "I have felt dreadfully in love with a character in a book I have been reading lately."

"What is his name?" she asked.

"Lord Francis Fitzjames."

"What kind of fellow was he?"

"Oh," said I, "he is represented as being a man of genius, very eccentric, melancholy, a poet, very handsome, with features regular as a Grecian statue and fine dark hair."

"And don't you know anyone who answers to that description?"

"No indeed," said I, "there are no such men in these parts, or I should fall in love."

"Well, I know," said she, "one person who exactly answers to that description."

"Who is it?" I enquired.

She refused to tell, and as I have every reason to be convinced it was *Brother,* I would not ask her; I suppose if I had added fifty other complimentary epithets, she would have fitted them all on to him. Strange!

Do tell me what Mr. Smith said, Ma cannot remember a word of it.

I am very much obliged to Mr. Cumming for those books. I think I shall be very much interested in them. Ma says I owe thanks to you for the box of Hooks & Eyes. Your reputation for generosity, Julia, stands very high in the family. *I* at least have reason to attribute it to you. My love to Anne. Tell Sarah, Henrietta says Brother Augustus was "very much taken with Sarah." Write soon.

Yours very affectionately.

Do not forget needles if you please.

Chapter Three

RESTLESS MARIA

"It was dictated more from a vague will to see the world a little beyond the limits of the Mt. Zion horizon. . . ."

Here Ma and Pa plan to go to Washington, Georgia, and perhaps on to Petersburg. Situated at the juncture of the Broad and Savannah rivers well above Augusta, Petersburg was once a thriving tobacco center with a population of eight hundred. With the coming of the railroads in the 1830s and 1840s, the town died and vanished from the map.

Maria Bryan to Julia Ann Bryan Cumming

April 22, 1828 (Tuesday)

My dear Julia,

I do not know when I have been more disappointed than when I found there was no letter from you in the last mail. It was only a short time before that I was boasting of our mutual punctuality. We should have been afraid you were sick had *not* Pa seen Mr. Musgrove, who told him he had left you well.

Ma has been very unwell again. Today she has been mostly on the bed. They had fixed on this morning to set off for Washington, but last evening Joseph Cunningham came, and continues here until tomorrow, which compelled them to put off their journey until then; they have some idea of extending their visit to Petersburg. Mr. Cunningham is a tall, rawboned man, extremely pale in appearance and manners. He appears to be very much devoted as a minister, and displays considerable good sense though but little sprightliness in conversation. He is to preach for us tonight.

Mr. Hoyt preached here Sabbath. I had no idea that I should have been so much pleased with him. His subject was the depravity of the heart. Pa, Catherine and myself went to Sparta to hear him in the afternoon. We stopt at Mrs. Jones's where Mr. Glenn was waiting to receive him, met him with a great deal of cordiality, and walked with him to church. We heard afterwards that the Sparta people were delighted, and he staid all night and gave them another sermon after candlelight.

I saw Mrs. Terrill there, and I have never seen her look so pale and dispirited. I suppose you know that her cousin Eugenia died while she was at Washington. She had the fever, and they apprehended no danger until Dr. Terrill arrived, and he told them if they expected Mrs. Rembert to see her again, they must send for her immediately. They did so, and she just came in time to see her breathe her last. Mrs. Terrill desired me to stop long enough to get your articles. I did so, and will send them to you when Uncle Jacob goes down.

Ma says she wishes you to send up needles and four spools of thread, numbers 30, 40, 50, and 60.

They have some idea of taking Sophia with them to Washington, but I feel unwilling to have her break off from her studies.

Julia, do write as soon as you can conveniently. You don't know how *blank* I feel when the usually auspicious post brings me no letter. I am very anxious to see you again, and Annie. Anne told me in her last that she was not very well.

Remember me to Mr. Cumming, Anne and Sarah. Catherine is anxious to go and see you but has no way. Herself and Aunt Wales spent yesterday with us.

Have you heard of old Mrs. Robertson's distress? Pa says not one *"tittle"* of her property will be left, from this business of Carrington's. Mr. [Carlisle] Beman too, is in great trouble. Mr. Ponce is pressing him sorely and has threatened to send on to make his brother [Nathan], who is his security, pay the debt. This provoked Carlisle very much, and he is so angry with

Mr. Ponce's treatment to him that he says he is very much afraid he cannot do *Frank* [Ponce's son] justice in school.

I must stop. I have written in such a hurry that I hardly knew what I was saying. I expect the stage every minute.

Yours.

Maria Bryan to Julia Ann Bryan Cumming

April 27, 1828 (Sabbath Night)

My dear Julia,

I have a little time to write to you before I go to bed, and I will therefore anticipate your letter which I hope to receive tomorrow morning.

Brother has been quite sick again this evening, with his chill and fever. He returned this evening from Mr. Bonner's with Willis Alston, who staid until after supper. There was a great dining party there yesterday given to Fannis and his bride. I had fully intended to go, and expected to until the last moment, when Brother said the gig was not strong enough to carry us. I am quite alone most of the time. The other night I thought I should have had the house entirely to myself all night. Brother had been gone during the day, and Goode and the other boys went a-fishing after supper, but they had not been gone long before Brother came.

Aunt Wales is quite sick again with the chills and fever. She brought them on by standing on the damp ground planting cabbage sprouts. Richardson has arrived. I saw him today at church but did not have an opportunity of speaking to him, do not know how long he means to remain in the up country, or what Margaret's arrangements are. I spoke to her today after church, and thought she appeared agitated. Her mother, too, [Mrs. Bailey] I fancied, had a restless look and an absent manner, which betokened that something was on her mind.

Colonel Bailey [a Macon attorney] called here yesterday again (General I should have said) with no material change in him except that he has clipped his whiskers, I expect, to surprise people at seeing so youthful-looking a brigadier. He expressed himself most dreadfully disappointed that he was not permitted to enjoy the happiness of seeing *Mrs. Cumming;* it was so extremely tantalizing to come so immediately upon her heels as it were and yet lose sight of her notwithstanding. I told Brother if he [General Bailey] had been a vain man he would set it down that I was deeply in love with him, for when he got up to go, he came and stood before me in his usual way, bowing and smiling and complimenting, and saying agreeable nothings, and I felt so foolish that I looked this way and that, and simpered, and my lip quivered as if I was in great agitation. Brother says don't be uneasy, Sam has not one *particle* of vanity.

You don't know how silent and gloomy it looks down stairs when we all come up to bed. Brother proposed the other night that he should sleep below — for fear the house should lose its center of gravity.

In haste yours

April 28, 1828 (Monday Morning)

Goode has just now brought me your letter, and as I may have an opportunity of sending this today, I have concluded to finish it immediately. You complain of my short letters, but I always write everything material with regard to the family and neighbourhood. I feel quite interested in those gentlemen from your account of them; the youngest I feel more disposed to envy than to pity. It seems to me so blessed a lot to die in one's youth if prepared for the event.

Pa and Ma speak of going to Tennessee in about five or six weeks. The latter seems to consider it, however, as a very doubtful thing whether they go at all, though Pa speaks of it as certain.

Of Brother, I never speak because I have nothing to tell that would give you any pleasure. He sits in Ma's armchair, chewing tobacco and reading novels most of the day, when he is not asleep, talks of going to Tennessee without however making any preparation for doing so.

I saw Mrs. Rossiter Saturday. She was much better, and part of the time very cheerful, though she cried as she spoke of Maria who from all accounts cannot be long for this world. She has the liver complaint, and fever daily. Richardson has brought news that Mr. Gildersleeve is going to be married to a lady in Charleston; and that Cooper is coming up to spend part of the summer. Perhaps he and Catherine will arrange their affairs, then. I never felt so much convinced as I do now from various circumstances that they are attached to each other. Poor David still remains, hanging about her, but if he had any hope of getting her I know not on what it can be founded. She seems to have grown tired to death of the report and of him, and cannot refrain from frequently manifesting her disgust. Do write soon.

Yours most affectionately.

Mackerness Goode stops by the Bryans' with his new wife, whom Maria was prepared not to like. Instead she describes her to Julia as being very pretty, having a face like Mrs. Augustus Longstreet's, wife of the author of Georgia Scenes, *who was Frances Eliza Parke of nearby Greensboro and thus probably well known to the Bryans.*

Maria Bryan to Julia Ann Bryan Cumming

May 5, 1828 (Monday Morning)

My dear Julia,

I am very much afraid that some of you are sick, as I received no letter from you or Anne. I felt certain that I should hear by this morning's mail. I was quite sick last week myself, was taken Monday night, and the next day I had high fever, and never felt sicker in my life. I thought I was taking the billious fever, but Dr. Gilbert bled me, and I took medicine, so that I am now getting well though I am still weak.

Pa and Ma have not yet returned. We expect them however some time in the course of the day. Mr. Kelsey who was at South Liberty yesterday says that he saw them there. I wish you could be with us next Sabbath. We expect several will unite with the church, among others Mrs. [Carlisle] Beman. The members of the church seem very much engaged in hoping and praying for a revival. The ladies' prayer meeting at Mrs. Rossiter's has been again revived and several of the male professors [at Mt. Zion Academy], Mr. Kelsy, Mr. Little, and others, meet with Dr. Brown and Mr. Beman for social prayer. Mrs. Rossiter was very ill Saturday. I went down to her this morning, have just heard that she is better. Her general health is worse, I think, than I ever knew it to be.

I do not know when I have been so much shocked as I was the other day.

Margaret [Bailey] came up to see me a little while in the morning, and I urged her to stay all day. She said she could not, for she had left her mother very low spirited as she had determined to go to the Chattahoochie. I saw Mrs. Bailey the same day, and she could hardly converse without crying. Armstrong had persuaded her that it was the best thing she could do, and he is now gone to have dwelling houses put up [in the frontier country], and she will move at Christmas. I do feel very sorry, for though I supposed Margaret would be married and leave the neighbourhood in the course of the year, yet I thought we should still have Mrs. Bailey and have now and then an opportunity of seeing Margaret.

Henrietta [Alston] called Saturday afternoon with Augustus Kenan, and staid an hour or two. She is going to Tennessee some time next week. I must not forget to deliver the message Mrs. Alston sent to you the last time I saw her. She said as so many members of both families would be absent during the summer, you must be sure and spend much of your time with her. I told her I could tell you, but I thought at the time I need not. I will put up my letter until Pa and Ma come as you will like to hear from them. I cannot help from feeling very uneasy lest you or Annie are sick. After Goode told me this morning that there was no letter, I sent to the office to be certain about it.

May 5, 1828 (Monday Night)

Pa and Ma arrived this afternoon, very little or no alteration in the health of the latter. She spent considerable time with Dr. Pope, who examined her case critically. She seems to think that travelling will do her no good unless there is a change effected in her system by medicine. He has given her several preparations which, he says, he thinks will benefit her if anything will. In one there is a very small portion of calomel [used chiefly as a purgative]. They visited Thomson and John Watkins, and Ma was delighted with Martha, and ardently wishes that Brother had such a wife.

Who do you think is here tonight — Mack[erness Goode] (Uncle Sam's son) and his *wife*, returning from a visit to his father's. She is sister to Mary Anne's husband. From Ma's account I imagined her some low creature who had *taken* him in, and was prepared to give her a cold reception though I knew it was wrong; yet I felt provoked at being impelled into a relationship with any and everybody. When she was getting out of the gig, Sophy whispered, "Sister, you must call her cousin," and I, in a very improper spirit, had said, "I'll sooner cut my tongue out," but her modest deportment and interesting appearance would have disarmed much severer prejudice than mine. I have not lately seen a prettier girl. She is rather taller than Caroline Ringold [the step-daughter of Maria's friend Richard Henry Wilde, who married James Ringold in Augusta on May 30, 1827], quite slender, fair skin, hair about the colour of mine which she puts up in very becoming rolls, and a really beautiful mouth. Her face is not unlike Mrs. Augustus Longstreet's in her best days. There is nothing crackerish about her. She acts perfectly at her ease, and as if she had been used to seeing the best company all her life.

Richardson is in the neighbourhood very ill indeed; he was taken with the fever last Thursday. Ma saw Caroline Grant, she did not speak of going to see you, as it was getting so late in the season.

Write soon. I hope I shall get a letter from you by Wednesday's mail at least.

Yours affectionately.

Weak from her recent illness, Maria broods on her deficiencies as a Christian.

Maria Bryan to Julia Ann Bryan Cumming

May 7, 1828 (Wednesday)

My dear Julia,

I sit down to write to you again, though I dispatched a letter yesterday, because it seems so natural for me to sit down immediately and answer yours. I cannot imagine what detained your letters lately—I find from the date of them that they should come by Monday's mail as usual. I am so weak that I can hardly write. Indeed, I think I never was much weaker in my life. I can hardly walk about the house, and if I consulted my inclinations I should be in bed all the time.

Your complaint of coldness and a worldly spirit I can most entirely respond to. Indeed, it is my constant exclamation how greatly I live below my privileges and how little I do to evince that I am a follower of Christ. And, alas, how much we show our ignorance and want of foresight when, instead of cultivating a taste for spiritual pleasures, we vainly pursue the world and the deceitful enjoyments which it holds out to us! I have sometimes thought that from mere principles of selfish policy we should endeavour, while in health and prosperity, to lay aside those stores and keep in exercise those tastes which alone can comfort us in the season of trial and adversity which will so certainly come upon each of the fallen family of Adam. I find that everything so contributes to take off my attention from what should be the one grand pursuit with every Christian, the books I read, the company I am in, mere every day business and the like, that I am sometimes resolved that, as to reading at least, I will lay aside everything but my Bible, and those books which relate immediately to religion.

I saw Aunt Wales yesterday evening. She has had such a dreadful sore mouth that she could neither eat nor sleep. I believe I told you she had been sick with the chill and fever. She seemed very low spirited indeed, and looks badly.

Ma and I rode down to the Doctor's [Rossiter's] late in the evening, and when we stopt at the gate the Dr., seeing it was Ma, made the most unexampled effort to come out, and Mrs. Rossiter too came stepping over the clover as lightly as you ever saw her. They were so glad to see Ma again, and in a little while Mrs. Rossiter went out, and in a short time came back with a waiter of bread and butter and chipped beef and apple tart, and pressed us to eat after sundry apologies for what she was setting before us.

I have like to have forgot again to tell you what I have intended to every letter I have written for several past, that Catherine was very much pleased with the purchases you made for her. Mrs. Bailey has fixed her bonnet and trimmed it, and looks very handsome indeed. Nanny Brown too was exceedingly thankful for what you got for her. Ma told her you had advanced a quarter of a dollar, and she seemed very grateful and said she should always feel obliged to "Mrs. Cummins." I cannot bear to think that you are not *certainly* coming up to spend the Summer with us. I have been thinking so much of it as a matter of course that it will turn all my ideas topsy-turvy, if you should not. I cannot bear to think of giving up hoping to have that "*little blessed one*" [Annie] with us constantly, and I have been thinking with pleasure of having Mr. Cumming's society again. I should dislike to have you come up against his will or that of his father's, but I cannot but still hope that you will.

Your advice is very good, and I ought to take it. Indeed, I regretted having written that as soon as I sent the letter, but I was low spirited; yet whatever may be my opinion on those subjects it is one that should never be confessed. Your kindness and regard is very gratifying to me, and I hope that whatever may befall me in life, I shall never be deprived of them.

Ma has not yet begun on Dr. Pope's prescriptions, says she does not like to be sick during meeting, and is putting it off until that is over. She is rather better, I think, and if she could only persuade herself of it she would be better still.

Brother is going next week to Tennessee in company with the Alstons. I told him the other day that [it was] not long since he was congratulating himself that H. [Henrietta] had fallen out with him, and thus prevented him from being obliged to declare himself, and that now he was, by his attentions, getting himself into the same situation again. I cannot bear to think of his marrying her for I am constrained to believe you always see her at her very best, and that she would make him a very unsuitable wife, and more than all, I should deprecate the consequence of a more intimate connection with that family. They are so irreligious, and I would dread their influence on our younger children when they are grown up. But I do not think Brother means to court H. I have thought strongly of late that he is half in love with Anny, and I believe if she was well he would court her.

I have been in a ferment about sending you *Honor O'Hara* ever since you wrote for it, but I have not yet obtained express permission. Pa said today he intended to write to you before long, but I expect you may wait patiently yet awhile. Richardson is better today. Monday he was in a stupor, and they thought he would die. John Brown has been nursing him as assiduously as if he were his brother. Is not he a generous fellow?

Our new cousin [Mrs. Mackerness Goode] professed great admiration of my beauty. She said she expected I had a great many beaux, I was so handsome. I told her she ought to see *you,* and she would not look at me then. Write soon.

You complain of the shortness of my letters, but I keep you informed of everything that happens in the family and neighbourhood. I have a *summary* way of relating things—but if you choose I can be more *diffuse.*

In haste yours affectionately.

Maria describes the death of a neighbor, Mrs. Jane Smith, who dies in a bloody childbirth, a victim of her times.

Maria Bryan to Julia Ann Bryan Cumming

May [12], 1828 (Monday Morning)

My dear Julia,

You seem to be in such a painful state of uncertainty with regard to your summer arrangements that I concluded I would not wait until the usual mail, but answer your last immediately. And yet I am unable either to give you any information that will render your intentions more determinate, for we are almost equally undecided. I can however, state to you the plans of the family as far as I understand them. Ma has commenced taking Dr. Pope's medicine and she is in hopes that that will relieve her without the trouble of journeying, but if she should get no benefit from it, she intends to set off for Tennessee in about four weeks from today. She seems very unwilling to leave home, and nothing but necessity will, I think, induce them to go.

As for me, that need not give you one moment's uneasiness. If I said to the Alstons I could not go and leave you, it was not because I could go if you were not to come, for I have not the most distant idea of accompanying Pa & Ma. I have now and then expressed an inclination to go, but it was dictated more from a vague will to see the world a little beyond the limits of the Mt. Zion horizon than with a desire to visit Tennessee particularly. And I know I should enjoy myself a great deal better at home, and if I were to go it would cost me more effort infinitely than to give up the journey. Therefore, if you and Mr. Cumming come you will certainly find me here, and if you do not I shall assuredly spend part of the summer with you, wherever you are, if I possibly can.

Jane Armour [a friend of Maria's and Julia's from Savannah] was here the other day and she said I must tell you not to disappoint her about coming this summer. If you must even remain, at least put it off until the next for she did anticipate a great deal of pleasure in seeing you while she remained in the up country.

You really make me envious when you describe the pleasure you have in hearing those fine singers. I have heard the remark made, and I think so, that a gentleman's voice when it is good is greatly preferable to a lady's. There is the same difference that there is between sugar and water, and good punch; the one is so altogether sweet, and the other besides the sweet has other equally delightful properties. . . .

You appear to have taken my remark in a more extended sense than I meant it. I can hardly say that there is anything more than the anticipation of a revival and hardly anything on which to found that. The members of the church, some of them at least, seem very much engaged, and I believe the exciting cause was nothing more than uneasiness, with respect to the near coldness which prevails throughout the congregation in matters of religion.

Poor Jane Smith [who married Horace Smith in 1821] is dead. She gave birth to a child on Thursday last, and the instant it was born she said, "I shall die," and expired immediately. She had been in a very critical situation some time before, and to use Ma's expression, literally *flooded* to death. Gallons seemed to come from her without the possibility of stopping it, and this produced such faintness and exhaustion, that soul and body could remain together no longer. Poor Horace and his little boy look so sad and desolate that it grieves me to see them, and it would have made your heart ache to have gone there while she was dead in the house, and seen how neat everything looked, and the yard and garden and kitchen so clean, and all so snug and comfortable in their little way.

Mrs. Bailey intends to plant [i.e., settle] at the Chattahoochie. Her son, as she calls him, has bought land in Troup County about three miles from the river, and her principal design seems to be to enjoy "Armstrong's society," when she has to give up her daughters. Richardson has got well. Mr. Twiss is coming out to spend the summer in Sparta. This Mrs. Warne told me as a great secret, but I suppose there is no harm in mentioning it to you.

I thank you sincerely for the collar, it is very pretty indeed. The music I am learning — and like the Scotch song very much. Catherine tells me her Ma is greatly pleased with her bonnet, and it is certainly quite becoming to her.

You must feel quite lonely in town now, and I have several times wished that Sophia or I could be with you. Brother talks of starting to Tennessee Wednesday. Henrietta has concluded not to go. Remember me to Mr. Cumming. Excuse this bad writing.

In haste yours affectionately.

Dueling still had cachet in middle Georgia in the 1820s; schoolboys wrote pieces in praise of it, and the fiancé of Henrietta Alston, Augustus Holmes Kenan, engaged in one — cause unknown.

Maria describes her mother's illness and continues to arrange for book purchases — this time Blue Stocking Hall.

Maria Bryan to Julia Ann Bryan Cumming

June 2, 1828 (Monday Morning)

My dear Julia,

So you would not write to me. How *you* would scold *me* if I were to be so particular in waiting for a letter from you! However, I suppose your excuse will be having written to Pa.

I have never seen Ma more unwell than she was last week. Saturday she thought she was dying and, though I could not but hope it was only one of her nervous turns, I really had my fears that she would not live through the day. Indeed, I have never been as much discouraged about her as I am now. In taking Dr. Pope's medicine she has been dieting, and that has weakened her so very much that she is hardly able to sit up at all. Her mind, too, is in a very unhappy state. She says she thinks she must die soon and she is afraid to die. She seems to have no confidence that she is prepared for the event, and appears to look upon the Saviour as a Judge arrayed in terror instead of a merciful and compassionate Redeemer. Pa conversed much with her in the hope of soothing her fears and giving her comfort, but every promise he directs her attention to, she puts aside by saying, yes, if she were a renewed person, she might apply it to herself. She appears better this morning and has now gone to ride out. She has, I believe, nearly come to the conclusion that she will take no more of the medicine, and Pa intends setting off for Tennessee as soon as is practicable.

June 3, 1828 (Tuesday)

I intended writing last night, but Dr. Brown detained us until after ten o'clock in meeting, and after I went up stairs, before I could get ready for writing, my candle went out. I came down stairs as softly as I possibly could, but Pa and Ma heard and said, "Who is that?" I did not answer at first, in hopes they would not say anything more, but upon the enquiry being repeated in a still sharper tone, I answered, "It is me." "Maria, ain't you in bed yet?" So I was obliged to go skulking back to my room and to get to bed as I could.

Yesterday after dinner I persuaded Ma to go to Aunt Wales's. She did, and I think it did her good. She and Aunt Wales, who is also sick, sat talking over their ailments, and it seemed to soothe them. Today she is certainly better, but she is not willing to admit it.

I have been the cause, it seems, very innocently, of getting Mr. Beman into some difficulty with regard to his [end-of-term] exhibition. He had a number of orations to correct, and they were as rude efforts as I have ever seen in my life. He requested me one day to assist him, desiring me, however, to say nothing of it as the boys might not like to have their compositions exposed to the eye of a stranger. I corrected four of them, and Friday he brought me Colquit's on "Duelling." It was as complete a specimen of high sounding nonsense as you can imagine, and Saturday morning I gave it to Mr. Beman. He was going to South Liberty and had not time to look it over much, I suppose, before giving it to Colquit, and I had written in such a hurry that it was difficult to read, and, Mr. Beman hesitating, Colquit thought it could not be his own writing and asked him if it was. Of course he would not tell a falsehood, and the circumstance of having had a female to correct his composition has riled Colquit so much that he said he would not "speak it for a negro," and that he always knew that all women were fools. He said, likewise, that he would have no part in the dialogues and, as it is too late to find a substitute, this would produce much trouble. Whether he will do this or not I cannot tell, but yesterday he tore his oration into a thousand pieces and positively refused to speak it. The slight that it cast upon me I regard not at all, but I feel sorry for the anxiety and mortification it has occasioned Mr. Beman.

Pa and I went into Sparta last week to call on Mrs. Bird's, and while in town, went to Mr. Alston's a few moments. We found the house completely topsy-turvy, the sofas standing in the middle of the passage and the chairs in the middle of the floor, Collier whitewashing, and everybody as busy as possible. Henrietta said to me in a low tone that she wished I would come in for she wished to see me particularly. I suppose you have heard that Kenan (her intended) is to fight a duel on the twelfth, with Augustus Clayton. The grounds of the quarrel I do not understand. He is now in Sparta, and will set off tomorrow for Alabama [to fetch] Augustus Alston for his second.

Tuesday Mrs. Bird and Mrs. Terrill spent here. The former said to me that it was reported to her that Henrietta had discarded Brother four times, and that Mrs. Alston had told her a few days before that Brother said, if she married Kenan, he should never see another happy day or something to the same purpose. I really felt provoked, knowing so well what was the actual situation of the case, but to confess the truth I am really afraid to affirm or deny anything on Brother's authority alone. He may have told Mrs. Alston this, for he seems extremely desirous to keep on good terms with the family. [Henrietta Alston married Augustus Holmes Kenan later in the month on June 19, 1828.]

I have seldom seen Pa and Ma so grieved and beset as the other day. We had been expecting a letter from Brother, agreeable to his promise to write at every post office, and have received none until Friday. Mr. Alston sent out one that he had gotten from him, a most affectionate epistle, in which he mentions all their household with kind solicitude, and sent "*love to every member of the family.*" On Monday, however, Pa got one which was written on the same day with the other.

Colonel [Thomas Flournoy] Foster [of Greensboro, Georgia] called on his way from Augusta. Your remark was true. He talks, if possible, more indefatigably than ever, and is in fine spirits about going to Congress. He asked for *my* support, but I told him I considered my influence as tacitly pledged to Mr. Wilde and Dr. Hanes, they having the prior claim. [Foster was elected to the Twenty-first Congress later that fall.]

I hope you were interested in *Honor*. Keep *Blue Stocking Hall* till you come up, if you would like to read it. Uncle Jacob will hand you the money for it. Mr. Alston brought word that Sarah is coming with you. Can it be so? I am really pleased with the idea of seeing Mr. Cumming again, for of late I am hardly more acquainted with him than if he was in Europe.

I will thank you to get me a frock like that you sent Sophia, the checked muslin, or of the same kind of material. Three and a half or four yards will do. I do not wish anything but a plain hem to it. Write very soon. Tell Annie the "tarrage will tum" before long. Oh, the little cretur! how I do want to squeeze her to death!

Traveling in Tennessee to take the waters for Ma's health, Maria writes her sister Julia, who is in Mt. Zion where she is summering in the Bryan home with her husband and daughter. Julia remained in Mt. Zion from June 18 to November 8, 1828.

Maria Bryan to Julia Ann Bryan Cumming

Athens, Tennessee
August 16, 1828 (Saturday Evening)

My dear Julia,

Ma, who seems to be thinking of you all at home most of the time, has insisted on my writing to you again this evening. We arrived in this State yesterday afternoon, and crossed the river Hiwassee (the dividing line between the Cherokee Nation), at a small town called Columbus. We put up at the house of a Mrs. White, and there was such an appearance of comfort and neatness in everything that Pa and Ma determined to spend the night. The lady and her daughter were striking in their appearance, and very polished in their manners. I at once set it down in my own mind that if these were a specimen of Tennessee ladies, that the State had great reason to be proud of them. We soon learnt from them, however, that they had been but a short time in the place, having removed from Abbingdon in Virginia, and as Pa judged, the Father of the family is a broken merchant, and that they have seen better days. The daughter is very much like Caroline Ringold, only handsomer, and one of the pleasantest and most interesting girls I have ever seen.

We set off from there this morning intending to go to the McMinn Springs, about twelve miles from Columbus, but we stopt for breakfast on the way, and the people told us that the accommodations were very poor, and the houses or huts in which the company staid miserable, although there are a number there. Brother was very anxious to have gone there, as he heard that there were two young lawyers at the Springs from Savannah, one of whom was Nat. Bond. However, he came on with us. The gentlemen from Georgia are in this town and we have found out that they are Banks from Elbert and young Charleton from Savannah.

I asked Ma just this moment what I should tell you about her health, and she said, "Oh, I don't know, I am a little better now *but* I do *not know* how long it will *continue.*" Pa said, "Oh wife, wife—a little better! You are a great deal better, and we are not talking of the future. We are talking of the present." For my own part I think she is considerably better. She is trying the limestone water, and as Pa and Brother say, drinks two drops and a half at a time. I do not think you need be at all afraid of their coming to live here, for they neither of them seem to be so much pleased as to give up home.

The night we spent at McNairs was very pleasant. The old lady, though a half breed, is fine looking and presides over her household with a great deal of dignity. Martha, the youngest daughter, is really handsome. She has a noble forehead, fine teeth, and as pretty eyes as yours, and not unlike them. She plays tolerably well on the piano, sings some songs in the Cherokee, and converses as well as most of the well educated girls in Georgia.

I hope you are all well, and enjoying yourselves. I sometimes think of you, and everything at home, until I feel as if I could not contain myself. I would not leave Georgia to live here to be as rich as Croesus, it seems to me to be entirely out of the world, and is, measurably; the women dress very unfashionably, though cleanly, and I have had articles of my dress cut three times since I left home. Dear little Annie, how I long to see her! Give my love to Mr. Cumming, Goode & Sophia. Pa and Ma send their love. Write to Nashville again.

Julia Bryan Cumming's first son, Alfred, was born in Augusta on January 30, 1829, and Maria had attended her sister during her confinement.

Maria Bryan to Julia Ann Bryan Cumming

March 4, 1829 (Wednesday)

My dear Julia,

I received your letter this morning and avail myself of the earliest leisure moment I have had during the day to write you a few lines. I felt sympathy for you on the expression of your lonely state and am half disposed to scold you, too, for with your ten thousand comforts, my dear Sister, what room can there be in your mind for anything but gratitude and content? You do not know how very much I want to be with you again. It does appear to me that

I could sit down by you now so quietly and happily all the day long, now that you need not be all the time groaning and sighing with bodily pain.

You cannot imagine, my dear Julia, how very gloomy we are now in this neighbourhood. Poor Mrs. [Carlisle] Beman's child is still very ill, the parents watching and trembling with bleeding anxious hearts, and little hope except that which strong affection excites. I am writing now in great hurry, for Mrs. B. has just sent down to request me to go up and sit up with the child tonight.

But ten times more awful, even horrible, is the death that has occurred this evening. Poor miserable Carrington has just gone into eternity with all his aggravated sins upon his head. Literally he has murdered himself with strong drink. Last Saturday he was taken, I think, in a fit, and from that time has been most confined to his bed, his senses wandering, little signs of rationality except now and then calling out for spirits. They have been obliged to give him some toddy to keep him alive but Monday when he got an opportunity so that no one could see him, he stole off into the kitchen and sent old Milly with a snuff bottle to get some on the hill. This evening he expired, and is literally a mass of corruption. Such a distracted family you never saw.

Yesterday Pa took old Mrs. [page torn] into town to sell her property — and I was with her. It seemed as if she thought her affliction greater than she could bear. Tom Lundy would not give the least indulgence. She was obliged to part, among others, with her favourite servant Bob, and coming home late in the evening, she said, "Well — my negroes are gone and I feel as if I was coming back from a funeral."

Pa requests me to mention to you that he is under the impression that he made a mistake in writing to Mr. Cumming today. He thinks instead of saying one *ream* of paper (which he meant), he said a *quire*. He wishes Brother Henry to procure half a ream of each kind of paper, foolscap and letter paper. Ma says I must say to you she was unable to procure a single pound of butter to send to you, but she will endeavour to get some, and have it go down by the first opportunity. Catherine is here now, and desires me to have you send up the bonnet, with the bill. She says she don't know what is necessary until she sees the bill. I really have been perplexed and annoyed in being the agent in this business, for there never has been a word since about money, and I really disliked to say anything about it to you, but you know it requires considerable delicacy to speak to Catherine on a matter [of this kind]. Finally, I determined, and did [ask her] and she then sent the message above.

Mr. & Mrs. Reid Golding made their appearance today at Dr. Brown's. Sophy, who went up today, as much from curiosity to see Reid's wife, as from a desire to visit Anne, has returned with rather a ludicrous description of her, but you know she finds something *"funny"* in every person and thing. Mrs. Rossiter, to whom I delivered your message about our little darling, sent you a very long and loving one in return, but for my life I cannot remember it. She says, "Dear Julia would be pleased to know how much good these oysters do me. And it does amuse me, the doctor is constantly relinquishing his part to me, and every day he'll say, 'My dear, my stomach craves a raw oyster, just one, my dear, I'll only take one.'"

Ma desires me to request you to get her two or three ounces of isinglass, and a couple of moulds and make Uncle Jacob pay for them. Tell Anne I will write to her soon. My love to Sally.

I saw Mrs. Terrill yesterday. Louise is well. She says she is very anxious to see you and your son. I called a moment at Mrs. Alston's. Anne was laying on the bed sick, and at last they waked her up, and she jumped up immediately and with her eyes half open said, "How's Mrs. Cumming?" She says she did want to see you very much, and her mother says she is desirous to have you pay her a visit.

Pa, Ma, Catherine and Sophy send their love. Kiss Annie for me. My most affectionate love to Brother Henry. Brother has offered to take Catherine down, whenever she will go, and she would consent in a moment with all her heart, but she hates to leave her Ma alone. Write soon, my dear Julia, and believe me to be ever your most affectionate Sister.

Long-forgotten books and authors figure in Maria Bryan's correspondence. In this letter are two such authors: James Beattie (1735–1803), Scottish poet and philosopher and a member of the Johnson circle in London, and Henry Home Kames (1696–1782), a Scottish lawyer and Presbyterian philosopher. Maria also notes in this letter that Mrs. Joseph White, wife of the congressional delegate from Florida, supposedly was coming to Augusta. Should Julia Cumming call on her?

Maria Bryan to Julia Ann Bryan Cumming

March 16, 1829 (Monday)

My dear Julia,

I received your letter this morning, and we were very glad to learn that you are again restored to your usual health. The family are all pretty well except Ma, who has been much more indisposed than usual for a week past. Indeed, she has been very uneasy for fear she would have one of her violent spells of colick, but I am in hopes it will not be the case.

I have forgot to say, too, that Goode is not well. He caught a dreadful cold the other night when he was out "possum hunting," and has a cough which racks his whole frame, and, I was going to say, shakes the whole house. You know what a cougher he is. Ma has kept him at home today, for you know how careful and tender she is of her sons, and she says he's of the right age now to have a cold settle upon his lungs.

He got a letter from his friend Colonel [William] Cumming [Henry Cumming's eldest brother] this morning, and I never saw a fellow so pleased in my life as he is. The Colonel told him that it was not necessary to go to any particular place in order to be a great man, but that study and perseverance would do more than the situation. The remark has had a very good effect so far. He's been sitting all day with a dictionary by him, and reading in a volume of Beattie's works, but how long the fever for acquiring [knowledge] will last, I cannot say — hardly the usual term of *nine* days, I fear. Sophia is very much engaged in her studies, and I think her temper is improving very much indeed.

Tell Mr. Cumming the book he sent will do very well, but I am sorry "Kames" could not be procured. Catherine's bonnet arrived safely the other day, and she is extremely pleased with it. I never saw her look as handsome as she did yesterday with it on, and the crimson mantle that we got for her. She talks often of going to see you, and when she was here the other day, she said, "Well, I will make up my mind soon, and let Julia know whether I can go or not." I do wish Anne or Sarah [Cumming] could come up and pay us a visit. The former, I think, speaks more discouragingly of it every letter she writes. I really should like to see Jemmy Ringold; it would make me think so of old times.

It is well you are relieved from the dilemma into which Mrs. White's arrival would have thrown you. Ma and I were talking of the matter the other day, and were disputing as to the course you would pursue. Ma thought you would not call, and that if you felt disposed to, Mr. Cumming would not be willing to have you, and I thought you would, and said I *hoped* you would. I do not believe she is anything but a very imprudent woman, and I do like Mr. Wilde so much, and think him so clever and amiable a man, that I should be unwilling to hurt his feelings by any appearance of slight or want of attention to his feelings. [An Augusta social scandal was the attention Congressman Richard Henry Wilde, a former mayor of Augusta, was paying the wife of Joseph M. White.]

I believe I wrote to you that Pa got a letter from him [Wilde] a short time since, in which he said he had been using the little influence he possessed for Goode and should continue to do so. The latter, however, is very incredulous, and seems wholly to have stricken Mr. Wilde from his books. He took his letter [from Colonel Cumming] out of his pocket just now, and turning it over said, "I don't know where I shall put this. I want to keep it as long as I live." I offered to take it and lock it up in my dresser, but he seems unwilling to have it so far from him, at least for the present.

Emily [Brown] Walker is staying with her mother now, and last night Pa and I walked up to Doctor Brown's after supper. I never saw her appear so well, and notwithstanding your remark that she was, to you, the most insipid personage in the world, I think she is growing to be quite agreeable, and seems disposed to do all the good she can. Brother we have not seen in a week. He went to Greenesborough and has not yet returned. Mr. Alston staid all night with him some short time since, and I believe Pa was half vexed at his laughing at the plain way in which Brother lived. Said he laughed out immoderately. "I suppose it would be very proper to have him go in debt for this one year," said Pa, "but Mr. Alston is a very weak man. He don't know how to appreciate things according to their usual value. He goes by appearances."

You ask me why I do not write longer letters. Why, are not my letters long enough? There is nothing of very great importance to write about ever—and I think my letters often suffer from want of dignity in the subjects. I know you do not care for sentimental letters. *Dissertations* on this or that or the other topic I know you do not desire to have, so I am confined to the news of the family and the neighbourhood, and you know this is not the region of events.

Pa and I called to see Mrs. Richardson the other day, whom we understood was sick. There was a general cleaning and putting to rights before we were admitted, and we found her in bed with a volume of *Wesley's Sermons* by her, apparently very cheerful and happy, and talking of her children being troublesome by their attentions.

Love to Brother Henry and Annie. Ma very readily believes your account of Alfred's beauty, and listened to the account with a very emphatic "See, I told her so."

Yours very affectionately.

Maria and Catherine Wales are leaving the next day for Scottsboro, not far from Milledgeville, to attend a Presbyterian meeting and to visit friends.

Maria Bryan to Julia Ann Bryan Cumming

March 26, 1829 (Thursday Evening)

My dear Julia,

As I expect to leave home in the morning, to be absent for some time, although I have had a dreadful headache all the evening, I concluded to drop you a few lines. How were you spending last night? I thought much of you, and imagined you might be gay and happy, unconscious of our trouble and anxiety.

Pa was over at the plantation yesterday, and assisted in lifting a very heavy piece of timber into the cart, and strained himself so much that he was taken violently ill with the colick, or that complaint of the kidneys to which he is subject. For five hours he hardly appeared like living, so great was his distress. Dr. Gilbert was here, and they bled him copiously, put him in the warm bath several times, and gave him a vast quantity of opiate. Between eleven and twelve he grew completely easy, and he said the sensation of rest and freedom from pain was so delightful that he never felt happier in his life. Today he is weak from loss of blood, and has remained about the house and bed nearly all day, and says he feels totally relieved from all symptoms of another attack.

I feel very unwilling to leave home tomorrow, and if I were the only person concerned would certainly give up the journey, but Pa insists upon me going and Catherine [Wales] would be very much disappointed, besides our being looked for by our friends according to our promise. We will remain in Scottsborough, after the [Presbyterian] meeting is over, until Wednesday, when Pa and Ma intend to meet us on their way, the former to Presbytery, and Ma to Clinton to which latter place Catherine and I will probably accompany her.

I hope Annie is relieved from her indisposition before now. Dear little soul, how I do long to see her. I was relating tonight how I used to entertain her with stories about feeding the chickens until I actually got into a figit to see her. I received a long letter from Margaret [Bailey] yesterday. She has delayed writing because the water courses were so high that the mail could not cross them. She writes cheerfully and gave me a minute account of her situation, and the family, I should judge, are quite comfortably situated. Pa just this moment requested me to say to you that he still indulges the hope that you will be up to the meeting in May. He says the carriage will be entirely subject to your order after we return. Give my love to Brother Henry, Anne and Sarah. You must really excuse the brevity of this letter, my dear Julia, for I feel very unwell indeed, and must lay down soon.

                              In great haste yours most affectionately.

In Clinton, about twenty miles southwest of Milledgeville, Maria wrote this letter to Julia from the home of Ma Bryan's niece, Caroline Goode Holt Iverson, and her husband, Alfred Iverson. The future Georgia senator was then thirty-one years old, a Princeton graduate, a practicing lawyer, and a representative in the Georgia Assembly.

Maria Bryan to Julia Ann Bryan Cumming

                                        Clinton, Georgia
                                        April 3, 1829 (Friday)

My dear Julia,

    Catherine [Wales] and I were at Scottsborough yesterday morning when Pa and Ma arrived and brought me your letter. Its contents made me really sorry that I had left home at all, as I do not like for Anne [Cumming] to defer her visit, and am extremely sorry to have missed seeing Mr. Wilde. Pa was in Sparta the day after your letter came, and requested Mr. Sayre, if the latter [Wilde] arrived and spoke of going out to our house, to inform him the family were all from home.

Catherine & I left home a week ago today. We have had a tolerably pleasant visit, and no pains have been spared to enable us to pass our time pleasantly, but I believe we have both wished ourselves at Mount Zion now and then. We had promised Emily Walker to stay with her, and we dined and took tea at other places and spent the nights with her while the meeting lasted.

Monday I spent with Julia Forsyth, and Tuesday went out to Scottsborough. Catherine has really been very much admired. A great many were very much struck with her appearance in Milledgeville, and indeed she did look remarkably well. Her new bonnet is very becoming, and she wears a black veil now, and her complexion, being better than usual, altogether made her look very striking. Colonel Carter's family go on much in the usual way. The girls were both at home, and they all spoke frequently and very kindly of you. I felt very sorry for Mrs. Carter. She is in a very common situation, and seems to be languid and weak, and was most of her time lolling on the bed or sofa. Mary Brantley left them late Tuesday. She had received a letter from her father directing her to return immediately with a lady who is now in Charleston, and accordingly she went with Mr. Sherwood in the stage.

We arrived here yesterday about two o'clock, found the family well and Cousin Caroline [Goode Holt Iverson] looking really stout for her. Her child is very good looking, and I think is by far the finest she has ever had. She is just the same woman she was when you saw her last; time has not changed her one whit, either in appearance, manners, or character. Mr. [Alfred] Iverson, too, is pretty much the same, as agreeable and pleasant as ever. You know he was always a favourite of mine.

We were considerably surprised to find Cousin Goode [Thaddeus Goode Holt, Caroline's oldest brother] and his wife here on a visit. He appears to be pleased with himself and his wife, and looks happy and satisfied. His wife is a young childish creature of sixteen, but extremely pretty, everybody would call her, and yet I cannot say I admire her appearance much. Her form is beautiful, about your height or rather taller, and they all say here that she is like you, I suppose, because she has large black eyes and dark hair. I was amused at Ma this morning. When somebody was remarking how much she was like you, Ma said, "She is not unlike Julia if her brow was not so heavy — if her brow was as light as Julia's she *would* be like her." She is of a very poor family. Cousin Goode has had his eye on her, from his own account, for some years, and she told Cousin Caroline that several times when he first courted her she insulted him, and flung out of the room, for she suspected his designs were not honourable; and she and her mother both thought he never meant to marry such a poor girl as she was. He & she were dressed very much, and his carriage & horses, which he has just purchased, is one of the most splendid establishments of the kind I ever saw. . . . Cousin Caroline sends her love, and desires me to say to you that she is very anxious to see [you, and] hopes that you and Mr. Cumming will visit her in the course of the year.

You can't imagine how the place is improved since you were here. The house is enlarged, and is as neat as a new pin, the garden and yard are really beautiful, there are three summer houses handsomely built, and altogether it is as tasteful an establishment as I have seen. Ma and Catherine send their love. Don't let Anne give up her visit. We'll be home probably by next Thursday. I am very sorry you cannot come this Spring. I should like to return with Anne and could do so were it not for Sophia. My love to Brother Henry.

Yours very truly.

Cousin Caroline has asked me a great many questions about Annie, and I have tried to remember all her smart little sayings that I could, which has amused her very much. Kiss the dear little soul for me and don't let her forget her "Aunty."

Yours.

Back from her trip to Milledgeville and Clinton, Maria recalls that in Macon she met again the Reverend Joseph Stiles, Henry Cumming's cousin, who was accompanied by his second wife, Caroline Clifford Nephew, whom he had married a year earlier. Puffed up with flattery, Mr. Stiles refused to preach at the presbytery, much to Pa's dismay and Maria's anger.

Maria Bryan to Julia Ann Bryan Cumming

April 9, 1829 (Thursday Evening)

My dear Julia,

We have just returned from Milledgeville and, after eating our supper, although I am so tired that I ache all over, I must write you a few lines to tell you how much we were all disappointed in not finding a letter from you. We have heard with equal regret and astonishment of the dreadful fire you have had in Augusta. What distress and ruin it must have occasioned!

Last Sabbath, Ma, Catherine and I were sitting together when Cousin Caroline [Iverson] entered the room, and with a very grave face said, "I am the messenger of ill news for you." I was so alarmed that I was nearly breathless, for it immediately occurred to me that she had heard some misfortune relating to Pa when she gave me the paper containing the account of the calamity. We have not yet heard the particulars of it, and were hoping that we should find a letter when we arrived. [On April 3, 1829, the Augusta fire destroyed about five hundred buildings, including the new theater, the new markethouse, and the hospital.] Ma has not been very well since she has been gone, and tonight she complains very much of fatigue, but I hope she will be better tomorrow.

Did I tell you in my letter from Clinton that I had seen Mrs. [Caroline] Stiles? I believe not. Mr. Iverson proposed to Catherine and I to visit Macon to look at the place, and Saturday we went. When we drove up to the tavern, who should we see standing in the door but Mr. Stiles. He came to the carriage and handed us out and told us his lady was within. We were introduced to her, and I really was very agreeably disappointed. She is very interesting in her appearance, and was pleased and affable in her manner, and it seemed to me evident that she was willing to take the pains to make an agreeable impression. There was a Miss McIntosh with her, a niece, in bad health. They expect to remain three months in the up country, and have promised to honour us with a call. She says she "has come prepared to like this part of the world, for Mr. Stiles is so much attached to it, and she has made up her mind to go with him wherever he may choose to reside, and to do nothing to obstruct his usefulness."

Pa has been very much delighted with this meeting of Presbytery, says it was very numerously attended. Mr. Stiles, however, refused to preach, without assigning any particular reason. I have never liked his manners so little, and Pa says he has never seen him when he appeared to care so little about him, or paid him so little attention. His manner to me positively made me angry; it was a mixture of stiffness and condescension and reserve, no more like he had met with a person with whom he had lived month after month than I would treat a perfect stranger. However, allowances ought to be made for the man. He is so much flattered that really it is above human nature to stand it, without being injured. Such a general excitement, now it is known that he is passing through the country, and with his wife, so I was told, that when they first came into the church everything was suspended and all turned to look at them. Every one that had known him so anxious to be presented to Mrs. Stiles.

I have a vast deal of love and many kind messages from your friends whom we have seen in our journey. Cousin Caroline, I think, loves you far better than she ever did. Maria told me that after your last visit she was so delighted with you, she said she believed you were nearer perfection in all aspects than anyone she knew. She intends coming to visit us the first of June, and Cousin Goode's wife with her. Perhaps you may see them. Mr. Iverson is really one of the finest young men I know, a most excellent husband and father, and, I think, would ere long be a Christian if he had any encouragement from his wife. I knew not before that he liked Brother Henry so well. Cousin Caroline said one day, "There are very few men that Mr. Iverson likes and admires as much as he does Mr. Cumming, and you know what I always have thought of him." "Oh yes," said Mr. Iverson, "Cary thinks he's faultless. He's her standard and model for everything."

Dr. Brown, when he was going to the village last week on his way to Presbytery, was thrown out of his sulky and his collar bone broken. He came home with us today, and took Pa's seat in the carriage, and appeared to suffer very much. Anne Apling, they hope, is recovering. There was an abscess formed in her side which has been lanced; it discharged a vast quantity of matter, which has relieved her lungs, and consequently her cough has nearly, or quite, ceased. Mrs. Beman's little boy continues poorly, but hope is entertained of his restoration. Do not let Anne give up her proposed visit if you have any influence with her. Is Mr. Bates still in Augusta? If he is, will you get Mr. Cumming to request him to send me the *Albion* [a New York weekly founded in 1822 by a British naval surgeon named John Sherren Bartlett, who edited it for a quarter of a century], from this time forth, or if he has left there, to speak to his agent to forward it. [The *Albion* brought to its readers British politics, literature, drama, and general news and culture.] Do write soon I beg you. My love to all.

Yours ever.

I am glad you lent *Calham* to Mrs. Campbell, for I have not suffered for it as I had not read far enough to be much interested in the book. I should be very much pleased to see Miss Hickman's criticism. Have you read *Is This Religion?* I am very anxious to see it. I read some of it in Milledgeville and was disposed to like that. My love to Brother Henry and Annie. I can't say I feel a very heart warming affection for Master Alfred [her nephew, who was at this writing an infant, just over two months old], being so slightly acquainted with him, but have no doubt but I soon should. Excuse this very badly written letter.

Yours ever.

In Mt. Zion religion was in earnest, and doctrinal disputes among the Presbyterians were as fierce as their opposition to the Baptists. Maria writes to her sister of a current dispute in the Mt. Zion Presbyterian Sabbath school.

Maria Bryan to Julia Ann Bryan Cumming

April 13, 1829 (Monday Evening)

My dear Julia,

I received your letter this morning, and hasten to answer it in readiness for tomorrow's mail. I am sorry for the state of excitement in which you are in Augusta, and hope sincerely the fears of the people [following the fire] are groundless. Anne [Cumming] arrived on Friday evening. I had gone down to Mrs. Rossiter's to deliver some money which was sent from Scottsborough, and hearing a knock turned round and, to my surprise, saw Alfred [Cumming. Anne Cumming, twenty-four, and Alfred Cumming, twenty-seven, were Henry's sister and brother.] He has spent two days here, seems to be in good spirits, and I have never seen him when he appeared more amiable and interesting. I sent, by him, a small present to Annie, a little frock which I made her, and I trust it will fit her, but as I had no pattern, nor guide of any kind, I fear it will have to undergo some alterations.

We have just returned from the Sabbath School prayer meeting. We have, of late, been much encouraged about our school, and I have never known it more interesting, but yesterday a circumstance occurred which has thrown some damp upon our spirits. While Pa was absent at Presbytery, Mr. Reeves had the Superintendance, and, hearing a class of little children in Brown's catechism, he objected to some part of it and, without consulting anyone, took the catechism away from them. The question which displeased him was this, "From what sin and iniquity were you delivered in your infancy?" When Pa returned, and there was no other book which could supply the place, he gave that one back to the children, but, in order to satisfy Mr. Reeves, he struck out the offensive passage. Mr. Little, who has always more zeal than humility, was in arms at this, said it was relinquishing an important doctrine of the church, and that it was our duty to contend earnestly for the faith. Moreover he would not teach if that was given up, nor his children should not teach or come. He has given up consequently his class. Eliza, who partakes of her father's spirit, has resigned hers. Mr. Reeves did not attend, and was not present tonight, and this, besides depriving us of teachers, and the Baptist interest and influence, perhaps will no doubt have an unhappy effect upon the minds of children, to see Christians falling out about such trifles, and giving up their duty. Pa really seems annoyed and grieved by the affair, for he has taken so much pains to cultivate peace and maintain harmony in the hope of doing good in this particular way.

Goode has heard that he will probably go to West Point and is all agog with joy and expectation. Ma, however, says she cannot give her consent, and indeed seems very much opposed to his leaving the state at all.

Pa is not very well now. He has still symptoms of his colick. He and Ma are very anxious to see yourself and the children now, and he speaks of going to Augusta in the course of a few weeks. Uncle [Isaac Bryan] left here this morning. He was very unwell, and disliked to go extremely. His voice faultered and his eyes filled when he bade us farewell. He appears to be in miserable spirits generally and says he has the hypochondriae very bad sometimes.

I received a long and very kind letter from Mr. Douglas this morning. Said he wrote "while Harriet was sitting by tending baby." Said he wished Alfred had been born the same day that his child was, and that I must tell you that nothing could give him more pleasure than to have yourself and Mr. Cumming next door neighbours, and gives me a pressing invitation to spend next winter with him.

Mrs. Beman, I fear, will at last be compelled to give up her little one. He is very low, appears to be in as complete a consumption as you ever saw a grown person. Anne Apling is a little better.

Write very soon. Excuse this short and hurried letter for I am almost sick with a violent cough and cold I have taken, and it is bed time. My love to Brother Henry.

Ever yours.

Ma wishes you to tell Uncle Jacob to procure her a couple of small jars for planting in and bring them up with him.

Chapter Four

MARRIAGE PROPOSALS

"Love, heard from most lips, is to me the most disgusting word in the world."

Maria, entertaining Anne Cumming, Julia's sister-in-law, takes her to call in Sparta. There, Maria learns that she is to be married soon and to go north for the summer. Sophia Bryan, at the age of fourteen, is a sore trial to her family.

Maria Bryan to Julia Ann Bryan Cumming

May 4, 1829 (Monday)

My dear Julia,

I was truly sorry that my obligation to you for a letter today was increased by your writing it while so much indisposed. It seems as if you cannot pass a Spring without suffering from debility of some kind or other. I wish you would take the charcoal. It is effecting most happy results upon some of the invalids of this place, and it is extremely pleasant to take a spoonful or two at a time several hours in the day. I do really wish I could go down. I never wanted to be with you more, but it appears to be my duty to remain here at present for the reason I assigned before.

I believe what you say about Sophia in some measure, that when she gets to be older she will learn to control herself better, and my hope would be very strong, were it not that I am convinced that she has not the religious principles and the religious fear that you and I have had even before our remembrance. But with regard to her I cannot ascertain that motives of this kind even influence her at all. Her mind is remarkably well informed in Scripture, but as to its special bearing upon herself or her own responsibility, it appears to me that she never thinks of it, or at least never realizes it.

I declare to you that oftentimes she makes my very heart sore. She frequently comes to me to recite her lessons or to attend to her music, and her manner throughout is as if she were conferring a favour upon me, contemptuous even, and petulant in the extreme. Ma she treats worse still in general, and I sometimes cannot refrain from taking a hearty cry when I think of her. It was only this evening when I thought I should be injuring her to keep it concealed any longer that I told her, "Sophia, I must certainly tell Pa of your conduct." "Tell him," said she. "I don't care if you do. You get your living by telling."

Anne [Cumming] and I went up to the log meeting house today to hear Mr. Norman. You may remember something of him, a very singular looking, hard-favoured man, but whose piety and mind seems to atone for his personal defects. There is really a wonderful contrast between his countenance and the sentiments and language which he utters. He preached today from these words in Revelation. "Blessed are they that do His commandments that they may have right to the tree of life and enter in through the gates into the city." I do hope you were comforted and blessed on the Sabbath. Ah, how I could sympathise in your feelings of unfitness to engage in that holy ordinance, from the whole tenor of my life and conversation. Yet if Christ has pardoned our sins He has promised grace to subdue them. It is often and often a comfort to me to think that we are, as I cannot but hope, both travelling that straight and narrow path that leads to endless life, and if we will be faithful we shall meet at last and be no more separated.

We found Pa gone when we returned from Sparta, and were very glad to learn from your letter that he got down safely, for Ma of late is always uneasy when he is from home without some of the family, for fear he will be attacked with his colick. We were both glad enough to get home, Anne especially, for there is very little about Sparta to prevent its being an irksome place. The day we spent at Mrs. Terrill's was rather pleasant. She was kind and in good spirits and temper, and the Doctor is always an agreeable man to me. As for the Alston family, I never knew them to appear as poorly. Henrietta was in bed sick and she really looks wretchedly, but she bears her affliction so little like a Christian, and is so peevish and fretful and irascible, that I could not forbear thinking repeatedly of the kind Providence which had prevented Brother from connecting his destiny with hers. I called to see Frances Davis who has another daughter. Mrs. Lucas told me she had seen you, and she was apparently very much pleased when she said, "Yes, I went to see July. Nothing would do but I must go to see her, though I told her I had mighty little time to spare. Tell your Ma, honey," said she, "that I'll try and get out and spend a day with her before the wedding—your wedding."

"I am not going to be married, Mrs. Lucas," said I.

"Now, will you," said she, "deny it when he came up post haste and killed two horses on the road, and went out at night and got there so late that you were all gone to bed and had to be knocked up."

And from Mrs. Terrill I learnt that the public had fixed the interesting event to be in May, and that Uncle Jacob had come up loaded with articles for the occasion, and that I was going on to the North to spend the summer and would take Goode as far as West Point.

Dr. Hanes and Satterlee spent Saturday with us. I never saw the former so low spirited, and I was induced to believe, from some of his remarks, that Mrs. Telfair had deprived him altogether of hope. He said to me, "Your sister once paid a very high compliment to me, which I often think on with pleasure—that I would be most successful when I was best known."

I wish you could be up at our meeting. It commences Thursday evening. I am afraid Dr. Brown will have very little resistance, however, and he is hardly able to preach, not having yet recovered from the effects of his fall. Anne Apling is improving astonishingly. Have you forgot to send the crape to Mrs. Carrington? I have been ashamed of myself whenever I remembered that I have not yet thanked you for the gloves you sent me by Anne—but I was not the less grateful, and it was what I was wishing for. I thank Mr. Cumming for wishing me to come down, but I will continue to hope that I shall see a great deal of him and you both during the Summer. Dear little Alfred, how I do long to see him and Annie! I was not aware that I had written shorter letters than usual lately, or that they appeared wandering. I have not been in very good spirits, and it may be in some degree owing to this.

Ma is rather better, but the thought of Goode's going away keeps her unhappy, and he, poor fellow, is beginning to feel very bad. Emily Walker is now at her father's and looks as if she were going to supply her loss before very long. Of Catherine you enquire—she is spending several days with Mrs. Wiley since the birth of her child. I dare say she would return with Anne if she had a convenient opportunity. Oh, that I could, dear Sister.

Ever yours.

Goode Bryan won acceptance to West Point and finally the approval of Ma, who accompanies him to Augusta for his departure to the academy. In this letter Maria and Sophia had gone to spend the day with Mrs. Ponce. Dimas Ponce and his wife, Isabella, a Savannah couple, owned Pleasant Valley Plantation near the Bryans.

Maria Bryan to Julia Ann Bryan Cumming

May 26, 1829

My dear Julia,

I was again disappointed in not receiving a letter from you this morning, but I suppose you have been in so much confusion in the preparations for Goode's departure that you did not feel like writing. It must have been a very severe trial to Ma; it is most kind in you to permit Annie [Julia's toddler] to come home with her, for no one will be so likely to control her and to fill Goode's place. We have had such rainy weather that we have been very much confined to the house lately.

I saw Brother yesterday and he seems very much out of spirits about his crop, says there will be no possible chance of clearing it of the grass any more this year. He intends to set off soon to Columbus where he promised to go to attend to some business for David Smith. Saturday evening we had a short visit from Colonel Erwin, whom I suppose you have seen before now. He brought me a letter from Mary, in which she expresses very great anxiety to come to Georgia, and her desire to become acquainted with you. Says she has past a delightful winter in New Orleans, and has been learning to play on the guitar, of which she is very fond.

I often wish you were at home now to eat strawberries. There is a great abundance, and Robert, careful as he is, is willing to spare quite as many as we can eat. He says he "don't like to pull 'em quite all, he likes for some to drop off and rot, and the beds will be richer arter it." He seems to take on very much on account of Goode's absence. [Robert was Goode's slave companion and their Mt. Zion gardener.] The other day I was leaning with my head in my hand, looking sad I suppose, and was hardly conscious of his presence, when he said in a very whining sympathetic tone — "Feel ugly about Goode?" "Yes," said I. "So do I too," said he. "I couldn't work in my garden all day for thinking of him."

Catherine and Sophy and I spent last Friday with Mrs. Ponce. We walked over having no way to ride. Mrs. Ponce is very friendly and kind but, I think, even more affected than ever. Jane Armour [the Ponces' twenty-nine-year-old house guest], I think, is one of the finest girls I ever saw, so unpretending, cheerful, and kind. It rained in the afternoon, and I was very anxious to come home for we had left Mary Hall by herself. And when Mrs. Ponce saw that I was determined on it, she ordered Dick to put the horse in the gig. You know the slowness of their operations. Well, before the gig was ready they had lit candles, and it was then thundering, and the appearance of another storm arriving. However, we determined to brave it. I was obliged to drive myself, but Dr. Williams who is there working, gallantly proffered his services to attend us. We could not go the nearer way, by the creek, but was obliged to take that terrible road of Mr. Wiley's. It grew darker and darker, only now and then a vivid flash of lightning which blinded me still worse by confusion, and the difficulty of driving was increased by Williams who, in his zeal to be useful, would every now and then brawl out, "Miss Bryan, keep clear of that rut"; "Miss Bryan, there's a stump at your left, make the horse walk in the gully." Finally the rain came, and all three of us (like Mrs. Lacee and her sister), rather than spoil our calashes [hats with hoops] took them off and rode bareheaded and, what with Sophy's laughter and Catherine's terrors, and the responsibility of their bones upon my shoulders, I was glad enough to get home. Mary met us at the door saying, "Miss Maria, Henny said she wished it would rain so all day tomorrow so you moutn't get home." I never did feel so much like slapping anybody in the mouth, all dripping and tired as I was, to receive such a welcome.

You will be very much alone when the family go to the Hill. [Sand Hills was a term applied to the ridge of hills lying three to five miles west of Augusta. Many well-to-do families from Augusta including the Cummings had established summer homes there because they thought the climate to be safer from the fever.] I really do wish sincerely that I could go down and remain with you until you come up. I cannot urge you to hustle your journey, though I am very anxious to have you here, for I know you will contribute materially to Mr. Cumming's comfort and I like to have you do that. Sophy was in the room just now and desired to be remembered to you. Aunt Wales and Catherine informed me yesterday that they would do themselves the pleasure of calling upon Miss Anne Cumming soon as she arrived, so you may be assured she will not suffer from want of polite attention, and we shall do everything to render her visit as pleasant and agreeable as possible, so that she may not have cause to regret the gaieties of the city.

Mrs. Warne says Mrs. Twiss's child is one of the finest and most sprightly infants she ever saw, and the father is infinitely happy and proud of it. Mrs. Rossiter sent a kiss to it by Mrs. Warne, and in return there came a large pound cake in the child's name. Mrs. Warne is hurt that Anne and I did not go to see her when we were in town [Sparta], says her call was specially for Anne [Cumming], and she makes visits of ceremony so seldom that she does not like her calls to pass for nothing. I suppose it was partly my fault, but there seemed to be no very convenient opportunity of going when we were in town. Write soon. My love to Mr. Cumming.

Yours truly.

Maria writes of a local Presbyterian missionary, patently afflicted with venereal disease, who went to Columbus, Georgia, preached and administered communion until the people rose up against him, stoned his house, and threatened to thrash him.

Maria Bryan to Julia Ann Bryan Cumming

June 1, 1829 (Monday)

My dear Julia,

It was really very gratifying to receive a letter from you again. You can't imagine how we all felt when we learned that Annie had not the measles — to think she might have been with us. I hope Alfred is well before this. Brother will go down for you, I believe, whenever you fix upon the time for coming home.

Ma is quite unwell at present. She has borne Goode's absence quite as well as we expected, and has been tolerably well, but today she has been very much indisposed. We have been trying to persuade her to take some medicine, for I do not doubt but it is bile, but she is afraid to venture, I believe. Catherine has been dangerously ill with the fever for several days past. Indeed, her symptoms are very alarming, and for some time the medicine she took entirely failed of the desired effect. Her mother, of course, has been very unhappy, although I could not discover that Catherine was uneasy respecting herself.

Mr. & Mrs. Hill have been paying us a visit. To give you an idea of the appearance of the latter, if you can conceive a handsome, softened, refined resemblance of Sarah Jean Thorp, you have her before you. Her complexion is extremely fair, and her skin is as young looking and delicate as Annie's. Her talents have not been overrated; she is very smart indeed. She is anxious to see the family in Augusta, but dreads the introduction, she says. I think she has a more favorable impression of Brother Henry than any of the younger members, for when I came to him, in giving her a high sketch of them, her face brightened and she said "Ah, I have *heard* of him."

Yesterday Mr. Stiles went to visit Mrs. Russell. She is, if possible, a more pitiable object than ever, decaying by piecemeal, and apparently calmly unconcerned about her soul. He was not conscious of producing any effect, but says he was very plain with her.

I have not seen Pa so terribly distressed in a long time, as at a piece of intelligence we have lately heard. That wretched Holinbec who, you know, went to Columbus as a missionary, has been preaching and administering the ordinances of the church with the venereal disease upon him, until finally it became so bad that concealment was impossible. The people are loud in their indignation. One night his house was stoned, and a gentleman in the place threatens to beat him because he dared to give his wife the sacramental bread with such polluted hands. Add to this, he is said to possess the most consummate vanity, is going about inquiring for ladies of fortune, says he rates his education at fifty thousand dollars, and in one case, a young lady went so far as to consult her friends upon the expediency of marrying him. Pa says our church has received an irrecoverable blow in that part of the country, besides the wound that religion itself has received. Oh human nature, what a desperate thing thou art!

The people in the neighbourhood are very busily engaged in preparation for the exhibition. I wish you could be here, but I expect we shall miss poor Goode very much. Pa got a letter from him yesterday morning, dated Savannah. He wrote quite cheerfully.

Tell Annie she must be a very good little girl, for Aunt Maria has got a beautiful little kitten for her when she comes up. Margaret writes as if she were more and more pleased with her new residence. Nat Bond, she says is in Columbus and is a great admirer of Eliza Bird. Says the Indians are in the habit of assembling on the opposite bank of the river at night, and he goes and walks up and down upon the bank half the night, declaiming upon Indian innocence and simplicity. They had a *"talk"* not far off and Nat attended. In coming home he lost his way in the woods. The Indians gave him shelter and food and stole his saddle from him.

I was very much disappointed that Ma did not bring my apple geranium with her. I think I have been quite self-denying in letting it remain so long, and must beg you to send it up by Uncle Jacob. I value it for its own sake and especially as being the gift of Mrs. Cumming [Mrs. Thomas Cumming, Henry Cumming's mother]. Ma says you think I gave it to you, but I assure you it never was my intention to do so, and if I did, must beg permission to play Indian in the matter. Pa and Ma think you had better hasten your departure as the weather is growing so warm.

Affectionately yours.

Julia Cumming, with her daughter Anne, three, and son Alfred, ten months, has just returned to Augusta after visiting Mt. Zion since mid-June. During Julia's long visit home her husband pictured her writing expressions of love to him in the room "where they read together . . . while little Annie slumbered." Here Maria resumes her correspondence with her sister.

Maria Bryan to Julia Ann Bryan Cumming

November 14, 1829 (Saturday)

My dear Julia,

Pa and Ma arrived in safety last night. The latter is, I think, benefitted by her journey, but she does not seem to think herself that her health is any better. They arrived just in time to see poor little Ben [the son of their slaves Patty and George] breathe his last. I can't tell you how sorry I felt for George. He had not more than taken his seat, with his child in his arms, before his breathing grew short and thick, and he died immediately.

Thursday morning Patty sent in a request for me to come down and see Ben. I did so, and found him in the first stage of the croup and breathing with a great deal of difficulty. No physician could be had. *I* did everything I had ever heard of for that complaint, gave him an emetic and applied garlic, and towards evening Dr. Gilbert came. *He* gave him calomel and bled him, but it did not relieve him at all. I sat up with him till about one o'clock for I thought he would probably die before morning, and as I was sitting there I thought I would look in Ma's receipt book [to see] if there was no remedy there for the croup. There was one, to cut up onions and stew them with tallow and sugar, give the liquor to the patient—apply the onions to the breast, feet and wrist. We tried this and I felt really very much encouraged. But everything was vain. I never saw a mother appear better than Patty. She made no fuss at all and was quiet and almost dignified. Her good discipline was very perceptible throughout the child's illness. She had only to speak to him and he would take medicine, or do anything she bid him. He would frequently say he wanted to get well and play with Miss Anne again. Patty is very much distressed indeed.

What a state of confusion and uneasiness you must all be in. I do really feel for you, and have hardly thought of anything else since Pa and Ma came home. Robert who takes a great interest in the fires and troubles in Augusta has asked a thousand questions about the late one. I was amused at his earnestness last night. After hearing Pa talk about it he said, "Well, I would not own property in Augusta for a hul *kingdom!*" The day after you and the children left here he looked troubled and forlorn. He would bring forth such deep groans that I could not bear to hear him. . . .

I hope we shall hear from you by Monday's mail. Sophia, I think, will go down with Pa. She is very anxious to do so and I do not believe Ma will object. I wish she could be with you while Mr. Cumming is confined in court. She is now sitting hard at work making her dress that Ma brought, and has hardly lifted her eyes from her work today. You know her propensity to have something new for Sunday.

Sam Wales has been paying a visit to his mother and sister [his stepmother, Aunt Wales, and his sister, Catherine]. He made Catherine quite a present—a pair of ear rings and breast pin, and one of those large twisted chains. I have no very great opinion of Sam's character, but I do think he deserves credit for his kindness and generosity to Catherine. He still dwells upon his visit to you last Spring, and says he shall go down again in the course of a few weeks.

You remember your urging Mrs. Alston last Sunday evening to persuade her husband to repair the office. She did not mention it to him at all, and this afternoon Pa said, "Norton, you'd better lay out the money you assign for fitting up that old house of yours, in fixing up the office for a residence—it will not take more than double the sum." "How can it be done?" he enquired. Pa said, "Step around and look at it. I will explain how it can be done." He said the idea struck him with great force and he would think further of it.

Give my love to Mr. Cumming and kiss Annie and Alfred for me. My love to Mr. & Mrs. Cumming [Sr.] and the girls. Well, Julia, I have begun my course of letters and it really sickens me to think of them, they are so stupid and uninteresting, that I am sure, were it not that they afford you means of hearing from the family, you might desire me to discontinue them altogether. Much love.

Yours affectionately.

Anne Alston is about to be married. She asks Maria to be an attendant at her wedding. Maria, who dislikes the Alstons, tries to wriggle out of the invitation without offending the younger woman.

Maria Bryan to Julia Ann Bryan Cumming

[Postmark: November 24, 1829]

My dear Julia,

Your last letter was so very short that I hoped you would write again by the succeeding mail. I suppose, however, that you have not had an opportunity of doing so. Ma has been more unwell for a day or two, although for some time after she got home she was much better, I thought.

We had a tolerably good exhibition [at Mt. Zion Academy], and there were a number of people present, a great many from Sparta, and other places at a distance. I do wish you could have witnessed Mr. Rood's examination, his pompous strange manner, and the thoroughness with which they had been taught would have amused you. Catherine is still quite unwell. The day of the examination, while sitting in the school room, she was taken with a chill and had to come in here and lay down.

Aunt Wales complains greatly of loneliness and low spirits. All her boys are gone [Aunt Wales operated a boardinghouse mostly for the young men attending the local academy], and I should think she would be really glad of it, for with Iverson, in particular, she had constant trouble. He told her, a few days before the exhibition, that he had long ago made up his mind to seek another boarding house next term. She told him she was very glad of it, for she had made up her mind not to take him. Mrs. Mathews has been staying at Aunt Wales's, and Catherine amused me relating various conversations she had held with her. Among others, one concerning you. Among other things, she said she did admire you very much indeed, your very white skin, and beautiful hair, and you were so commanding, one of the most lady-like persons she had ever seen in her life. Indeed, "in her whole appearance, dress and manners," said she, "Mrs. Cumming is a complete lady." You know how you laugh at me for always telling compliments.

Dr. Ellenson and Mr. Barness called here the other day, and I saw the former then for the first time. I do not like his conversation particularly, for he is very affected, and has a sort of dying away languor, and talks of feeling and sentiment and sensibility and impulses too much, but he is really very handsome. He told me a great deal of Mrs. Hitchcock, at whose house he stayed in Mobile, says she is certainly the most lovely woman he ever met with, and indeed, said he, "while I was there I had to keep a constant guard over myself lest I should fall in love with her." I forget whether you ever saw Barness. He is very much improved since I saw him before, and is really a very agreeable, modest young man.

I suppose you have before this received Anne Alston's commissions. She told me she had written to you. She came out the other day for me to go in town with her on special business, she said. I could not go then, but went in to pay Mrs. Skinner the visit I promised her. I called at the Alstons and she [Anne Alston] took me one side and begged me to be an attendant. I hesitated, almost refused, for I felt a special repugnance to filling the office to any one, but especially in that family. She looked very much chagrined and mortified, and asked me what was my reason. I told her in the first place I was a great deal older than her, and I supposed that she could find someone else who would do better, and I was not at all prepared to appear in this character, and there was very little time to be ready. After much coaxing on her part, which I could not get over without offending her, I concluded to think further of it, as I wished to ask Pa and Ma's advice. They seem inclined to have me consent, not from any other cause but from sympathy with their condition, that Anne has few or no friends to perform that office for her.

Since writing this, I received your letter, and am surprised to find you did not receive the one I wrote sooner, but I sent it by Monday's mail. We are very glad to hear that Mr. Cumming is getting better, and especially rejoiced to find that the public agitation, as well as the causes of the uneasiness, are subsiding.

How very sorry you made me feel for Mr. Wilde. Poor fellow, the world has indeed proved to him a "broken reed, a pointed spear." And his *Friend*—you made me hate him! Ah, what kind of friendship is this, to avoid and neglect one because he has fallen in to misfortune for what is *error*, either in principle or conduct, but misfortune of the worse kind? Why not go and remonstrate with him, he could have influence if any one could, but he will stand aloof, as though *he* were not a mortal man equally exposed to temptation and crime, etc. It is *envy*, it is the fear of dividing with him those honours which superior genius is so justly entitled to—and not the righteous indignation of pure and holy principle.

You surprise and distress me in what you relate of Richardson. Poor

Margaret, she is another of those who seems *doomed* through life to disappointment. You ask me not to mention it. May I not mention it to her, is it not my duty?

The General [Bailey, who visited Mt. Zion earlier] does indeed inspire me with as much awful respect as ever. My lips quiver, my face burns, I stammer and hesitate when I speak, so that if he understands the signs of the hidden passion, he certainly may feel himself assured of the existence of it in myself. He said to me that he understood I was about entering into the discharge of some very awful duties. I did not deny or confess, but avoided the subject.

Anne Alston seems to think it probable that Anne, Alfred, and Sarah [Cumming] at least will come up to her wedding. Mrs. Mathews is there sewing for her. She has a watered silk white petticoat, linen cambric morning dress, three new bonnets, and lilac silk pelisse, very rich and beautifully trimmed, a handsome new watch and a chain the facsimile of yours.

Mrs. Rossiter says she would like much to go and see you, but she has lately had one of her worst headaches, and is very unwell. Sophy is proposing to go down with Pa if he can get a gig to take her. Dear little Annie, how I want to see her and kiss her sweet mouth again. "And Alfred too," as Mrs. Ponce says. I did not think she would understand about Ben's death. [See the letter of November 14, 1829, concerning the death of the Bryans' young slave.]

I do not know when I have talked and listened so incessantly as I did the day and night I spent with Mrs. Skinner, of all her own affairs and [her daughter] Jane's and everybody else. The woman has twice the sense and shrewdness I gave her credit for, and really has a great insight into character, though I never saw anyone who observed everybody's words and actions so narrowly. Upon the whole, I like her very much. Mrs. Baxter was there, and they are as affectionate sisters as any two that I know. Mrs. Tom Baxter is expected at the house of the latter and Maria McDonald with her.

Margaret Bailey wrote me a dreadful account of Dr. Bird. Eliza had been there, she says, their child is extraordinarily smart, but has the united temper of both parents. And withal she is most wretchedly managed, sometimes whipped severely when her mother is in a passion, and then indulged in every whim as if to make up to her for the severity that has been used.

I thought you were going to send me something to make my niece some pantalets. You know, Julia, how willingly I would get something myself and not trouble you, but it is out of my power. Write soon. I am in much better spirits than I have been, and I hope I shall continue if not happy, at least composed and contented, for besides the pain it causes, those gloomy moods makes one so petulant and selfish, that on that account, if no other, they ought to be represt. Give my best love to Mr. Cumming. I would like much to see him and yourself. Pa talks of going to Savannah and I do suppose if Mr. Joseph Cumming [Henry Cumming's older brother] comes up and urges him to go down he will accompany him. Tell Annie not to forget her Aunty.

Affectionately yours.

Maria's persistent rejection of a suitor is described here at length to Julia, who apparently had advised her sister to accept this marriage offer and "take up [her] abode on the sea coast" at Camden, Georgia. The Bryans, in this letter, are also harassed by a slave patrol entering the house late at night, striking their slaves and quarreling with Pa for trying to protect his blacks against their intrusions.

Maria Bryan to Julia Ann Bryan Cumming

December 13, 1829 (Sunday)

My dear Julia,

Your letter, as usual, was most joyfully received, and though I wrote to you a day or two ago, I fear you may be disappointed if I do not write by this mail. I can sympathise in your suffering from a cold, by same experience at present. I hope, however, that yours is better by this time.

Ma and I are alone again tonight. Pa set off for Milledgeville this morning, to attend to some of Mrs. Robertson's interests, and we do not expect him home until Wednesday. Aunt Wales and Catherine have been with us this afternoon assisting us to quilt; the former was very much pleased at the proof of Annie's remembrance. I was really amused at her sober way of talking of the child's excellencies. "I know," said she, "that I am impartial, perfectly so, and I do think she is the most interesting child I ever saw. To be sure, blood runs thicker than water, but I'm sure that don't influence *my* opinion in the least." Mrs. Rossiter has amused everybody in relating her efforts to entertain her by singing "Charlie is my darling." Tomorrow is the day General Bailey promised that Margaret should be here and I shall look most earnestly for her.

I suppose you have heard of the dreadful occurrence of poor Gideon

Alston's death. The family are very much distressed indeed. Many persons I am told attended the funeral. Poor Pepin continues raving as if he would go distracted. Poor little fellow, my very heart is sore for him. He seemed to dread, at first, that the family, if they did not blame him for wilfully committing the misdeed, might yet look upon him with involuntary loathing, and Satterlee went up to him and said, "Ferdinand, go down to my office." "Oh, Mr. Satterlee," said he, "where shall I go? I have no place to go to."

I received a most affectionate letter from Caroline just this morning, urging me to go and see her. She tells me she has promised you a visit of a week or ten days about Christmas; seems to be very cheerful, and condoles with me on my low spirits. I am truly glad to be released from the necessity, or the *duty,* of being low spirited. Julia, is not all the high pretensions of nobleness in those Clays' and Stiles's a mere puff? I do believe so. Real generosity they do not understand and can not exhibit (*entre nous*).

I had just been reading your advice, that I would yield to my destiny and take up my abode on the sea coast, when I heard a rap at the door, and as I went out to meet the visitor, there stood Major Floyd filling the front door with his august person and the majesty thrown around it. I was taken so upon surprise that I was frightened as bad as if it had been General Bailey himself, and blushing, and in a voice hardly articulate, I let him into the room and motioned him to a seat. I soon recovered myself, but I wish I could give you some idea of his manner.

You have read in novels of those men who gaze and look as though they were going to take one in bodily—well, instead of taking a chair, he just looked at me as if he could think of nothing but the lovely vision before him, and when he came to himself sufficiently to sit down, it was not long before he commenced the engrossing subject. He hoped I had been considering the subject he had the honor of proposing to me. I told him—however it is no matter what *I* said. I wish I could tell you his conversation, for although much of it was rhapsody, still there were indications of good sense and good feeling in what he said. My endeavour was to give as decided a negative as possible, at the same time that I avoided any personal objection, or anything that would wound his self-love. Were it that I dreaded to leave my parents, he said, one half, one *third* of my time, if I chose it, should be spent with them, only what time I pleased in Camden. His friends would love me as my own did. Was it from aversion to marriage? He hopes, he intreats, that a mere whim, as he must call it, would not prevent him from devoting his life to the business of making me happy. Was my negative founded on a supposed difference in religious opinion? He knew I was a member of the Church, and he never should interfere with my feelings or actions in that respect. If he were not himself religious, he might be permitted, in justice to himself, to say he was a *moral* man.

Still, as I continued to say nay to every argument, he said, "What can I do, or propose, that will induce you to be favourable to me. Ah, you have some perfect character drawn by your imagination that you are waiting to meet. Believe me, this dream can never be realized. Oh, accept the attachment of a living feeling being who offers you genuine love, warm from his heart! Don't shake your head and tell me no. I will not receive that for an answer. You must think more of it—if I must lose you it should not be without a struggle. If I cannot win you, at least it shall not be my own fault."

He said for several years past there had been little or nothing to bind him to life. Now that he felt once more something to interest him and draw forth all his energies, I must excuse him for his obstinate determination to persevere in his suit, although I forbade it. If I did not finally relent, he felt now as if he could not remain in this country. Since he could not hope for happiness in domestic life, he would go to Europe, join some army and try to forget his failure. I can't tell you how sorry I felt, when I looked at him, for his face, when not possessed of its usual pompous, self-satisfied expression, looks more sad, and yet more placid than any one I ever saw. However, I suppose I have given you a detail long enough of this matter.

I do not wonder you want to see Brother. We are really growing uneasy about him. There is a report in the neighbourhood that he is married.

Rakestraw and Kitty are busily engaged putting up meat and sausages, and Pa seems very much pleased with Rakestraw's conduct and the interest he takes in everything. [Rakestraw is probably the Rakestraw who worked for the Cummings in Augusta in the next generation and accompanied Julia's son, Major Joseph B. Cumming, to the Civil War as his body servant.] He boasts very much of a feat he performed the other day. He was at the mill and killed six wild ducks at one shoot. "Insatiate ache—could not *one* suffice?"

It is generally thought, at least in this country, that a man's house is his castle, but it would seem that this is not always the case. We really are troubled by the patrol lately. They come in the cellar at all times of the night, waking up the family, and making an uproar. The other night they struck Jack over the face, and his nose bled nearly a quart. Pa went out to protect him, and they became dreadfully angry with him, said he "upheld his negroes in their rascality." "You are a liar," said Pa. A few nights ago somebody took Mercer's horse out of the stable (quite a valuable riding nag worth 80 or 90 dollars), took him off to some distance, and knocked him in the head. Mercer has been whipping and examining and cross-questioning, but the offender is not yet more than suspected.

Tell Sophy, Ma was really angry and hurt when she found that she wished to stay away from her longer. Just now, when I was writing on the last page, she says, "Ask Miss Sophy if it can be that she wants to stay in Augusta longer." Tell her that Frank is learning to play on the flute and the only tune he can or does play is "Day of absence sad and dreary," and that he has sent forth with a dismal wail every night since she has been gone. I wish Anne would go to the low country if she will not come here. She informs me she still suffers from symptoms of vertigo.

Indeed I fear, Julia, that all the ingenuity with which you compliment me will fail to teach me how to make any frock. I have a perfect horror of beginning it unless I knew how to do it, and believe I'd rather not wear it this winter than undertake to make it by guess. Tell Sophie — Tailor Smith has bought Plunket out, and they are going to live there. Polly is as industriously making breeches as he is.

Tell my dear little Annie how glad her Aunty is that she does not forget her. Ma says, "Tell Julia if she wants to see me so bad, I wish she would come up and eat Christmas dinner with us." Oh will you not? My love to Mr. [Thomas] Cumming [Sr.]. I suppose he is still living though I can only guess at it. This is a wretchedly written letter, but Pa has gone off with my knife, the paper is bad and I am in a great hurry, for I must write to Anne. With love.

Affectionately yours.

Mrs. Caroline Goode Holt Iverson died in Clinton, Georgia, on Tuesday, March 16, 1830. She left two children. Caroline was not a member of a church, and Maria has some doubts about her salvation.

Maria Bryan to Julia Ann Bryan Cumming

March 20, 1830 (Saturday)

My dear Julia,

We arrived home about ten o'clock this morning, and I take the first moment of leisure to write to you. Our poor Cousin [Caroline] is dead. She died Tuesday night about eight o'clock, and we did not receive Mr. Iverson's letter, or set off, until the morning after. I could not but hope all the day, as we were travelling, that she might live, that we might find her better, and I had taken my trunk full of clothes in case she should desire me to stay and nurse her for a few weeks. We stopt for a few minutes in Milledgeville, and Pa went to speak to some gentleman, leaving me in the gig. Mr. Hines Holt saw me and came and spoke to me. I told him we were going to Clinton to see Cousin Caroline who was very ill. "She is dead," said he. I was almost as much shocked as though I had not heard of her sickness.

We went that night to Scottsborough, and the next morning being cloudy, Pa went on without me, wishing to see Mr. Iverson and to know his arrangements about the children. He says he has seldom seen any one more deeply afflicted than Mr. Iverson. She was buried the evening before. Every one had left the house and he was sitting alone in it when Pa stept in at the door. He heard and went to meet him, and, Pa says, threw himself upon his neck and wept aloud. She had been indisposed slightly for several weeks, and on being taken worse, she complained of pain in her head. This afterwards removed to the bowels. The physicians were sanguine, and thought the disease was entirely under the control of the usual remedies.

From the first, however, she told her husband she thought it was her last sickness, and expressed a great wish to see us, particularly her Uncle. When she found she must die, she was very much distrest, and sent messages to her friends, pious persons to pray for her. The physicians bled her four times until she fainted and until nature seemed quite exhausted, but when aroused to consciousness of her situation she would earnestly desire "to see Uncle." There was a young woman (whose name I do not remember) who was attending to her during her sickness, a member of the Methodist Church, and a very good girl. She said to her, "Oh pray for me, I have many sins to answer for." "Yes," said the other, "but you have a great Saviour to go to." Mr. Iverson says the last words he heard her utter were "Lord, have mercy on me." But a little before she expired her eyes were closed and Mr. Iverson put his mouth to her face and kissed her. "Is that you?" said she. "Remember your poor Carry."

Oh, if I could cherish a hope of her future happiness, how different would be my feelings, and yet I cannot but hope. Last Spring when she was here, I gave her a little book, Dodriys' *Rise and Progress,* and I wrote some thing to this effect in the first pages, that "I trusted my dear Cousin's name would be added to the long catalogue of those who had been converted by means of this book." Mr. Iverson said he had observed that she often read in it; that she read much in her Bible, and during the last year she had been more interested in the subject of religion than he had ever known her, had attended church regularly, was fond of the society of Christians, and of conversing on religious subjects.

Oh, how deeply I do regret her death. Each day since, I seemed to realize the loss more than I did at first. Her very peculiarities, as I remember them, only impresses her image more strongly on my memory. I trust, my dear Julia, that it may be sanctified to us both, as I have often thought since the event took place, no doubt whatever situation she may now be in, she thinks if she had her life to go over again that it should be wholly devoted to the service of her Maker. Let us, to whom God yet gives an existence on this earth, act upon this belief and spend our remaining days more consistently and more piously.

Mr. Iverson says he cannot, at present, think of sparing his children. Yet he cannot keep them. He wishes Julia [Julia Maria Iverson, his young daughter] certainly to come here, that he frequently heard her [Caroline Iverson] say that if she were to die, she hoped I would take charge of Julia. When her Mother was carried away she [Julia Maria] seemed greatly grieved, but Pa says is utterly unconscious of her loss. The infant [a year-old son] is very ill and is now at the Doctor's. Mr. Iverson, Pa remarks, though so much grieved, is yet totally free from a disposition to murmur. He says the Lord is a Sovereign and has a right to act his own pleasure.

Anne told you probably, that I would have returned with her had it been convenient for Mr. Cumming to have given me a seat. Ma's health is rather better than when I wrote before. Captain Lacee died last night, and will be buried up at his Father's plantation tomorrow morning. Oh what a destitute family he has left. Give my love to Catherine. Tell her I thank her sincerely for her letter, and would have answered it immediately had I not left home. I will however write to her in a few days. The family are well at Scottsborough, enquired with great affection of you, and Catherine sent to Annie the long-talked-of gingham dress, which by the way you will probably be obliged to transfer to Master Alfred. Patty's infant is lying dead in her room [just four months after the death of her son, Ben]. It has been the greatest sufferer I ever saw, such piteous groans every moment as it would make, it would have pained your heart to hear. Do write soon. Tell Catherine her Mother is well. Give my love to Brother Henry, Anne and Sarah, and Caroline if she is still with you.

Very affectionately yours.

Will you be so kind as to procure me Harneds *Lecturer for Young Men* and send it at the first opportunity. I will send the money by Brother.

Yours truly.

Uncle Isaac Bryan, now in Mt. Zion, is subject to periodic fits, possibly epileptic. He fears he will die in one of these seizures. When not preoccupied with his ail-ment, however, the miserly uncle keeps himself busy shuffling his business papers (probably notes and mortgages) and talking about money matters. Alfred, Julia's fourteen-month-old son, is teething.

Maria Bryan to Julia Ann Bryan Cumming

March 29, 1830 (Monday)

My dear Julia,

This is the evening in which I usually write to you, otherwise I should not now write, as Brother can tell you in person of anything which I could inform you. I suppose you will be almost sorry to see him come as he will be obliged to take Catherine [Wales] away from you. But yet if you could realize how much her Mother wants her to return, I think you would resign her with more cheerfulness.

Uncle is with us tonight and it makes me low spirited to see him. He is now anticipating one of his fits, and he dreads it so much, as he says, he knows not but it may snatch him out of the world in a minute. And poor man so entirely unprepared as I fear he is, and yet in his intervals of repose, he is as busily engaged as ever sorting and arranging his papers, and talking about money matters.

We have all been very industrious lately making a new carpet for the parlour. I think I never remember being so tired in my life as I was Saturday. After sewing hard in the morning, I spent the afternoon with the others, pasting cloth over the cracks in the floor to stop the smoke from penetrating.

I think it is altogether the better plan for yourself and the children to come up early in May as your health will thereby be more ensured than by remaining later.

Brother has probably told you that Miss Stebbins [their former teacher] thinks it probable she will come out in the Fall. Sophia seems as if she can hardly wait with any patience to be instructed by me, since she has heard of it — however I have endeavoured to be faithful in instructing her through good and evil report, to the best of my ability, and trust I shall continue to do so until I resign the charge into abler hands.

Tell my little Annie her Aunt Maria loves to see her too. I hope I shall hear from you by the next mail, though this letter is hardly worth a reply.

Very affectionately yours.

Tell Brother I wrote, according to his request, to Lucy Sperry today and urged her to accept the invitation to Monticello. I shall write to Dr. Broddus as soon as I hear from her, which I hope will be tomorrow. My love to Brother Henry, Caroline and Catherine. Master Alfred's formidable increase of grinders seems to threaten devastation to his Grandfather's provender during the ensuing Summer.

Maria in this letter to Julia is in a self-critical mood and is evidently going into mourning for her cousin, Mrs. Caroline Goode Holt Iverson. In this confessional letter, Maria nevertheless longs for beauty and the fashionable life of the city.

Maria Bryan to Julia Ann Bryan Cumming

April 5, 1830 (Monday)

My dear Julia,

I received your letter this morning, and although I have nothing special to write, I sit down to answer it. You complain of the shortness of my letters, but

one a week written from a place where there are so few events worth record-
ing as in this, may be supposed not to be long. You, by your own confession,
hate sentimental epistles and, by the way, I have come over to your opinion
and heartily wish I had never written one in my life, and when I attempt
anything in the way of reasoning, advice, or grave moralizing, I almost fancy
I hear the far off echo of your voice "Humph, Maria is taking great airs upon
herself."

Catherine [Wales] arrived home safely, and has confirmed our suspicions
that she did not care about returning to the humdrum sort of life we lead
here at Mt. Zion, after quaffing so largely of the sweets of fashionable life in
Augusta. She is very much improved indeed in health and in her appearance.
I never saw her look so handsome, and everyone notices her acquisition of
"the indescribable air of ton."

What is it in the atmosphere of your house that communicates this in such a
remarkable degree to your guests after they have been a while in your family?
All but me. *I* must have been insulated in my infancy, for this certain something I could never *take*. Sophia, Catherine, after they come home awhile,
seem like creatures of another order whereas I, if I may trust the reflection
from my mirror and my own judgment upon it, as unpolished and inelegant
as ever. My only resource is to affect to despise it, but I cannot impose upon
myself. These airs and graces (if not appearing as if *put* on), this look of high
life, these marks of refinement betokening a soul of superior cast, is what I
have always desired next to beauty, and, alas, neither have been granted to
me—but why do I say alas? In my better moments I am wise enough rather
to be thankful for the absence of these things.

But, as I was saying, Catherine is very much pleased with her visit indeed.
I never saw her manifest more exhilaration of spirits, and Sophy's poor little
head is almost turned with her account of the theater. Catherine was telling
her of having seen *Venice Preserved* acted, and in the course of the evening
Saturday when I went in the room, where I supposed she was getting her
Sunday School lesson, I found her poring over the woes of Belvidera [daugh-
ter of a Venetian senator in the work *Venice Preserved, or a Plot Discovered*,
by Thomas Otway; first presented in 1682, it remained a stock piece on the
stage until into the nineteenth century]. And yesterday, just before entering
church I heard her and Catherine laughing at the appearance of the Senators
of Venice.

"Pretty conversation for the Sabbath day, Sophy," said I.

"Why la——— Sister, what harm is it?"

"Don't you know," said I, "we are commanded in Scripture not to speak our own words, or think our own thoughts on the Sabbath, but keep it strictly holy to the Lord?"

"Whose thoughts must I think then?" said she, and so my lectures are generally received with a sneer.

I believe I did not tell you in my last that Mrs. [Carlisle] Beman has a son whom she calls Henry. You can rarely see a more delighted Father and Mother than they are.

How sorry it makes me feel to hear of your restless discontented feelings. If, as you suspect, they be hereditary, then there is double reason for resisting them, lest you should thus inflict them upon your children in turn. Ma very often retorts upon me when I announce some of my maxims of conduct, "Ah it is so much easier to preach than to practice," and I have no doubt but it is so, but yet it does appear to me to be so clearly an interest in the way of promoting our own happiness, as well as a duty to be acquiescent in every situation of trial in which we may be placed. How often I have admired the spirit which dictated the beautiful language of the Mother of our Saviour "Behold, the handmaid of the Lord, be it unto me according to Thy word."

I would willingly, nay, even gladly, go and spend several weeks with you now—but I rarely consult my own convenience in my visiting arrangements, and it would be far from being proper to do so now. Ma is really in wretched health, and it is absolutely indispensable that something should be done for her. This moment I would give a thousand dollars if she could go to the North. Her heart is set on it, and she feels firmly convinced it would improve her health vastly, and poor little Goode writes such pathetic and earnest requests that they would come on and see him [at West Point], that I never desired anything much more. How I wish you and Mr. Cumming would persuade Pa. When I see Ma dragging out one day after another in constant pain, languid low spirit, hopeless of relief, I cannot help from blaming Pa for denying her what she so much craves, and what would in all probability benefit her greatly. For myself I would willingly relinquish the prospect of going with them—if only they two would go.

With regard to the articles for which I sent, I have from some association or other, acquired an invincible dislike to a grass bonnet, especially when trimmed with black, and have determined never to wear one. I have been told that black mode trimmed with lease [lace] or crape makes very handsome mourning bonnets, and such are very much worn at the North. Will you, therefore, be kind enough to order one for me. I will send down a bandbox by Uncle Jacob. The other things which I requested—a pair of black stockings, black gloves, a calico, or gingham, the crape, and two yards of black belt ribbon. Sophy does not wish to wear mourning. I know you are so much troubled with commissions that I was very unwilling to send to you and urged Pa to let me get Mrs. Sandwich to make me a bonnet, but he preferred my sending to you.

Nancy Carrington is very much to be pitied. Since her Mother's death she has had an hysteric fit, she is very weak and low spirited, lays down most of the time, and fancies she is unable to be up—besides being terribly uneasy if alone.

Tell Annie she must make haste and come to Mount Zion, for Aunty wants to see her very much.

Yours truly.

A restless Maria Bryan at twenty-two is finding home life at Mt. Zion getting on her nerves. She yearns to go to Europe. Despite her mood, she rejects yet again an earlier suitor.

Maria Bryan to Julia Ann Bryan Cumming

April 19, 1830 (Monday)

My dear Julia,

It hardly seems possible that I am to see you so soon again. I suppose we shall never, while we live, get over the delusion of looking upon future time as very long, while the past appears truly to have fled most rapidly.

Pa and Ma, notwithstanding your prognostics, are actually gone. They set off last Thursday, and expected to spend the Sabbath in Macon. Brother had been speaking, most of the time, of going with them and I believe that was Pa's principal reason for desiring to go to Florida—that he might induce him to settle there and, in that case, purchase him lands. But the very evening before they went, he came down and said he could not leave home just at that time. I have never seen Pa and Ma when their feelings were more hurt. After they had left, Brother, I thought, seemed to feel very bad on account of the way he had acted, and so yesterday he came down from his plantation and said he would set out and try and overtake them.

We are lonely enough, I can assure you. You may have heard me say I do not generally suffer much from this feeling, and indeed I cannot tell why I do now, but I believe we are so constituted that we must have some excitement, and I actually have nothing in this world at present. I wander about the house like a troubled ghost seeking rest and finding none. I read with no comfort, for it appears to me that every book in the house has grown dull. Music is discord, and sewing is worse than all, for then I have nothing but my thoughts for my companions, and they give the lie to the old saying that bad company is better than none. I do not wonder that persons destitute of religious principle rush into dissipation of various kinds to rid themselves of ennui, for it is surely as insupportable a thing as may be.

We received a letter from Mr. Iverson last week, requesting that Julia Maria may be brought here, and Ma has of course given her consent. When she will come I do not know.

I received a letter this morning which has really vexed me, from Colonel F. to use his own expression, making a reavowal of his regard. He begs me to "lay aside my *peculiar* and *romantic* notions," and deliberate on the matter. I am sure that I am sufficiently averse to the thing without deliberating, and if his self-love did not blind him, he would know that deliberation would only increase this aversion. But I wonder if he does not think that his being a Congressman will batter down all my prejudices. Glorious prospect he presents, to visit the metropolis the ensuing season — and with a companion I could be so proud of, too. Love, heard from most lips, is to me the most disgusting word in the world, and you may imagine it to be nauseous in the extreme in this instance. He reminds me of what Louisa D'Albeman (in *Delphine*) [a character in the Mme. de Staël novel of 1802] says of herself — she has a soft and tender heart, but it would be ridiculous for such a looking person as her to love. I shall write that our correspondence may now cease, since the terms of it are so little understood. When he wrote of fashion and politics I was content to read his epistles.

You ask me why I have not mentioned Mrs. Rossiter. I saw her only an hour ago. She is at Mrs. Alston's where she had been spending the day. Her health is very bad now indeed. She has very frequent attacks of the headache, but seems wonderfully cheerful and happy. And as to the Dr. [Rossiter] time and infirmity seem as if they dared not lay their hands upon him. He reads newspapers with as much pleasure and swigs his buttermilk with the same relish as ever.

Mrs. Lacee says she is very much pleased with the article you purchased, and says it was a "great favour for Mrs. Cumming to do that for her."

Yesterday afternoon I was in my room laying down, when Epsey came to tell me there was some ladies had come in a carriage. I could not imagine who had favoured me, until I found seated in the parlour Sally, Mary, and Henrietta Bonner, with their sister Mrs. Ridly. They had been to Sparta to church, and hearing of my being alone, had called. You know I have a perfect abhorrence of visits on Sunday, and from such persons. They seem to speak and think more of Brother than anyone else and very familiarly call him "Joe." Anne Floyd [possibly kin to the rejected Major Floyd] has again gone to Camden, on a visit of four or five weeks, with Mrs. Everett Hamilton. Among the various talk with which the ladies regaled me yesterday evening, they were looking at some geraniums, and it seems that Anne had told them that Miss Floyd had a cockroach geranium, and whenever she wanted to give a gentleman a piece of geranium she pulled it off of that one, for it smelt exactly like cockroaches.

I am truly sorry for Mr. Cumming's indisposition. I think he had better go somewhere this Summer. How much I do want to go to Europe—I never did desire it so much in my life.

I am very much obliged to you for the things you obtained, and am pleased with them. The bonnet is light and sufficiently becoming, but I cannot say I admire it particularly. Robert gave us some strawberries yesterday and they were delicious. Who would have thought of Annie's understanding this expression. I shall hope to see you at the appointed time.

Yours affectionately.

Brother received a letter from Storrs the morning he left home, telling him he should be here the twenty fifth of the month, and requesting him and Satterlee to hold themselves in readiness to accompany him to Vermont where he is going. He says, "Shall we not form a glorious trio! Our friends will be delighted to see us." Brother would have given his teeth to consent to the proposal, I believe.

Sophia who is sitting by me reading suddenly broke out by saying just now, "Sister, do you intend to be married at night?"

"Yes—if I were to marry."

"Well," said she, "[I] will not. I intend to marry as they do in England. There, they marry in the morning, and call it marriage in high life."

"But consider," said I, "that in this case, it can't be called marriage in high life—so it will be ridiculous if that's your aim."

Since the last letter, Julia has had another son, and third child, Julien Cumming, born August 1, 1830, and Julia Maria Iverson has come to stay with the Bryans. Maria in this letter makes a veiled reference to Harford, a suitor of whom her father evidently disapproves.

Maria Bryan to Julia Ann Bryan Cumming

[Postmark: November 13, 1830]

My dear Julia,

I suppose if I were to attend strictly to the business rule in such matters I should write to Mr. Cumming tonight instead of you. However, as I feel well assured he will very gladly excuse me, I address myself in the usual way. I was sorry not to receive a letter from you this morning, and sorrier still for the cause of it. I hope your cold is, before this, relieved. Ma says she always dreads to have you take cold in the beginning of the season. Brother did not reach home until Sunday morning, and is, I fear, more unwell than before.

Last week was a constant scene of bustle with us. You remember I told you I was going to help Mrs. Brown sew. I went, and so did Ma and Mrs. Rossiter and Catherine and Eliza Beman. We were all very much engaged in the midst of vests, pantaloons and dresses, when Mat came for me to go home as Miss Caroline Grant and her brother [Anderson] had arrived. I found that their father had dispatched them in great haste for Oakly, understanding from you that he was extremely ill. C. says her Papa is deafer than she has ever known him to be, and she supposed he did not hear distinctly what you said. Oakly [a student at Mt. Zion Academy] has a very important part in the dialogue and on Mr. Beman's earnest entreaties that they would allow him to remain until after the exhibition, Anderson took the stage and Caroline remained two days longer.

Poor girl, how much pity and interest I feel for her. I do not know that I have ever met with anyone whose character I think is more improved by the influence of adverse circumstances. She is mild and quiet, perfectly equable, and I have rarely met with anyone more unselfish and free from envy and malevolent feelings. She was very anxious for me to go home with her, and said she came on purpose, as she supposed I would not like to return with her brother alone, but I could not go from a variety of reasons. My clothes all need mending and putting in order for the winter, besides having to do the same for Julia [Maria Iverson] and what is more important still, I should hate to leave the latter entirely under Ma's care, for I believe sick and unwell as she is, she would eat herself to death if I were not always watching her. She will go down into the cellar in spite of me, and all that I can say or do, Creasy will give her food. Catherine went to Columbia with C., the latter offered to take her to Augusta to see you and spend a day or two. I believe indeed she expects to return home with Pa when he goes to Synod.

We have had a visit from Daniel Watkins, his wife and Susan, last week. Mrs. Watkins, I think, is a very clever person, and does not lack sense, or information either, and as for our Cousin Daniel it is marvelous to see how his respectability and dignity is increased by having someone to love him and look up to him. And oh, what a kind husband he is. I began almost to believe in the truth of Ma's assertion, that a woman can in time love any "decent man" who will treat her kindly. They had an infant of about six months old, but I can give you no idea of the little mortal's appearance. Oh, how different from my little Julien! If you can conceive the features and countenance of an old man with the smooth skin and diminutive size of a very small child. It reminded me of the fairy tale of Prince Abdullah whose mother foolishly desired that he might live a thousand years, and when he was born he had anticipated at least fifty of them. It holds up its head though and tries to be sprightly—but to finish all, the nurse keeps it in a very careless manner. I could not but smile the other day. She had been listening to her sister Susan's singing and playing, and was sailing out of the room, when she met the nurse and child at the door coming to her. I heard her say, and it was so true, "Poor little thing, it lookth tho forlorn thumhow or other."

Mrs. Brown is so charmed with everything you sent. She says, "*What* a cloak for only eight dollars," and her eyes she believes will soon be restored by the use of Thomson's Infallible Eyewater. Mrs. Mathews is going to make her caps for her, and if she will only take care of her clothes she will have quite a comfortable wardrobe for winter.

I am fancying Colonel Foster [now a United States Congressman] at your house tonight and I know he so much anticipated spending some time with you. I can almost hear and see him as he is laughing and joking. I have not heard one word of the man this winter. Does he not come to see you at all, or do you fancy the *impossibility* of my taking no interest in his sayings or doings? "Sooner would my right hand forget its cunning."

We heard from Goode lately. He is well, and petitions for money. I cannot imagine how he disposes of what he receives as his expenses are all paid. Pa sent him ten dollars which I suppose will make him happy in view of oceans of tobacco.

I hope you will write to me this week. Give my love to Annie and tell her Aunty loves her very much for remembering to send the corset string. Brother unluckily dropt it out of his pocket, however.

I smiled when I found the inquiries you had been making from your inter-est in Harford. He would have great reason to thank you if he knew how much interest you had manifested for him, when everybody else was angry or indifferent. Pa, whenever he sees a letter, looks so grave, and says to me, "Strange that this young man should hang round the Army yet. Why don't he study a profession? I expect he's one of your *mere* literary men, like Twiss." I do not think it need give him much uneasiness, for I expect the denouement of this will be like everything else of the kind.

Ma liked her calico very much, and the shoes suited equally well. Pa says it is by no means certain that he shall attend Synod. Give my love to Brother Henry and thank him for his letter and kind invitation. Brother seems quite pleased with your Cousin Joe Stiles, and delivered Pa his message to accom-pany him to Florida. I believe I have written myself out, my dear Julia, only begging you to take much more for granted of my love and devotedness to you than I can expect.

M.

Maria has evidently been to Augusta to visit her sister Julia and has now returned to Mt. Zion. In this letter, buried among reports of neighborhood sickness and death, is a dramatic account of a white woman who had evidently given birth in the woods to a black infant. In the Old South a white woman who gave birth to a black child would be shunned, if not imprisoned. Although the intermixture of the races was severely frowned upon, many white men fathered children with black women and were still accepted in society in the antebellum South. As noted by the diarist Mary Boykin Chesnut, "the Mulattoes one sees in every family exactly resemble the white children—and every lady tells you who is the father of all the Mulatto children in everybody's household, but those in her own she seems to think drop from the clouds or pretends so to think."

Maria Bryan to Julia Ann Bryan Cumming

March 11, 1831 (Friday)

My dear Julia,

I was somewhat in hopes that I should receive a letter from you by Monday's mail, but was not so fortunate. You have received mine, I presume, before this. The family are not very well. Sophia has been very sick with the canker sore throat and fever. It is delightful weather now, not warm enough to be enervating to the system, and you can't think how beautiful the flowers look. I have been asked twenty times when you were coming up, and Ma is very anxious to see you indeed, but she said I must tell you she has no chance at all to go down.

I went to visit Mrs. Rossiter the other day. I got into the door before she or the Dr. saw me. They expressed great pleasure at my coming home, and I have seldom heard such a tale of woes, as that evening. We had no conception, from what we heard, how very sick Mrs. Rossiter was. It was a kind of inflammatory fever she had. While engaged in some household occupation she was suddenly struck with a violent pain, and for nearly or quite a fortnight was confined to her bed, much of the time was in a delirium, and it being the week of the snow and dreadful cold weather, none of the neighbours knew she was sick, nor came near her. The Dr. was nearly torpid from cold. Mary was in her worst mood and her wants were entirely unattended to because she was supposed to be raving. When she grew a little better, she was shocked by the circumstances of the child's being found dead. I never saw her look so badly, old and wrinkled, and Ma thinks her mind is much impaired, but I did not perceive that.

You asked me if I had taken the choir bag. I had not practised for several days before I left, and to my surprise found it in my instruction book where I had it last. I will send it to you by Uncle Jacob—if I can see him, before I leave here. I have had the misfortune to break my smallest guitar string, and coming away without getting any additional ones, have been very much put out.

Caroline Alston is as well behaved and pleasant a girl as I ever saw, and gives very little trouble, if it were not that we do not like to have so large a family.

Brother, when he returned, brought a strange account of a circumstance that took place in Clinton. A few weeks since a woman was found in the woods with no clothing on but her under dress, an infant a few days old, to which she was trying to administer nourishment although she said she had not eat one mouthful since its birth, and the child was a black one. She was taken to some charitable person's house, but positively refused to tell her name. She was apparently so overcome by shame as to have wandered away from her home, wherever that might be, and when her child was born she had no assistance at all. Brother said he saw the woman who had one night entertained her, and conversed with her. She told him that she could find out nothing of the person's name or family.

Satterlee was here Tuesday. He has recovered, though his limbs are stiff to what they were. He intends going to Florida in a few weeks to settle if he likes the country, otherwise he will go (he says) to New Orleans.

I hope I shall hear from you soon. Caroline and Marcia, I presume, are gone, and I fear you feel quite lonely. Do make Uncle Jacob bring my trunk for the India rubber shoes and several other things I want much. Send, if you please, *Consolation in Travel* as Colonel Cumming does not want it, or would not have it, and my red guard chain if you can find it. Tell Annie I hope she is a very good girl at school and at home. My love to Mr. Cumming.

Yours very affectionately.

Though the year of this letter is uncertain, it was presumably written a short time
before Maria's marriage to Lieutenant William Harford. In it a well-known his-
torical person, William Lowndes Yancey, appears fleetingly. Yancey, here a boy
of seventeen, had run off. His mother was Caroline Bird Yancey, who after the
death of his father, Benjamin Yancey, married in 1821 Nathan S. S. Beman when
he was still principal of the Mt. Zion Academy. Young Yancey accompanied his
stepfather back to Troy, New York, and went to school there. In this letter he is
evidently visiting his Bird relatives in Sparta. Yancey did not join the navy but did
attend Williams College and later studied law in the offices of Nathan Sayre of
Sparta and Benjamin F. Perry of Greenville, South Carolina. Still later Yancey
moved to Alabama and became a leader in the secession movement for southern
independence.

Maria Bryan to Julia Ann Bryan Cumming

[1831] (Thursday Night)

My dear Julia,

You perceive I am still at home; we expected to have gone Tuesday but the
weather was too bad to venture, and it was fortunate for us that we did not
leave here, for we should certainly have been detained in some place much
less pleasant than our present quarters. I was disappointed that I did not get a
letter from you last Sunday, and I suppose that you are under the impression
that I have gone, and have not written since.

Ma has been rather better lately than I have seen her for some time, though
today she has been made quite sick from a scene of Pa's with Brother's horse.
The horse has been used so little of late that he had become quite wild, and
several have urged Pa not to drive him on the journey. Today he brought him
out and put him in the buggy to try him, and he acted like a mad creature,
rearing and plunging. Pa and George kept hold of the bridle all the time,
and finally he got George under him, and we were afraid he would kick his
brains out. We all screamed, and prayed and besought Pa not to attempt to
drive him, but he was determined to conquer him, and got in and drove him
several miles until he seemed to have discovered that he must obey though
he looked to the last as if he was not willing to do so. This evening Pa had
him put in harness again, and made me get in with him not much to my will,

for I have been so little used to horses for the last two years that I have grown quite timid. Ma entreats him not to drive him, but he says, "Wife, how can you get to Augusta if I take one of the carriage horses?" She says, "I'll send down to Julia, and I know Mr. Cumming had rather send his horses to draw our carriage than have your life jeopardized." But he will have his own way, you know.

Sophia and I went to Sparta one day last week. We discovered as soon as we saw Mrs. Bird that something was the matter, and she told us she was in hourly expectation of hearing of Dr. Casey's death. [Mrs. James Wilson Bird is the former Frances Pamela Casey.] There was an abscess in his side, and his physicians were in doubt and hesitation about opening it, and death was apprehended in either case, whether they opened it or whether it broke; Mrs. Berrien and Weems had gone on, when they heard of his situation, and they wrote to her every other day.

She [Mrs. Frances Pamela Bird] and Mr. [James Wilson] Bird were likewise in much distress about William Yancey who, I presume you know, had left them in a clandestine manner, telling someone that he intended to try and get a place in the Navy. They had both written to beg he would come back, but they have not received one line in reply.

Old Mrs. Beman was in Sparta, staying at Weems's for ten days. I only saw her for a few minutes.

We heard that Mrs. Terrill was quite sick, and, as Pa had business with the Doctor, we called. She received me in a very friendly manner. We found her in bed, looking as pale and wasted as one in the last stages of a consumption. The tears would fall from her eyes on the pillow as she was telling us how sick she had been. Her complaint the Dr. calls the inflammatory rheumatism, and her hands have been drawn up like Mrs. Richardson's, and it was thought necessary to bleed her six times, and blister one of her wrists. The baby was quite well, and is a sprightly, though not a pretty, child. We saw likewise Eliza Crawford, and Mrs. C. and Mrs. Rembert.

Dr. & Mrs. Rossiter have both been sick lately. The Dr. was taken in the night with an affection which they say was produced by what they called Spasmodic Wind, and his pain was for some time so violent that he, as well as Mrs. Rossiter, thought he would die before morning. I saw them today, and they are both better. They are much annoyed by their boarders who are noisy boys, and Mr. Brantley's son in particular is a wild torn down youth.

I presume we will not go until Monday. I have been begging Ma to go with us, for I think she needs the journey. No news from Brother. My love to Mr. Cumming.

Yours affectionately.

Patty has a daughter. I hope Annie has her books by this time. Sophy says I must tell you Miss Judy Fontleroy is at Mrs. Skinner's. Mrs. Skinner and Mrs. Richardson spent a day here last week, the old lady [Mrs. Richardson] was all suavity. By the way I paid Mrs. Wade a visit the other day. Wade was in and had many pleasant and polite things to say, regretted that I was going away, and says: "When Mrs. *Cumming* leaves, we all feel a void. I suppose Mr. Harford could not do so well here as where he is, but if he could I should be glad for you to settle here, for the little acquaintance I have had with you, Madam, has been so very agreeable that I dislike to part with you."

M.

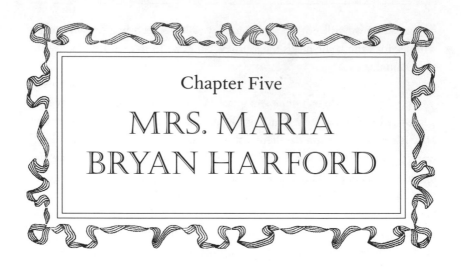

Chapter Five

MRS. MARIA BRYAN HARFORD

"I wish I was going where this letter is."

Maria Bryan married William H. Harford sometime between March and December 1831. Maria Bryan, almost twenty-four, and William H. Harford, age twenty-four, had been married a few weeks or months when she wrote this letter to Julia. No letters have been found to tell how or where she met Harford, what her real feelings toward him were, or where and when they were married. Maria's marriage and departure from Mt. Zion apparently had made her father unhappy. She was grateful to learn from Julia that Pa was growing "resigned."

Maria Bryan Harford to Julia Ann Bryan Cumming

Savannah
December 7, 1831 (Wednesday)

My dear Julia,

We returned from Liberty County last night, in the stage, about eight o'clock. Mr. [Joseph] Cumming [Henry Cumming's elder brother] had given us a most kind and pressing invitation to stay at his house and, as I feel infinitely more at home with him than with anyone else in Savannah, I was very glad to accept it. I had been in the house but a short time, before he told me there was a letter at his counting house from home, for me. You may imagine I was very restless, under the idea, but I found I must e'er wait quietly until this morning. I was extremely glad to hear that you were all well, and you were right indeed, my dear Julia, in saying it would be a gratification to me to know that Pa was composed and resigned, for I can truly say that the greatest aggravation of the trial of leaving home was the idea of the unhappiness it appeared to occasion him. How very glad I should have been to have been present at the baptism of the little one [Julia's fourth child, Thomas William Cumming, had been born October 14, 1831]. I hope and pray that the obligation you then laid yourself under, to train him up in the fear of God, you may be enabled faithfully to perform.

I was quite pleased during the visit we made to Mr. Harford's friends. Some of them are very agreeable and really superior persons, and others are plain and had nothing to recommend them to me but their apparently great affection for him, and kindness to myself. One of his half-sisters Mrs. Baker I took at first a most unpardonable dislike to, and I told him that I felt there was a mysterious influence which would even drive us as far as the poles asunder. My feelings, however, quite changed in a few days, and although she is not one whom I would seek to associate with from any congeniality of feeling, still I learned to respect and to do her justice before I came away. His sister Mary (Mrs. Way) would, I think, be remarked in any circle for her fine air and appearance. She has not near the regularity of features that you have, and yet there was something in her size and form and complexion that was constantly reminding me of you, and Jenny [Maria's personal slave] was continually saying "How much that lady looks like Miss Julia."

I never was in a more well ordered, interesting family than that of Mr. [John] Dunwoody, his cousin. It consists of five boys from the age of fifteen down, and one girl. Mrs. [Jane] Dunwoody is a really charming woman, uncommonly fine looking and ladylike, and her mind is as well cultivated as that of any female I have known. She treated me like a child or a sister, used every means of curing my cough that kind attention and prescription could do, and when I left her fitted me up with conveniences for the voyage at sea. She gave me a great many charges about my health. "Now do, my dear," said she, "be careful of that cough," as she was fixing me off. "I am uneasy about it, and I think so much of your parents, when I hear it."

We rode yesterday in the stage with the elder Mr. [Thomas] Spaulding from Sapelo Island [Spalding was fifty-seven years old, a wealthy planter and former congressman]; and I was really very much entertained while I leaned back in the corner, with his varied chat, and the smooth and easy flow of his words and ideas. I spent an evening last week with his son Charles (who I find is quite distinguished here at Mrs. Richardson's). His father has given him a plantation and one hundred negroes, besides which, he is just returned from a three years' visit to Europe, both of which considerations conspire to make him irresistible to the ladies. I was not a little amused at the attention that was paid him by a group of young women, and to observe his shrugs and grimaces and contortions and affected laughter while he was talking to them of Paris and London, and the English ladies, and "riding in the park," and so forth and so forth. Richardson, however, says he is a very smart and very accomplished fellow, and that he puts on so many affectations to conceal embarrassment.

The letters from Eliza Bird contained a most dismal account of her troubles, and of her separation from Dr. Bird. She says he struck her down in the street, that Joseph Clay rescued her, and that Dr. Bird told him that it was his intention to have killed her and the child, and then himself. Poor woman, she seems greatly afflicted, and says she is now thrown completely upon her father, who is obliged to make hard exertions to maintain his otherwise large family.

I am very much pleased with Mr. [Joseph] Cumming, and find him exactly the sort of man I expected to see. Truly, as Judge Montgomery said, talent is the failing of this family, for I know he is considered as possessing as little as any other member of the family, and I am sure I should anywhere be struck with him as a man possessing strong intellect and rich and varied cultivation. He professes to be very much attached to you, says in his decided way, as if there were no appeal from his opinion, "Julia is a fine woman," and he says he is extremely anxious to have you visit him. I really would if I was in your place. You and Anne [Cumming] might come down [to Savannah] for a short time. I am certain you'd be pleased, for it is a remarkably pleasant and ordered establishment, I assure you. Himself and Mr. Harford have been out all day, and it being rainy I have had to amuse myself as I could. I read the latter [her husband, William Harford] your advice to me. He smiled and repeated *"dutiful."*

We shall sail in the ship *Tybee,* which is now taking in her lading, but I am not able to say when we shall get off.

I can hardly tell you how much I took it to heart that I could not see Mr. Cumming [Sr.]. It would have been a pleasure to me to have remembered the interview, although painful to have taken leave. How is Annie and Alfred and all of them?

I received a letter from Anne, which, if I can, I should answer before leaving, and then you will hear again. Do write to New York. Mr. Harford has this moment come in and desires his most "affectionate regards" to you. My love to Brother Henry and kiss the dear children for me.

Ever yours most truly,

M.

After Savannah, Maria and her new husband, whom she always refers to as "Mr. Harford," spent a few weeks in New York. Then they journeyed to Washington, where Maria dispatched this letter to Julia. Maria, at her literary best, describes the people she meets. Among those singled out are Congressmen Richard Henry Wilde and Colonel Thomas Flournoy Foster.

Maria Bryan Harford to Julia Ann Bryan Cumming

Washington City
January 17, 1832 (Tuesday)

I return you a thousand thanks, my dear Julia, for your kind letter which was like a draught of refreshing water to the hot and thirsty life of the worn-out pilgrim. I meant to have written to you at length from New York, and was prevented from the hope each day that I should hear from you. I knew that in general you were so punctual, and I had so repeatedly requested you to write to New York that I used to send *every day, every day,* to the office, until the Post Master, Mr. Harford said, appeared really tired out with looking.

I was quite pleased with my visit there, and made some rather pleasant acquaintances. The people at the house where we were, were, as Mr. Iverson would say, "very genteel," and kind to me. I became quite sociable with George Curtis, who was engaged to Susan Skinner. He is certainly as smart and witty a fellow as I ever met with, but a man of no *refinement* in thought,

word, or deed. The Wallaces [Sarah Clay Wallace was Henry's aunt] I cannot
say I much liked, except the eldest son; but indeed, I saw but little of them.
They were kind and polite, but distant, I thought, and as to Elizabeth, the
youngest daughter, I took a positive dislike to her; she was so pert and as-
suming and ugly. Don't say anything of this except to Brother Henry, and
I'm afraid it would half vex him. To my surprise I met Eliza Clay there. She
is spending the winter with her relatives. Mr. Harford, who seemed to understand something of the nature of our claims upon the Staples's [Mrs. Staples
was a Wales, a sister of the late Mr. Wales of Mt. Zion and an aunt of Catherine
Wales], said to me before carrying Catherine's letter, "What will you do?
Refuse if they should ask you to stay with them while you remain in the city?"

"Don't puzzle your mind about that," said I, "there's not the slightest danger that they will." I laughed at him heartily when their civilities proved to
consist in an invitation "*to tea.*" I believe, however, they endeavoured to be
very friendly and polite, though there was so much of stiffness and precision
about them that I did not forget for a moment that I was among strangers.
Mrs. Douglas was in Troy. Mrs. Staples and Mrs. Goddard enquired about
you and your children with seeming interest. Upon my remarking that the
children were very beautiful, Mrs. Goddard said with emphasis, "I should
think they might very well be so." They spoke of your having gone to bed
one night, before a young admirer's calling to see you, and the surprise he
felt when he heard that you'd retired for the night—and many other little
circumstances were related in which I could plainly see the Julia Bryan of
those days. Mr. Staples is a very fine looking man. The whole evening I spent
there he did not exchange a sentence with me, but sat apart, conversing with
Mr. Harford upon what appeared subjects of *grave import.*

Old Mrs. Wales asked me a thousand and one questions—about "my Aunt
'*July,*' " and about Catherine, and Sam, and John. She wanted to know much
what Pa said about the way the Georgians acted toward the missionaries. . . .

I found, at first, considerable difficulty about shopping in New York, and
having work done. I was surprised to find, at first, that goods were very nearly
the same price as with us. Anne [Cumming] directed me to call for Miss
Anne Wallace's assistance in shopping, but this I could not do. The woman to
whom Miss Philly directed me, as first rate dressmaker, Miss Watson, I found
decidedly the *finest lady* in New York. She would neither do any work for me,

nor give me any directions, received me in her parlour, drest up like a queen, and to all my inquiries professed a very genteel ignorance. But when we went to private lodgings, I found there an English lady and her daughter, the latter, Miss Micage, one of the most complete veterans and devotees to fashion and gaiety that I ever came across. She without anything said on my part proffered her services to assist me in shopping. She was assuredly of great service to me, as she took upon her hands what I never would have done, beating down the clerks, so that in several cases I got articles at one fifth of the specified prices. She took me likewise to her own milliners and mantuamakers to whom she invariably introduced me with a flourish of trumpets, "that I was a lady from the South, and I wanted everything in the very best style, and in the highest fashion," and so forth and so forth. I only purchased three dresses, one merino (brown) and a black and coloured silk.

The first night we got here, we staid at Gadsby's hotel, and the next day we came to Mrs. Bronaugh's where we now are. I am tolerably well pleased with the place, though the room is rather small.

Mr. Harford called to see Miss Stebbins [a former teacher at Mt. Zion] and told her I was in the place, and the same day she called to see me. I cannot express to you how much she is changed, and how very much she is the same. Every year of the ten since we saw her is legibly marked upon her face, and instead of that eager, hysterical appearance, and great excitability when anything pleased her, she is now as apathetic and cold and unmoved as a statue. She does not wear her own hair as she *did,* and she has false teeth, both of which circumstances contribute to change her, but her voice is the same, her mode of picking in her teeth and working at her chin remind me of 1821. She is not much pleased with her situation; Mrs. H., she says, loves to dictate too much, has not much society and is quite homesick. Says she'd go to Georgia again but fears she could not stand a summer there — and then said how very much she had suffered with cold this winter, especially as she has to sit in her room, and it has neither stove nor fireplace. Poor old lady, how I felt for her!

Colonel Foster, of course, you know appeared very glad to see me, scolded violently that I had not let him hear from me the moment I got to Washington, and, according to his way of flattering his acquaintance, I almost believed that the whole city had been waiting for a month and a half in eager expectation for my arrival, and were in readiness to do me honour en masse.

He is the same bustling, alert person as at home, talks as if he knew every body, thing, and place, and I discover from those who know him that he is quite a favourite in society here.

Mr. [Richard Henry] Wilde, too, has been to see me, and Judge Wayne. The former came this morning and took me out to ride. He spoke much of you, of your extreme beauty, said that, "In looking at you there was an impression made of *fragility*, that interested deeply, and that dignity mingled with that produced the highest respect."

You remember the letter Mrs. Bird gave me to her friend Mrs. Thornton? She called immediately after it was sent, and last night we took tea with her. She is distant and reserved in her manner, and I do not feel as if I could ever be intimate with her, though she begs me to visit her often and unceremoniously, and has offered to take me in her carriage to pay any visits I may have to return. Among the few I met there—I was introduced to Mrs. Edward Smith. I got a seat next to her on the sofa, and I was very much pleased with her indeed. Mr. Smith was not there, having gone to attend a meeting of the temperance society. She is extremely plain in her person, has an unpleasant voice in speaking, but you soon get over the impression of these disadvantages, by the evidences of very great intelligence and amiability.

Who do you think came to see me this evening—that never ending Plummer, bringing with him Dr. Paul Eve—the Polish Champion. The Dr. considering how much of a lion he is considered, behaves very well, and I was quite grateful to Plummer for affording me the interview. He is going to leave next Wednesday for Georgia and offered to take letters. I had rather, however, send this by the mail, assured that you will sooner get it that way. [Dr. Paul Fitzsimons Eve, the "Polish Champion," was the son of Oswell and Aphra Prichard Eve of Augusta. He volunteered his medical services to the Poles in 1831 in their unsuccessful revolt against Russia. He was the nephew of Mrs. Christopher Fitzsimons of Charleston and a first cousin by marriage to both James Henry Hammond and Wade Hampton II.]

I can truly say with dear little Annie "I wish I was going where this letter is," for I long to see you all. My very heart melts within me when I think of the [four] children. I hope Mr. Cumming will sometime or other write to me. I fear I shall rarely hear from home except through you. Sophia has not written one line to me since I left. Tell Anne I would not have believed she would have allowed so much time to pass without letting me hear from her. Give my affectionate love to her and Sarah and Mr. & Mrs. Cumming [Sr.]. Tell Mr. Cumming I have all manner of kind thoughts of him. I hope you will very soon write again to me. Give my love to Annie and Alfred, and tell them I wish they'd come on to see their Aunty. Mr. Harford desires me to "present his most particular remembrance to you, and begs that you will sometimes speak of him to your sweet little children."

I have not mentioned Goode to you yet. In some respects I was gratified, in others disappointed in him. If he has talent he gives but little evidence of it in his talk, for his conversational powers are as yet as completely in their infancy as when he left home, and consist of exaggerated expression of "the ugliest, or the prettiest, or the most splendid thing in the world," and of school boy slang. He seems, too, to have that wavering vascillating mind that we feared he'd possess. Sometimes he means to be a farmer, then he's going into the Army, then he's going to be a civil engineer and fill Georgia with railroads from one extremity to the other, and so on. But he is affectionate and kind, retains the deepest feelings of affection to all at home, his eyes will almost fill when Pa or Ma's name is mentioned, has no affectations or airs at all. His standing, he says, is now very good at the school. Oh, how much I pity poor Mr. Henry and pray God that his sufferings may be relieved, and that he may be led to obtain mercy of the Saviour. That you may always be under God's keeping and direction, my dear Sister, is my daily prayer for you.

Ever most affectionately yours.

In July 1832, Maria Bryan Harford, separated from her army husband by the necessities of military duty, traveled down from the North by ship to Savannah and then through Augusta, accompanied by her brother, Goode, on leave from West Point. She spent the remaining part of the summer and early fall in Mt. Zion with her sister Julia, also home for the summer. Henry Cumming advised his wife Julia to do all she could to patch up the breach between Maria and her father.

By November 1832, the Harfords were reunited at Fort Mitchell, a military post in eastern Alabama, just across the river from Columbus, Georgia. Henry Cumming at this time, in a letter to his wife, snidely remarks that Maria's "ruling passion" is admiration, which she is probably receiving in full measure from the

idle young officers at Fort Mitchell. Henry also mentions to Julia the "state of high
excitement over the [nullification] ordinance of the Convention of South Caro-
lina." When the convention met, the delegates defiantly nullified within South
Carolina's borders the tariffs of 1828 and 1832. President Jackson responded to
South Carolina that he intended to enforce the federal laws within the state despite
the nullification ordinance. South Carolina immediately prepared for a military
showdown with the national government. The danger of war ended in the spring
with the passage by Congress of the Compromise of 1833.

In the meantime, the Harfords had journeyed to Montgomery on their way to
New Orleans, where Harford had secured a position as an engineer on the New
Orleans–Pontchartrain Canal project. Eighteen thirty-two was not only the year of
the nullification crisis but also the year of the great cholera epidemic, and as a sea-
port New Orleans was especially hard hit by this plague. With the cooler weather
the disease was already subsiding as the couple approached their destination via
Mobile.

Maria Bryan Harford to Julia Ann Bryan Cumming

Montgomery, Alabama
November 26, 1832 (Monday)

My dear Julia,

Just as we were setting off from Fort Mitchell, on Thursday at two o'clock, they called us to stop and get some letters that had just come. I was very glad that we did not leave yours for I was extremely anxious to hear from home. We had a very unpleasant journey to Montgomery. The roads were wretched, we came near turning over several times, and riding constantly for nearly twenty four hours, I don't know when I ever felt more battered out and weary. Zac. Watkins keeps the hotel at Montgomery, and it is miserably kept, bad fare, and uncomfortable lodgings.

Uncle [Samuel Goode] sent in to town for us quite early, and as you may suppose, we were very kindly received by the family. Anne and her husband is visiting here at present. I heard him preach yesterday. He is a pleasant young man and very sensible and cultivated in mind, and I never saw a couple apparently more attached to each other. Uncle and all the family are very much pleased with the marriage, and seem to think she has done very well for herself in forming the connexion. [Anne Eliza Goode married a clergyman named Witherspoon.]

I take it for granted that you have returned to Augusta before now. [Julia's husband wrote on November 24 that he was preparing for her return.] I did not understand from your letter whether you expected to live on the Hill or in town. I trust you will never remain so long in a similar state of uncertainty again. [Julia and Henry Cumming were able, after Julia's return from Mt. Zion, to move into their new house in town, located at 243 Broad Street, Augusta.]

I feel great regret when I think how much Pa and Ma have suffered from uneasiness about me, with regard to going to New Orleans. I presume you hear constantly from there, and know that the last accounts are very favourable, that at present there are few or no cases of cholera. We are waiting the arrival of a steamboat, which is hourly expected, in which we shall go to Mobile. I have been so long in such an unsettled state that I am extremely anxious to be at our destination, that I may be quiet and industrious once more. Yet, all things considered, it has been extremely fortunate that we have been detained from the place, while disease was raging there so violently.

Uncle is in fine health and spirits [at age sixty-six], as kind and hospitable as possible. Aunt Tezon is just as she used to be. She enquires very kindly after you (as they all do), and says she does want to see you worse than almost anybody else. Hamilton [their eldest son, age thirty-one] is at home. He is not, I believe, engaged in any business at present, which seems to be the occasion of much annoyance to his Father. Mack [age twenty-nine] and his wife have gone to Georgia for a visit. Watkins [Samuel Watkins Goode, age twenty-three] is in Montgomery in a druggist's store, and Emily is at home, a very pretty and interesting girl indeed. I saw Street in church yesterday; Eliza is still at his mother's, in Greensborough. I hear no one speak in his favour, but I have been asked why her friends permitted her to marry him. His judgeship, which was an executive appointment, has been taken from him by the Legislature.

I hope I shall receive a letter from you when I get to New Orleans, or very soon after. Since I commenced writing this, Mr. Harford has received a letter from New Orleans, from a gentleman concerned with the canal, who says the cholera has subsided, and that there are now three hundred labourers employed in the work, and consequently his presence is desirable as soon as he can return. I hope your children are entirely well before this time. Give my love to Mr. Cumming, and to the girls when you see them. The [Goode] family are all sitting round talking, and I hardly know what I write, so I will conclude.

Yours affectionately.

The Harfords had been in New Orleans at the army garrison for about two months when Maria writes this letter to Julia.

Maria Bryan Harford to Julia Ann Bryan Cumming

New Orleans
January 26, 1833 (Saturday)

I have several causes, my dear Julia, to account for what you call the infrequency of my communications. In the first place you must know in what a disordered state the mail carriage from this place is at present. Everybody is speaking of its tardiness and uncertainty. Again, it is not because I am unwilling to "devote an hour," or more still, of each week to you. Every day I think "Well, I shall write to Julia," but then a thought occurs to me — "I should get a letter from her by this mail or the next, and there will be something in it that I should wish to reply to, so I will wait a little longer." Your letter was dated the sixteenth and I did not receive it until the twenty fourth. I should have answered it the same day, but it found me very sick, and I am now just able to sit up.

I have had a cold and cough almost ever since I came to this place, for the climate is so damp and the houses so wretchedly built. Every door and window has cracks and crevices that it is impossible to stop, and when the weather suddenly changes which it often does, you have no means of guarding yourself from cold. However, I grew daily more unwell until I was obliged to lay down most of the time, suffering with fever and a dreadful pain in my side. Mr. Harford was continually begging me to let him send for a physician, and I with Pa's obstinacy refused, until he thought it absolutely necessary, and without my expecting him, Dr. [Thomas] Lawson, the surgeon from the garrison, came. He said I had the Bilious Pleurisy, a common disease in New Orleans, gave me some very severe medicine, and confined me to my room and to my bed. I do not know when I ever was so sick in my life.

Dr. Lawson is very much such a man and physician as Dr. Terrill, about his age, and soft and kind in his manner. He is a Virginian, and has many of the characteristics we attribute to one. Every sentence he addresses you is always begun or ended by "Madam." He comes in smiling so kindly and says, "Well, Madam, and how do you find yourself today?" "Be very cautious with regard to your food, Madam." "Indulge yourself as much as possible in sleep, Madam." [Lawson was appointed surgeon general of the United States in 1836.]

I was very sorry to hear that Ma has been sick. I do hope that she is now with you, and I have no doubt that she will be improved in health and spirits. I feel certain that it is this affair of Goode's that has affected her so, and if he has exhibited such an unbecoming spirit towards Pa, it is enough to distress her. When I read that part of your letter and thought of the interest Pa had always taken in his children, and his meeting with such a return, I could not refrain from bursting into tears, and as I looked up at Mr. Harford his eyes were full, and he said, "I do hope, Maria, that some day or other we may be a great comfort to your Father and Mother." I am sure I hope so too, and it is one of my greatest anticipations, that of getting to Georgia and not leaving the vicinity of my friends again.

I saw your neighbour Mr. Ben. Sims the other day. He called and offered to take a letter or anything I might wish to send. I thought at first that I would go out and hunt up something for the children, but he seemed to be so absent and flighty that Mr. Harford said he did not believe we ought to commit anything to his care.

I have formed a number of acquaintances among the ladies, some quite pleasant, and what is a little singular, there are two French families who have been to see me, and I am extremely pleased with their manners and conversation. So you have seen Miss Walton and admire her — I have always thought *I* should admire her. [Octavia Walton, born in Augusta, allegedly was *the* reigning belle of the South.] Bowman I frequently see, he always speaks of her, and when I tell him I have learnt anything favourable of her it seems to put him in an ecstasy.

Captain Allen whom you know is the commander of this post is a very singular man, rather rough and plain spoken, but has very good sense, and is very amusing. He was for some time in Pensacola, and the account he gives of Miss Walton and her mother [Sally Minge Walker Walton] is very vivid. He spoke of one young lieutenant that had just been sent on to join his command, and as soon as he arrived the Captain says he let him into Miss Walton's ways, and told him to be on his guard or the same fate would befall him that had happened to everyone before him. The young fellow called of course, and again and again, he says, evening after evening he spent there, until one night he said to him, "Now you are going to make a fool of yourself, I see plainly." He says the young man looked him in the face and said, "Well Captain, *how* can I help it?"

You inquired if Catherine ever writes to me. Yes, I have received one letter from her, two from Sophia, and one from Pa, and that is all that I have gotten since I came here. I am sure I never received so few letters in my life, and I am sure I never desired them more. I forgot to mention that Mrs. Nevin called to see me the other day. She said she had just received a letter from Mrs. Henry who begged her to come, and she did not know who I was before. Mr. Nevin had told her that Mr. Harford was living here, but she thought he had married somebody in St. Mary's.

I am truly glad to hear that Annie is learning so well. Tell her that I shall certainly write her a nice little letter one of these days, for I have a great deal to talk to her about, and I shall put it all in that, and I hope she will learn to write herself so she may write me a letter back again. I am sure you will not have much trouble in learning Alfred, he is so good and docile, dear little fellow. I often think of him and tell Mr. Harford of him as I last saw him the morning he set off for Augusta. When I put up the basket I said, "Here, Alfred, is something for you to eat today." "Yes Ma'am, thanky Aunt," said he. "I'll send you something from Augusta." Tell him his Aunt Maria says he must be sure and send her something from Augusta.

I suppose you heard Sophia speak of the resemblance between Julien [Julia's two-year-old son] and a young officer whom she saw at Columbus. He is stationed here, and the resemblance is indeed very striking. He is bashful and generally holds his head down, and I never see McKeen without thinking of Julien in one of his pouting fits.

Can it be possible that Brother has really gone to Florida? Well, I never shall believe he is going to be married even if he were actually engaged, so I expect he will rather have it fancied that Miss Fantlecor has actually discarded him than to marry her, or he will make out that she is going to marry someone else, or there will be some reason or other. I have no patience with ———— much less than with Brother, she does not pretend to love him, she knows that she has influenced him unhappily, and yet she is weak enough, and unkind enough, to gratify her foolish and selfish vanity at his expense. How she satisfies her conscience, correct as her principles are, Heaven only knows.

I hope you will write again very soon. I must conclude this, for though I have written it at intervals I am very much wearied, and I wish to get it off today.

Give my affectionate love to Mr. Cumming, I am much obliged to him for his promise of attention to Larned for my sake. In truth, I never expected he would please either of you much, and perhaps he would not have pleased me but for the peculiar circumstances of our acquaintance which interested me in his favour. He is talented and, as a classmate of his here, Lieut. Wilkinson, says, "The man's erudition is quite astonishing."

No more at present but that I am as ever

Your affectionate Sister.

Maria in this letter confesses to Julia her heartbreaking loneliness in New Orleans. Her only acquaintances are a few fashionable women who pay perfunctory calls and then promptly forget her. Even her husband provides her with little companionship and less conversation.

Maria Bryan Harford to Julia Ann Bryan Cumming

New Orleans
March 20, 1833

My dear Julia,

I was very glad to receive your last letter for I assure you I was beginning to think it a long time that I had not heard from you, or anyone at home. I need not tell you, for I am sure you can divine it from your own feelings, that

I sometimes get very low spirited and homesick, and feel very much as if no one cared for me in the world. Indeed, I have a fair right to imagine so sometimes, for I do not think there are many people who have been accustomed at all to society, who have much less of intercourse with their kind than I do nowadays.

The few acquaintances I have here are mostly fashionable people who, after paying me a call about once a month, and perceiving little to attract them in my abode and much elsewhere, say adieu and, I presume, do not think of me again until they look over their visiting debts, or hear the bell ring at their own houses and, after rubbing their foreheads, perhaps remember who I am, and where they have seen me before.

I have little, very little, of Mr. Harford's society for he is entirely engrossed in the most perplexing business, and even when I am with him, I have but little of his conversation, for while he is in the same room, or even walking in the street with me, he is calculating to himself or aloud, and I often perceive him knitting his brow, and saying, "The square root of so & so is so & so, or so many cubic feet make so many yards, miles," or whatever it may be. Oh, if I could only live at home in Georgia! But I need not talk of that, the prospect is too distant to afford me any comfort or the anticipation, and I often think that I shall, in all probability, lay my bones in a strange land, and not even "find a *grave* in the land of my birth." However, it is selfish to trouble you with moody thoughts.

I received a long letter from Pa yesterday. He spoke of Ma's absence and said he felt rather lonely; informed me that Brother had gotten back and seems to be very much disappointed that he came as he went. I presume Ma and Sophia have left you before this. I am very glad to hear that the health of the former has improved, in consequence of her journey. Oh, if she would only take one now, to see me.

Ah, it is so tantalizing to hear of your being so near as Montgomery [visiting their Goode relatives] and not to come further. As to my going there, it will be impossible. I should have no one to go with me, and I do not indulge the thought of it because I know full well that it cannot be accomplished. But why can you not come here, Julia? We have lately got another room fixed up so that there are three bedrooms, and consequently we can accommodate you all—Celia, Tom and all. I assure you that the journey when once you get to Montgomery is nothing, in comparison with the previous one, and the spring weather here is so delightful, and besides the happiness it would give me to have you all here, you would thus have an opportunity of seeing this far famed city. Mr. Harford says I must tell you that you must come, and then the pleasure that Annie and I should have there's no telling. I am sure that when you get to Uncle's you will not desire to make a long tarry. He will give you a sincere and kind welcome, and make you as comfortable as he can, but Aunt Tezon's department is not so well managed as it might be.

How very sorry I was to hear of Jane Skinner's illness. I hope she is better. Poor girl, has not hers been rather a melancholy lot? Such a mother that her girlhood could not be very pleasant, and such an espousal? I am truly thankful for your attention to Mrs. Wharton. Indeed, I feel very much indebted to her and the Dr., for I certainly never was treated with more kindness by people upon whom I had not the slightest claim whatever. And though my stay at their house was lengthened out day after day until a fortnight and more had passed, their attentions never flagged, and there was no symptoms which could have been construed with an indication of weariness of my residence with them.

I must not forget to tell you that last Saturday Mr. Harford received a letter from Larned telling him of his present situation, that having lost his pay as an Army officer he was, of course, cut off from all means of support, and requesting him if there was any place in the work under his direction that would suit him, to let him know, as he would be extremely obliged to him, and that nothing but the circumstances in which he was there would have induced him to take such a freedom, and demand such a favour. There was no such place at all, but Mr. Harford busied himself among his acquaintances to find some opening for him.

With Captain Crozet, the State Engineer, he is very intimate, and to him he applied first. Captain Crozet was one of Napoleon's officers, and is a very intelligent and agreeable man, and has been in America eight or nine years. When Mr. Harford told him of Larned, and described his character and capacities, Captain Crozet appeared pleased and said, "Can he be here in four weeks, for if he can I think it probable that I shall appoint him my assistant."

Larned, you know, intends to be a lawyer as soon as he has the facilities of acquiring that profession. So, after talking with Captain Crozet, Mr. Harford endeavoured to make some further arrangements. There is a gentleman here of some eminence as a lawyer, and is at present a Notary. He is extremely kind and friendly to Mr. Harford, and is (that aside) a most amiable man. Mr. Harford went to Mr. Pollock and told him he wanted his assistance for a friend of his, and gave him an account of Larned. Says he to Mr. Pollock, "You are at least familiar with the name. The Mr. Larned who lived here as a clergyman was his cousin." "Ah, indeed," said he with great interest, "and he was a most superior young man." Said he further, "He shall study in my office (rent is so high) *gratis*. I will give him all the facilities in my power for pursuing his studies, and will throw what business I can in his hands." Mr. Harford wrote immediately to Larned.

I got a letter today from Anne Apling, written, it seems, at the earnest request of the Doctor. Ma and Sophia had not returned when she wrote. I hear nothing further of John Brown's gold mine and hope it was not a failure.

How is your *cidevant* pest Daphne [Julia's servant] behaving nowadays? I hope better than Henny. Mr. Harford, whose heart ordinarily overflows with kindness to the living creation, dislikes her, I believe, more than anything in the world. He says if anyone was to make him a present of a plantation full of slaves, poor as he is, he would not accept the gift if the condition was that Henny should always be around him.

Jenny does very well but her head is nearly turned with flatteries. She has as many compliments to tell me of as Sophia used to. A great many suitors among the bond and the freemen of colour, Captain Allen [commandant of the post] has a servant who, with all the pretension and pomposity, has likewise all the wiles and none of the virtues of the Camp. He set his eyes admiringly upon Jenny from the first glance and was in the kitchen night and day. The gate is always locked at nine o'clock. One night at the usual hour Barnill refused to go home, and when they told him we required everybody to depart after that time, he jumped up and ran into Jenny's bedroom. She, I suppose, to show to him the exceeding purity and delicacy of her character, came in the house and told Mr. Harford of the shock she had been compelled to sustain. Mr. Harford, who knew his character and did not desire him to be intimate with the servants, told him to go off and never put his foot in the yard again. He, it appears, is sorrowful but not despairing, sends her messages, begs her to ask "the Lieutenant" to take off his injunction, and makes her presents, and the other Sunday he sent her three dollars for her to hire a hack and take a ride into the country. But I consume too much of my paper.

Do write soon again. Pa's letter was the first I had gotten from home in six weeks, but I know you never neglect me, and consequently when you do not write I become uneasy. Mr. Harford has not been at all well during the winter. He has lately been troubled with an acute pain in his forehead just over his eyes, which is very trying. He has consulted a physician and others, and is told that it is caused by intense application, united with cold. I long to see Mr. Cumming and the children. Give my love to him, and kiss the children for me. Mr. Harford says, "Tell Alfred that if he will come to New Orleans, he will buy him a nice saddle and bridle to ride the Spanish horse that his Aunt Maria is going to give him, and he shall ride out with him upon the Canal and see all the men digging."

Give my love to Mrs. Johnston, the Bennetts and their sister, Mr. & Mrs. H., and Mrs. Reid. Tell the latter that her name is a fortunate one for me, for the best friend I have met with in New Orleans is a Mrs. Reid. My kind regards to Mr. & Mrs. Cumming and to Mrs. Davis.

Yours most affectionately.

Maria writes to Julia that a miniature of her husband has been sent from New Orleans. This miniature of William H. Harford, a photograph of which appears in this book, is the only known likeness of him to survive.

Maria Bryan Harford to Julia Ann Bryan Cumming

New Orleans
March 29, 1833 (Friday)

My dear Julia,

I received your letter two days ago, and also one from Sophia by the same mail. I should have answered it immediately, but have been quite sick since from a violent cold I have taken. I was very glad to hear from Sophia that Ma's health is so much improved by her visit to you. Sophy tells me she had a delightful visit herself, and had so many parties to go to, and saw so much company, that she had not any time to write to me until she got back home.

It seems that Pa is perplexed about land for Brother during the coming year, and I can readily imagine how much he is troubled. Mr. Harford has written on to Satterlee [a close friend from Sparta of their brother, Joseph] to come to this place immediately, and I hope he will be inclined to accept the offer. It is connected with the canal, and the business is to take charge of some labourers on Lake Pontchartrain, about three miles from the city. He will receive sixty dollars a month and will be at little or no expense for board, for there is a snug house, and every convenience already provided, and it may at least serve for Satterlee until he can look about and obtain some employment that will be more agreeable to him.

Did I mention in my last letter how much New Orleans is at present disturbed by robberies? There is no watch in the city, and every day we heard of some daring attempt and mostly successful, but I little thought we were to have our turn also until a few nights since. As I was sleeping quietly I heard the most awful yell I ever remember, except that of Leatha's when she was disturbed by little Dick. It was Jenny who came running in, and crying out that some men had broken open the door. We ran into the room where she had been sleeping, and it was as she had said. The door had been prized open in some way or other. The noise and the sudden light flashing in upon her from the lamp in the street woke her up, and the terrible noise she made induced them to run off. I was dreadfully alarmed though for a minute. Mr. Harford had seized up his pistol which was loaded. I went to the open door and I heard it go off, and was feeling so awfully under the fear that someone had been killed. He shot it off without seeing anyone, however, and because, he said, if they were lurking near that he might convince them that the house was on the alert.

It is said that it is a regular gang of robbers and housebreakers from Europe, and you would be equally amused and astonished if you could hear of some of their doings. They are so expert that they have even stolen different articles from under the head of gentlemen without waking them. They take off every thing they can find, even to chairs and sofas.

I am sorry to hear of the pecuniary misfortunes of the people of Augusta. Mr. Erwin had been here a few days before your letter arrived and gave me an account of it. I suppose it will fall with as much heaviness upon Mr. McKenzie's family as any other, as his family of children is so large.

The officers at the [Augusta] Arsenal must have been quite delighted this winter at the attention that has been paid them by the people of Augusta. I suppose Miss Walton has been in her element. I am glad you like Clarke. Your opinion of Crittenden [Lieutenant George B. Crittenden, twenty-one, son of Kentucky's famous John J. Crittenden] is precisely that of mine; he is coarse and rough, and has precisely that manner of the western or Kentucky gentleman that Mrs. Trollope describes as characteristic of all Americans [Frances Trollope's *Domestic Manners of the Americans,* published in 1832, Maria had already read]. How different from Larned's! I never saw that young man guilty of a single thing that did not show him to be refined and perfectly well bred. Among the officers stationed here the only thorough gentleman is Dr. Lawson. Him I esteem and almost love, but some of the others are intolerable. But indeed I have no intimate, as I would say "congenial spirit," if you did not laugh at the word, of either sex, not one individual with whom I "can take counsel." You have heard me mention Mr. Pollock. His family are agreeable and extremely kind to us, and I should take pleasure in his society if he was not so completely a man of business, that I see him but a little while at a time. You know the New Orleans Creole custom of never calling to see strangers but waiting until they visit first. This family have set aside that custom in our favour and, though we had no claims upon them by letter or in any other way, have treated us with marked attention. Mr. Pollock has an excellent library of Spanish, French and English books. This he presses us to use whenever we wish and retain any works as long as we choose. His wife is very pretty, and his two daughters are beautiful.

Jenny is sick, or at least keeps her chamber, for some days past and I have to depend upon Henny for everything — to cook, wash, milk, etc. Don't you pity me? Mr. Harford, after suffering a great deal with the pain in his forehead, is at last relieved.

Give my love to Mr. Cumming, and kiss the children for me. Write very soon and believe me ever

Affectionately yours.

P.S. Mr. Harford has obtained a furlough for six months [from the army to work on the canal], after which it is his present intention to resign. He desires me to send his remembrances to yourself and Mr. Cumming, and says I must tell you he regrets very much that you have been so long kept out of [i.e., deprived of] the miniature, and hopes that when you do get it you will not be disappointed from its want of resemblance to the original.

Maria describes with sadness the death of her cow in the backyard of their New Orleans quarters.

Maria Bryan Harford to Julia Ann Bryan Cumming

New Orleans
April 15, 1833 (Monday)

My dear Julia,

I have not written to you of late because I knew it would only lie in the office in this place, as there is at present no mail conveyance between New Orleans and Mobile, one of the steamboats having sunk and the other being out of repair also.

I sympathise with you much in your family troubles, but am truly thankful that there is a prospect of their terminating without any loss among your beloved little group. As to my dear little Annie, I hope it is Heaven's will to take me ere she leaves this world. The thought of her death is like distraction to me. I regret very much to hear of so much trouble among our acquaintances in Augusta. I do hope, my dear Julia, that you will be able to persuade Pa to come on as far as New Orleans. I dreamed last night that you had all come to see me, and I had taken particular pains to have everything cooked to suit your peculiar taste, and was much mortified to find that you were not at all pleased.

You know that your letters are always sufficiently welcome, but none ever was more so than the one that was sent to me this afternoon from the garrison. I had felt particularly sad, and have been sitting in my room alone from nine o'clock until four, the day one of those dark gloomy ones so common in New Orleans which weighs upon your heart so, that you feel that it has lost all its elasticity and can never spring up in mirth and joy again.

I have really been in sorrow today from having lost our poor cow last night. The pecuniary loss is something to cause regret, but it is not that, but a feeling of pain at the death of a creature to whom I had become really attached as to a faithful domestic. She was a most valuable animal, furnished us plentifully with the richest milk, and such delicious butter that I have often and often said, I know Julia would like this butter. The affections must go out upon something; there are no children about the house, and indeed so little call upon mine that I loved this creature from seeing her constantly, and she was so sagacious and gentle, and any time as I past near her in the yard she would lick my hand.

She appeared drooping several days past and last night when we were sound asleep, we were all woke up by a tremendous noise, and on getting up we found the cow had run into the piazza and was dashing from place to place, beating her head against every obstacle like a mad creature. I declare it was an awful sight, and it would have rent your heart to have witnessed the manifestation of suffering she showed. She trembled all over like a leaf, lowed most piteously. Finally from exhaustion she lay down, and her breathing could be distinctly heard in the house when all the doors were shut until she died. It may appear more ridiculous than pathetic, but when I saw the good creature laying dead this morning, in the place where I had often seen her stand to be milked, I can't tell you how it made me feel, and when a nice plate of her butter came on the table, I actually burst into a flood of tears and could not restrain myself.

I am glad you have received the miniature at last, and am rejoiced that you can see any likeness at all in it. Now I think I ought to have yours. Tell Annie that her Aunt Maria is very sorry that she has been so sick, and wishes she had been there to sit by her and help her mother take care of her, and tell her little stories when she began to grow better. Tell her I shall write her another letter the first time anybody goes from here to Augusta. I hope she will come and see me, and try and take us all back to Georgia, that we may live close by her. I realize, I think, nowadays what the feelings of the Israelites were in exile pining for their own land, and truly this is a Babylon, a very Sodom of sin and iniquity. How I do wish, my dear Julia, that I could see you and have a long talk with you. Give my love to Mr. Cumming, tell him I long very much to see him.

I am glad that my music book will probably reach me before long. I should, therefore, welcome Colonel Twiggs [David Emanuel Twiggs, of Augusta (1790–1862)], but I suppose I am the only one of the Army establishment who will, for there is trouble, consternation among the officers here at the very idea of serving under him, and some of them talk of trying to get away from the post. He is very much disliked here, principally because he is so fond of parades and show that he makes them turn out upon all occasion, and in all sorts of weather, and as they say, just to give himself eclat. They say he is very selfish and imperious, with divers allegations of a similar kind.

You did not mention Alfred in your letter. I suppose he is still at Mount Zion, and I have amused myself sometimes in thinking of how happy he was there at his plays, and in the society of his Grandparents. Do you hear anything of Satterlee's coming on here? Bonner seems to be afraid to remain here during the sickly season. He has applied to Mr. Harford to get permission from the Canal Committee to let him leave here during the Summer, and he says if they refuse he will throw up his office altogether.

I was sure you would like *Henry Masterson*. I have lately been reading *Philip Augustus* by the same author. [George Payne Rainsford James (1799–1860), English novelist, wrote about one volume every nine months for eighteen years. *Philip Augustus,* a long book, was produced in less than seven weeks and was published in 1831. *Henry Masterson* appeared in 1832.] I have as many of those kinds of books, and more than I can read, furnished me by Mr. Pollock. He still talks of going to the north in the summer, and passing through Georgia. I hope and trust you will see him. I'm not *certain*, but I think Mr. Cumming will like him. He is not prepossessing in appearance, but is a gentleman, and I do not think from all I know and hear of him that there is a more amiable man living, and I can't tell you how much I like him.

Mr. Harford is sitting by and sends a message to you. He says, "Give her my *warmest love.* Tell her I am very sorry she finds the miniature not so perfect a likeness as could be wished, and that I hope she will have it in her power to come to New Orleans."

His eyes fairly swam in tears as I read him the account of Annie's sickness. Do, my dear Julia, write very soon again. I shall not feel easy until I get another letter, informing of the entire convalescence of your family. I am rejoiced to hear such good news from Goode. I hope it will recompense Pa and Ma for their uneasiness. Remember me to Mr. Wilde. Tell him I owe him a letter and would promise to pay but that he may possibly think mine [to pay] those debts more honored in the breach than in the observance.

Affectionately yours.

Have you read Mrs. Trollope's delectable novel, *The Refugee in America* [published in London in 1832 and reprinted in New York in 1833]? Write very soon again.

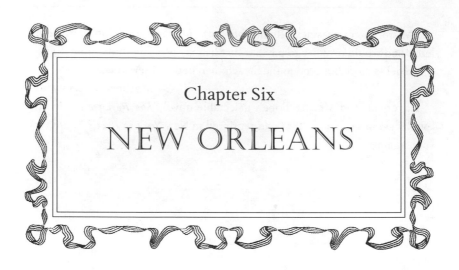

Chapter Six

NEW ORLEANS

"The cholera has been raging dreadfully again."

The cholera season had begun again in the Crescent City, and Maria had been extremely ill but was now well. In the awful early summer heat death seemed cool and quiet to her, but she wrote Julia, "I have such a horror of being buried in New Orleans that I conclude I'd rather live on." Cholera claimed at least five thousand lives in New Orleans during the epidemic of 1832–33. Yellow fever, which raged simultaneously, caused almost as many deaths as cholera in that unfortunate city.

Maria Bryan Harford to Julia Ann Bryan Cumming

New Orleans
June 3, 1833 (Monday)

My dear Julia,

I expect you will think I have been very negligent of late in writing to you, but I have unfortunately had a very good reason for I have been extremely sick for a number of days past, and am really very much reduced. This is the first day in several that I have hardly set up at all. It has been cholera, I suppose, of a mild kind, in all the symptoms but the cramp. I suppose you have by this time arrived home again. I received yours written at Mount Zion two days ago, and it has made me almost heartsick to be at home and see them all.

Mr. Harford and I have both been confined to our rooms at the same time, and you might hear us groan alternately. He has had an unlucky affray with one of the assistant engineers on the Canal. I may have mentioned the man to you (his name is Harper) as giving him a great deal of trouble. He and Mr. Livermore, who appears to be a bitter enemy of Mr. Harford, had brought matters to such a state that Mr. Harford had resolved to resign his office when Captain Delafield arrived and in a meeting of the Canal Committee openly approved of everything Mr. Harford had done, and even the alterations that had been made from his [Delafield's] plan, he said it was his intention to have made them had he remained. This changed the face of things so much that I suppose Harper was doubly irritated, and on his way home he met him [Harford] in the street and asked him why he had made such and such statements. Mr. Harford replied that the statements he had made were correct, upon which Harper said, "It's a lie." Mr. Harford struck him a blow in the jaw, and so they had it. As it is but fair the aggressor should have the worst of it, I am happy to tell you that I understand Mr. Harper had decidedly the worst of it, but you may imagine how I felt when I saw the carriage drive up to the door and Mr. Harford get out of it with his head and face tied up and bloody. I hope if you live a thousand years you may never see one you love so horribly disfigured and changed as he was at first.

Colonel and Mrs. Twiggs arrived about ten days ago, but did not come into the city, at least the ladies did not. They remained at a public house kept at Lake Pontchartrain, two or three miles from town, and I did not see them, for Colonel Twiggs, after having a slight touch of cholera, was so uneasy about his family that he gave immediate orders for the removal of the troops, and they have all gone to Bayou St. Louis, about 80 miles by water from New Orleans. Miss Peggy made an almost immediate conquest of Captain Allen, which is something to pique herself upon. He came home from his first interview saying that for years he had not seen such a pair of black eyes.

I have received the packet you sent, which Colonel Twiggs was so kind as to send by his servant. Mr. Harford was confined to the house and did not see him at all. I am very much obliged to you for your present. I think they are beautiful, and tell Annie I was so delighted with the gloves that I could hardly wait for Sunday to come before I wore them. Tell her I shall keep them just as carefully and as long as I can for her sake. I was very glad to get my guitar book. It is beautifully and tastefully bound, and I plainly see whose judgement directed it. Indeed, the tokens of remembrance did me no little good, I assure you, my dear Julia, for when Satterlee came and did not bring me a line, nor one single evidence of being remembered by my friends at home, I shed not a few tears. For indeed, you can't realize how lonely and forlorn I am here, and since Summer has come on, almost everybody that I know has gone away. Satterlee is quite well and appears to be in pretty good spirits, though he has been a little sick once and was alarmed and very much cast down for a while. He lives several miles from the city, as he says, in a very pleasant place, and I have not seen him before yesterday in a fortnight. I gave him your messages. He says you must recollect your promise to write first.

I received a note from Leon Brut the other day, offering to take charge of anything I might wish to send to Augusta. I regretted very much that I could not go out and get some little toys for the children, but we live entirely out of the way of the trading part of the town. I hope they and yourself were very much improved by your visit home. I am truly sorry to hear of Ma's poor state of health. I wish she would consent to go without Sophia and travel about. Much to my gratification I heard from Mrs. Rossiter the other day. She seems to be in good health and spirits. To my utter astonishment who should I get a letter from a short time since but Elizabeth Bailey. She writes like a sensible girl, and I suppose they are all going on very prosperously at La Grange. Dr. Ellenson who I often see says she is very pretty and very smart, but added with his usual impudence, "a little careless in her dress as you used to be." I denied that he had any right to say that of me, but he insisted with a drawl, "Oh—you waas." Mr. Harford desires me to send his love.

Write soon. Remember me affectionately to Mr. Cumming. Oh, it is terribly, terribly hot here. I long for a cool, quiet, shady spot sometimes, and feel almost as if I would be willing to leave this earth to get it, but then there is but one way from it, and I have such a horror of being buried in New Orleans that I conclude I'd rather live on.

Farewell yours very affectionately—

M.

Cholera continued to rage in New Orleans with some days a hundred deaths. All who could fled the infected city, but Maria is calm and is putting her trust in Providence.

Maria Bryan Harford to Julia Ann Bryan Cumming

New Orleans
June 11, 1833 (Tuesday)

My dear Julia,

I wrote to you not long since, but have concluded to drop you a few lines by today's mail, thinking that if you see the New Orleans papers you will, of course, feel anxious to hear particularly early. Our family are all perfectly well, but the cholera has been raging dreadfully again. On some days there have been upwards of a hundred deaths. The panic is excessive. Those who can fly have gone, saying in some cases that they would not remain in New Orleans a night longer for thousands, and those whose circumstances have compelled to remain suffer death, and worse, from apprehension.

I am not at all alarmed, and have not been. I certainly must feel awed and solemn, at seeing many suddenly cut off, and hearing of death every moment, and in the idea that there is an awful visitation of God's anger upon the place where I now am, but otherwise I feel quite as composed as usual. I fear you will all blame me at home, and say it is rashness and folly to remain here under such circumstances but what can we do? By going to any part of this state we are liable to encounter it, and by taking our servants and going else-where, Mr. Harford would spend all he has in the world, besides forfeiting his obligations, and throwing himself completely out of business for the future. So our only plan is to remain, and trust to the protection of Providence.

I was in hopes to have received another letter from you since your return home. Satterlee is well but very low spirited, and poor Bonner, I imagine, is compelled to keep his heart strong through the influence of brandy toddy. I think he has the horrors awfully. I am all the while anxious, but Mr. Har-ford, he thinks himself obliged to make certain surveys now, which take him nearly all day from sunrise, and the swamp is at this time nearly immersed in water. But he is just as obstinate and imprudent as ever Pa was, and it is perfectly useless to remonstrate. We have just seen Larned who has arrived from New York. He could not stay long in the city, and has gone to his post at Baton Rouge.

Poor Edwin Harford! I suppose he is now in the penitentiary. If sorrow and mortification could break his Brother's heart, this has produced enough of both. It seems to me a hard case — but it must be endured.

I hope you are all well and happy at home, and that the children have recovered their health entirely. I shall be glad to hear that Ma is travelling, for I trust much in the advantage she would gain from a change of scene and air.

Do write to me very soon. We get the Augusta paper which Mr. Cumming is so kind as to send regularly, and I have resolved every time I have written for the last two months to mention it, but I always forget it. It is a very interesting paper, and furnishes us with the only means of hearing of public events in the State that we have.

Remember me kindly to Mr. Cumming, kiss the children for their Aunt, and believe me, my dear Julia, ever yours.

M.

The cholera epidemic suddenly subsided in New Orleans. In this letter Maria, perhaps more interested in him than she would admit, gives a long sketch of Dr. McMahon, a French-born bachelor who has replaced Dr. Lawson as the garrison surgeon.

Maria Bryan Harford to Julia Ann Bryan Cumming

New Orleans
July 9, 1833 (Tuesday)

My last letter, my dear Julia, was concluded in such a hurry by persons coming in while I was getting it ready to send to the mail that I have since had an unsatisfactory feeling in remembering the circumstance. I suppose Ma and Sophia are with you now. I hope you had influence enough with Pa to persuade him to stay at least several days with you, if for nothing else but to keep him away from his work, as Sophia tells me he has been quite unwell. I had an unpleasant dream about Pa a fortnight ago or more, and when I waked up in the night the first thing that struck me was that he had the colick, and it has been, it seems, verified.

We are all well and the physicians say there is no cholera in the city now. I suppose there never was a greater demand for fish in time of Lent than there has been for Irish potatoes in New Orleans for the last few months, for that is almost the only vegetable that the people have eaten from dread of their effects in producing sickness. You never saw such quantities of melons in your life, large fine ones, sold for nothing almost, and very few will eat them.

I believe I have hardly ever spoken to you particularly of the few acquaintances we have here. I am not very much in the way of giving descriptions, because if an acquaintance is uninteresting I feel unwilling to take the trouble to do so, and if I admire them, I am always so certain that the picture will fall below the reality that I do not even attempt a sketch. At this time, the greater part of the few we know are gone away for the summer. Among those who remain, and from whose society I derive most pleasure, are Captain and Mrs. Crozet, and Dr. McMahon, the surgeon of the garrison. I believe you know that my dear Dr. Lawson is gone, and has been away for nearly two months travelling at the North, and in his beloved Virginia to regain his health.

Dr. McMahon fills his place, a man of a character totally different. He is likewise a bachelor of forty or thereabouts — and is just one of those men that you do not see every day of the world. You know, I almost always compare men that I admire to William or Henry Cumming. In this case there is indeed a most remarkable personal resemblance to the former. Dr. McMahon is stout, but not so tall, and has just such a complexion as Colonel [William] Cumming, [Henry's older brother] with this resemblance further, his conversation is sprinkled with sketches of character, conveyed in that peculiar striking phraseology altogether his own. He is a Frenchman born, was educated in Paris, at the Polytechnic school (they say), but has been in this country and in the army so long, that he is as much an American in manner as in language. He is universally known and respected here where he has lived a great deal, and indeed, he seems to be personally acquainted with everybody of any note in the country. He is very unassuming in some respects, is perfectly well bred when he is in company, but you see plainly he is not an amiable man, and I often think delightful and exciting as his conversation is, that it costs more than it comes to, for I am always afraid of making some faux pas that will put him in a fluster.

He is universally spoken of in the army as a man of tremendously strong passions and prejudices, that it is as much as one's life is worth to offend him, and great as his accomplishment and good sense and his mental power of forming a correct judgement of character, some accidental circumstances bias his likes and dislikes. When he is offended, for a moment or two, even in company it seems as if he could not control himself. When, however, he gets the reins back again into his hands he seems to be so shocked at his own dereliction from good breeding that he seems to endeavour to make atonement by the most perfectly bland and gentle manner. I thought he would have annihilated me one day for asking him some question about Miss Walton. He had had a duel with her Father, which he took it for granted I had heard of, and so concluded I either meant to take a great liberty, or to insult him. [Octavia Walton's father, George Walton, was secretary of West Florida during the governorship of Andrew Jackson, 1821–22, and secretary of the East-West Florida Territory, 1822–26. Walton, who was the son of George Walton from Augusta, Georgia, a signer of the Declaration of Independence, remained with his family in Pensacola until 1835. In that year, the Waltons moved to Mobile, Alabama.]

He is as quick in his observations as lightning, and withal somewhat suspicious. For example, the last time he came here I was in our little parlour busily engaged about something, not expecting to see anybody, when Dr. McMahon knocked at the door. I suppose my manner was not so cordial as usual, for he said instantly in a very peculiar and somewhat haughty tone, "I hope I do not *interrupt* you, Madam?" But really, I did not think my description would have taken up so much room, so I will barely add what will interest you more for our sakes, that he is a most excellent physician, and has the reputation of being more scientific and thorough than Dr. Lawson.

I meant to have told you a great deal of Mrs. Crozet [wife of the state engineer] who is really a charming woman but I will reserve that for a future occasion. I often think when I am with her, that she is just the person whom you would particularly like and admire.

I saw Satterlee Sunday, he is well, says *you* most certainly promised to write *first*. Mr. Harford's great enemy [on the canal] and persecutor, Mr. Livermore, is very ill of the cholera. Dr. McMahon, who hates him bitterly, says he will not die for Satan has too much for him to do on earth yet a while. I hope Ma's health and spirits are both good while she is with you. Tell Ma, lest I forget it, Julia, that there was a lady here the other day who said her house had been infested with cockroaches. She put elder leaves in the closets, they ate them and totally disappeared. This is said to be effectual.

Ask Sophia if she has seen an account in the *Albion* of the "Hon. Miss Ada Byron's" court dress? I thought of *her* while reading of the "Queen's drawing room." I should prefer appearing in a dress like Lady Cecil Delafield's. Write soon. My love to all. I long to see you all once more.

Yours most affectionately —
M.

William Harford sends in his resignation from the army effective September 1833, and the canal company is about to raise his pay to three thousand dollars a year. Maria reports to Julia that yellow fever is beginning to appear in New Orleans, but it is not yet an epidemic.

Maria Bryan Harford to Julia Ann Bryan Cumming

New Orleans
August 12, 1833 (Monday)

My dear Julia,

I received your letter today, after having been looking for one a week or ten days past. I have been intending every day lately to write to you, but truly I have not had an opportunity.

Satterlee has been here for a fortnight past, part of the time sick, and you may imagine how much things must have been out of their usual course in a small house, and with only two female servants [Henny and Jenny]. He left here day before yesterday. His physician was Dr. Rice who was recommended by Dr. McMahon to Mr. Harford, when *he* was about leaving the city. Satterlee liked him very much. He is an elderly man, is said to be very skillful, and is very fat and good natured, but very blunt, and talks to a patient as if he was giving orders to sailors in a storm.

By the way, I cannot avoid telling you of his visit to me. I had not been well with a headache for a few days, but thought nothing of it. Mr. Harford who knows nothing about sickness, but is always uneasy when I complain, with some indefinite notion that it may turn out to be cholera or yellow fever or some other of the violent diseases of this climate, without telling me, as he knew I would object, asked Dr. Rice to call. He came in the evening, and I was sitting by the table with my head tied up. Mr. Harford had stept out of the door to see something about his horse, and the Doctor made the best use of his absence to question me, which he did in his usual loud rough way, as if a little sickness was the most insignificant thing in the world. "Subject to the headache, eh! How long since you had it? Le'm me look at your tongue. Ha, ha! Clean as the palm of my hand. Sick at your stomach?" I knew where all this was tending and I said as loud as he, "*No sir!*" "Sick at stomach 'a mornings?" "*No sir!*" "In the family way?" "*No sir!*"

I heard from home a few days ago, from Sophia's letter in which she informed me that Pa had been quite sick. How truly distrest I am to think that he has that terrible disease. But yet I feel assured that if it be so, it is a kind dispensation of Providence to wean him, as I hope it will, from the world. I know of nothing that would give me such comfort as to see Pa living a quiet contemplative life, only anxious for himself and his children, for those blessings which every day convinces me more and more can make one happy who has nothing else, and without which nothing else on this earth can.

Poor Mrs. Campbell, hers is truly one of the most severe of any trial that can befall one. I realize it to myself by thinking how I should feel were either you or Sophia bereft of reason, and to see nothing in those with whom I had been accustomed to take sweet counsel, or have entire sympathy, but the foolish ravings of insanity. You remember how we all felt when Brother was even slightly and temporarily affected.

I am glad you have so near a prospect of getting into your house. I feel as if I should spend many a pleasant hour with you in it. Sophia writes me that it is the most beautiful house she ever saw. I told Jenny what she said, and I very believe you could have counted every tooth in her head as she replied, "Is it?" It certainly has been completed very soon.

When I told Mr. Harford what you said of Mr. Cumming's occupation, and the little you had of his society, he said, "See there how your sister is situated, as bad off as you in that respect." "Yes," said I, "but she is among acquaintances and I among total strangers." I sometimes do not eat one single meal with him in the day, and very rarely breakfast. However that is a much less evil than an opposite one would be to us. He has lately sent on his resignation to Washington as the Canal Company have proposed to increase his salary to three thousand dollars, and his furlough expires the thirteenth of September.

Some of the young officers have lately been to the city from their summer retreat, the Bayou St. Louis, and give flaming accounts of Miss Hunter [the daughter of David Emanuel Twiggs and his wife, Elizabeth Hunter of Virginia]. She is universally admired by the officers, as well as by others who are spending the summer there, and great triumphs are anticipated for her next winter when she enters on a wider field. Mrs. Twiggs, too, was considered something uncommon, for you must know that it is a thing universally admitted, that the ladies of the Fourth Regiment do not do much credit to the Service, and from the specimens I have seen, I am entirely of the opinion. The Colonel's wife Mrs. *Clinch*, it is said, would ornament any circle or situation, but for the rest. . . .

I do indulge the hope of going home with great satisfaction to myself. When I think much of it, I feel like a bird in a cage, and it seems as if I could not contain myself, I am so very, very anxious to see you all. I should prefer going now to the winter, but that I know I should feel so uneasy for the health of those I leave behind that the pleasure of my visit would be marred. How I have thought of old times since you told me that Annie and Julia Maria [Iverson] go to the same school. Just to think of Cousin Caroline and yourself, and your children under such circumstances being together.

Have you seen from the papers that the yellow fever is in the city? One physician has died of it, and another has been given out. Dr. Rice tells Mr. Harford it cannot be called as yet an epidemic.

I hope I shall hear from you very soon again. My best love to Mr. Cumming and the children. It seems hard for little Tom [twenty-two-month-old son of the Cummings] to recover entirely. Mrs. Campfield must be all bustle. Mr. Harford desires his kind regards to you, and often speaks of you with interest and admiration. His opinion that you pretended to triumph over me for, last summer, I find fire cannot melt out of him. Well, I'll try and convert Mr. Cumming to the opposite one. Give my love to Mrs. Henry, and tell her

I hope soon to see her. Have you read Mrs. Child's *Biography of Good Wife?* [Lydia Maria Child (1802–80), author and abolitionist, published the book *Biographies of Good Wives.*] I think she makes women shine quite as much as Mrs. Jameson. The latter's shine like mahogany, Mrs. Child's more like the deal table. Tell Annie I say *when* is that letter coming. 'Tis very late. Goodnight.

Ever affectionately yours.

Yellow fever is on the rise in New Orleans with many deaths. William Harford is especially exposed to fever infection in his superintendence of the digging of the canal. Maria thinks only Providence protects her husband.

Maria in this letter refers again to her husband's unhappiness concerning his brother Edwin. Edwin Harford, a young banker, had been convicted of embezzlement and confined to the state prison in Milledgeville.

Maria Bryan Harford to Julia Ann Bryan Cumming

New Orleans
August 24, 1833 (Saturday)

My dear Julia,

A cold which I have had for some time has made me feel so heavy and dull for several days that I have not hitherto fulfilled my promise of writing very soon. You must be very much occupied yourself nowadays, for it appears to me that your letters come not so frequently as formerly. We have had some sickness since I wrote to you before. Henny has been very sick indeed, and for nearly a week past I have had no servant but Jenny. She was attacked with great violence, high fever, dreadful pain in the head, and throwing up great quantities of bile. The worst of it is over with her now, I hope, but Bird is still sick, and was obliged to come home from the place where he is working. The poor fellow has the most forlorn and despondent look of any human countenance I ever saw, and seems to think he is suffering more than the ordinary lot of misery.

I have lately heard from Pa. He wrote to me from Scottsborough on his way to the Chattahoochie. I presume he has recovered his health, as he does not mention having been sick even. I thought Ma and Sophy were going with him, part of the way, but it appears not from his letter. I have recently heard from Catherine [Wales] who gives me more of the news of the place than I have had in a long time; among other things that Mrs. Lansing Beman (or Houghton, rather) would perhaps marry Jem Smith, and that Miss Jane Armour and Mrs. Reid were spending the summer at Pleasant Valley. She gave a sad, though not to me surprising, account of Frank Early, that he has formally renounced his religion.

Tell Annie I am very glad to hear she is going to school so willingly, and ask her if I shall bring her some little books when I come to see her. Tell Annie that we have got a little dog here that I often wish she had, as I think it would just suit *her*. It belonged to a poor crazy man who had been working on the Canal, and died in the hospital about ten days since, and the dog followed Mr. Harford home. Tell her it is white with yellow ears and yellow spots upon it, and it has a most beautiful countenance with the prettiest eyes I almost ever saw. Withal, it is certainly the most affectionate little creature in the world, and has not one single bad trick. Every morning when it wakes up it must have a formal good morning with everybody, and then does not solicit any more special notice from that person. It comes into my room and as I sit yawning and trying to wake up, it sees me through my mosquito net and barks and whines, and when I call it or notice it at all, it appears in perfect ecstasy. I say half a dozen times every day, "Oh I wish Annie had this little dog."

The yellow fever is much talked of in the city, and many have died, and many are now ill with it. I must confess I dread it far more than I did the cholera. I am not much afraid of having it myself, but it is a disease which strikes me with more terror than the other. I am sure it is owing to the interposition of Providence that Mr. Harford is not sick, for he is more exposed than you can conceive. He has all the superintendence of the works at present, for Bonner has left town and is staying with Satterlee at the lake, and the poor fellow is so alarmed and in so much fear of sickness that he has sold his horses and hardly stirs out of the house from one day's end to another. Mr. Harford is expecting his friend Johnson as an assistant but he will probably not be here before October or November.

He [Mr. Harford] is extremely unhappy sometimes, and I am sure it would wring your heart, as it does mine, to see what he suffers. I do not suppose he would wish me to speak of his feelings to anyone, but it certainly can do no harm to mention it to you. You have never been enough with him to know how much he was attached to Edwin. He was very proud of him, and was always quoting his sayings and telling me anecdotes of him. With the pain which his affection causes, is added the deepest mortification and a sense of even personal disgrace that I vainly try to reason him out of. He says 'tis a blow which will follow him to his grave, and will always put a drop of bitter in his sweetest draughts through life. He certainly needed no additional care to make him grave, for he had before but little of the lightness of heart that men of his age ordinarily have. For the last two years, whatever he may have been before, the anxiety of acquiring the means of living respectably has constantly thrown a shadow upon his brow. By now unfortunately it is too often that of the deepest gloom. I can give you no idea of what I feel when I hear him, after a long and gloomy silence which is often the case, burst out with those two words "Oh, *Edwin, Edwin!*" It expresses such grief and affection and pity combined, as if his heart would break.

Pa told me he had visited him [Edwin Harford] and mentioned how he was employed. I read part of the account to Mr. Harford, but omitted the part which related to his specific occupation, for I know that the *vague* idea he had of Edwin's situation was better than any particular description. Sometime after, he took up Pa's letter and read that part. My first impulse was to take it from him but I feared that he might suspect something still worse. But the effect far exceeded even what I had anticipated. He often says to me, "Oh Maria, to think you are the wife of a man whose brother is confined in a prison with outcasts, for such an alleged crime." I *might* reply, but it will be better still in actions

> *Did I but purpose to embark with thee*
> *On the smooth surface of a summer's sea. etc.*

I hope I shall hear from you very soon. I am glad you have such pleasant neighbours as the Miss Telfairs, and hope you will see them often. Remember me affectionately to Mr. Cumming and the children, and believe me ever truly yours.

M.

Tell Anne I shall look for a letter from her very soon.

Almost seven months have passed since the last extant letter from Maria Harford in New Orleans, and she and her husband are now in Washington, where Harford is working hard on some drawings to accompany a report on "the Florida excursion." Congressman Richard Henry Wilde's suspicious relationship with Mrs. Joseph White, wife of the congressional delegate from Florida, comes under Maria's direct observation. While Mr. Wilde, a widower, has been very ill, Mrs. White attends all the large parties, flirts with men, and flaunts her disregard of social opinion. For Mr. Wilde's sake, Maria refuses to believe the worst about her.

Maria Bryan Harford to Julia Ann Bryan Cumming

March 17, 1834 (Monday)
[Postmark: Georgetown, D.C.]

My dear Julia,

I received your letter yesterday with the pleasure I always feel in hearing from you. I hope Alfred is recovered before this. I really wonder how you could have gotten your own consent to part with Annie. She seems to be so indispensable to your comfort. I am truly happy to hear that Pa appears in such good health and spirits, and wish I could have flown to you and spent at least the few days of his visit with you too.

I cannot realize that you all wish to see me as much as I do you, for you have so many of those you love around you to fill up the small vacuum my absence created; but I have literally nobody but Mr. Harford, and there is precious little of his company I have during the day. He has almost made himself sick from his assiduity in finishing the drawings, and this, with an influenza he has had, has made him look as if he were going into a consumption, and I have sometimes felt really uneasy about him. Mr. Pekell, the principal officer of the Florida excursion, has left all the drawings and calculations to be done by Mr. Harford and Leach, while he has been using his privilege in drawing up the *report,* visiting the ladies, etc. Leach and Mr. Harford divided the labor equally between them, and such was his anxiety to finish the work that he will have completed his portion next week, while Leach will probably, he says, not have finished *his* in three weeks or a month more. He has obtained leave from the higher powers to go to Philadelphia to await orders (as they call it), and intends studying law in some office with what diligence he can. If you were to inquire why he does not stay here, I believe his principal reasons are to be more retired, to live cheaper, and avoid the gaiety of this city, for which he has a greater aversion than I can give you any idea of.

I am glad you told me of Uncle [Isaac], though the report was little gratifying, for I have not heard a word about him since I left home. I should write to him sometimes to give him an idea of my situation, and signify my interest and regard for him, but he would inevitably think I was aiming to acquire some of "the plunder," of which, I suppose, he thinks I would be more desirous than usual.

I saw Miss Stebbins a day or two since. You must know she had been exceedingly anxious to be introduced to the President [Andrew Jackson] and as I had an opportunity of going, I called for her to accompany me. We were led into the General's cabinet where we found him immersed in papers. He was extremely gracious to us, very sociable, said he always felt honoured when ladies called upon him. I asked him if he remembered Brother. "Very well," he said, enquired if he was married, and told me to send his regards to him, and say he should always feel interested in his welfare.

Miss Stebbins was struck all up in a heap, as the saying is, when she beheld the great man. She had had a dozen things to say to him, and did not get out one, but that she had long been desirous of calling, and that she was "from Massachusetts." I am always so filled with interest and pity for the poor old lady when I see her. Her situation, as I am sufficiently able to perceive, is very unpleasant. She is treated as a complete underling of the family where she lives, and I do think really, she is one of the excellent of the earth, so humble and conscientious, and kind in spirit to every human creature. I gave her all your messages which gratify her very much, and she desires me to send a great deal of love in return to you. You may tell Brother and Sophy they are both mentioned in the tale of the "South" and nothing said to the disparagement of either. Catherine is not mentioned but Aunt Wales is.

Oh, by the bye, Pa was as much mistaken as I was, with regard to the news she [Aunt Wales] wrote to me. I heard frequently of her forthcoming letter, and I anticipated a treat, an epitome of everything that had been said or done at Mt. Zion, of which no one had written me much, but it was a complete disappointment. Whether it was that she bore in mind my professed hatred of gossipping, and my sometimes hard rubs to herself, I don't know, but her lines were far apart, and the whole of the first page was taken up in telling me why she had not written before, and that her advancing age prevented her from visiting as well as formerly, and she concluded the letter by saying she believed she would not tell me any news as she supposed I heard all of importance through other channels.

But Mr. Wilde! I had almost forgotten to mention him. Oh Julia, I am afraid he is not long for this world. He has had another severe attack, though he is about again now. When he heard your message he said, "Ah, the traitress! She avails herself with true feminine dexterity of my good nature or weakness. Because I knew well there was no hope of a reply, I did not disdain to be again mortified. She *assumes* that I decline her correspondence. Tell her she cannot deceive me, though I almost thank her for the kindness of the artifice. It is less intolerable to have it said that I do not desire than to have it intimated that I do not deserve a line. I am sure I have a sufficiently humble opinion of my deserts," said he, "but I confess it is rather painful for me to suffer the indifference or contempt of those whom one admires, esteems, loves, if the last much abused word may ever be admitted again into good society on earth."

I am sure if they, who conceive Mrs. White to be so guilty, could see her flaunting away in all the gaieties of Washington, in those large parties, dancing, promenading and smiling with the young and old men who seem to consider a smile or a word from her as conferring distinction, while Mr. Wilde is at home, amusing himself in his solitary sick chamber as best he may, I am sure they would not think much of her tenderness for him *now*, whatever it may have been. She evinces the most silly love of notoriety, the greatest disregard of the prejudices of the society of her own country that I've ever seen. She's been playing my lady patroness of late to Mrs. Drake, the celebrated actress, who was a Kentuckian as well as herself, carrying her to shows, inviting her to tea, and so forth. Mr. Harford saw Mrs. White at the levee the other evening, and she told him she wished to speak to him on a subject which she was anxious about, lest she might not see me in time. Mrs. Drake, she said, was going to play several nights again soon, and she was particularly anxious that I should be there the night of her benefit.

I never, in my life, was so amazed as in hearing of Mr. Alexander's and Mrs. Veach's supposed misconduct. Oh, poor human nature, as Pa says. I have not heard a word from Mrs. Bailey, or Margaret, since I came here. So you did not go to Savannah at last.

I presume we shall set off for Philadelphia about the second week in April. There will be some whom I shall regret leaving, for some here are kind to me. There is a family of Hutchinsons (Quakers) who live a little ways off, who are very good and really affectionate to me. Just before I commenced my letter, about twelve, I was leaning over the fire to toast some bread and cheese, which Mrs. B. had sent to me to break my fast or before dinner, when a servant came in with a basket of cakes covered over with a clean white towel which that family had sent me. They were warm still, and there was pound cake, and hearts, and all very nice and, as you must remember my taste for *nick nacks,* may suppose they were quite acceptable.

Jenny inquired of me the other day if I had written home that I had had three parties given to me. I told her no, upon which she seemed very much grieved and astonished. You may imagine the situation was as surprising to me as to her, for I was not aware that anybody here cared enough for me to show me any extra attention whatever.

I am very glad to hear that Sophy behaves so well, and doubly rejoiced that Pa is disposed to look with a favourable eye upon Brother. It is very cold, unpleasant weather now. From my window I see the air thick with the falling snow.

I think there must be a mistake in the report of Colonel [Thomas Flournoy] Foster and Miss Gardner. He denies it, at any rate. I am sure if she would have him he ought to embrace the chance, for no one else hardly would. [Elizabeth McKinne Gardner (1810–93) married Colonel Foster.] You cannot imagine how much hauteur Colonel Foster assumes toward Mr. Harford. He evidently dislikes him, though why I can't, for the life of me, imagine. Mr. Harford is always perfectly respectful towards him.

Remember me affectionately to Mr. & Mrs. Cumming, Mr. & Mrs. Henry & Mrs. Reid. I need not send a formal message to your beloved lord who is always so well assured, if he would take the trouble to think of it, how much I love and esteem him. Write soon (every week).

Ever truly yours.

How is your health now? I have almost as much colour as I used to have when I was a school girl. I have a picture (borrowed from a young officer here) that I wish you could see. It is a portrait of Mary Queen of Scots, the very image of you, without any flattery.

Mr. Harford does not know Lieut. Baldwin, he says. I go every Sunday that the weather will permit, morning & evening, to Mr. Smith's church in which we have rented a pew. It is nearly a mile from here, so that in the course of the day I do not walk much less than four miles. He is an admirable preacher. I have seldom heard such eloquence as from him, and he is always interesting and never flags. He is an indefatigable student, and all his theological studies are pursued in the German tongue. Have you read *Eugene Aram* [a three-volume work written by the English novelist Edward George Earle Bulwer-Lytton and published in 1832] yet? I am engrossed with Miss [Maria] Edgeworth [an English novelist]. Is not she a charming writer?

Yours ever.

Five months have passed. Maria and her husband are back again in New Orleans, and she is spending the summer outside the city at "Summerland." This letter is written to Julia at Mt. Zion, where Julia has gone to await the birth of her fifth child.

Maria Bryan Harford to Julia Ann Bryan Cumming

"Summerland"
August 7, 1834 (Thursday)
[Postmark: New Orleans]

My dear Julia,

I was glad to find from the reception of your letter that you had health and spirits to write. I think it possible that this will find you at home. Who was it that said of his daughters which amused you so much, "They thought it was so pleasant to go to Pa's"? It certainly is to you, and I know it would be to me.

I was very much surprised to hear of Mrs. Cuthbert's death so soon. [The former Sally Jones, the wife of Alfred Cuthbert and a first cousin of Henry Cumming, died on July 12, 1834.] You and Anne [Cumming] had informed me of her being there, and of her poor health. It must have been really a melancholy time, and yet it seems better for her to have died there than in that out of the way place of hers in the country.

I was surprised and grieved at what you told me of the lady of Mr. Talmage's *choice*. What congeniality can he hope to find in such a character? Yet it would seem that he is not long for this world. It seems a wonderful thing on both sides. She, from appearances, would hardly have a right to anticipate anything but being the relict of a very good man. I *did* think that sooner or later he and Anne would be married—but it was not to be.

I am very comfortably and pleasantly situated here, and have my health perfectly. I have lost all the languor which rendered life a burden in New Orleans, am strong and active, not a pain or an ache and, if it were not for the uneasiness I have about Mr. Harford's exposure, should have nothing to complain of. He always comes home sick and that keeps me uneasy about him all the while he is gone. One of my annoyances here is from the visits of the people in the neighbourhood. They come and sit and sit and have nothing to say, and I rack my brain to talk to them, and no matter what I am engaged about, all must be stopped when they come to entertain them. You all know well at home how little patience I ever had with those sorts of things.

When I read to Mr. Harford what you said about Annie, he said, "Maria, tell Julia that I beg she will keep that child occupied in thoughts and studies more suitable to her age. She is so peculiar that she must be watched over very closely. Let her health and her bodily developments be attended to now, almost entirely." Much more he said very sapiently, to the same purpose. One should have thought, to hear him talk, that he had had the most ample experience in bringing up children.

I wish I had her and your little boys here now. There is at least a dozen watermelons and muskmelons lying on the hearth. They would associate the image of their Auntie with that of so much plenty and delight, with watermelons of glowing red hearts, and muskmelons with their rich salmon tints. Alfred would think me a descended goddess. Mr. Harford laughed very much at your description of Julien, and the necessity of your interference between him and Tom to allay their mighty causes of dispute.

I shall be very anxious about you now for several months to come, not precisely uneasy but thoughtful and solicitous, as even those will be who are with you. Absence at this distance, I assure you, increases the natural feeling much.

If you could see Susan Griffin now, she would beset you to "eat, drink and sleep upon" *sweet oil*. Everybody almost has a favourite medicine and a favourite doctor; her medicine in such cases is *sweet oil*. Such wonders as it works, you would think some one had found means to battle the effects of the sentence upon Eve and her daughters, or else it was the chosen means of fulfilling the promise communicated through the apostle that they shall be saved in childbearing if they continue in faith and charity with sobriety. She is greatly favoured in consequence of taking it, she says, and her sister who had had two children, I think, before Susan was married, suffered so much each time that her life was almost despaired of. Dr. Griffin, who recommends it to all his patients (and who you know stands very high in his profession), induced her to take it, and now she feels as if she were in the possession of a precious treasure. I heard enough of its virtues one night, in particular, as we were coming down the river. Before she had often spoken of it, but one evening a lady and her two children came on board. I went to bed early and waked up again; I could not get to sleep for the talk of her and Mrs. Griffin. They were asking each other, which is usually the first question among ladies, how many children they each had, and after some time spent in talking of their children, the other lady said she hoped she would never have any more for she suffered dreadfully. It was like death each time, and she said she sometimes felt right awful when she remembered the discontented and mumbling speeches she had made when her last child was born. Mrs. Griffin told her of the wonderful properties of the sweet oil. The woman seemed greatly pleased and vowed if she ever had occasion she would take it. The dose is one wine glass of the purest and freshest that can be procured, taken every night before going to bed, and this taken three or two months before confinement. Mrs. Griffin says it does not affect the child in the least.

How do you like Mary Kelsey? I hope she has behaved well and been a suitable companion for Annie. I have not been pleased with any of that family of late — except Mr. Kelsey.

Mr. Harford came home from New Orleans quite out of humour with Mr. Porter. Mary [Porter] is now staying at Pascagoula [Mississippi, a town on the Gulf of Mexico] and will remain during the summer as her health was quite delicate, but she does not like the society. Mr. Porter inquired after me, and asked Mr. Harford if he did not intend to take me to Pascagoula during the summer. Mr. Harford said I would like very well to go, but that I had got settled here and was busy in making little improvements. He paid no attention to this, but still insisted upon it that I should leave all and go to Pascagoula, as Mrs. Porter would be so pleased if I were with her. Mr. Harford says "[He] just wishes you for the comfort it would afford his wife. Our affairs must suffer and our arrangements be totally altered that Mrs. Porter may have society that will suit her." I told him he was too suspicious of their motives, though I am perfectly convinced they have an infinite deal of self-importance and selfishness, and think of people rather relatively to themselves than in any other way.

I do not love Mary Porter now though she is a woman of good principle and intelligent. I prefer her, though, to most others of the Americans. She is daily becoming more and more like Mrs. Hitchcock. You cannot deny her the possession of many virtues, yet you yield her praise with reluctance because she seems so aware of her virtues, and is such an object of esteem and admiration to herself. She is like a great many women I have known, who estimate themselves in the degree in which their lovers or husbands estimate them, not having the good sense to be pleased with even the exaggerated, though perhaps elusive opinions of their husbands as proof of their love, yet always bearing in mind that the world sees with very different eyes. Have you read Allen Cunningham's, *Painters and Sculptors?* [Scottish poet and author Allan Cunningham (1782–1842) published *Lives of the Most Eminent British Painters, Sculptors and Architects* between 1829 and 1833.] It is a delightful book. Write when you can. Mr. Harford sends his love.

Very affectionately yours—
M.

If you ever do not hear from me again soon, attribute it to the worst of opportunity of sending to this mail. My best love to Mr. Cumming and Annie.

A fifteen-month gap occurs here in Maria Harford's letters, from August 1834 to November 1835. In that period Julia gave birth to her fifth child, Emily Harford Cumming, born in Mt. Zion on November 16, 1834. The proud father wrote his mother in Augusta that Emily was "a blue eyed, black haired little girl" who resembled very much their son Julien. He wrote that he feared "for a young lady, she is rather too much like him in the size of her hands and feet." During those fifteen months, Maria had visited her family in Georgia. At the time of this letter she and her husband are back in New Orleans, and Julia is pregnant with her sixth child. Yellow fever still persists as the autumn weather is unseasonably warm.

Maria Bryan Harford to Julia Ann Bryan Cumming

New Orleans
November 20, 1835 (Friday)

My dear Julia,

You have doubtless received a letter from me (written about ten days ago) before this time. I was just about commencing another, not thinking of exacting a regular answer from you in your present circumstances, when I received yours. You remark that it was to have been brought by Mr. & Mrs. Slaughter, but I perceive that it was mailed in Augusta, and I have not heard one word from them. Should I learn that they are here, or if they come hereafter, I will render them all the attention in my power, and perhaps Mr. Harford may be able to be of some little service to Mr. Slaughter, as he has acquaintances among many of the business men of the city. It is enough that they are friends of yours and Mr. Cumming's to insure our *exertions* to be kind to them.

I have had one letter from home since I came back, that was from Sophia, and gave a favourable account of Ma's health. God grant that the expectations of her friends may be realized. If it be a medicine which can "minister to a mind diseased," or, but its seeming effect upon the body, have a sanitary influence on the mind, I shall have hopes of her cure in time. If that tendency to diarrhea can be checked, the effect upon her feelings I am sure will be wonderful, for with her dread of death, it has always of late operated as a sword suspended over her head. She would not be encouraged even when she was better. She was continually thinking that at any moment she might be reduced to the lowest ebb by an attack of that kind. . . .

In my last letter home, I informed them of the death of Jacob Turner of the yellow fever. It has been, and is, still quite sickly here, owing to the unseasonably warm weather, and he, finding so many subjects of curiosity, was going everywhere and at all hours of the day. He suffered a great deal, and it must have been a very aggravated case of the disease, for Mr. Harford, who saw the body, says he was as yellow as an orange. Mr. Bryan took the charge of funeral expenses, and so forth, and was desired by him to write to his family.

I often see Mr. Bryan and think him a very clever man, with some very marked peculiarities. I have seen Mrs. Reid very often since I came back. She seems more completely devoted to the world than ever, and appears to be making many projects for her winter campaigns. Lucy is as amiable as ever but looks thin and has lost a good deal of her bloom. We are now living near them; we tried hard after our return to obtain a house rather more pleasant than the one Mr. Harford had occupied, but it was impossible to get one and we are compelled to stay here. We are obliged always to seek a house which has stables connected with it and they rarely build them in this city, and it is owing to that circumstance that we cannot be readily suited. If you have ever occasion to direct your friends to us, we are living at No. 18 Union Street.

Why will you not try and go home and stay some there? I am sure the journey, if conducted with proper prudence, would not hurt you, and Dr. Gilbert seems to be your best physician. Poor little Annie was not more disappointed than I was, in not coming up. It gives me a feeling of the most unsatisfactory and painful kind to think how little I was with her and all of you. Give my love to her, and tell her she must write to me. She has never answered my letter that I wrote her last Christmas yet.

You see in the papers, I suppose, that N. P. Willis [Nathaniel Parker Willis (1806–67), journalist, editor, and author] has married an English lady and is gone to France, and I have heard today that Bulwer[-Lytton] has run off with some married lady. Well done for the author of *Falkland!* [Rosina Bulwer had separated from her author husband in 1835, and he established a long-term relationship with another woman. Of this tie Edward Bulwer-Lytton wrote in his private diary, "Had we but been married, we should have been cited as models of domestic happiness and household virtues."]

I am glad to hear that Annie's health is better. When did she see Mr. Henderson? I have not had any letters from him since the one that I found at your house on my arrival in Augusta. He is not coming back here any more. I have not been to church since my return, for it is too far to walk, and we have no horse at present. Mr. Harford sends his kind regards to you and Mr. Cumming.

Affectionately yours.

P.S. A young man has lately died with the yellow fever, who has excited our feelings very much. He had been in the city a year, but was absent part of the summer. He came down a week before his death, strong, hearty, robust, in perfect health. He was sick only three days. The disease took a sudden turn in the night, and he threw up. He asked if that was the black vomit and they told him no (deceiving him). "Don't attempt to deceive me," said he. "Let me have a minister." You may not know that in this complaint for some time before death there is a stupor, an irresistible inclination to sleep. A number of young men, intimate friends of his, were sitting around him. They would occasionally arouse him to moisten his lips, and he would exert himself to throw off sleep, perfectly conscious that he must soon die. "Boys," said he, "pray for me. I am too wicked to pray for myself."

Write soon.

Most truly yours.

Mr. and Mrs. Slaughter, friends of Julia's, arrive in New Orleans, rent a large house, and receive a call from Maria Harford.

Maria Bryan Harford to Julia Ann Bryan Cumming

New Orleans
December 5, 1835 (Saturday)

My dear Julia,

I have been constantly intending to write to you for a week past, but have really been so busily engaged sewing, that I have not found a moment of leisure. I had the pleasure of hearing from you directly through Mrs. Slaughter, to whom I paid a long visit a day or two ago. She says she never saw you look in better spirits and so beautiful, as when she last saw you. She is in very fine spirits herself, and is perfectly delighted with New Orleans, she says. They have rented a very commodious house, and on most excellent terms for this place. Mr. Slaughter has taken an office in a spot which, he is told, is very eligible for business, and they seem to have a reasonable share of attention every way, considering how lately they have arrived. I was sorry to hear from Mrs. Slaughter that Anne [Cumming] did not look so well as her friends had hoped she would do after her journey. Give my love to Anne and tell her that a trip to New Orleans would be the best thing she could do, and if she will but come, I will lay myself out to make her as comfortable and happy as I possibly can.

I have received but one letter from home since my return, and cannot but feel uneasy, knowing the fluctuations of Ma's health, and am only comforted by recollecting the want of punctuality of the family with regard to letter writing. I hope they have been paying you a visit or that they are still there.

I received a letter from Watkins Goode about a week since, in which he mentions that Mr. Sayre had been in Montgomery, and told them that Brother was daily expected home, and that Pa was anxiously expecting to hear from him. I do hope that he has been home, or written, before this time.

It has been very cold here lately though the weather has been clear and delightful. The city is all in a bustle, with gaiety and business, ladies shopping from morning to night, Sundays included, the milliners and dressmakers crowded to death with business, and more insolent than ever. Having a little more money than usual to sally out with, I concluded to indulge myself in the rare luxury of having a dress made to serve as a sort of model etc., but after a proposition or two, in which I was but little satisfied with their high airs, and their *"tant d'ouvrage Madame"* [so much workmanship] often repeated, I returned home thankful that I had skill and industry enough to render me independent in this respect, and rejoicing that I was not forced to dance a servile attendance upon any such folks, which many ladies from their excessive devotion to fashion do at this season.

You will perhaps hear talk of a famous theatre that they are just finishing in St. Charles Street. They have been using it this week, and I am told by those who have been there that the *coup d'oeil* is magnificent beyond anything that is to be seen in America. They have a number of actors of note here now, among others the celebrated Miss Fanny Durman, whom you may have seen praised in *Blackwood's Magazine* [published by William Blackwood and Sons in Edinburgh] as one of the "three Fannys."

I see Mr. Bryan pretty often. He comes and sits and talks by the hour of his family, his brothers and sisters. He says there is an estate in Ireland to which the Bryan family in this country have claim, as there is no heir there. He saw a gentleman in New York who was making enquiries about the family, and who informed him of the circumstances. Pa is the heir, it seems, by good rights.

I presume you have gone to town by this time and are settled for the winter. Remember me affectionately to Mr. Cumming and Annie. Do write to me as often as you can. I received the book and scissors sheath and the packet from

Mr. Henderson. Mr. [Joel] Parker's church [First Presbyterian Church in New Orleans] is finished and is crowded on Sabbath to overflowing. The pews are to be sold soon. I hope that we shall buy one, or we shall be excluded entirely after the sale. At present the seats are free.

Affectionately yours.

This is Maria's last extant letter from New Orleans. In it Maria wonders aloud if she and Julia "will ever live near together in this world."

Maria Bryan Harford to Julia Ann Bryan Cumming

New Orleans
December 11, 1835 (Friday)

My dear Julia,

I was sitting yesterday by my table sewing, and looked upon the paper and pen and ink with a very wistful eye, thinking that if I had time I would write to you again. But I cannot delay saying a few words, since I have heard from Pa's letter of your affliction in the loss of poor Letha [a favorite house slave of Julia's]. I know from my own feelings at her death what yours must be, and besides the *regret* you feel. I know you will miss her in a thousand ways. But I cannot say what I feel in a letter. How I wish I was near you! I wonder, my dear Julia, if we will ever live near together in this world, or if we will not sometime have an opportunity of being more in each other's society than at present.

Pa writes me that he found you suffering considerably from indisposition yourself. I was in hopes, from what Mrs. Slaughter told me of your healthful appearance, that you were getting quite well comparatively. I shall think of you often and with great solicitude. You *must* exert yourself and try and keep your spirits up, and trust to the mercy of the Good providence which has always watched over you and so kindly brought you through many trials and dangers. [Julia is more than seven months pregnant with her sixth child.]

You remember I told you that Mrs. Slaughter was in fine spirits when I saw her, and that they had obtained a comfortable house. Tuesday last we called to see her again. She had just changed her abode the day before. On our way there we met W. Huntingdon, who had just returned from paying her a visit. We enquired the way from him, and he gave us directions saying, "It is a miserable place but don't say anything to discourage her." After he left us I said to Mr. Harford, "W. Huntingdon thinks every place is miserable because he takes the splendours of the Julia Street establishment as the standard" (Mr. Miller's house). But we found on our arrival that there was no exaggeration in his account. The entrance was by a low hotel called the "Strangers Coffee House" in a dirty, obscure part of the upper Faubourg, and the alley was damp and dirty in the extreme. She had given the stairs and the parlour a somewhat comfortable and neat appearance, but still it looked unpleasant. Mrs. Slaughter made an effort to appear cheerful, but her lips quivered and I did not know but she would burst out a-crying. She said she could never stay there, there was not a lock on the house, the landlord had refused to do anything, and the night before there had been several fights in the street just before their window. On our way home we met Mr. Slaughter. They were to give 45 dollars a month for that house, and he told us he was making arrangements to get it off his hands and take another at 60 dollars.

I was truly glad to find from Pa's letter of the continued improvement in Ma's health. He mentioned that he was himself lame from a fall off his horse. I hope you will write soon. Tell Annie I do long for her to begin to write to us, and I hope I will then have a little correspondent that I can depend upon. Is Julien still at Mt. Zion? I hear that Dr. Brown is to leave there. What a pity! I know it is much against his will for he frequently said as much to me in my conversations with him.

I am writing this in a hurry for Mr. Harford is preparing to go, and if I do not send it by today's mail it will not go in three days. My love to Mr. Cumming and the children. Jenny was very much distrest at the death of Letha. Poor Aunt Sal, I have thought a great deal of her since I heard it. Mr. Harford sends kind remembrances to yourself and Mr. Cumming.

Ever yours truly

M

Maria Bryan Harford (1808–44).
Portrait painted by George Cooke in Mt. Zion, Ga., June 1840,
a year before her marriage to Dr. Alva Connell.

Joseph Bryan
(1768–1861),
father of Maria Bryan.
Portrait painted by George
Cooke in Mt. Zion, Ga.,
June 1840.

(George) Goode Bryan
(1812–85). This picture of
Maria Bryan's younger
brother is copied from an
illustration in Virginia
Cousins—The Goode
Family. During the Civil
War, Goode held the rank of
brigadier general of the
Sixteenth Georgia
Regiment.

*Henry Harford Cumming (1799–1866). This is the earliest known likeness
of Maria Bryan's brother-in-law, husband of her sister Julia.*

William H. Harford (1807–36), first husband of Maria Bryan.
Miniature painted in New Orleans, 1833.

Maria Bryan Harford as the young wife of William H. Harford.

Julia Bryan Cumming (1803–79), sister of Maria Bryan and recipient of her letters, and her daughter Emily Harford Cumming (1834–1911). This portrait of Maria's sister and niece was painted by George Cooke in Augusta, Ga., May 1840.

*Maria Bryan as a young woman, presumably before her marriage
to William H. Harford in 1831. A posthumous steel engraving made by
Charles Fenderich of Philadelphia in 1845.*

Cumming home. The home of Julia and Henry Cumming built by Henry in the Sand Hills, outside Augusta, early in his marriage to Julia. It was here that Maria Bryan visited her sister frequently. This photograph was taken shortly before Julia's death in 1879.

Mt. Zion Presbyterian Church, photographed in 1940.

Three sons of Julia and Henry Cumming. Joseph Bryan Cumming (1836–1922),
Thomas William Cumming (1831–89), Harford Montgomery Cumming
(1838–72), photographed in 1844.

Anne Maria Cumming (1826–55), eldest daughter of Julia and Henry Cumming.
She is holding her youngest sister, Maria Bryan Cumming, born in 1844 and
named for her recently deceased aunt.

Henry Harford Cumming. This portrait by an unknown artist was painted just before the Civil War when he was in his early sixties.

Julia Bryan Cumming. Probably a Brady photo of the 1850s.

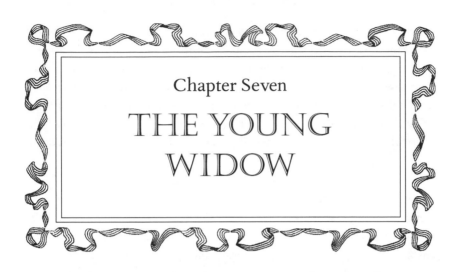

Chapter Seven

THE YOUNG WIDOW

"I am sorry you think I do not bear my sorrow
as becomes a Christian."

Five weeks after Maria's letter of December 11, 1835, William H. Harford died
suddenly, on January 16, 1836, in New Orleans. Shortly after her husband's death,
twenty-eight-year-old Maria returned home to Mt. Zion, took up her old life again
as the dutiful daughter, and devoted herself to her parents and to helping with the
education and upbringing of her six Cumming nieces and nephews.

This letter is the first extant letter of the young widow to her sister Julia. In it she
reports on the fragility of women's lives especially during the childbearing years.

Maria Bryan Harford to Julia Ann Bryan Cumming

Mt. Zion
August 27, 1836 (Saturday Morning)

My dear Julia,

We were becoming (in our turn) very anxious to hear from you before the
reception of your last letter. We had heard that Goode was sick there, and Ma
had an unpleasant dream some time since, and she was sure, she said, that
she should hear he was dead; it was in vain we reasoned with her, that the

state of her health and nerves was such that her dreams should not make any impression on her. She made herself very miserable and sick from uneasiness.

The journey has been delayed on account of the blindness of one of the horses, and this week there has been so much sickness in the neighbourhood and in the family. Tom has been very ill that they said they could not think of leaving. Mr. & Mrs. Little and Mr. & Mrs. Brewer have been sick with the fever, all but the latter dangerously ill, though at this time they are considered out of danger.

The account Mrs. Richardson gives of Lavinia [Richardson Holt, wife of the Bryans' first cousin, Pulaski Holt] is this. She had gone over the week before, hearing that she was sick, and found that she had had a little fright (I believe from a dog), and was trying to keep off an abortion. But she was up, had workmen in the house who were finishing it in great style, and took her about to explain her plans and open some boxes of furniture to show her, but not intending to make use of it until the birth of her child which was expected in two or three months. She was so well that in two or three days her mother, at her own permission, left her, but two days after, it seems, she had an uncomfortable night, and early in the morning her husband proposed sending for Dr. Branham. He arrived about six o'clock, and expressed the opinion that her health would, in time, be materially injured by her remaining in that state, and proposed that she should take a small portion of ergot. She consented, but immediately felt an unpleasant effect from it. She was sitting upon the edge of the bed, and suddenly exclaimed, "Oh Doctor, I'm blind," and fell back upon her pillow in a convulsion, and died in seventeen minutes after she had swallowed the dose. Pa called to see Mrs. Richardson, but he could not learn anything from her as to the state of her mind, and indeed, I believe, said nothing which gave him any idea of what her own opinion of her was.

Caroline Lesly spent the day here yesterday. She is staying in Sparta while Mr. Vanness is gone to Washington city. She enquired particularly after you and your family. Her health is delicate, and she seems to be very much afraid of a Southern climate as she has not spent several summers so far South. She expects to go to her sister's, who lives in Greene County, Alabama, as soon as they can safely pass through the [Cherokee] Nation. Her mother is there, and I presume she expects to remain there until after her confinement, which Ma imagines will take place in two or three months.

Mary Porter [whom Maria knew in New Orleans] died at Smithland, which you know is a small town in Kentucky, not far from the Tennessee line. What she was doing there I do not know, unless she was on a visit to her brother. Her child died about a fortnight after, and her remains were carried to her Father's (where *we* were). What a trial to poor old Mrs. Erwin! She left there a bride, and never returned but under such circumstances.

I have never received but one letter from Mr. Bowman. This was a long and consoling one, but I never answered it. I feel a great disinclination to write now, which I never had before. I cannot exactly explain why it is. Indeed there are things in the philosophy of woe that cannot be known but to him who suffers. May you never, if it be the will of Heaven, have occasion to know as much of it as I experience. I hope that you may have grace given you by your deportment and by your prayers to discharge your duty faithfully to all those who are so dear to you that all may, after the purifying discipline of this world, meet an "unbroken family in Heaven." I am sure that even in reference to this life alone, that our happiness is increased in proportion as we live near to the Saviour, and subdue our evil and unholy passions and dispositions.

Dr. & Mrs. Rossiter are on the hill and seem to be very well pleased so far. We heard yesterday that Susan Halsey (Mrs. Hill) is very dangerously sick at her mother's, after having given birth to an infant.

Tell Alfred we all want to see him very much, and his Brothers and Sisters too. Pa and Ma were delighted that he wanted to come again. The time now fixed upon for going is next Monday, but I do not think it certain. My love to Mr. Cumming and the children.

I remain affectionately yours.

M.

Pa says I must tell you that he has not forgotten your flour, but he has been getting his grain out and trying different mills to know which made the best flour, and has not yet had an opportunity of sending you such as he would like.

Pa Bryan is opening up a new plantation in Alabama. He takes a party of his
slaves with him and is accompanied by his daughter Sophia, now twenty-one,
leaving Ma Bryan and Maria alone in Mt. Zion.

Maria Bryan Harford to Julia Ann Bryan Cumming

Mt. Zion
December 19, 1836 (Monday)

My dear Julia,

Ma and I were very glad in our solitude to receive your letter, as we had
been expressing a wish to hear for several days past.

We feel much sympathy for Mrs. Cumming and poor John, and have often
spoken of them today. Anne [Cumming], when she was here, said he had some
idea of going to the West Indies. Surely he must have become much worse
within a few weeks. The idea of a marriage at all, under such circumstances, is
disagreeable, and that of a *party* appears to me shocking and unfeeling. Surely
they cannot be aware of his danger. I am rejoiced that Celia is recovering and
hope that it may be Heaven's will to spare her life many years as it is so useful
a one.

Pa and Sophia left home Wednesday morning; they had been delayed by
the bad weather, and getting the negroes off. The night they left, Pa went with
them. They got as far as Wm. Guin's plantation and camped out under a tent,
and Pa staid with them, I suppose, to see if they were comfortable. He had
not said that he should stay, and as it was a dark night, and he rode Goode's
young horse, we were quite uneasy about him. Ma was very unwilling for
Sophia to go, but she appears to be quite reconciled to their absence and until
yesterday and today, has seemed tolerably well. Her general health however
is very poor, and her cough at times distressingly bad. I wish it was in your
power to come and see her and spend some time, but I presume that is now
almost impossible. Tell Julien he must come up as soon as he can, and keep us
company, for his Grandmother and I are very lonesome.

I got a letter today from Maria McDonald, in which she inquired if you had
sent her silk to Milledgeville, and to whose care you had directed it. She left
the money with Ma, who forgot to send it by Uncle Jacob as she intended.
Did you know Dr. Boykin's son Burwell; she gave me an account of his death

which, she says, has been a very heavy blow to his father. His disease was dropsy, and he died sitting in his chair. His father had left to go and see his sister, Mrs. Rutherford, who is not expected to live long, and while there informed the family on their inquiring after Burwell, that he considered him as decidedly better, and a moment after a servant came to inform him that he was dead.

Eliza Brantley has returned, having had the misfortune to lose her trunk containing all her winter clothing by the way. I suppose it is probable you will see Maria and Catherine in January as they intend going to Charleston to pay a visit to the Furmans. Aunt Wales and Catherine have been here a good deal since we have been alone, the former has been very unwell lately and has looked so wretchedly that we have felt quite uneasy about her, though now she appears to be mending a little. They are going to take Mrs. Smith's family to board. I suppose you know Lem Smith has sold the doctor's place, and that they intend going to the North in the Spring.

Catherine is at present very much annoyed, and not a little provoked, from having taken the itch from Cornelia who got it at Midway, and visited and slept with her without letting her know it.

You remember hearing of the sickness of Mr. Shivers who lived at Mr. Norton's old place; he died about ten days ago leaving his family in great distress. I never felt sorrier for anyone than for Mrs. Shivers. You know what a handsome ladylike looking woman she is (or maybe you never saw her), and she seemed always to be very fond of her husband. She sat crying on her work, and the tears falling in her lap. She said they got along badly enough while he lived, but it would be worse now — she expected everything to be sold to pay their debts, and if they had a friend in the world she did not know it. Barefield was on the point of refusing to let them have materials for making a shroud as, she said, they already owed him more than he expected to get, and she told me she did not expect to be able to get her a frock even.

Mr. Hooker [the Presbyterian minister at Mt. Zion] has determined upon committing the "suicide" of remaining here another year. Nothing had been said by anybody to him on the subject, and at last he appeared to grow uneasy and the Sabbath before Pa left home, he called in the morning and proposed that there should be a meeting of the Congregation. Mr. Little filled the chair, and put the question whether the Church desired Mr. Hooker to be their pastor the next year. [The remainder of this letter is badly torn. Evidently the congregation voted to extend Hooker's tenure, but without enthusiasm.]

Remember me to Mr. Cumming and the children.

I remain affectionately

M

Ma and Maria are joined by Goode for their nonfestive "apples and oranges" Christmas. Goode graduated from West Point in 1834 and resigned his army commission in 1835. Pa and Sophia have reached Columbus, Georgia, on their westward trip and are met by Brother, who is now practicing law in Tuskegee, Alabama.

Maria Bryan Harford to Julia Ann Bryan Cumming

Mt. Zion

December 26, 1836 (Monday Morning)

My dear Julia,

I write you a few lines this morning, that you may not be disappointed in hearing from home at the usual time.

Goode came Saturday evening, much to Ma's satisfaction, who was anticipating a very dull Christmas. He speaks of going to Augusta next Friday.

Ma is somewhat better, I think, than when I wrote last. She has received two letters since Pa and Sophia left home, the last was dated at Columbus, where they met with Brother. He told them that he could not return home until the court at Tuskegee had adjourned, and that would not be until Spring or Summer.

We have just heard of the death of Mrs. Brown at Fort Gaines, by a letter which Dr. Gilbert received, but we have not learned any of the particulars except that it was rather sudden.

I suppose Anne has left Augusta by this time, agreeably to her expectation. We heard of the fire by the papers of last week. [The Augusta fire of December 23, 1836, burned for four hours and destroyed sixteen stores and numerous dwellings.] We are very much obliged to you for the apples and oranges; as the box was not marked, Uncle Jacob carried it with him to Milledgeville, so that we did not get it until yesterday.

My love to all. The mail is closing.

Affectionately yours,
M.H.

Still in mourning for her husband, Maria plans to send her winter coat to Augusta to be dyed black if Julia thinks it can be properly done there. In this letter is the first mention of Emily, Julia's fifth child, now two years old. Julia's sixth child, Joseph Bryan Cumming, named for her father, was born on February 2, 1836, two weeks after the death of Maria's husband.

Maria Bryan Harford to Julia Ann Bryan Cumming

Mt. Zion
December 29, 1836 (Thursday Morning)

My dear Julia,

Goode left here this morning, saying that he should set off tomorrow for Augusta, but as you *may* not see him until next week, I sit down to answer your letter.

Ma is, I think, better and her cough for a week or more has not troubled her so much as common. She says she would gladly accept your offer and go down, but she fears the damp climate of Augusta on account of her cough.

With regard to the cloak, it is already so dark that I think any dyer of the least skill might color it black, and if convenient I should be glad if you could examine some specimens of things dyed there, so that if you think it will answer, let it be done as soon as possible. But should you judge it best not to let the dyer in Augusta undertake it, I had (upon reflection) rather it should not be sent to the North, as in that case I shall be obliged to do without it until it is so late in the season that I shall not need it, and you can, therefore, send it to me, by Uncle Jacob, some time when he is coming up.

We have not heard from Pa since I last wrote, and are uncertain when he will be back. Goode expects to bring Julien with him, if you should be willing to let him come. I am sorry to hear that the children have been so unwell, and hope that they and Celia have recovered before now.

There has not been near so much noise and disturbance as was expected on the hill during Christmas. John Bonner has killed a man by the name of Caldwell at the White Plains, though it is said it was in self defense and I do not think that they are going to do anything with him.

You forgot, I suppose, to say anything about Maria's dress. Ma is anxious to know as she can, in that case, tell what disposition to make of her money whether to send it to you or to return it to her, in case you are unable to procure the material which she wanted. Mrs. Matthews has commenced the quilt; she sent for thread which was furnished her, and for cotton, and sent the lining to have it shrunk, so I suppose she is at work upon it, but I never see her nowadays but at church. I sent her word to come and look at a quilt here which I thought was done in a very pretty pattern, but she said you had told her *how* you wished it done.

Mrs. Rossiter has been better of late. She has hired the old negro woman that used to cook for Mrs. Smith, and Ellen is to live at Mr. Little's, so it is to be hoped that they may get along much better the coming year than they have in a long time. Aunt Wales confines herself so much now that Mr. Smith's family are living there, that we have not seen her in ten days or more, Catherine too, though the latter spent a night with us this week. Ma gets along better than I expected alone, and says she did not know she should have missed Sophia so little. She is very anxious to have you come up and stay awhile, and thinks it would do Emily a great deal of good.

I must take back my request about the watch, which I find I shall not be able to get at present without inconvenience, therefore hope you will not trouble yourself about it. Ma says if you can send her up some nitting cotton she can have some stockings nit for the little boys.

Lindy has left the family, to the regret of all. Her master came for her and would not consent to hire her, or sell her for any price that was considered reasonable. Tom [a Bryan slave] is with Pa, so that she did not see him when she left, and I never saw any one more distrest in my life. She is an excellent woman, an exemplary consistent Christian if I ever saw one.

My love to Mr. Cumming and the children.

Yours affectionately,
M.H.

Pa and Sophia have not yet returned from their Alabama trip, and Ma Bryan is ill again with a return of her chills and fever.

Maria Bryan Harford to Julia Ann Bryan Cumming

Mt. Zion

January 5, 1837 (Thursday)

My dear Julia,

I intended writing to you by Mr. [the Reverend Francis William] Bowman, thinking you might get the letter sooner in that way than by the mail, but he left so soon after breakfast that I had no time.

Pa and Sophia have not returned yet and we have not heard from them in more than a fortnight, and I think if they are travelling they must suffer very much from the cold.

Ma has been very unwell for four or five days. There seems to be a return of her fevers and chills. She has night sweats which weaken her very much, and make her cough very distressing. Uncle [Isaac], too, is very unwell indeed and looks wretchedly. He is sometimes in such pain that his groans are loud and frequent. But he will not confess that he is sick, but constantly speaks of growing better.

I went to see Mrs. Matthews a few evenings ago. She was quilting and I really felt sorry for her in that cold, open house, sitting alone at work, and she has laid it off so thickly that it will take her a long time, I think, to finish it. I should go and help her quilt at least one day, if it were not for leaving Ma entirely alone. She intends going to Mrs. Skinner's to stay three or four months, and is expecting her to come for her before long.

Carlisle Martin [who married Margaret Little] has commenced his school, with about twenty scholars. Mr. Little has bought Russell's house for him, and the second night after they moved in Margaret [Little Martin] had a son. Mrs. Beman says she had been stooping down cleaning her hearth, and before the hearth was fully dry, the child was born. Joseph Ponce was here yesterday, and told us that Richardson and Margaret had returned, but he could not tell anything about them, but said the health of the Dr. appeared to be pretty good.

I am glad that Celia is recovering, and sorry that you have so many cares as you speak of. You must feel the want of a seamstress very much.

Mr. Bowman was at Uncle's [Sam Goode] in Montgomery, and found out that he was Ma's brother from asking the little boy his name, who told him it was Joseph Bryan [Goode]. Anne and her husband are going to live at Nashville. Mr. Witherspoon is to take charge of a religious paper there. He (Mr. Bowman) spent more than a week at Mr. Hitchcock's. To my surprise he informed me that Mrs. H. was in very good spirits, and that they expected to go to Europe in the Spring.

Aunt Wales and Catherine desired me to send their love to you — the latter is here, so I must close.

Affectionately yours,
M.H.

Julien Cumming, aged six and one-half years, is visiting Mt. Zion under his Aunt Maria's tutelage. In an earlier letter Julia must have taken Maria to task for not bearing her widow's sorrows "as becomes a Christian."

Maria Bryan Harford to Julia Ann Bryan Cumming

Mt. Zion
February 26, 1837 (Sunday)

My dear Julia,

I suppose that Sophia, as well as Pa, has explained to you that I have not been able to write, or do much of anything lately, on account of a violent pain in my right shoulder. Blistering has relieved me of the spasms which made the suffering nearly intolerable, but it is still at times in such a condition that I was afraid of using it for fear it may again be as bad as before.

I do not know whether Sophia writes to you by this mail or not. She has been ready to pay you a visit and is only waiting for Goode, from whom we have heard nothing of late. I wish she could go, both on her own account and yours, as she is very much confined for a young person.

Ma continues pretty much the same. Her cough is at times very trouble-some and is only relieved by the use of Morphine. We would all be glad if you could come up, but your reasons for not making a visit appear perfectly satisfactory to me. She says she is so tired of remaining in one place that she intends to go to White Plains next week, if she is well enough, and stay two or three days. You know Ashley — perhaps she may stay at his house, as there is no public house at the place and he lives only a mile distant.

Julien is in excellent health and behaves very well. Ma and Aunt Wales say I keep him too much confined, but I see that his health does not suffer, and his little employments vary so much that they are not irksome, and I find that leisure is the very worst thing for him, as he is sure to get into some mischief unless he is pretty constantly occupied.

Uncle [Isaac] came one day last week, and at first looked a great deal better, so much so that everybody was struck with the difference in his appearance, but he is again sick, and seems to be threatened with a fit. I presume he has been making an imprudent use of his nostrums again.

Dr. & Mrs. Rossiter have both been very unwell for a week past, and their old woman, of whom they think so much, is now at the point of death for several days with the influenza, which she caught from washing a great many clothes for Loraine during some very cold weather. Poor Loraine came yesterday to make an apology to Mrs. Rossiter, and she had made the agreement (as her own health was bad) upon the express condition that Mrs. Rossiter consented. She said she had hardly slept for a week past thinking of it, but "seem like she *was* born to bad luck." I think she is the most humble, meek, good creature I ever saw.

Tell Mr. Cumming I am truly grateful for his kind offer to come for me. As to your "attempts at consolation" as you call them, my dear Julia, they are perfectly "understood" as they are meant, as evidences of affectionate sympathy, and I assure you, you need never refrain from them by imagining that I can think you cannot feel because you have not suffered in the same way. I am sorry you think I do not bear my sorrow as becomes a Christian; I am sensible that I do nothing as a Christian should, but I endeavour to do so, and trust that slowly as the resemblance progresses, I may gradually be moulded more and more into the likeness of Him whom I try to take for my pattern. I am truly sorry to give you any pain, even reflected from my own sufferings, and so much do I desire *you* to be shielded from sorrow, that I would willingly relinquish, if that were possible, the interest you feel in mine.

Tell Annie I was very glad to get her letter and I want to see her very much indeed. My love to Mr. Cumming and the children.

Affectionately your Sister,

M.H.

Maria reports briefly to Julia about their ailing mother. Ma Bryan, she writes, cannot live long.

Maria Bryan Harford to Julia Ann Bryan Cumming

Mt. Zion

March 16, 1837 (Thursday)

My dear Julia,

As it is the opinion of the family that you will be here before a letter could reach you, and none has been prepared, but as it is possible you may not find it convenient to leave home, and in that case will be very anxious to hear from here, I have thought it best to write you a few lines before the mail closes.

Ma continues in the same state as when Pa wrote to you last week. She keeps to her bed the whole time from feebleness, and is wasted to a shadow, and it seems as if she could not live unless there should be a change for the better. She talks a great deal about her absent children and expresses a constant desire to see them.

Julien has been quite sick but is now as well as usual. He is very anxious to see you and is very much delighted to think you may come before long. I suppose you have seen Uncle [Isaac] before this, as he left here for Augusta Monday morning. Sophia talks of going down with Goode, but I do not think she ought to leave home under present circumstances.

If I thought you would certainly receive this before leaving I should write more, so must beg you to excuse the brevity of this and believe me as ever your affectionate Sister.

M.H.

Julia Cumming and her daughter Annie have just left Mt. Zion after visiting Ma Bryan. Julia has taken her son Julien back to Augusta with them.

Maria Bryan Harford to Julia Ann Bryan Cumming

Mt. Zion

April 15, 1837 (Saturday)

My dear Julia,

I have concluded to write one mail earlier than the time we spoke of when you left, as I have an opportunity of doing so, and am at present entirely free from the pain in my shoulder.

Ma has been quite comfortable yesterday and today, at least as much so as I ever see her now. She was not so much agitated at your departure as I thought she would have been. She was quite composed on hearing of Patty's death [a favorite slave] and seemed to be considerably surprised, for she said she [Patty] had been so desirous to go, and had so much faith that she should receive benefit from the steam doctor that she [Ma] herself rather thought she would.

Robert is decidedly better, Pa thinks, and so does Doctor Ridley. It will indeed be wonderful to me if he should recover, for his case has appeared so very strange that I had but little expectation of his living.

Aunt Wales I have not seen since the evening we visited her together, for we have been in such a bustle and I was so fatigued that I could not go, and the report has uniformly been that she was growing better; it was, however, found necessary to bleed her again, as she continued to raise blood and had other inflammatory symptoms. Mrs. Wiley staid with her last night and today.

We missed you and the children very much indeed. At supper there were only three of us and Sophy looked quite tearful and forlorn in the absence of her little love. I hope you got to your night's lodging safely, and found Mr. Cumming there, and well. We were all day, after you left, cleaning and arranging the dining room for Ma, and she has moved in it. She has her small bed in the same position in the room as it was upstairs and suspended from ropes, so that she can swing, but Ma does not like the motion as yet. Your room is fitted up for an eating apartment, so that everything is completely changed since you left. Poor Ma, it seems to me, is even more impatient of pain than she was, and calls for Morphine incessantly, until she seems almost stupified, and sleeps constantly.

I sent Jenny to look for your key, and she professes to have made a thorough search for it, but in vain. Creasy and Cynthia say that Celia found a key with a twine string in it which she gave to some of the men connected with the menagerie. I found the second volume of *Female Sovereigns* on Julien's table soon after you left. Julien probably in one of his absent fits a la Sir Isaac Newton carried it there for one of his own. I will send it to you in the trunk. I hope that his father will not find that his bodily constitution has suffered very materially from his mental efforts, notwithstanding his apprehensions. Pa says he thinks he had some uneasiness on that score.

Tell Annie my room looked so gloomy without her last night when I went into it that I had to read very hard to keep from thinking of her. If she had been with me, she would have waked me before I had nearly suffocated from the most horrible nightmare than even I ever had almost.

Pulaski Holt was here this morning and staid an hour or two, though I did not see him as I was very busy and in my loose gown. They report him to be in uncommonly good health and excellent spirits.

Mr. & Mrs. Bird came out this afternoon. She regretted much that you had gone without her seeing you again. She told me of the death of an acquaintance of mine in Washington, at which I was surprised and shocked — that of Mrs. [Joseph] Lovell, wife of Dr. Lovell, Surgeon General of the Army (you probably heard of *his* death which took place last Summer, and that Dr. Lawson who was next in rank [Dr. Thomas Lawson was Maria's old friend from her New Orleans days], now fills his place). Mrs. Lovell was a young and handsome woman with eleven children, but very fond of dress and company and of the highest ton in the Washington view of her. She has left ten children, and Judge [John MacPherson] Berrien [attorney general of the United States (1829–31) and United States senator (1825–29, 1841–53)] has adopted [the eleventh] one which is named John MacPherson, and is going to send him to Sparta to go to school to Mr. Moneghan.

Mrs. Matthews was very sorry that you had left without her knowing it, as she wished to have written to her sister by you.

Remember me to Mr. Cumming and the children.

Affectionately yours,
M.H.

Saturday morning.

Ma complains of being very feeble, but had a tolerable night. Says she has been looking at the hills through the window, and they certainly are the most beautiful things in the world. Robert [the house and garden servant] is not so well again. He says I must tell you he is getting better, and hopes he shall yet "live to see you." He was very much "hurt" in parting from you. I forgot to tell you to say to Mrs. McKenzie that I would have sent her book but just as I was finishing it, Pa commenced reading it and I hated to take it from him. Sometime when it is convenient, I wish you would look at the book stores and ask them if they have *Horae Solitairae*, and get Mr. Plant to send for it if he has not. [*Horae Solitairae*, written by Ambrose Serle, a Calvinist writer, was first published in 1780.] Please send me a paper of black pins and a roll of shoe ribbon, when you send the mittens, and let me know the prices of all, that I may send the money by Uncle Jacob.

Yours,

M.

Maria reports that Ma Bryan is a little better and a little stronger.

Maria Bryan Harford to Julia Ann Bryan Cumming

Mt. Zion

April 17, 1837 (Monday Night)

My dear Julia,

I received your letter this morning and was very glad to hear that you had arrived safely and found all your little family in health. I am sorry indeed to hear that *you* have that pain in the shoulder. Try Jewetts Ointment, my experience has almost persuaded me that it is a specific.

I write tonight though there is nothing in particular to tell you, but as of course you are anxious to hear often, and there will not be another mail until Thursday, I am hoping I may find some way of sending it tomorrow.

Ma has been very comfortable during the day, and sat up in her armchair for about half an hour perhaps. I wish she could be induced to sit up oftimes, for it would rest her much from the fatigue of lying. Dr. Terrill came out yesterday. He sat and talked with her for some time, and says he does not consider her case by any means as a hopeless one. He feels assured that her lungs are not materially affected, but that the mucous proceeds from some other part which is inflamed. He wishes she could allay her cough in some other way than by such frequent doses of Morphine, which he says has a tendency to render the system very torpid (and this we know is true with regard to her). He thinks a small portion of digitalis would be useful for her cough, and recommends air, and riding in the carriage as often as the weather will permit. She was quite excited in talking to him, and gave a full account of her various symptoms.

I received a letter from Maria McDonald Saturday morning. She expressed great anxiety to hear from the family, and begged me to write to her immediately, which I have done. They are going with the Miss Furmans to visit their relatives in the interior of the State, and will not be at home until July. She gave no account of Catherine's health.

We have not yet heard from Brother. Mr. Wiley set off to Alabama last week, without Pa's knowing it until he had left, who regrets very much that he did not have an opportunity of writing by him.

Robert is much better, and has been walking all about today. He went into the garden and seemed a good deal disturbed to find it in so unpromising a state as he considers it. Catherine came up this afternoon and congratulated him that he was so much better. "Yes," said he, "I've been in our gaardin and I can tell you it looks bad enough." Aunt Wales is much better; she is exceedingly reduced, and looks really ghastly, I think worse than Ma does.

We have been eating the salmon and find it very nice. Pa seems to relish it very much indeed.

I am sorry to hear that Anne is not well, as I had supposed she would be like a new creature from spending so mild a winter.

Mrs. Cumming must be excessively wearied in body and mind. I feel very much for her, and hope she may experience the fulfillment of the promise that "as thy days shall thy strength be."

Uncle Jacob left home today for Augusta. He took your red trunk, containing the bed quilt, *Memoirs of Miss Hilene*, a volume of *Female Sovereigns*, and *Robinson Crusoe*.

Tell Anny I want to see her very much and hope I shall have an opportunity of writing to her before long.

Remember me to Mr. Cumming and the children. Ma says I must tell you she is "about as common, if anything she is a little stronger." It has appeared to me as if her countenance looked better today than I have seen it in some time.

Very affectionately yours,

M.H.

Brother has returned home to be with his dying mother. Maria, after describing Ma's condition, inquires how Henry Cumming's mother, Ann Clay Cumming, supports herself now. She does not mean financially but rather physically and spiritually. Her husband, Thomas Cumming, died in 1834 and left an estate of three hundred thousand dollars on which his widow lived comfortably until her death in 1849, when she died at the age of eighty-one.

Maria Bryan Harford to Julia Ann Bryan Cumming

Mt. Zion
April 25, 1837 (Tuesday)

My dear Julia,

I sent a letter to Sparta to put in the office last Tuesday by Barefield, which I have been afraid did not reach you as early as I had hoped—as we did not hear today.

When I wrote by Saturday's mail Ma had appeared more comfortable for several days. Since the weather has changed, however, she has seemed much more unwell and is exceedingly feeble. Saturday night she was so ill, appeared in a perfect stupor and could not be roused at all, that Pa was so seriously uneasy that he proposed our sitting up, and himself, Sophy, and I sat up until nearly one o'clock. She then roused up and expressed her surprise to find anyone sitting up. I do not know what to say of her to you, but it seems impossible that she should long survive in the situation in which she now is. She lies and sleeps and this evening, for instance (though sleeping) coughs almost every breath, and yet keeps all that she raises in her throat, so that you would think she must suffocate.

Pa is again in violent distress with his tooth, and cannot get much relief from anything he tries. He often speaks in a very sorrowful manner of the afflictions of the family and seems almost borne down by them frequently.

Goode was here Saturday and Sunday. He is very well and says he intends to get leave of absence to come and stay some time.

I hope we shall hear from you tomorrow and that your family are all well. I am sorry that Julien gives you trouble again, and trust that when he gets established in home habits he will behave well.

Aunt Wales spent yesterday with us. She looks very much reduced, but says "excepting weakness she feels quite well again." She is very low spirited, as indeed she always is when she has no boarders.

Mr. Bowman wrote to Pa and I by Mrs. Allen who was in Greenesborough last week. He sent his love to you, and said that Mrs. [Harriet Byron Minor] Bowman and himself were sorely disappointed that you did not come. They looked for you for several evenings but in vain.

Brother has been to Sparta settling his business, and has paid all his debts there except to Mr. Sayre, who has taken his note without security. He is very much as he was when I wrote last. Mr. Mallory who, you know, was his college mate, spent an evening here and had a long conversation with him on the subject of religion. He told him candidly that he was very much concerned on the subject, but he could not realize that one who had wandered as far as he had should ever become a Christian.

Poor Sophia, who has certainly less tenderness of feelings toward the infirmities and troubles of others than anybody I almost ever saw, gets out of all patience with him [Brother]. She wishes he had never come from Alabama, and wonders that "*a man*" can be so weak. And as for his religious concern, it is nothing but "rightdown servile fear of dying," she says. I do not know how she can feel so, for he has really gone through a great deal of trial and has met with heavy losses, after what has been to him unexampled exertion, added to all, confinement of body and intense application of mind has left him in a state of nervous irritability which he cannot help until his health is better and which is most pitiable. He is very uncomplaining and generous and pleasant to everyone, and a body must have a heart of stone to feel harshly towards him. Dr. Sydney Brown says he has had an exactly similar case, and that it is an inflammation of the palate of his throat. He says there is a constant sensation like the sides of his throat were rubbing together. The dizziness of the head, of which he complained, has been relieved in a measure by bleeding. He has a letter since you left from Mr. Swain at Columbus. I knew you had some little solicitude about it.

How does Mrs. Cumming support herself now? I received a letter from Mrs. Carter yesterday; her family has been sick. She intends coming up this week or next to see Ma, about whom she expresses much concern.

Ma has proposed that a fast should be kept in the family, and Pa has determined on Monday next. He desired me to let you know of it, and say that if you felt inclined to unite he would be very glad to have you.

Remember me to Mr. Cumming and the children.

Yours affectionately,

M.H.

A week before her mother's death, Maria's chief concern in this letter to Julia is again with the sad and serious case of her brother Joseph.

Maria Bryan Harford to Julia Ann Bryan Cumming

Mt. Zion

April 28, 1837 (Friday)

My dear Julia,

I thought you would have heard by this time *particularly* from us all, through Brother who had made up his mind to go immediately to Augusta. But Goode who, you know, has great confidence in the professional skill of a certain Dr. Foster of Crawfordville sent him here bearing a letter of introduction. He appears to be a man of good sense and to take a probably correct view of Brother's case. He thinks his nervous system is very much deranged, which he attributes to application and anxiety of mind, and says the feeling in his throat proceeds from the ulceration of the nerves of that region, and the first thing he prescribed was an emetic which he accordingly took yesterday.

Brother is really out of health; he has fever and other symptoms which indicate it, but the gloom of his mind is more distressing than anything else. He has it impressed upon his mind, he says, that he shall become insane, and yesterday he sat and made many inquiries of me about John Bird. He has a wild glassy look from the eyes, which I do not, however, consider as an indication of anything but his internal agitation of feeling. Did I tell you what a dislike he has taken to books? He won't touch one hardly, just sits brooding all the time over his own train of ideas, and though Sophy and I have recommended different books to him, and got them, and put them into his hands to beguile him into some light and gay reading, he will not read. He does not like to be alone at all, and to give you a specimen of his complete *abandon* in every respect, last night when he was taking his Ipecac, though Catherine and Aunt Wales were here to supper, he lay upon the sopha with his bowl beside him in a chair, and in the midst of our meal, had to get up and go into the porch and throw up.

Pa is better of his toothache but he is very much broken of his rest at night, and looks cast down and out of sorts.

Since commencing this, Brother has resolved to set off this evening [for Augusta], but I will not destroy it as it will give you more knowledge of him perhaps. He will tell you about Ma—she is very low, truly.

I was a little at a loss about the length of Emily's calico frock as I have nothing to measure by, and neglected to take the length before you left. I hope the white one I send will fit her. I did not put the same sort of trimming around the neck and sleeves for I thought the narrower would look better. Please send me some needles, from No. 7 to 11 inclusive, silk for a black apron, 2 pieces of tape ordinary width, and a couple of bunches of bobbins, and two pairs of the black stockings I tried to get in Sparta, also a coarse calico for Jenny, and be sure and send me the bill, that I may send you the money by Uncle Jacob.

Brother is going, so I must stop.

Eleven days later, on May 9, 1837, Mrs. Anne Goode Bryan died in Mt. Zion at the age of sixty-two. Ma was buried in the family plot in the neighborhood cemetery, just behind the Mt. Zion Presbyterian Church. A month after her death, the Bryans' home is still racked with troubles, and Maria is kept busy nursing Pa Bryan.

Maria Bryan Harford to Julia Ann Bryan Cumming

Mt. Zion

June 7, 1837 (Wednesday)

My dear Julia,

You complain that I do not write more particularly about myself, but there is never anything cheering to say, and any discussion about myself always agitates me so much that I endeavour to avoid it as much as possible. If we could *talk* together the case might be different, but even then it is impossible for me to contemplate with anything like calmness that wreck of past happiness which I have suffered.

I would bow in submission to God's will, and if I cannot acquiesce, at least be silent and uncomplaining. I would endeavour too to interest myself more about others' happiness and others' sorrows, for I may and can, I doubt not, be of some use by doing so, and for myself I expect nothing and wish for nothing in this world but that satisfaction which flows from a sense of performing my duty to my fellow creatures and to God. I may say though that if my mind was not so perpetually clouded by doubts and fears and darkness, even on those matters where I rest my dearest hopes and indeed all my hope, I might not feel faint so entirely, as I sometimes do, under the "chastenings and rebukes of the Almighty." But perhaps this itself is but a necessary part of the discipline, and I cannot but sometimes hope that, sorrowful and unworthy as I am, that even for me there is a "rest remaining."

As it regards going to Alabama, I have never had but one thought about it since I found that Pa was determined to go. Had Ma lived to have been with him, I should have thought myself excusable in indulging my reluctance to make any movement whatever, but now broken as he is in spirits and failing in health, my own self-reproach would be intolerable, if I could do anything but seek his comfort first or if anything were to occur during his absence from home. If you could see for yourself how little dependence for comfort and judicious nursing there is from any one else, you would urge me by every consideration to go. Both [Sophia and Brother] feel, the one more than she feels for anybody else, and Brother so much that it parylizes him completely, but they are unknowing and unskillful in nursing, or administering to mind and body.

You would have been distrest had you been here the other day. Pa was exceedingly ill, his face like purple, an excruciating pain in his back and one of his limbs, and threatened with the cholic besides, there was a hard lump like a ball or knot in his bowels, and he was every moment trying to throw up. No physician could be had, and I proposed giving him an emetic, to follow out the very indications which nature seemed to point out, and he wished to take one, but Brother and Sophia were so alarmed that they implored that he might not take it. I sat myself down with such quietness as I might, to see him suffer without being able to do anything, when finally it was thought he was so sick that he had better take one. I weighed out the proportion. Brother came up to me looking like misery personified and said, "Well, I never saw so large an emetic given in my life." To gratify him I lessened the dose (but afterwards had to give more). Very soon his whole system was relaxed and the pain gone, and he in a complete perspiration, and therefore all the dangerous symptoms abated. I never saw such quantities of bile; they then became very much frightened, and begged me to give him something to stop the operation. Brother's eyes looked like distraction and him and Uncle both said his perspiration was "cold and clammy," and that he "was sinking," while I *knew* that it was not so, that his pulse was good, and every symptom just as favourable as could be desired. I gave him some anodyne [medicine for pain], and I think his fever was not so long, by four or five hours, as the previous one, or as it would have been, and he said he was easy and really comfortable after so much pain. When Brother's alarm was subdued, I said to him that I felt thankful that I knew something about sickness, and that I had some degree of self-reliance, for if it were not so, the way he acted would so completely alarm and unnerve me that I should not be able enough to do anything.

Dr. Ridley came at last, and directed that the morning of his next chill he should put a blister upon his bowels. A very large one was drawn, and he took, the succeeding day, rhubarb and cream tartar. He missed his chill, but was so exhausted by the medicine that once I was very much alarmed and did not know but he would die immediately, but he would go outdoors constantly, hot as the day was. I [gave] him some thickened milk, and gave him a little anodyne which soon, *the two,* revived him. He is much better, has no fever now, but is more reduced without any exception than I ever saw him in my life. The disease was a bilious intermittent fever, and one of the most violent kind. He has not fixed upon any time for his journey.

Brother is in a deplorable state part of the time, not so much like one insane as idiotic, and his countenance looks really destitute of intelligence at times. Yesterday he was very bad. He cried and sobbed like a child, and I could not comfort him. I asked him what ailed him. He said all was gloom, and death was staring him in the face and he had no preparation for it. I told him he ought, if he thought so, to endeavour to meet the event with manliness and decency, but that it seemed strange to look in his face and hear him talk so. He seems to me deprived of nerve and energy, utterly. I am sure he is diseased, and I *long* to have him go to the North, and that some decisive measures may be taken while there is hope. I feel no impatience towards him, though it is very trying, but *now* he cannot help himself much, I think. He worries me (his case), of course.

I am much obliged to you, my dear Julia, for your offer about my frock and, indeed, for all your kindness. I feel it far more than I can ever express, but I shall not need a new one this summer. I hope Mrs. Barth can bring my watch for I miss it very much. I am truly glad that Joseph is out of danger. I will look after Goode's shirt. Tom gave me the towel agreeable to direction, and with much emphasis. I do not know why Sophia does not write. I never am with her but at mealtimes and prayers, for she is in her room with closed doors all day, and almost every evening with Catherine.

And now, my dear Julia, does not the sight of a letter from me, and any communication with me, forewarn you of gloom? But you always request me to let you know how things are, and I know I do not exaggerate though I endeavour to state exactly how things are. When I can be the organ of more encouraging information, you cannot doubt how much more willingly I shall communicate it.

P.S. Some time when you have the opportunity, make one more effort to get my little cross. It is not the value so much as the feeling with which I regard that and my ring, the one reminds me of ———— but I need not say.

Your Sister

M.H.

Pa Bryan, recovered from his illness of "bilious fever," talks of going to his Ala-
bama place. This property, to which he took a number of slaves the December
before, was at Oakfasky (or more properly, Oakfuskee), and the nearest town was
Wetumpkee (or Wetumpka), thirty miles away, or fifteen miles north of Mont-
gomery. By 1837, this former frontier region had been opened to settlement. Maria
is in a dilemma over whether to go with Pa or to stay in Mt. Zion.

Maria Bryan Harford to Julia Ann Bryan Cumming

Mt. Zion
June 29, 1837 (Thursday)

My dear Julia,

Why did you mind what Uncle Jacob said about the journey to Alabama?
Pa and all of us are extremely sorry that you did not come [to Mt. Zion], especially as you found it possible for you to do so. Uncle Jacob knows very little
of what is going on in the family, and indeed, I am unable to say myself when
Pa will go; he has always said not until his wheat was secured, and that seems
to be a very heavy piece of work. He almost breaks himself down attending
to it, and comes home almost bent double with fatigue. Perhaps if you had
come you might have had some effect upon this Alabama arrangement, which
appears to me about as inauspicious and unpromising an undertaking as was
ever planned.

You have no idea of how few comforts there are at Oakfasky, and you
may have heard that Wetumpkee, where supplies of any kind are procured, is
thirty miles distant. When I was there last, and I believe there is no increase
of comforts, there was but one mattress, or straw bed rather, one or two little
dirty soft pillows, and I am sure not two changes of bedding. I was obliged
to raise my head with my cloak, and Pa, who slept upon the least comfortable
place, could hardly rest at all, it was so hard and the cords of the bed cut him
so much. They make no butter there as their cows are all turned out to range,
seldom or never have flour, no poultry, as the "wild varmints" like them for
their own table. There is no physician, and if one or more of us were to be
sick the prospect is rather gloomy.

If I were to urge these considerations to Pa he would immediately reply, as
he always does, when I suggest any objection to the plan, "Don't go if you

do not wish. I never desire a child of mine to do what is repugnant to their own inclination to gratify me. It is absolutely necessary that I should go, and if none of you wish to go with me, I shall go alone."

I am utterly at a loss sometimes to know what to do, for if we remain, it would probably shorten his stay, and if we do, and he should be sick, we should feel very unhappy, so that I am, and have been, in that most unpleasant situation, a dilemma as to that course which it would be most expedient and the most my duty to take. If Pa would say positively that he means to spend all the season there until frost, I should think, under all circumstances, that I ought to be with him, but he always says he don't know how long he shall stay, it will depend on circumstances.

I am sorry that Emmy has hurt herself so much. What a strange little thing she is! I wonder if her fall will have any moral consequences upon her pride?

I am much obliged to you for hunting up the breast pin. I have often felt ashamed for giving you so much trouble and for seeming so pertinacious about so apparently insignificant a thing.

Aunt Wales and Catherine expect to set off alone, the fifth of July. Samuel will meet them in Athens. They have both been sick since I wrote last, and are far more low spirited than I ever saw them. Aunt Wales says distinctly she does not think *she* will live through the summer, and I believe all Catherine's friends, who understand her situation, think that she will not. She is certainly (Brother always excepted) the most miserable person at present that I know, for *death* is, without the mere exaggeration of the phrase, the "king of terrors" to her, and she fully believes that her warning is to depart.

You may suppose from all that I tell you that times are not very cheering with us here at present. I assure you that they are not, and to add to it, Mrs. Rossiter is sick in bed, and a night or two past thought that she should not survive until morning, and in that state was alone and could not wake anybody. She dreads being left alone this summer, and plaintively inquires who will close their eyes, if either of them should die while all their old friends are absent.

It would be very agreeable to me, my dear Julia, if one of the children could always be with us, but I could not ask it, knowing the opinion that Mr. Cumming and yourself have of the unhealthiness of this place, and that there is no physician here on whom you would greatly rely. When you are willing to send any of them, I shall be gratified and shall take all imaginable care of their health, morals and mind that is in my power. I wish indeed that Mrs. Campbell could have come and spent some time with us. Pa has repeatedly said since your letter arrived, "Well, I do wish Julia had come, indeed."

I believe that I mentioned to you that Mrs. Ponce had come up for the summer, and expects Mr. Ponce and Jane Armour in a week or ten days. Sophia and Catherine are invited to a picnic given by Frank next Saturday; thirty young ladies are expected from Sparta. It is to be on the creek. All the neighbors are invited to Mr. Harris's to dine in the grove near their house on the Fourth of July, and the evening is to conclude with a party at Mrs. Kelsey's, she having happily overcome her grief sufficiently to preside on such an occasion. What think you of such a temperament as that, is it desirable or not? I hope you will write soon. Your letters now come by Wednesday's instead of Monday's mail as formerly.

Give my love to Mr. Cumming and Annie.

Affectionately yours,
M.H.

P.S. Mrs. Bird spent a day here last week, bringing with her Dalton, Eliza Spring's little girl. She is not quite so large as Annie, and is a very smart and well behaved child. I shall let you know precisely when Pa goes when it is determined.

Pa Bryan, Brother, and Sophia departed for Oakfuskee in Alabama, a six-day journey on horseback through semiwilderness, leaving Maria at home. Uncle Isaac Bryan is visiting, and he and his niece are getting along harmoniously "so far."

Maria Bryan Harford to Julia Ann Bryan Cumming

Mt. Zion
July 13, 1837 (Thursday)

My dear Julia,

You have mentioned in both of your last letters that mine did not reach you at the usual time. I cannot account for it, as I write on the same day (Thursday) and send in time for the post boy.

All have gone, Pa, Brother and Sophia; they set off Monday, and expect to reach Oakfuskee Saturday night.

Brother was exceedingly agitated when he took leave of me, for he is confident in the belief that he shall not live long, and I think he supposed we should meet no more. Notwithstanding the apprenticeship I have served to sorrow and disappointment in this world, I avoid habitually to "cast the fashion of uncertain evil," but in this case I could not but think there was an additional reason for some of that misgiving that friends always have in parting, even under the most favourable circumstances. The indications of disease have increased with Brother of late, at least they are more apparent to me. His throat is covered in the inside with I know not what to call them, but pustules or something of the kind, pushing out under the skin, and all very much inflamed. I could tell you of other unfavourable symptoms if I were speaking instead of writing. He is exceedingly languid, was very unwilling to go to Alabama, and I finally began to think it was improper for him to go, particularly as he was to ride on horseback, but the journey may do him good. I trust and hope it may — poor fellow, my heart is pained within me whenever I think of him.

Pa left us very undecided as to his return, whether in the course of a few weeks or not until fall. I never saw him more excited about everything connected with Alabama than now. Indeed, hardly anything else seems to interest him much. He has had a very nice barrel of flour prepared for you which Uncle Jacob, who starts this morning, is to take with him.

Sophia told me to tell you that she had been reading the "three eras in the life of women and had become acquainted with Lady Sophia Barron." [*Three Eras of Women's Life*, by Elizabeth Elton Smith, was published in 1836.] I saw Mrs. Rossiter yesterday, and we were talking about you, and she desired me to give her "affectionate love" to you when I wrote. Her health is very bad. She is exceedingly weakened by a constant diarrhea, and that is so much the attendant of old people, and so often takes them out of the world, that I sometimes think she will not live through the summer. One thing strange for her is that when she lies down, or I think she says *sits* down, a moment alone, she falls asleep. I am struck, when I see her and think of her, with the truth of your remark that she has survived most of her old friends, and now especially that Pa and Aunt Wales are gone [out of town], she seems like the last of her generation lingering upon the stage, for the Doctor is so childish and so very deaf that he is hardly a protector or companion to any great degree. Added to this, since the affliction of her eyes, she can not work, and is deprived of that great solace to her solitary hours as to anybody's that is fond of it, I mean reading. But she has a "hope full of immortality," and her time here is undoubtedly short. I often in my own mind apply these lines to her, which I have so much admired since I came across them.

> Pilgrim, is thy journey drear
> Are its lights extinct forever?
> Still suppress the rising fear
> God forsakes the righteous, *never!*
>
> Storms may rage around thy path;
> All the ties of life may sever,
> Still amid the fearful Scaith,
> God forsakes the righteous, *never!*
>
> Pain may rack thy aching frame,
> Health desert thy couch forever.
> Faith still burns with deathless flame,
> God forsakes the righteous, *never!*

[In fact, Mrs. Rossiter does not die until 1845 at the age of eighty; her husband died four months after her death at the age of ninety-two.]

I send Emmy some gooseberries. I wished that I had had a large jar to send you, but Robert had but few, which I preserved, thinking they would be very nice in sickness from the agreeable acid taste they have.

Uncle is here and we all get along very harmoniously together *so far,* and I have no doubt but we shall continue to do so if he can see as much economy pursued in the use of articles of flour, candles etc. as he desires, and I have no disposition to disturb him by a lavish expenditure.

If you have any books that you think would interest me, French or English, please send them, and they shall be carefully returned after I have read them. Write soon.

Affectionately yours.

A month later Maria is still alone in Mt. Zion.

Maria Bryan Harford to Julia Ann Bryan Cumming

Mt. Zion

August 9, 1837 (Wednesday)

My dear Julia,

I am sorry to hear so bad an account of the health of your family. Entire freedom from care and anxiety is not often our portion in this life, and the burden of every one is so much increased by the corruption of our hearts and by the want of faith and patience and forbearance and humility. What a blessed thing if we are among the number towards whom it may be said, "All the paths of the Lord are mercy and truth."

I did not understand Pa's letter in the way in which you did. At any rate I have not inferred from that, that he would return so soon; indeed, I shall not be surprised if he does not come back in a month or more.

Tell Annie that I wish her letters would come along, notwithstanding the bad spelling. She must receive comfort from the reflection that Miss Theodosia Burr [Aaron Burr's daughter] had to *learn* to spell as well as herself.

Do you remember seeing an account in the papers about a year ago of the pirate who was executed in Mobile, and who said he had boarded the vessel in which it was known that Mrs. [Theodosia Burr] Alston had sailed, and that she was killed? What a fate for one so interesting and happy, or indeed for anyone, but the imagination has so much to do with the sympathy we feel for sufferings at a distance from us, and I have always had a peculiar feeling for Mrs. Alston and her husband [Governor Joseph Alston of South Carolina], both so much attached, and so highly endowed, and so unfortunate.

Mrs. Rossiter is still very unwell. I believe she thinks she shall not live long. She is so exceedingly nervous now, as I think I have before mentioned to you, that it is painful to be with her, and her mind weakened proportionately.

You were so kind as to tell me to mention any book I would like to read. If you still have that volume by the author [the Reverend Charles B. Taylor (1797–1875)] of *Records of a Good Man's Life* please send it.

Mrs. Matthews has spent two or three nights with me since I have been alone, but not a day, and, indeed, seems very much indisposed to leaving home. She is now very busily engaged quilting and I presume I shall not see her until that is finished, for whatever she has to do she does it with her might. Do you ever hear of any friend who has work to put out? It would be a great act of Charity to secure such things for her if you could do it, and I would undertake myself to manage the transportation part. She gets nothing to do sometimes for months, and her spirits seem greatly affected by it.

My best love to Mr. Cumming and the children.

M.M.H.

When this letter to Julia was written, Goode Bryan, who had resigned his army commission in 1835, had a job as a civil engineer for the first railroad being built in the state of Georgia. Goode Bryan and his construction crew had been working in the vicinity of Crawfordsville, fifteen to twenty miles from Mt. Zion. The Georgia Railroad will cut the traveling time between the Cummings in Augusta and the Bryans in Mt. Zion from forty-eight hours by carriage to twelve hours by train.

Maria Bryan Harford to Julia Ann Bryan Cumming

Mt. Zion
August 23, 1837 (Thursday)

My dear Julia,

I received a letter from you on Monday dated the 14th, and Annie's also by the same mail.

Maria and Catherine McDonald did not come here as Julia tells me that the Miss Brisbanes were very anxious to reach Scottsborough, although Catherine was so much fatigued that she said she did not know how she could travel all night.

I did not expect you would like Mr. Bryan [a Bryan cousin from Alabama] though, in justice, you must lay aside your suspicions about his *temperance,* as his complexion was occasioned from riding on horseback in Alabama on one of those hot days in July, and I have reason to believe that he has no excesses of any kind except an excessive love of money, and that, I believe, the world in general is allowed to call a tolerably respectable excess. He was indeed pertinacious, as you say, if he still continued to talk about my going to the North with him. When ever he mentioned the subject I replied as if I could not believe him in earnest in speaking on the subject, and when his return to it became annoying, I finally said, "I have not money enough to take me to Charleston, and certainly could not afford a Northern tour if I was inclined to go."

Mr. Joseph Cumming [Henry Cumming's older brother who lived in Savannah], I think, affords the best practical comment of the sustaining power of his faith of any body I have almost ever known. I do believe his cheerfulness, under all the various changes he has undergone, arises from *his faith,* and that "he endures as seeing Him who is invisible." *I* have a faith which carries me to the full and realizing conviction that I am a stranger and a pilgrim and, in the words of John Wesley's hymn (is it not?), can say, "Nothing on earth I call my own, a Stranger to the world unknown." But mine is not the cheering, exhilarating conscience of the wayfarer who feels that the celestial city is soon to burst upon his sight, and that its eternal towers are his bourne and his final home. I should like much to see him [Joseph Cumming], and have often thought of him since his pecuniary troubles commenced, for I know from close observation of their effects how fretting and care-consuming those things are to men.

Uncle Jacob did not bring me the box which you mentioned, and I am not able to find out where it is. I am sorry the preserves turned out so badly, but think if you had boiled them over they might have done for ordinary times. I am glad you like the pickles.

I expect to set off in the course of an hour for Crawfordsville to see Goode. I got a short note from him saying he was sick, and Swinney, who brought it, thinks he is *quite sick* and advises me to go and see him as "Every body," he says, "there is sick," and Peters [Richard Peters from Pennsylvania, an engineer who later became the first superintendent of the Georgia Railroad and a prime developer of Atlanta] has gone to the North. I have borrowed Mrs. Allen's carriage, and if he is well enough to come, shall return in the morning. If not, I shall remain with him as long as is necessary. How much I have thought of Ma since I heard it, but from all these anxieties she is free now.

Tell Annie I was very much pleased with her letter and shall answer it soon. Do not give yourself any uneasiness about hearing from Goode, as I shall write every mail while any uncertainty exists.

Affec. your Sister,
Maria H.

Maria Bryan Harford to Julia Ann Bryan Cumming

Mt. Zion
August 27 [1837]

My dear Julia,

It has been so many days since I wrote, and will be a day or two before the regular time of the mail, that I have concluded to send to Sparta lest you might be uneasy.

Goode has been very sick since I wrote, and is still very unwell and suffers, but the Dr. assures him he is out of danger. I believe I mentioned in my last that it was considered a disease of the lungs or chest, attended with bilious and inflammatory symptoms. He is very dejected indeed, but is as patient as could be expected. Uncle is so unwell that he cannot give me much assistance in nursing him, but as yet I continue pretty well, though fatigued.

Will you please send me by the first opportunity a box of Morrison's pills or Mirkin's (Plant has them). I have sent, by Uncle Jacob, four times — but in vain. They are for Mrs. Matthews. Please destroy my last letter, for the charges of life are so great that family affairs ought to be taken care of. I have much more to say but the messenger waits.

Affectionately yours,
M.H.

Julia Cumming, with her brother Goode, who had been ill, and her sister-in-law Sarah Cumming, were traveling north by ship, and this letter from Maria in Mt. Zion is sent to New York. Pa and Sophia have just returned from Alabama. They were away from Mt. Zion for two months, from July 10 to September 10.

Maria Bryan Harford to Julia Ann Bryan Cumming

Mt. Zion

September 14, 1837 (Thursday)

My dear Julia,

If I had not known that you would not have left Augusta until this week I should have written to you at my usual time. I presume that today you are on the water, and that your heart is heavy enough. I trust, however, that the improvement and pleasure you will meet with will compensate you for the effort you have made, and for the pain and self-denial it has cost you to leave your family.

Pa and Sophia arrived Sunday morning to breakfast. They could not reach home the night before in consequence of some accident that delayed them on the road. Pa says I must tell you that he is still very uncertain about going [permanently] to Alabama, and I will add that he does not appear to be near as anxious about it as he did. He seems to be willing that Providence should decide, and as if he would be contented, whatever may take place. His health is very good and he seems to be cheerful, though at times very much over-come, and says he is almost a child, and that it requires all his exertions to preserve anything like equanimity of feeling. But he seems to be very happy in his mind as it regards his religious hopes and comforts, and often says without that he should be, of all men, most miserable.

Sophia is, I think, out of spirits. She weeps frequently whenever she mentions Ma or hears her name spoken. Her [love] affair is in no progress at all. I told her of the report you mentioned and she said she was very sorry you denied it. She says I must tell you that she is very sorry you did not send some of the children here, and that she will write to you soon.

I hope Goode's health and spirits will improve and that we shall hear from you both frequently. Catherine, we learn, is again very unwell. Mrs. Rossiter is a little better, though, since I wrote last. It was thought that she and the Doctor would not stand it long. He has had a violent attack of colera morbus.

Remember me affectionately to Sarah and Goode.

Yours truly,

M.H.

Chapter Eight

AUNT MARIA

"I willingly assume the charge of the children. . . ."

A hiatus of four months occurs here in Maria's letters. Julia has returned to Augusta from her New York visit; Goode is back on the Georgia Railroad construction job at Greensboro, and Annie is studying with her Aunt Maria in Mt. Zion.

Maria Bryan Harford to Julia Ann Bryan Cumming

Mt. Zion
January 18, 1838 (Thursday)

My dear Julia,

We have not had a line from any of you since Uncle arrived and I have, therefore, feared that you had not received my letter written last Thursday.

I presume, from what Major Nelson told us, that you must have been very much disappointed that Sophia did not go last week, but it was well that she did not set off on the appointed day, as it appeared from a letter received from Goode that he was, at that very time, in Greenesborough. My impression is that she is either expecting a letter or a certain individual in *propria personae*, and therefore is reluctant to leave home; at any rate she seems to me very much discomposed about something. All of which I beg may be *entre nous*.

214

Pa spent Monday night at Scottsborough. They were all in usual health and prosperity, Maria still at Macon.

I hope Henny is improving. Lindy has been here, and Pa has written to her Master that he is willing to buy her, and Tom seems as happy as can be with his Hannah and Pensimah. [In Maria's letter of December 29, 1836, Lindy's master refused to sell her to Pa.]

We are anxiously expecting to hear from you.

Your affectionate Sister,
M.H.

Presumably, Pa and his grandchildren, Annie, aged eleven, and Alfred, aged nine, have just made the trip up from Augusta on the railroad as far as the train was built. There was evidently some accident during the journey but no injury to them. Maria is to take charge of the Cumming children and their education.

Maria Bryan Harford to Julia Ann Bryan Cumming

Mt. Zion
January 25, 1838 (Thursday)

My dear Julia,

One thing after another has occurred today to cause me to put off writing to you until it is so late that I shall only have opportunity to send you a few lines.

Pa and the children arrived safely about seven o'clock and I was very much disturbed, as you were certainly, on hearing of their accident. But there was, and is, great cause for thankfulness that they received no injury. They were very cold but a warm supper soon restored them to comfort and talkativeness. Annie has a cold which, she tells me, she had taken before she left Augusta. I have given her a dose of salts and hope it will not occasion her much inconvenience. Alfred went to school yesterday morning, accompanied by his Grandpa and was introduced in form. As he had muddied his clothes very much, I told him to put on his best suit, as it was always desirable to make a favourable impression at first and I hoped, in his case, that good conduct would confirm what good clothes began.

Pa has gotten all the books which Mr. Martin [the current Mt. Zion head-master] wished him to have, as they were at the stores. But I can neither buy or borrow for Annie and must, therefore, request you to send her Smith's grammar, with the books Sophia has on a memorandum, and her slate. Pa says Hale is his agent in Warrenton [twenty miles from Sparta, and the largest town near the end of the tracks]. You can, therefore, send the articles in a box on the railroad to his care, and Uncle Jacob, who will be in Warrenton Monday night, can get them.

I willingly assume the charge of the children's clothes and all, and shall endeavour to contribute to their happiness and improvement while they stay, of which, I trust, Mr. Cumming and yourself will feel assured, so that you may in some degree be compensated for their absence from you.

I am very much obliged to you for the ointment and the frock, and for your various kindnesses of feeling and expression. Give my love to all. Tell Sophia we miss her very much. Mrs. Rossiter has been dangerously sick, but is better.

Yours affectionately,

M.H.

The railroad has evidently speeded up the mail considerably. Maria received Julia's letter the day after it was written. Maria reports that she has had "a little scene" with her pupil and niece, Annie.

Maria Bryan Harford to Julia Ann Bryan Cumming

Mt. Zion

February 1, 1838 (Thursday)

My dear Julia,

Your letter came much more expeditiously than it usually does, as it arrived yesterday morning, the day after it was written.

I was sorry that Pa had so bad a day to go down, and the weather still continues so that he will not be able at present to attend to his business with much comfort to himself.

You are by this time, I suppose, perfectly relieved about Annie and Alfred who are both at this time in excellent health and spirits. The former, I believe, is astonished at herself that she does not have occasions of gloom, as I hear her commenting upon her feeling so pleasantly and good-natured. I hope I shall get her set to rights before Sophia comes, so that I need have no gloomy looks, when I feel myself obliged to exercise that painful and necessary prerogative of a good government being a "terror to evil doers as well as a praise to them that do well."

She (Sophy, I mean) often remarks upon my being affected by the looks and manners of people beyond measure. I confess that a cloud upon the human face divine affects my spirits much more unpleasantly than even clouds and storms on the face of Heaven, for I don't know always what the former portends, whereas I am assured in the latter case that though clouds and darkness are round about, that righteousness and judgment support His throne Who rules the elements.

Yesterday morning Annie and I had a little scene. She generally studies her lessons in my room, and while I was in there after breakfast, I saw under the cushion of my chair Judge Clayton's *Mysterious Picture* [a novel written by Augustin Smith Clayton (1783–1839) and published in 1825]. You remember the book perhaps. I immediately judged that she had placed it there to read during the time I supposed her getting her lessons, and called her and inquired if it was so. She said it was. I told her how sorry I was that she would allow herself to do those things, to attempt to deceive and so forth and so forth, and ended by telling her if she did not have confidence enough in my regard for her to suppose that I was willing to allow her to do any reasonable thing upon her asking permission, and not feel under the necessity of hiding and concealing her movements in a way displeasing to God, and highly dishonorable in the sight of man, I was indeed truly sorry. She did not seem angry but was mortified and cried, and said she would not do the like again.

At the usual time of day she came to me with the best lessons I ever heard from her, and one of the best because of the hardest I ever heard from anybody. She had committed [to memory] the names of the 15 Saxon Kings of England with the years they came to the throne and the year they died, and all the names of the successive Kings of England of the different houses until George III, without missing one word.

Catherine was very well satisfied with your arrangements about her things — do have the waist made large enough to allow her some comfort. She looks wretchedly and weeps frequently but on the whole, I think, is pleased with her prospects.

Tell Sophia she must not forget thread. I forgot to put down on the memorandum a white wash brush and some table salt. Ask her to get me a veil of the black bobinet.

I received Mr. Cumming's letter last Saturday, but need not answer it particularly. I am gratified at the trust he is willing to repose in me, and hope you both believe shall exert myself to the utmost of my power to discharge it well, and am sure you both know shall do it willingly and cheerfully. Remember me affectionately to him and to the children, and Sophia.

I remain yours truly,
M.H.

P.S. Aunt Wales says anything can be sent by Mr. Thomas's waggon.

Brother is on his way to Washington, D.C., where he became the legal agent for the Creek Indians of Alabama and pressed their claims against the federal government. Later he became part owner of the Metropolitan Hotel on Pennsylvania Avenue, a few blocks below the Capitol.

Maria Bryan Harford to Julia Ann Bryan Cumming

Mt. Zion
March 14, 1838 (Wednesday)

My dear Julia,

I received your letter this morning, and write in the hope of having an opportunity of getting this off before the regular Thursday mail from this place.

I was surprised to hear that Brother was still with you as when he left here he seemed very anxious to arrive at Washington as soon as possible.

I do not know what occasioned Pa's threat to Alfred, as I did not hear it, but I heard last night a very affectionate conversation between them (Alfred by his eyes only). Someone was reporting to Pa an expression of Alfred of how much he loved him, and Pa replied that he could "truly say the affection was reciprocated." Here Alfred's course of thought was impeded, as it easily is, by the difficulty of understanding so long and hard a word. This produced a reiteration of affectionate regard in language more intelligible but not less tender.

I hope you have received Annie's letter written last Saturday before this time. I mentioned to you in my postscript that she had a bad cold. I gave her some salts and she is now much better. She is like you in one respect, when she is a little indisposed her nitting is her greatest solace, and she is now sitting by me plying her needles most indefatigably.

Have you heard anything from Margaret Bailey, within a day or two? I received a letter from Savannah mailed the 9th. The first two pages was a most affectionate letter from Margaret, expression after expression of the kindest interest, but blotted and scratched out and corrected and not signed. The third page contained a postscript from Dr. Richardson, saying that she had left that letter for me undirected when she was taken with a brain fever, that her friends and medical attendants had the day before despaired of her life, but that he considered her, at the moment of his writing, a little better. I hope and trust, for the sake of her husband and children and mother, that her life may be spared: they are of course the first to be thought of, but truly I should be deeply grieved at losing Margaret, for I have always loved her very much and am confident that her regard for me is equally strong, considering how much nearer and more engrossing ties she has. She said in the first part of her letter that the last day of the year she had been thinking a great deal about me, and had pleased herself with the belief that we should meet and love each other in a better world. All my hopes with regard to almost everything are reserved for that place, for in this I can adopt the language of the Psalmist, and apply to myself what is said of God's people, "Thou feedest them with the bread of tears and givest them tears to drink in great measure." [Margaret Bailey, who had married Dr. Cosmo P. Richardsone of Savannah, died in that spring of 1838.]

Pa is very busily engaged in getting off your meat this morning. He says it is very fine indeed. He wishes you to send up the things you have procured immediately to the care of Mr. Hale, as he says he has frequent opportunities to get articles from Warrenton. Uncle Jacob leaves home today for that place. He feels very badly about his wife and says he does not know that she will live. She wishes very much to go to Dr. Durham's, and I suppose she and Henny will go sometime this week. The latter is one of the greatest sufferers I almost ever saw. As soon as night comes on she sends to me, and sometimes repeatedly in the evening, to please to give her something to cure her pain. The only thing which seems to give her a temporary relief is morphine and peppermint. She has fallen away to a mere shadow and it is distressing to see her.

I did not give you money for Julia's [Iverson] shoes for I forgot to, and also forgot to send (which I intended to by Brother), but be so kind, if you please, as to keep a strict account of everything for which you are obliged to advance money for either of us, and I will send you the amount the first opportunity which I consider a safe one. Remember me kindly to Mr. Cumming and believe me very truly and affectionately yours.

M.M.H.

P.S. Martin [at Mt. Zion Academy] has given orders for his boys to learn a speech and [nine-year-old] Alfred has pitched upon [Thomas Campbell's] *Hohenlinden* because his Uncle Goode spoke it—so we have gestures and "Iser rolling rapidly" in abundance at present. Pa is going to Dr. Durham's and to the factory for cloth, and as Henny is found unable to go, I am going with him, and Annie with us for the excursion and to see a cotton factory. We shall be back tomorrow.

Yours truly.

March 15, 1838 (Thursday)

P.S. I left this with Sophia to be sent and she has had no opportunity. I therefore open it to tell you we had a safe journey and arrived home last night. Annie and her grandfather were in a romp the whole way and to judge by her appetite she must have felt uncommonly well. Dr. Durham thinks Henny's a bad case. I found your bandbox for which I am very much obliged to you indeed. The shoes fit and I thank you kindly for the bonnet. I am very much troubled with one eye which is greatly inflamed, and part of the time has a dreadful pain which is communicated by sympathy to my head. I have had some misgivings that I was going to lose it, but hope the use of calomel will relieve me. Don't be uneasy about nitting Alfred's socks. He has a new pair done and two more in progress. Miss [Harriet] Martineau [the British writer who toured the United States and published *Society in America* in 1837] has done me the honour to record [in her book] a conversation I had with her. All are well with the exceptions stated. What a sad affair that duel in Congress is. I cannot keep the bereaved wife out of my mind. [The "duel in Congress" to which Maria referred occurred February 24, 1838, when Representative Jonathan Cilley of Maine was killed just outside the District of Columbia by Representative William J. Graves of Kentucky. Cilley left a wife and three children.]

Maria, although recently ill, continues to take charge of her niece and nephew and Julia Iverson, her cousin's daughter.

Maria Bryan Harford to Julia Ann Bryan Cumming

Mt. Zion
May 1, 1838 (Tuesday)

My dear Julia,

I do not know whether Sophia mentioned to you in any of her letters how very unwell (I mean sick) I have been. Indeed, for more than two weeks I have felt so wretchedly that I have not sat up a great deal of the time, and slight fevers almost every day and restless sleepless nights have reduced me considerably, and made me so weak that I am not able to do anything, and writing especially is a very great effort to me.

We had begun to feel quite uneasy about you before the arrival of your letter, fearing that yourself or some of the family were sick, and the news of poor dear little Emmy's sickness was a confirmation that our uneasiness was not unfounded. Sophia took a hearty cry when she heard of it for she had been talking about her, if possible, more than usual. I hope we shall hear again tomorrow that she is in her ordinary health. You said nothing about yourself, whether you were benefitted by your journey.

I am sorry you did not see Mrs. Bailey [Margaret Bailey Richardsone's mother]. We had heard she was going to Savannah to live and were in hopes that you would meet there. So Margaret's baby has followed its mother so soon! It is doubtless for the best, since it has been ordered so by Him to whom it was consecrated, but I had pleased myself with the idea that the two little girls would be a source of great comfort to Mrs. Bailey and in time almost, if not quite, supply Margaret's loss. Poor Richardson! "Ses beaux jours sont passès," I have no doubt; not that I take it for granted that he will necessarily always feel so miserable as he does now, but under almost any circumstances imaginable things will be so different. Margaret had such a decided control, mild as she was, over him, that she was the cause of his being less eccentric, and more happy and respectable. [In June 1839, Dr. Richardsone married Elizabeth Bailey, the twenty-four-year-old sister of his first wife, Margaret.]

Your children are very well, and happier than common today, for I have begged Martin out of a holiday for Alfred, and I had promised it to Julia and Annie for a long time past. They have been in the woods for flowers, and are to fit up the summer house and take their cake, candy, strawberries, etc. in the open air at six o'clock.

Alfred has had a very bad bile [boil] but has borne the pain very patiently and manfully. His fortitude in this respect and general good behaviour was the subject of conversation a day or two since, and he was standing by Pa, whose heart overflowing with the subject, he vented his affection and complacence with several very hard taps and as it happened upon the afflicted part. This was almost too much for Alfred, for it really hurt him greatly, but not so much as it probably did his Grandpa.

I was very sorry to find Uncle Jacob had actually set off to Augusta without my knowledge, as I intended (though you will not answer my request for a jar), to send you some pickles that I have for a long time had in reserve for you, and the volumes of Miss Martineau's book which, as a whole, has rather lowered her in my opinion. I have been wishing during this languid and lazy time of mine, that I had the book you promised me, *Stories of the Irish Peasantry* [by Mrs. S. C. Hall and published in Edinburgh], for really I cannot understand anything that requires much attention, and were it not a family weakness to imagine something was coming to the head, I should enlarge upon the very uncomfortable state in which mine is most of the time.

Perhaps Sophia told you that Aunt Wales has heard that Catherine [Wales, who married Alexander Erwin on February 28, 1838, and now lives in Clarkesville, Georgia] has been very sick, so much so as to have required the constant attendance of two physicians. She was well enough to write, but expressed herself very desirous to come here and stay while Mr. Erwin was absent on his Charleston trip. Aunt Wales herself is not very well but is in good spirits and appears to enjoy life as much as I ever knew her. Mr. Chamberlain demonstrated a reasonable degree of pleasure at the improvement of his boys (though he remarked, en passant, that they were "always exceedingly well behaved children") and this pleased her enough to animate her to new diligence if that were possible.

Mr. Iverson passed through Sparta the other day without calling, but wrote a letter to [his daughter] Julia inclosing $15. which, with 20 he sent to her some time ago, is all that he has allowed for purchasing her clothes etc., making them, and buying books etc. It is rather trying to be so exceedingly cramped in this matter as I am, as it almost compels me to have all the trouble in making her clothing, as well as other cares in relation to her, but I should endure everything of the sort with infinitely more cheerfulness if I had more encouragement in her own character.

Mrs. Rossiter is about as usual in health and spirits. Mrs. Matthews has gone to spend some time in Sparta at Mrs. Simmon's during the absence of the latter in Savannah.

I have been obliged to alter Annie's thin frocks as they are all too small for her, but I think she will not need any additional clothes until she goes home.

Please tell Uncle Jacob to get ½ pound of hops without fail, as we are entirely out.

I suppose you are too much worn out with your late journey to think with any pleasure of taking another soon, but I hope you bear in mind a promise to visit us somewhere about this time. I assure you we do, and very often talk of it. Try and get Mr. Cumming away from his business for a few days. I assure you it would do him good. I was on the point of writing to him the other day to make the request which Pa did in my name, but the sad cause which makes it my business to undertake such affairs almost overwhelms me whenever I attempt anything of that sort.

Wm. Bryan, who has always been determined to have Dinah, when he found there was no longer any reason or excuse for detaining her, sent her to Mr. Parker, who has written to me, as he says, at the request of Dinah, to beg that she might be permitted to stay as she had married and did not like to leave her husband. Mr. Bryan, I suppose, thought this plan would be effectual, and that touching me upon my religious scruples was assailing me at my weak point [of not separating slave husband and wife] and would complete his purpose. I hope *that* is my weak point, or rather, I hope it is my strong one, at any rate that I would make any sacrifice of interest to duty, but Dinah has a husband every few months, and I conceive it is far more for her good to bring her back, than to leave her to the uncertainty she would always be in there from changing owners.

Give my love to Mr. Cumming and believe me affectionately yrs.

M.H.

Maria Bryan Harford to Julia Ann Bryan Cumming

Mt. Zion
June 27, 1838 (Wednesday)

My dear Julia,

I have only a moment to write as Tom is going into Sparta, and am so unwell that I cannot hold my pen steady as you may perceive. That will account for the very short letter. The object principally is to ask you to go to Mr. Latimer's, Edgar's, or anywhere else, or send for Pa, to have a piece of unbleached homespun of the quality of your children's drawers, and another piece of the same quality bleached (for linings etc.) & vest patterns for Robert, and 7 yds. of brown linen, for a common suit for him, & 6 dozen buttons for shirt bosoms—that it may be sent up by Alfred.

The children are well. Pa has been quite sick with a diarrhea, and I began to grow seriously uneasy as his voice was weak & hollow & his eyes sunk, and he had fallen off considerably. Sophia & I begged him in vain to send for a physician. At last, at our urgent entreaties, he went to Dr. Barksdale's shop, & told him his disease, and asked advice. He gave him medicine which immediately relieved him, & he appears better & in better spirits than for ten days.

My love to all.

Ever affectionately yours,
M.H.

Pa says that Sophia and Tommy will be at the railroad Monday to meet Mr. C. I am always uneasy, now you are so unwell, to send to you for anything, fearing it gives you much trouble, but the stores here are so unreasonably

high that Pa almost refuses to get anything from them. The box sent by
Mr. Cumming, tonic mix & hops, have arrived. Ask Mr. C. to get at Barretts
1 lb. supercarbonate of soda. Pa has the heartburn a great deal & it is the only
thing that relieves him at all.

M.H.

*There is a three-month gap in Maria's letters to Julia. Maria has three of Julia's
children under her wing in Mt. Zion, Annie, Alfred, and now Julien, who is eight
years old. Julia is pregnant with her seventh child.*

Maria Bryan Harford to Julia Ann Bryan Cumming

Mt. Zion
September 25, 1838 (Tuesday)

My dear Julia,

I have just found out that I shall have an opportunity of sending this to
Sparta, and I write you a few lines to say that Julien is still growing better
and has just finished part of a custard which he has had great comfort in
eating. He had been looking for his Father every day until his letter arrived
Monday morning. He is a good little boy and as patient a one as I ever saw.
You seem to have been very uneasy about Julien from Mr. Cumming's and
Sophia's account, and I am not at all surprised that you should have been so,
but I can assure you that every attention and all the nursing by night and by
day that his case required has been constantly rendered to him. I think he has
been drooping for a long time, and it is my opinion that his liver was a little
deranged in its functions, as well as that he was troubled with worms. Indeed,
it seems to me that his sickness is very much such as one as Annie had at
nearly his age, and I hope it will end by confirming him with better health
and a better constitution than he ever has had before.

Alfred is perfectly well, and has been as kind and attentive and useful as
ever a child could be; indeed, he actually helps me more in the trouble of
housekeeping, or as much, as Tom does.

But I cannot write you a long letter for I have just returned from
Dr. Whitton's, where I sat up the whole of last night without a moment's
repose. Mrs. Whitton has been at the point of death with an inflammatory

attack of the liver. She has been in terrible anguish of spirit for her spiritual condition, more, I believe, than any one I ever saw. She sent for Mr. Hooker [the regular Mt. Zion minister] but he was not at home, and Mr. [William] Erwin, Catherine's brother-in-law, went in his place, and has seemed to be the instrument of imparting a great deal of comfort to her. I left her this morning much better and very composed in her mind, determined, as she says, "if God spares her life, to be no longer a cumberer of the ground as she has been."

Goode is at home now. He is in good health and spirits. I do not know what his purposes are, for I have not heard him allude to any plan whatever. He will leave Saturday.

Tell Mrs. Henry and Mrs. Campbell that their present arrived safely and I am obliged to them. The Dr. and Mrs. Rossiter was obliged to them for the gifts they received, and Mary Kelsey sends her love and many thanks to Mrs. Campbell and Fenwick.

Catherine has been very dangerously ill, but is better, can not come down, but is most urgent to have her mother go there, to which Aunt Wales has consented to do next month.

Tell Sophia I am pleased with the prospect of a cap from her hands, and very much obliged to her for thinking of me.

Give my best love to her, Mr. Cumming and Annie.

Very affectionately yours,
M.M.H.

Goode Bryan, aged twenty-six, is in Mt. Zion with a "severe attack of bilious fever." He is still working as a survey engineer with the Georgia Railroad. Because of his illness, Goode cannot any time soon return to the construction crew now located somewhere between Greensboro and Madison, Georgia.

Maria Bryan Harford to Julia Ann Bryan Cumming

Mt. Zion
October 1, 1838 (Monday)

My dear Julia,

I write you a line or two as I will not have another opportunity by the mail from this place until Thursday.

Julien is improving. Alfred is quite well, but Goode has a regular and pretty severe attack of bilious fever and is, as usual, very much agitated and alarmed about himself. Indeed, his peculiar constitution makes his situation alarming when he is much sick, for usually, and at present, there is a great deal of inflammation about him, an exceedingly flushed face, high pulse, and a cough, and as soon as there is an attempt to bleed him, or rather as soon as he is bled, or much of an operation takes place upon his bowels, his pulse sinks and he becomes alarmingly faint.

I shall have to stop for Philoclea Carey is down stairs and I hear her asking for me.

I hope you do not suffer quite as much as you did. I wish you were well enough to write a letter to poor Catherine. She is most dreadfully low spirited and thinks she shall die. Aunt Wales wishes to sell her house, and Pa has asked her to live here. She will go during the winter to Clarkesville. Tell Sophia she must be composed about it and always be willing for Pa to do what he considers his duty. Aunt Wales is these times one of the most unhappy persons I know, lonesome and disconsolate, and imagines herself forsaken by the world and her friends.

No news from Brother.

Julia, is there any one that you can get to make some shirts for Pa? He is very bad off, and I have so much nursing, and preserving etc., company, and no seamstress, that though I have begun him some I don't know when they will ever be done. If you and Sophia can get them done for him, he will settle it all, I'm sure, and you can get the material at Latimer's. He is well but is constantly miserable about Mr. Wiley's affair.

Love to all. I am sorry to send a letter so little agreeable intrinsically and extrinsically—but it can't be helped. Ask Sophia if she has forgotten my request about the stocking.

Your affectionate Sister—
M.H.

Maria, in the midst of quoting Scripture to her brother-in-law to prove that God alone is the source of every good and perfect gift, ruefully alludes to her widowhood in terms of having "nobody to please by the delicacy of [her] ancle." Here appears for the first time the name of the man she was to marry next — Alva Connell (or Connel, as it was sometimes spelled).

Dr. Rossiter was fined fifty dollars in court for his assault upon Mr. Gilbert. Probably his age (eighty-five) and his Revolutionary War record saved him from a hundred-dollar fine.

Maria Bryan Harford to Henry H. Cumming

October 15, 1838 (Monday)

My dear Mr. Cumming,

I received your letter and packet this evening by Mr. Williams, for which I return you many thanks. We are taught to believe that everything good that we receive in life comes from the benevolent Parent of us all, and however gratefully our emotions may flow out to those who are his instruments of good to us, they must also ascend to Him. I have often comforted myself by a promise recorded in Scripture to all who try to serve God, "Thy bread shall be given thee and thy water shall be sure," that then, at least, I had an assurance that the wayside expenses of my pilgrimage would be paid, but I shall begin to think myself greatly in the wrong by understanding this in its strict and literal sense. I observe a difference, as you remarked, but all suit me well as I have nobody to please by the delicacy of my ancle, that is a matter of less consequence than comfort and durability. I am glad to hear that Goode and Julien are doing so well. I miss the little boys more even than I expected. Jenny continues sick, and has had to be bled repeatedly and blistered. I can hardly say what ails her, though it appears to be a nervous attack, and Connel, who has been to see her today, says he does not apprehend fever. I was sent for to go and see Mr. Wiley's family this afternoon, and I had not much more than got there, before Wellington came riding post haste after Pa and I, saying that she [Jenny] was "most dead." I went home immediately, in considerable alarm as you may suppose, but found things not so bad as was represented.

I never saw a family in more distress than Mr. Wiley's in my life. He has been dangerously ill for several days, Mrs. Wiley also, a servant girl, and two of their children. Their youngest child, a boy of six years of age, died about ten o'clock today. The parents could not see it, nor each other to speak a word of comfort in their mutual grief to one another. They have sent for Pa and

I repeatedly, and seem to wish us to be there all the time. Mr. Wiley is so affectionate to *me* that it quite moves my heart. He takes my hand and holds it in his own fevered one and presses it repeatedly every little while saying some kind thing to me. I believe he would be glad if Pa was not out of his sight at all; indeed, weighed down with anguish of mind and languor of body as he is, he looks like "one whom the hand of the Lord hath touched," and no one could see him without feeling the utmost compassion and sympathy.

But I commenced this letter merely to acknowledge the receipt of yours, and to have a few lines ready by the morning's mail, and here am I in danger of pressing on through the whole sheet. But I will stop short after telling you the only piece of news which has interested the neighbourhood much, which is that Dr. Rossiter has been sentenced to pay fifty dollars for his assault upon Mr. Gilbert. The Judge told him it was his first intention to make him pay a hundred but some certain things having come to his knowledge had induced him to lower the sum.

May heaven bless you and yours is the wish of your very affectionate friend and Sister,

M.M.H.

In Mt. Zion are only Maria and her father. Annie, Alfred, and Julien have returned home; Sophia and Goode Bryan are also at the Cumming home in Augusta.

Maria Bryan Harford to Julia Ann Bryan Cumming

Mt. Zion
October 18, 1838 (Thursday)

My dear Julia,

I write you a few lines by today's mail, but as the children are not here we have not thought it necessary to write so punctually as formerly.

Isaac Williams brought us news Sunday evening, since which time we have not heard from you at all. We were very glad to learn that Goode and Julien were getting so much better and I hope by this time they have got perfectly well.

Pa has been intending to go to Augusta for Sophia this week, but he has been quite unfortunate with his horses. Gay, who was in the pasture, was so violently kicked by another horse on the leg that he cannot put his foot to the ground and it is doubtful whether he will ever be able to get the use of it. And a night or two after, someone took the other horse out of the stable and rode him so hard that he is perfectly stiff, and has the thumps into the bargain. Pa is very much distrest about them.

Tell Sophia that Peters from Alabama is here since Monday; his health is not good and he has taken cold, which detains him here longer than he intended to stay.

Mr. Wiley and the other sick ones in his family are better, and there is a prospect of their recovering.

Whenever you think proper to send any of the children back, we shall be very glad to have them come. I hope you feel better since the weather has become cooler.

Mrs. Whitton is again very ill. Catherine McDonald has been baptized by Mr. Brantley. The mail is about closing.

I remain affectionately yours,
M.H.

There is another three-month gap in Maria's letters; Julia gave birth to Harford Montgomery Cumming, her seventh child and fifth son, in Augusta on December 24, 1838. Dr. Connell, Maria's next husband, appears here again, attending Mary Richardson, aged fifteen, who seems to be in the final stages of tuberculosis.

Maria Bryan Harford to Julia Ann Bryan Cumming

Mt. Zion
January 12, 1839 (Saturday)

My dear Julia,

I write again, although I never receive one line from Augusta. I wish very much that for Pa's sake (not to speak of myself) that he could hear more frequently, for as mail after mail passes and he gets no letter from Brother, nor from yourself and Sophia, he feels hurt and neglected. I meant to have written by Goode but I had no idea he was going to set off so soon in the day, and I had ordered my horse to take a ride but a little while before he left, so had no time to prepare a letter.

Uncle Ned died the same day he left. I was with him when he breathed his last, and much of the time during the day, and he suffered very much indeed. It was a violent attack of pleurisy, and he probably was suffocated at last. He was mild and patient, said "The Lord's will must be done," and prayed earnestly and constantly. His only dependence, he said, was in "the Saviour who had suffered so much for us poor creatures." He said to Jenny, "My daughter, ask Master to have me laid close by the side of my wife Henny." He exprest a great wish to see his absent children. He looked very natural when he was laid out, was very decently drest, and had a neat coffin and a decent funeral in every way. James Thomas went with the body and made some remarks and sung and prayed at the grave. I tell you this particularly, as it will no doubt gratify Rachel and Cynthia [daughters of the slave Uncle Ned, who lived with Julia] to hear all that they can. I have never seen Jenny so much moved by anything in my life. She is deeply and unaffectedly distrest, and nursed him most faithfully to the last.

Mr. and Mrs. Bowman came Friday and left this evening. He will come and preach every second and fourth Sabbath in the month. They did not bring their children with them and did not stay here much, as they paid visits to Mr. Wiley, Mr. Little, and Mr. Harris.

Dr. Rossiter continues very feeble and has entirely lost his appetite. Nothing relishes, and I have exhausted our stock of varieties to get something that he could eat. Could not you or Mr. Cumming find some little delicacy in the way of eating or drinking to send him? He is so much of a child that it would delight him to have anything sent by either of you, and from so far. I meant to have requested Goode to hunt him up some salmon, a delicate fish, but entirely forgot it.

There is an object of distress in the neighbourhood at present, though, that excites even more of my compassion than the Doctor. It is Mary Richardson, Daniel Richardson's youngest child. She returned from Eatonton where she had been at school, in the vacation, her grandmother dead, Mrs. Skinner gone, and she, not finding herself very welcome at Mrs. Baxter's, strayed off to Mrs. Green's, a distant relation, you know, of the family. She had had the chill and fever in the fall, and everybody saw she was not well, but she grew worse and worse, raised blood and had a terrible cough. The impression is that she is suffering from the effect of *obstruction*, as she is fifteen and many symptoms seem to indicate that as one of the difficulties under which she is labouring. Connel and Sydney Brown are both attending her and have exhausted all their skill, apparently in vain, for she does not seem as if she could live but a few days. She is one of the most interesting looking objects I ever saw. Her skin is about the colour and texture of the noisette rose leaf, no cap upon her head, but a profusion of yellowish brown hair falling over the pillow, her features very delicate and regular, and her eyes shut, and looking so languid as if it were an effort to her to breathe. She never speaks when she can help it, but while she is awake keeps up a piteous melancholy groaning, as if she suffered greatly — Mrs. Green is so kind to her as if she were her child.

Pa intends sending to the railroad Tuesday morning for Goode and Sophia. He has caught a bad cold which has given him a crick in his neck and such a pain in his back that he can hardly straighten himself. He is very anxious for you to come up, and I do wish you could come to see him oftener. He says if you had rather come in the carriage he will send down for you at any time. Give my love to Mr. C. and the children.

Affectionately yours,
M.H.

Alfred Cumming, aged ten, returns to Mt. Zion to resume his schoolwork at Mr. Martin's academy. He came up on the train to Double Wells, a stop on the Georgia Railroad, with his Uncle Goode. "Mr. Harris arrived this morning and everything appears to be going on smoothly" is a reference by Maria to Robert Y. Harriss and his courtship of Sophia Bryan. Maria consistently misspells Harriss.

Alfred Cumming to Julia Ann Bryan Cumming
Maria Bryan Harford to Julia Ann Bryan Cumming

Mt. Zion
January 23, 1839 (Wednesday)

My dear Mother,

I want to see you very much. We got to the Double Wells about half after ten and Uncle and I staid in the room with a Catholic priest who stood praying for a long time. Rideing here in the carrige made me sick but as soon as we got through Powelton I walked a mile, and a half. I study Ancient History and arritmetic and Latin and Geography and Music, and Aunt Maria says that as soon as I get along in my other studies she will begin to teach me how to pronounce French. Tell Emmy and Josey and Tommy that I want to see them very much.

Yesterday morning Aunt Sophia and I and Dr. Connel went to hunt partridges with a net. We went 8 or 10 miles and we had to go through briers and jump over gulleys and we got home about four o'clock and we were very tired and hungry. Aunt Sophia rode her poney and I rode Essex, and we saw two or three droves but as soon as we had set the net they flew up. Tell Mammy that I gave the handkerchief to Uncle Dicky and Aunt Sophia gave him the bundle. Tell Tommy that the next time he comes up here he must learn to ride Essex. Tell Emmy that the next time I write I will write to her. Tell Jule that I want him to write to me. Uncle has been reading *Nicholas Nickelby* [only published as a book by Charles Dickens in 1839] to me and I like it very much. Give my love to Pa and tell him that I intend to study hard and learn as much as I can this term.

Give my love to Grandma and Aunt Sarah and Uncle William and all the children and tell them that I want to see them very much.

Your affectionate son
Alfred Cumming

My dear Julia,

Alf is quite distrest about the number of mistakes in his letter, and says it is the worst letter he ever wrote yet, and somehow he says he could not help making mistakes. The truth is he has not been working in harness quite long enough to be used to it yet, though he behaves and studies very well indeed. We have concluded to send this by Sam Wales, who leaves tomorrow for Augusta. I was amused at Robert's pros and cons whether the letter should go by the mail or in the way I spoke of, "*I'd* send it by *him*," he says, "it'll *save* the postage, that is, unless he should break open the letter, but I guess he wouldn't do that."

I am going to give you a little trouble, but as Aunt Wales says, "I'll do as much for you." I send some pieces of bombazine which I shall be glad if you will get Miss Draper to make into a waist, sleeves and cape for me. (I think there is enough of it for that purpose.) I send the measure of my waist. Your dresses, you know, fit me. You can have the sleeves made like those of yours with buttons, or any other one (I am not particular), and the cape like that one on Sophia's dark frock. Send the bill to me and I will settle it immediately.

Mr. Harris arrived this morning, and everything appears to be going on smoothly. Goode and Sophia talk of going to Scottsborough in a few days. Pa received letters from Mr. McLamore and Mr. Lawson, who told him that Dunn Pickard and others broke open his doors while he was at church, and took out ten bags of cotton which they have carried off, and they earnestly request Pa to come out immediately. He will go to Augusta the first of next week.

Affectionately yours,
Maria M.H.

P.S. I forgot to ask you to get Miss Draper to try and have this ready for Pa to bring up next week, and ask her to be so kind as to send me all the pieces she saves for I find it impossible to get a piece in the stores here to match or mend or alter with. Dr. Rossiter is greatly improved and he and Mrs. Rossiter attribute it principally to the use of one third of the bottle of the Wonderful Spiritus Vitae that I, at an amazing cost of self sacrifice, gave him. Give my best love to my dear Brother Henry, make him as happy as you can, for he deserves everything from those who love him. Once more, your son is improving in mind and his manly exercises, I hope and believe. He sleeps with Pa and the latter is always happier when he has company at night.

Your Sister and Friend

The comings and goings of the Cumming children in Mt. Zion are difficult to follow from their Aunt Maria's intermittent letters. On January 23, Alfred Cumming had just arrived in Mt. Zion, and now less than three weeks later he has evidently returned to Augusta and his place has been taken by Annie and Julien. Uncle Isaac Bryan in Mt. Zion extols Thomsonian steam doctoring to Julien. (Samuel Thomson [1769–1843] was a New England "botanic doctor" whose herbal treatments included vapor baths.)

Maria Bryan Harford to Julia Ann Bryan Cumming

Mt. Zion

February 10, 1839 (Sunday)

My dear Julia,

It has been nearly a fortnight since we have received a letter from you or Sophia, until last Friday. I am glad to hear you are improving.

All are well here, but I have been almost worn out nursing Mrs. Rossiter and sitting up night after night with her. I never saw her so sick, and we all supposed she was near her end. It was a most violent attack of Diarrhea which, you know, is a very dangerous complaint to old people, and she has been reduced very low indeed. She seems better today but is exceedingly feeble, and I think any return of the disease would probably take her off.

Today was the sacrament in this Church. Pa did not commune and as I did not wish to see him stay away from an ordinance that he values so highly, and for such a reason, I thought myself furnished with a sufficient excuse to stay with Mrs. Rossiter during the service at Church. She has been in a most enviable frame of mind during her sickness, has evinced very little of that agitation and nervous irritability that I have always seen about her when she has been ill, which has made me think more that it was probably her last sickness. She has talked a great deal about you, and spoke of what she has often mentioned to me before. She says that when you were here at Catherine's wedding, [February 28, 1838] when you parted last from her it was with the promise of seeing her again before you left, but you did *not* call, and as she was awake the morning you set off, she heard the sounds of the carriage wheels, and she never was sensible of such an "exceeding depression of spirits and load at her heart" in parting from you. While you were sick she did not know but that her presentiment would be realized by something happening to you, and since her own attack she has thought it probable you would never meet her again in this world. She has said "dear Julia, what a situation of responsibility she fills, in an exalted station in society looked up to and admired, and surrounded by the world and its allurements, and so many children to bring up, how fervently I hope and pray that she may have grace given to her, according to her need."

The children are in excellent health and spirits and behave as well as could reasonably be expected, and I think are improving in their studies. They frequently ride out on horseback, and inherit to the full the hereditary passion for that exercise, and for horses, and everything connected with them. Annie has made improvement in singing and has quite a notion of learning hymns and sacred music, which is something of the rage about here at present.

Jule [eight years old] is most desperately smitten with Miss Jane Adams, and you can tell Alf that he admires her even more than he did. Uncle is trying to persuade him to consent to be a Steam doctor, and is initiating him into the mysteries of the system by making him read the Thomsonian theories. I hear them in the other room now, Jule reading aloud in an emphatic voice and Uncle acting the part of delighted listener. I have no trouble with Jule's temper or behaviour whatever.

I had a little scene with him the other day. I had left a box of medallion wafers which Sophia sent to me on the mantle piece, and being at the Doctor's all the morning, on my return I found he had had them, and broke at least half a dozen of the prettiest. As he is very much in the habit of touching what does not belong to him, I reasoned the case with him about taking advantage of my absence etc. and punished him a little, and then asked him how much money he had. He told me he had a quarter. I made him give it to me, telling him it was only fair that as he had destroyed my property that he should *repay,* and that I should take the quarter as part of the price of another box. I concluded that a punishment which would fix itself upon his memory would probably do him more good than a whipping which would only be associated with other whippings without any distinct impression as to the cause.

Pa *delights* in him, and any time when Jule has a lesson to say or any exhibition whatever to make, no matter how busy Pa is with his papers or accounts, down all go, and his eyes are over the spectacles, with a look and manner only paralleled by the pleasure Brother sometimes occasions. Jule has a great reputation for smartness about; I was amused today with the boys in my [Sunday school] class; he was reciting the III'd chap. of Proverbs, which is part of his daily lesson, and said it almost perfectly, and every boy that had a Bible, opened to the place and overlooked it while he was reciting with great apparent approbation.

Adeline Thomas seems to have been pleased with her visit to Augusta. She is quite unwell now. Louisa Kelsey was married to Dickinson, Alfred's friend,

Thursday night. I have not seen Mrs. K. since she got her cap, but Mary tells me she admires it very much.

I wish you would ask Sophia to get me a long veil like the one she sent up on my bonnet, as that one is almost as short again as it ought to be. I will send and settle all my accounts by Mr. Cumming. Can you send me the other volume of Henry Milner, and can the *Life of Wilberforce,* and Lockhart's *Memories of Scott* be procured for me? I am anxious to see them both. Mrs. Harris has an infant of a fortnight old, and has been dangerously sick. I rather think she is not yet out of danger. Mrs. Matthews has been confined to her room with putrid fever.

Be assured, my dear Sister, of my earnest and best endeavours to benefit and make happy those you have committed to me. Love to all.

Your ever affectionate Sister
Maria Harford

Maria is busy nursing the sick, cutting out and basting clothes for the Bryan slaves including pantaloons "for the multitude of little fry," and looking after her niece and nephew. Nevertheless, Maria, a fast reader, is always out of books in Mt. Zion and is regularly asking for more from Augusta. Her book requests in her last letter for John Gibson Lockhart's Life of Sir Walter Scott *ran to seven volumes, and the* Life of Wilberforce *included five volumes. The latter — the life of William Wilberforce (1759–1833) — published in 1838 by his sons Robert, Isaac, and Samuel, is especially interesting as reading matter for a planter's daughter. Wilberforce was chiefly associated with the abolition of the slave trade in England and the establishment of the English antislavery society, which culminated in Parliament's passage of the Emancipation Bill, a month after Wilberforce's death.*

Maria Bryan Harford to Julia Ann Bryan Cumming

March 11, 1839 (Monday)

My Dear Julia,

I am afraid you have not only felt the want of my usual punctuality in writing to you, from being deprived of the communication that one friend naturally loves to have with another, but that you have thought me unkind in not oftener acting as the medium of special information with regard to your children. But there have been many things which have left me less time than usual to write, for until the Miss McDonalds came I was obliged to be with Mrs. Rossiter day and night as much as I could be from home, and I have had the negroes' clothes to cut out and every garment to baste and fit, and this is very troublesome, particularly for the multitude of little fry to be fixed up with pantaloons etc. Besides, I knew you were hearing through the children themselves in a general way of their health and welfare, and this prevented me from making the extra exertions I otherwise would have done to write to you.

I am glad that Sophia has been so much of a comfort and society to you and that she has been inclined to it herself, and feel much for you in the loneliness you will at least for a time experience from her absence. Mr. Cumming can tell you better about the children than I can in a letter. Annie has a cold at present, but they ordinarily enjoy good health and spirits, and seem perfectly contented. They anticipate your coming with much delight, and for that matter we all do, and hope you will stay as long as you possibly can make it convenient to remain from home.

I am very much obliged to you for my share of the cake and oranges, the latter are indeed welcome since my appetite is weakened by a week's fever and indisposition.

I have been greatly disturbed, my dear Julia, to find that you are so overcome by the sickness and apparent danger of your child. You must, for your own sake, and from the trustful spirit of submission you owe to your wise and kind heavenly Parent, endeavour to cultivate that state of mind which will make you always desire that He should rule over you and yours, and arrange every thing concerning you. "Be careful for nothing but in every thing by prayer and supplication with thanksgiving make known your requests unto God, and the *peace of God* which *passeth understanding,* shall keep your hearts and minds through Jesus Christ." You know that in our sense of the word my all has been taken from me, that with a heart overflowing with affection I have neither husband nor child, those natural outlets to a woman's love. There is too, but one life in a certain sense between me and a situation still more lonely and unprotected, but I endeavour constantly to feel that though a stranger and a pilgrim in my journey to a better land, I will nevertheless be assuredly guided in "the *right way,*" and delivered from every thing that is "*evil*" however difficult some of the passages of life may be for flesh and blood to bear.

I am obliged to you for *Fielding* and am glad to get something to read, for, not being strong enough to work, I have more time for reading, and I have acquired and was ready to say the unfortunate habit of reading so fast that I get through what I have and not being where I can command books am at something of a loss. She [Sophia] did not bring Charles Lamb or Henry Milner. I shall endeavour to write oftener to you.

Your affectionate Sister
M.M.H.

Sophia has been ill with symptoms of "inflammation of the brain." She perks up when her suitor, Mr. Harriss, arrives. Maria continues to ask for and receive books, including three volumes of Jane Taylor (1783–1824), who, with her sister, Ann, wrote moral verses for children. Jane, alone, wrote Display, a Tale for Young People *in 1815, which Maria anticipates reading with "great pleasure."*

Maria Bryan Harford to Julia Ann Bryan Cumming

Mt. Zion
April 2, 1839 (Tuesday)

My dear Julia,

You must blame Sophia that you did not get a letter from me some time since for one night when I had taken my writing materials to commence a letter to you, she begged me *not* to write, for she was then very unwell and she said she had rather you should not hear until she was better. She is considerably improved in health within a few days, but is still unwell, and very thin and weak. I think she was very dangerously attacked indeed, and we were all very much alarmed about her, for there seemed to be symptoms of inflammation of the brain, or that her disease would finally terminate in something of that sort which would prove fatal, and what made us still more anxious was her determination and that most of the time acted upon, to do nothing for herself. I think she seems out of spirits and troubled, though I suppose she would not like to have me think so or make you think so. She herself attributes her sickness to the constant excitement of mind and body in which she was several weeks previous to her coming home.

Uncle Jacob brought the bundle you sent, and goes back today charged with some more clay, which we hope you will receive in safety this time. I am much obliged to you for the books and the whistle. The latter I needed very much indeed. I send you back a specimen of the piece from which I would like you to get me a dress. I don't know the width and therefore must beg you to judge what will be enough for the frock and cape. I do not know that this is the prettiest figure but it seems to be a good black, and the material will wear well I think.

Pa is very much encouraged to hope by the information you sent him from Colonel Downing that Brother will be at home this week, particularly as next week is the sitting of court. Mr. Wiley has returned from Alabama in somewhat better humour, and he has received a long letter from Mr. Bowman which has had a softening influence upon him. He had a long conversation with Pa a few days since, in which he told him that he had never *had* a hard thought of *him* personally, but it had been his impression that he had been milled, and had had incorrect views about his claims, and of the affair generally. [Pa rented a plantation in Alabama from Mr. Wiley.] He said for many years Pa had been the friend in whom he had most confided, that whenever he wanted advice he had always gone to him, and *now* he was at a loss to whom to apply in any strait, etc. Pa himself is much more cheerful than he was, although he thinks Mr. Wiley's claims when they come to be settled will be unreasonable, as in a statement which he requested him to make out, that he might know what he actually thought due him, he put the rent of the plantation for three years at 22 hundred dollars. Pa was likewise disappointed in his expectations from the Cotton Crop in Alabama, by a letter he received from Mr. Lawson [the overseer]. He had expressly directed that the cotton should not be sold, and Mr. Lawson informed him that he had had an application from Brother for four hundred dollars, and had sold the cotton before the advance in price. This has deranged his plans, as he intended making use of it to pay a debt of Goode's (who has never received anything from the place) to Tom Grimes, who is really clamorous for the money, and has rather annoyed Pa, as his (Goode's) security, by often demanding it.

I shall be very glad to get my watch and breast pin, as I am constantly needing the former in regulating my scholars' arrangements. I am very much pleased with the volumes by the author of *Tremaine* [*or The Man of Refinement*, written by Robert Ward Plumer (1765–1846) and published in 1825], and have not read anything this long time I admired so much as *Atticus;* it is just to my taste. I have been pleased with a little book someone lent me lately, called *The Three Experiments.* Have you seen it? Catherine McDonald sent me by Pa, who returned Saturday from Scottsborough, three volumes of Jane Taylor's works, and in them was the story I have heard so much of and never saw called *Display.* I anticipate great pleasure, and I hope I shall be profited by reading her works and that I shall be better for life by it, for her standard of piety is very high, and her writings are more practical than almost anybody else's. At least I always feel for a time after reading them that I shall begin practising what she recommends with great energy.

Uncle Jacob will tell you that his wife has a daughter again. She was dreadfully sick and I did not know but she would die, or that the child would be born dead, but it is a very fine and a very pretty baby. Pa says he thinks Eliza Brantley's is rather a weakly infant, though the family appear to consider it a fine child. She has determined not to go to Texas this Summer, and Judge Franklin will return in July to Georgia. Mrs. Rossiter's health is improving though she is very feeble and full of pains and aches. I have told Annie to ask you to send her some good quills by the first opportunity, as I find they never bring any to this place, and I do think the children would improve faster in their writing if they had better quills to make their pens of.

Remember me affectionately to Mr. Cumming and the children. Tell Emmy I do want to see *her* very much indeed.

Yours ever,
M.M.H.

Mr. Harris arrived this evening and is now in high chat with Sophy or rather the latter is with him for I only hear her voice. I have barely seen him.

Annie Cumming is twelve and a half years old when she writes this letter to her mother from Mt. Zion, heavily footnoted by her Aunt Maria. Maria complains in her footnotes that Annie exaggerates.

Annie M. Cumming to Julia Ann Bryan Cumming
Maria Bryan Harford to Julia Ann Bryan Cumming

Mt. Zion

April 2, 1839 (Tuesday)

My dear Mother,

I am greatly in hopes that my turn for a letter will come tomorrow. I have gotten none in more than two weeks. I've tried to keep from laughing for pleasure at the sight of a letter from Alf and he did not laugh much.

We have been thinking of your coming with a great deal of pleasure and me and Jule both had rather you would come up as soon as you can, than wait so long a time. I hope when you do come it will make Harford quite well. We are all such a family of beauties I wonder they have not been stolen from you; Aunt Sophia makes out that Harford is the greatest beauty ever seen. We have been preparing for you, already fixing our garden for you. I don't know what Robert thinks of doing to show off his own. Grandpa, Aunt Sophy, and Aunt Maria get him so mad sometimes, though Grandpa gives up very soon. The other night Aunt Maria was asking him to keep a dog in the garden and he got so mad, and you would have thought of the tower of Babel, Aunt Maria quoting and gives "instances" and tells him he is like Mr. Little and he don't like that.* I expect he is in hopes that "July" will take parts with him but I can assure him that July is as obstinate as the rest of them.

I am certain you would have music enough if you were here, for besides the *song humming,* mine and Jule's practising, Aunt Maria and Aunt Sophy play a good deal on the organ, and Aunt Maria plays on the guitar. I believe that there is hardly more than three hours that there ain't some instrument agoing. Aunt Sophia is a fiddling away now.** The other day Aunt Sophia was playing on the fiddle and Aunt Maria on the organ, "Tessie the Flower

---

* Annie relates so many of Robert's and my arguments that I fear you think we get along but badly, but in truth there are no better friends.   M.H.

** Altogether an exaggeration of Annie's. I am very sorry to say that she is entirely disinclined to practise and I can only depend on her doing so, or at any rate playing her pieces correctly, when I take my work and sit by her. Jule really loves his music, but I think in her other studies Annie advances. This letter is not written as correctly nor in so fair a hand as the original for she copies with the idea of a ride on horseback in her head, and she hurried very much for fear she should be too late.   M.H.

O'Durblane." Jule came into my room and asked me what that was. When I told him he said, "It thrills through me." I hope Alf and Mr. Palmer have no difficulty and that he improves his music. Tell him that if he don't take care Jule will best him in his music and Latin. He can play several pieces very well; he plays "In My Cottage," "My Country," and "Bruce's Address."

Grandpa says that he will look for Uncle Joe every day, he says he will begin to look for him tomorrow. I should have been glad to have seen Mr. Downing and hear him lisp.

I am very much obliged to you for all that you sent me and though I have not tried on the frocks they look as if they would fit.

Give my love to Em. Franklin and ask her if she remembers the time when I took her to walk to the City Hall to all the rooms and to see the queen of May. I wish you would send me and Jule some quills by the first opportunity as Aunt Maria says these up here in the store ain't fit to make a pen with. Give my love to all.

Your affectionate daughter,
Annie M. Cumming

P.S. Pa wishes you to get at Mr. Edgar's some coloured homespun for frocks for the house servants, enough for five dresses, and five chemises of the unbleached northern homespun. Also, grey satinet for a suit for Tom, of the quality you judge suitable and a set of brass buttons. Please get at the same place a Sunday calico for Creasy.

Yours — M.H.

P.S. 2. Since writing this I have received your letter and the contents by Mr. Harris. I enclose you $60 to pay Sophia's bill, for Pa, I know, cannot command the money at this time, and has lately been very much fretted by having fifty dollars stolen out of his desk. Besides, at this particular moment I have not the heart to trouble Sophia by letting her know of the affair, for she is unwell and excited and anxious and embarrassed. Give the bill receipted for her that she may see that it is paid, and at some future occasion I can let Pa know that I have paid it, and it may be convenient for him to return it to me. I know you would be willing to do it for him but you have far more claims on you than I have, and I can spare this at present.

Very affectionately —
M.H.

Pa's debts have become a serious problem for the Bryans in Mt. Zion.

Maria Bryan Harford to Julia Ann Bryan Cumming

Mt. Zion

April 9, 1839 (Tuesday Morning)

My dear Julia,

I believe Sophia wrote you by the last mail, but I have concluded to drop you a few lines by Pa who is going into Sparta this morning.

Brother came last night, and I am truly glad on Pa's account that he did come. But he is greatly distrest by Mr. Wiley's conduct. Indeed it does seem to me that it will take his life if the thing cannot terminate soon. Mr. Wiley's claim is about three thousand dollars, and Uncle's [Isaac] as you know five thousand. These two, he says, he shall be obliged to meet and they cannot be unless by the sale of property, and of negro property which he is so unwilling to engage in. I am just telling you his views, and the effect of them upon his mind. I wish Mr. Cumming could have come up, for what with restless and sleepless nights and anxiety of mind, his health is impaired so that he has a complaint of the bowels, and his nervous energy from this wear and tear upon mind and body seems to be totally gone, so that now when he is required to act, and to act with decision and promptness, he is as weak as a child and sheds tears almost as readily.

Uncle too! how I hate to use a term implying relationship to such a man. The miserable old usurer! If I could just shake my fist in his face this morning and tell him what I think, I should feel better, I am sure. But he and Mr. Wiley are great cronies, and he, we have reason to think, really wishes Mr. Wiley success. Pa says he must settle on some terms, he cannot live so, and this morning said if it were not for Sophy and me he would walk out of his door and give him up his house and let him take possession, and he would go and board somewhere. I tell him if that were needful we need not hinder his plans or wishes, for I could go wherever he did, and Sophy could always go to you.

I reckon you'll hate after awhile to see my letters, Julia, but I just tell you things as they are. I know I do not exaggerate, and I do as I should like to be treated when my friends are in distress, and I think it is the way you wish to be treated as it regards information.

Mrs. Terrill has twins, one is dead, and she is very sick. Sophia is getting much better, and the children are perfectly well. Brother is delighted with Jule. They are going so I must stop.

Your Sister,
M.H.

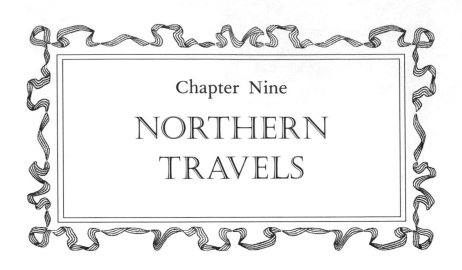

Chapter Nine

NORTHERN
TRAVELS

"I wish you were going."

Three months have passed since Maria's last extant letter, and she writes Julia of her plans to go by sea in about a week to New York accompanied by Catherine McDonald, Margaret Kelsey, and the local minister, Mr. Hooker. Maria has a "sinking of heart" about going out among strangers as a widow. Sophia Bryan in an addendum to Maria's letter reports that Miss Jane Armour (who will become the second Mrs. Joseph Bryan) is summering nearby with the Ponces at Pleasant Valley Plantation.

Maria Bryan Harford to Julia Ann Bryan Cumming
Sophia Bryan to Julia Ann Bryan Cumming

Mt. Zion
July 7, 1839 (Sunday)

My dear Julia,

I did not receive your letter written Saturday until the last mail.

Pa and Sophia are still at home, and the former has been, and is, still quite sick with the chill and fever; he has had it for three successive days and is so much weakened that he cannot sit up much. If he would use decided and judicious measures I should not feel very anxious, but he is always so unwilling to take medicine or have a physician in attendance, that while Pa is sick I suffer in the flesh. I feel very much disinclined to go away from this specimen of how he is liable to suffer, but he is very anxious and indeed, determined that I shall go.

We, at present, intend setting off Monday week. The party will consist of Catherine McDonald, Mr. Hooker, Margaret Kelsey and myself. The plan is not projected farther than to New York by sea. You will probably hear from us again in the course of the week, but if nothing unforeseen happens you may expect to see us the evening of next Monday. I wish you were going, or Mr. Cumming, for I dislike so much to travel without some relative, and such a sinking of heart as I sometimes experience at the prospect of leaving home and going among strangers with the change that has past upon me since I was similarly situated, I cannot describe.

Give my love to Mrs. Ringold and tell her I am glad that she thought of coming. As to bringing her children, it would be pleasant to them I have no doubt, and we should not consider the trouble. I shall remember her promise and claim it when I return. I do feel very much for her, and wish she could feel the comfort arising from a trust in God, and a belief that he was directing all the changes and trials of her life in mercy.

The Doctor and Mrs. Rossiter are in the same condition as when I wrote you last. They feel very badly at the prospect of losing so many of their friends' society at the same time, Pa's, Mr. Hooker's and mine — particularly as they are in that state of health now, and at that age, when literally they know not the day of their death.

You were so kind as to offer me your straw bonnet to travel in. If you have not given it away, please get a black ribbon and have it in readiness for me. Robert is waiting.

Yours,

M.H.

My dear Sister,

I intended to have written to you tonight a long letter, but Sister Maria wished to write and let you know of her plans for traveling this Summer.

Pa gave up his journey to Alabama last week on account of Uncle's absence. He took it into his head that he should loose [sic] the debt Dr. Gilbert owed him unless he went to see him about it, and he left without giving notice of his intentions to anyone until just as he was setting off. Pa has been quite sick for three days with chill and fever and we are afraid, from his symptoms, that he is going to be sick for some time. He has not taken any active medicine yet and I am afraid he will not consent to take anything, as he thinks it is a cold he has.

Tommy is very well and still improving in health. He is becoming quite impatient to go to Alabama, and says he expects we will not go after all. He is standing by the table and I asked him what I should tell you. He said almost despairingly, "Oh! Aunt Sophy, I don't know what to tell her. I *wish* I could *say* something."

I have seen Mrs. Ponce and Miss Jane Armour quite often since they came up. The latter I think looks better than I ever saw her. They expect to spend part of this summer at the Indian Springs.

Tell Alf and Jule that Tommy went with Pa to Mr. Harris's one day last week, and spent the whole day, and he came back exceedingly delighted with his visit, and says he wishes he could live there. He saw the Rabbits and Guinea Pigs, and when he (Mr. Harris) came from the North he brought on a good many different kind of birds, and among them a parrot. He says I must tell Josie [his brother Joseph, aged three] that the parrot kept talking all day, and told his mistress that "poor poll wanted a cracker." He says "Tell Ma to tell Josie *that anyhow.*"

Pa thinks we should leave for Alabama next Tuesday week.

You must allow me, Sister, to plead not guilty to the charge you laid against me in your last letter; that is, of influencing Brother Goode in *any* way about [Frances] Maria Myers [of Savannah, whom Goode marries years later]. I do not think we exchanged ten words about her at all during the time he was here, and I assure you I did not say one word *against* her. But he cannot sit and hear any woman praised, without wishing he was at liberty to appropriate her charms, for he never has one doubt about his success in any quarter.

Give my love to Brother Henry and Annie. Tell Emmy that I have got a beautiful little fly brush to send to her by her Aunt Maria. Write to me this week, and I shall get the letter before I go away.

Very affectionately yours,
[Sophia]

Maria Bryan Harford to Julia Ann Bryan Cumming

Mt. Zion
July 12, 1839 (Friday)

My dear Julia,

I have just time to write a line by an opportunity of sending to Sparta which occurs, to answer the message from Mr. Henry. Please say I am under obligation to him for proposing to wait; but it will be unnecessary, as our route will be different. C. McD. [Catherine McDonald], Mr. Hooker, M[argaret] Kelsey and I will set off, as at present designed, next Wednesday, and expect to take shipping to Boston, New York or Norfolk, which of these places will depend on circumstances.

Your letter which ought to have been here much sooner, only arrived this evening.

Pa is a great deal better. He has had a very serious attack and has been much weakened. He will not set off until after I go.

Hamilton and Mr. Alexander Robertson are here tonight. I have no time to write more. Tommy is well, and pleased with his letter.

Yours in haste,
M.H.

Four days after her departure from Augusta, Maria, having traveled by carriage, railroad, and steamer, arrived in Wilmington, North Carolina. Here she wrote Julia a humorous description of a stylish and haughty lady and her poodle whom she met on the train.

Maria Bryan Harford to Julia Ann Bryan Cumming

[Wilmington, North Carolina]
July 22, 1839 (Monday Morning)

My dear Julia,

The journey so far has been prosperous and pleasant. My side is not yet free from pain but I do not have those terrible spasms that I had while with you, so that at present it is quite bearable. Indeed, I think it grew better from the moment I swallowed the dose of Buchu [a mixture of aromatic leaves used in medicine as a stimulant or diuretic].

I suppose Robert told you that we got to the cars [at Hamburg, terminal of the South Carolina Railroad] considerably before the time. When the omnibus arrived, a lady of very stylish appearance entered the car where I was sitting and took her seat in the corner opposite me, with a small Spanish poodle in her lap. She gave divers directions in a loud and commanding tone about her baggage which, for the information of all, she stated, was two trunks, two carpet bags, a wooden box. Three or four gentlemen seemed in attendance and travelling with her, who stood ready to obey every order. "Mr. Carpenter," said she screaming aloud, "take special care of my bandbox. It has that gipsy [hat] in it that I told you about last night." etc. etc.

After all had taken their seats, the agent came to the window of the car and said, "That dog has not been paid for."

"*This dog,*" said she, holding up the little thing. "What, you don't pretend to charge anything for this poodle that I carry in my lap, it's unheard of."

"I will not pay," said her husband, "it's an imposition." At last the agent begged him to come into the office. He did so (while all the party were exclaiming in different phraseology on the unreasonableness of the demand) and returned saying, "I have paid the fellow a sovereign, and he insists that I owe him a seven pence, but let him get it if he can."

Just at this moment another agent, a large, red-faced man, thundered out, "That dog has not been paid for."

"I *have* paid for him," said the master of the poodle.

"The car shall not leave this place if it be till twelve o'clock," said the agent, "until that dog is paid for."

Again was the man summoned out, and the lady evidently enjoying the pleasure of causing such a "*to do,*" though enraged at the charge, and urging her friends to take part in the settlement of the matter.

"Go, Mr. Leach," said she. "See it out."

"Mr. Thornton, have you paid for your cane? Do pay for your cane."

"Well, I'll never travel this road again if I live a hundred years."

I confess my feelings went with the agents, for I saw they were contending for the regulations of the road, and had some excuse for their irritation in the insulting remarks that were made to them.

After all had seated themselves in the car the husband of the lady, rather a poor looking man who seemed just waked up after a night's revel, and seemed as if he had rather play "Sneak, that even bully in any farce," declared he'd publish the affair when he got to Charleston.

"Look here," said he to the agent, "what is your name, sir?"

"Sturges," said the man in a loud tone.

"I *thought so*," said the other.

The agent then, as if giving direction to some of the attendants of the car, said, "Let that dog be put in the baggage car."

"Well then, sir," said the lady, "you put me there too, if you send my poodle there. Let's go back. Was there ever such treatment!"

By this time several young men started up, and there seemed as if there would be a mêlée in good earnest, and the person who was called Mr. Carpenter, an exceedingly pleasant-looking stout young man with a very dirty shirt collar, stepped forward and, making a motion with his hands as if about to roll up his sleeves, and 'oint [anoint] his hands by spitting upon them, said "Let any one attempt it. That's more than I can stand. Whoever enters the door to remove this dog shall trample first *over my cold corse.*"

He really said this in so heroic a style that it was quite exciting, and I only wished within myself that he had said his *warm* corse, because of course, as I reasoned, his corse will not have time to become cold. However, the agent, who evidently had no design to enforce the latter threat, did not answer to the invitations made him "to come on" but quietly kept at his writing, and the train moved off, much to my satisfaction.

They came with us (this party) as far as Wilmington. I think [they] were from Mobile, and the lady and her husband were Mr. & Mrs. Guy Johnson. She was going to Petersburg, Va. to see her mother, an exceedingly pretty woman with manners a l'Alston, and as fond of dogs as Lady Bulwer, for in the progress of our acquaintance when we got on board the steamboat and she had nobody to talk to but women, she gave me many anecdotes of the Canine Species, and seemed positively delighted when "Pauline" actually without any inviting on my part got up in my lap and went to sleep. "I never saw her do that before," said she. "Buffon is certainly right when he says dogs understand the countenance and know who are their friends. When I visit at a house," she continued, "and see the dogs and cats badly treated, they may devote themselves to please me but my *happiness is positively destroyed. . . .*"

I am surprised that I never heard anyone say that Charleston and the environs are not exceedingly like New Orleans. Had I been suddenly set down in the place I should have declared it was N.O. The colour of the houses and ground, the stagnant water, the shrubbery and flowers, the quantity of West Indian fruit, and the complexion and dress of the women and the mulatto race make the resemblance complete.

When we got to the wharf of the Norfolk boat, where the omnibus first went to discharge some passengers, in the midst of the great crowd ready to go on board, who should I see but Mr. Henderson, dressed in better taste and looking altogether better than I ever saw him. My first impulse was to speak, but I did not wish to recognize him for the recollection of N.O. had been rolling in upon me before until I was very sad, and seeing him completed the illusion and the gloom. He looked earnestly at me, but my change of dress, and still greater change of looks and the scene, made him look as if he said I am not sure enough to venture to speak. There were not more than twenty on board our boat, the accommodations were excellent, and I was not much sick. Mr. Hooker [was] to his heart's content.

We have been very comfortably situated in Wilmington at the Restons who are kind, and well bred people. Heard two most excellent sermons yesterday in the Epis. church from Parson Drove, brother to Captain D. of the Army.

You would not complain of the shortness of my letters if you knew the circumstances of writing this, this morning with packing up and Mr. Hooker who is fidgetty hurrying me.

Love to all adieu,
M.M.H.

Maria and her brother Joseph (whom she met as she made her way north) traveled up the Hudson River with a party of four "very agreeable people from Baltimore," including Miss Ellen Lee, to whom Joseph was most attentive. They had now reached Saratoga Springs and were staying at the fashionable United States Hotel.

Maria Bryan Harford to Julia Ann Bryan Cumming

[Saratoga Springs, New York]
August 5, 1839 (Monday)

My dear Julia,

You will be somewhat surprised to find me here, and it was a very sudden resolution for me to come. But in New York I heard so much of the virtues of the mineral waters here, and being anxious to see the scenery of the North [Hudson] River we determined to come.

We are travelling with a party of very agreeable people from Baltimore, with whom we became acquainted in Philadelphia, and it was well if we came at all, that it was with them, for they had previously written for rooms and have divided with us, or I suppose we could not have gotten in at all. Every hotel is crowded to excess and the "United States," where we stay, has between four and five hundred persons in it.

While I was in New York I was taken with a pain and soreness in my right shoulder, which has continued ever since, and been increasing indeed. I was directed to take the advice of a physician on coming to this place in order to find out from which of the springs I should drink and in what degree and manner to make use of the water. He says that the pain in my shoulder, as well as my complexion, are undoubted indications of an affection of the liver. All I can say is that I continue to feel very unwell, and do not know that I am any better since I left home.

There are a great many persons of distinction here, and I have met with a number of acquaintances. The President [Martin Van Buren] is at the house where we stay, and is a much finer looking man than I expected to see. Mr. [John] Forsyth [secretary of state] and Virginia are here, Colonel and Mrs. White, and the rich Colonel Thorn of Paris. Everybody seems trying to make a display; you see servants in rich livery, and splendid carriages and four dashing about the streets. You remember hearing me speak of Colonel Denton of New Orleans, he is staying here. Mr. Henry [an Augustan] and Maria Myers [who marries Goode Bryan in 1849] have just left for the Falls. George Imes and his two sisters and his mother are here. Tell Mrs. Campbell that I have seen Edward, who is with them, and is very well indeed. I have also seen Mr. & Mrs. Lamon and Rebecca, and Mary Anne Gardner.

I have been relieved about Mr. Cumming, from Miss Gardner's telling me she had received a letter from her Mother, and nothing was said of his being sick. I have felt very anxious about Mr. Cumming and this is the first information, direct or indirect, that I have received. I hope I shall hear from you very soon, as I believe Brother intends writing to New Haven to have the letters sent from there. Please direct your next here, as I shall probably remain some time longer if I find the waters are good for me.

I staid in Troy one night and the next morning got directions to the house of Mrs. Beman [Caroline Bird Yancey Beman, the second wife of Nathan S. S. Beman. Caroline Beman and her husband were legally separated in 1835]. She was very much surprised at seeing me and, indeed, did not know me at all at first. She lives entirely alone, says sometimes she does not have even a servant with her, and does all her own work, even cooking. She appears quite cheerful, and if one might judge from the *words* of another what the character was, I should say she was a Christian. She says she feels that notwithstanding her heavy trials that God is dealing with her in mercy and that he is preparing her for a better world. She expressed an earnest sense of her own faults and errors and said God, she hoped and believed, was making use of these means to draw off her affections from the world for, said she, I have loved it too much. We are made, said she, to love God and, Oh Maria, said she, nothing inferior to Him can satisfy an immortal mind. She says some nights she goes to bed after the labours of the day are over, and though separated from her husband, and not a child near her, she feels so happy and thankful, and through the hours of the night (for she sleeps but little) her feelings are lifted up in thanksgiving to God for all his mercies.

Brother saw Mrs. Parmelee for a moment in Troy. She was much better, and intends going to Ohio to pay a visit to her Sister.

The Countess of Westmoreland and her train are here. She is an elderly and very ill looking woman and dresses wretchedly. Mr. Fenwick Kollock is here, too.

I give you the news in not much order, but as I recollect things in the hurry of writing them, and I am writing this in haste to prepare it for the mail.

Mary Jones is, I think, one of the greatest belles here. Mr. Forsyth notices her a great deal, and she receives a great deal of attention from a young man, the Minister from Texas, and from William Henry Dangerfield, the son of Mrs. Bird's friend. Brother is said to be the handsomest man at the Springs, and I assure you his dress brings him out very much. He is devoted in his attentions to the ladies, particularly to Miss Ellen Lee, the young lady who is travelling with us. If I had not seen him in the same way so often with other ladies, I should think that certainly something would come of it this time, as she seems perfectly fascinated with him.

I take a warm sulphur bath every day by the direction of the physician, and it is very pleasant and I hope it will be useful to me.

Give my very best love to Mr. Cumming and the children and to Mrs. Cumming [Sr.], Mrs. Davis [Henry's older sister] and Sarah [his youngest sister who never married]. Mr. Forsyth asked very particularly after you and says, you are "beautiful, *beautiful*." Here ends this chapter on the vanities and follies of the world.

Affectionately yours,

M.M.H.

Maria and her brother have stopped over at Plattsburgh deliberately to part company with the Maryland people who had made up their party at Saratoga Springs. These travelers were Miss Ellen Lee, daughter of a Harpers Ferry planter; Mrs. Mitchell, an amiable woman, who was chaperoning Ellen Lee; Mrs. Mitchell's twenty-five-year-old son; and a Judge Hanson of Baltimore, "friend and travelling companion of the three former."

Maria Bryan Harford to Julia Ann Bryan Cumming

[Postmark: Plattsburgh, New York]
August 14, 1839

"Back side o'Albany stand Lake Champlain
  One little pond half full o'water.
  Plattsburg be dere, too, justup on de main,
  One little town, he grow bigger dough herearter."

You may infer from this elegant stanza, that I am writing to you from the town of Plattsburg. My last was written to you from Saratoga which I hope you have long before this received.

A day or two after the date of that letter, I was taken very sick with a violent cold and cough and fever, and was confined to my room several days. Brother was so alarmed about me that he *would* send for the physician, who kept me sick (nauseated) several days with antimony, and then gave me a dose of calomel [mercurous chloride, a tasteless white powder used as a cathartic] which ended by satiating me. I had, until I took cold, felt much better, and do think that the waters at Saratoga were beginning to do me good, but the doctor said I could not drink them with the cough and constant fever which I had, and the very best thing for me was travelling, even better than seabathing.

So we left Saratoga Tuesday morning and spent that night at Caldwell, a little town at the southern end of Lake George, which for beauty of scenery I have never seen surpassed not even by the shores of the Hudson. We stopped and looked at Fort Ticonderoga, and took dinner at a public house kept near the old fort, and at three o'clock in the afternoon went on board the most complete steamboat I ever saw, and past up Lake Champlain, and arrived at this place about ten o'clock last night. I had a comfortable bed and room which I have not enjoyed before since leaving the city of New York, and I slept delightfully and feel refreshed this morning and better than in many a long day before.

I hardly know whether it is better to enter upon the details which have led to our present situation and change of plan, or defer it until I see you, but I believe I will explain a little. You remember I mentioned in my last a flirtation between Brother and Miss Ellen Lee a young lady who was travelling with friends, who had formed a party with ourselves. I don't know that I have ever said anything about the other persons of the party. We first saw them all as we got into the cars at Baltimore to proceed eastwardly; they consisted of Mrs. Mitchell of Baltimore, and her son an only child, a young man of five and twenty perhaps, Ellen Lee (whose father, a planter, lives in Maryland near Harper's Ferry), who was under the charge of Mrs. Mitchell; and Judge Hanson of Baltimore, friend and travelling companion of the three former. Brother soon became acquainted with Judge Hanson, who is a man of great pretensions, and who has undoubtedly very superior acquirements and a brilliant mind, and who appears to be vastly admired and honoured by the numerous Baltimore people we met at the Springs.

We all put up at the Amer. H. [American Hotel, in New York City] where

we staid several days, and then they gave us an urgent invitation to accompany them to Saratoga. As Brother [now thirty-eight years old] was travelling
solely to benefit me, and for no special occasion of his own, I was very glad
to have him interested in something which would relieve the irksomeness of
travelling under these circumstances, and I saw he was exceedingly anxious
to travel with these people. Besides, as the waters were greatly recommended
to me, I entered into the scheme very willingly.

Mrs. Mitchell is a Catholic, an intelligent and very worthy and amiable
person, and for the fortnight I have been with her, neither mother nor sister
could have been kinder. Judge Hanson I never liked, for I perceived at once
that he was vain and haughty, and as I wished to avoid all comment at the
Springs, where I saw many acquaintances, I decidedly, and as he thought
disdainfully, declined all particular civilities to myself from him, and attached
myself constantly to Brother. This he complained of frequently to me, and to
Mrs. Mitchell said he had never been so pointedly kept at a distance by any
lady in his life. He is an inveterate punster, and is frequently very successful
in his puns, and altogether decidedly *witty*. I frequently joined in the laugh at
his good puns, and ridiculed his many failures, until I found he was growing
rather testy, and then I determined to be on my guard.

Brother and Miss Lee were proceeding together most harmoniously; the
former without doubt, more in love than I have seen him since Anne inspired
his sighs, and the lady "nothing loath" to his demonstrations of devotion.
This continued at all times and under all circumstances; and in the public
salon of the U. States [Hotel] at Saratoga, they were as apparently rapt and ab-
stracted whether promenading the circle with the crowd, or withdrawn apart
into a corner, as if they were the solitary dwellers upon some desert island of
the Pacific. Mrs. Mitchell and her son were exceedingly pleased I know, and
often to me commented on their mutual liking wondering whereunto it would
grow. Judge Hanson often laughed at them to their face and elsewhere, and
never said or looked anything which indicated displeasure.

They wished to leave Saratoga for Canada three days previous to the time
we came away, and while I was sick, and I urged them not to suffer their
plans to be interfered with by me. However, they insisted upon waiting, and
Tuesday morning we set off to Lake George. The next morning Judge Hanson
called Mrs. Mitchell apart and showed her a letter which he had written to

Mr. Lee, blaming her and her son very much, and telling of the intimacy between Brother and his daughter, and adding that it was a current report at the Springs that they were engaged. This letter, he said, he would send unless they separated immediately. Mrs. Mitchell was astounded. She had taken a great liking to Brother and she saw the indelicacy of the proceeding, but she said Mr. Lee was a very particular man and would demand permission asked before love was made to his daughter. She told Brother the circumstance, expressed her great friendship to him, and said that if he ever felt inclined to go to Midwood (Mr. Lee's residence) she would take her carriage and go with him and introduce him to the family.

I never saw any one feel as badly as Miss Lee. She said she was shocked at the indelicate position in which she was placed, from having such a fuss made about those customary civilities which a gentleman thrown into a lady's society would, of course, render. However, my space is already too much taken up with the narration of the affair.

I boldly expressed to everyone my assurance that, had any personal wishes of Judge Hanson induced him to desire our company, he would have conveniently blinded his eyes to those proceedings which had long been apparent to him, before he thought proper to take notice of them. However, I have omitted to say that we took leave of the party last night at the wharf at Plattsburg. They were to proceed in the boat to St. John's and from there to Montreal and Quebec, and we, after resting a day here, will go to the falls of Niagara, from there to Canada, and from thence by the White Mountains to Boston. At least so we think at present though we may again and frequently change, as we are not set upon any particular plan.

I have thought all day how Sophia would be pleased if she were here, for there is a whole regiment of artillery stationed here, and the house is full of officers in their uniforms, from the Colonel to the merely brevetted Lieutenant.

I want to see you all very much indeed, and am exceedingly anxious to hear from you; you must write next to Boston. Tell Jule and Alf that I became very well acquainted with Peter Parley at Saratoga. [Peter Parley was the pen name of Samuel Griswold Goodrich, who, from 1827, wrote hundreds of books for children under the guise of a kindly and omniscient old veteran of the Revolutionary War.] He and his wife were there. He is a young man (instead of an old Revolutionary character) about as old as their father, and very good looking and agreeable. He wanted us to go with him to Boston and has invited us to come and see him while we are there, as he lives four miles out of the city. I told him that I had a letter of introduction to Mrs. Minot. He said that would be sufficient of itself, for Mrs. Minot had the key of all Boston.

If you can get the [New York] "Herald" read [James Gordon] Bennett's letters from Saratoga. He was there all the time we were. I was very much pleased with Mr. Van Buren. We left him there and Mr. Clay and General Scott, Mr. and Mrs. Wilcox, Mr. and Mrs. Hepburn, the Countess of Westmoreland, the Andersons of Savannah, the Rutledges, Heywards and Draytons of [South] Carolina, the Livingstons of New York, and all the elite of the land. There were said to be 700 at the U. States Hotel where we staid. [James Gordon Bennett published fourteen letters from Saratoga beginning on August 7, a few days after Maria arrived, and concluding with the appearance in the *New York Herald* of his final letter on August 20, 1839.]

You cannot complain of the shortness of this. Love to all. Write soon.

Yours affectionately,

M.H.

Maria and her brother Joseph have been traveling in Canada.

Maria Bryan Harford to Julia Ann Bryan Cumming

[Montreal, Quebec Province]
September 1, 1839 (Sunday)

My dear Julia,

I have not written to you within a week past for I have been in a constant bustle, and am not so well as I have been.

When we arrived here about a week ago we expected to stay only a few days and then go to Boston, but Brother met with Colonel Downing and a party from Florida who were going to Quebec, and that put him in the notion of a trip there. Colonel Downing afterwards changed his mind and returned to New York, but some of the others went and we accompanied *them*. They are part of a delegation sent on by the Governor of Florida to see the President and Secretary of War in order to obtain assistance in putting down the Indians and after transacting their business they came here. [The second Seminole War (1835–42) ended with the removal of the last resisting Seminole Indians from Florida to beyond the Mississippi.]

Everything in Quebec is different from what I expected, and its being a walled town, and completely garrisoned, made it a novel sight to me. We went to Wolfe's monument on the spot where he fell on the Plains of Abraham. It was a simple inscription, "Here died Wolfe victorious." On the plains we witnessed a grand review and an imitation battle by the British troops, and so much firing as to try my nerves very considerably. There were nine mounted officers on the field, and the whole reviewed by Sir James McDonald, who commanded the 93rd Scotch Highlanders at the Battle of Waterloo.

I went to see the Falls of Montmorenci about nine miles from Quebec. The scenery is beautiful, and all around Quebec it is exceedingly fine.

They dine in Canada at six o'clock, but one day that we were in Quebec we ordered our dinner at three, sent our baggage to the steamboat, and rode out to see some objects of curiosity, as the steamboat was not to leave for several hours. After this we drove down to the wharf without calling at our hotel, and just as we were getting in sight we heard the bell of the steamer ring. She was out of our reach and we were obliged to return and spend another day and night at Quebec. We felt great uneasiness about our baggage, and some of the party had put all their money in their trunks. As for me, I had no night clothes, nor a comb, nor tooth brush, etc. etc. But on arriving here today, to our great satisfaction we found the steamboat in the harbour and every thing safe and sound.

I have visited the black nunnery where Maria Monk was, and the grey nuns [the Sisters of Charity of Montreal] also. I never saw any churches to compare with those I have seen in this country, for the rich ornaments in gold and silver, fine paintings, and the superiority of their architecture. The cathedral in this place, just finished, will hold 16,000 people. Tell Emmy I have got a little needlehook made in the shape of a butterfly, which I got in the nunnery for her, and shall take good care of it till I see her.

We shall set off tomorrow at nine, and expect to spend tomorrow night at Burlington. I hope I shall find letters at Boston as I am distressingly anxious to hear from home. I shall let you know of my further arrangements as soon as I understand them myself, but I do not [because of traveling with Brother] have the control of our movements at all.

I have been considerably better until within a few days past, and I think my indisposition at present comes from drinking the water which they say has considerable magnesia in it. I have hardly been able to hold up my head today, but did not like delaying longer to write to you. That must excuse my not filling the sheet as usual.

Give my kindest love to Mr. Cumming and the children, and Mrs. Cumming, Sarah and Mrs. Davis.

Ever most affectionately yours
M.M.H.

Maria's brother borrowed half her cash in Boston and returned to Washington. Soon after his departure, Maria learned that a severe epidemic of yellow fever raged in Augusta in the late summer of 1839. Joseph Bryan wrote to his son-in-law, Henry, suggesting that his daughter Julia and his grandchildren come to Mt. Zion and remain with him until the epidemic passed. As the city's mayor, Alfred Cumming, the younger brother of Henry Cumming, led the fight against the pestilence in Augusta. Maria Harford, arriving alone in New Haven, is greatly upset at the indirect news that her brother-in-law, Henry Cumming, is among those ill.

Maria Bryan Harford to Julia Ann Bryan Cumming

[New Haven, Connecticut]
September 25, 1839 (Wednesday)

My dear Julia,

I have not written to you lately, not because I did not think of you, but because I have thought so much, and with so much anxiety of you and yours. Not one line have I yet received from you, and in all this alarm and the accounts in the paper, I can only *conjecture* what you are feeling or suffering.

I found on my arrival here yesterday, a letter from Sophia dated the ninth. That is the first word I have heard from home, and that relieved me some, though so long ago written. But today I went with Grace Daggett to the State House, where was an exhibition of the Agricultural and Horticultural

Societies, and saw David Smith. He told me he had just received a letter from Augusta which informed him that Mr. Cumming was just taken sick. I came very near fainting, and was taken suddenly so very sick that I had to hurry home as fast as possible. I must, therefore, remain in suspense and anxiety for I know not how long. I must endeavour to put my trust in Providence and quiet myself as well as I can, but just imagine how I must feel so far away from home and in a strange place, with no companion, and suffering as I do from anxiety.

Brother writes me that Mr. Forsyth [the secretary of state] has sent your letters to Mr. Goodrich [Peter Parley] at Boston, and I have today written to request that he will send them here. I believe I mentioned to you that Brother had left me in Boston, being obliged to return to Washington by the fifteenth.

Mrs. Minot was confined to her room, but was exceedingly kind to me, and so was Mrs. Clarke and her family. I have not seen anyone since I left home that I liked and admired more than Sarah Clarke. Mrs. Minot appears to be very much attached to you, and spoke of you in terms almost too flattering to be repeated. Mr. Minot is an exceedingly gentlemanly and pleasant person, and seemed really to devise methods of showing me kindness while I was in Boston. He came to take leave of me the morning I came away, and asked me if I had plenty of money, as he said that ladies who were alone sometimes made mistakes in their calculations.

I went to Newport in company with a gentleman and lady who were from Newark, and acquaintances of the Wallace family. They were so regardful of me, and the gentleman so mindful of my baggage and myself, that I hardly missed Brother, though it was my first experiment in travelling without him. A little before the boat landed, whom should I meet on board but your Cousin William Stiles [a Savannah lawyer later to become a congressman and United States minister to Austria], so that instead of having to go to a hotel alone, which I expected, (as my Newark friends were proceeding immediately to New York), I had his very kind and attentive care during my stay in Newport, where his family has been passing the summer.

At Providence I had seen Mr. and Mrs. Larned who urged me to stay with them or if not, to come back there and proceed to New Haven from that place. This I resolved to do as I dreaded exceedingly to be in New York alone; Mrs. Minot had given me a letter of introduction to the Miss Telfairs at

Newport, but they had left the very morning of the day I got there. I found the Bullocks, the Andersons, the Draytons, the Jones's, etc. etc. at Newport. I must repeat in the same phraseology what I will not fear you will be tired of hearing, that from all I received attention and kindness, was at once admitted on the most familiar and intimate terms, and every thing done to contribute to my pleasure while I remained.

It was late in the season and cold at Newport. Besides, everyone whom I had spoken to on the subject seemed to be so convinced that I had decidedly an affection of the liver, for which seabathing is not considered good, that I did not attempt it, and did not stay so long as was my first intention. I was to leave Newport at four o'clock in the morning in the boat to Providence, which I dreaded as the hour was so unreasonable, and the never ending care about baggage rendered doubly troublesome by its being too dark to identify my own from others, but to my great surprise as well as pleasure, Mrs. Nuttall and George Jones offered to accompany me and return to Newport the same day. So you see that Providence has in every case provided for me.

I spent four days at Mr. Larned's. They are as agreeable a family as I ever knew, all of them well bred in the greatest degree, and talented, and so sweet and amiable in their tempers that you could hardly imagine they were relatives of the Larned you know. They tell me that he has named his youngest child "Maria Harford." I saw William Brantley, who is just finishing his course there (at Brown University), and who has already commenced preaching. Mr. and Mrs. Andre came to see me, the former very often; and I was invited to a small evening party at their house which, however, I did not attend.

I left Providence last Monday, three days ago; they were very unwilling to have me set off alone, and their son William, who is in business in Boston, and was home on a visit, proposed to come with me to New Haven, requiring me to wait two days longer while he could go to Boston and make arrangements for leaving his business, but I could not consent to receiving such a favor from a comparative stranger, as there would not only be *time*, but considerable *money* expended on my account, so I set out with a stout heart, *alone*.

I arrived at Hartford the first night, after having past through a beautiful country, and finding several ladies who, like myself, were without a male protector. Found there a polite and kind host and an obliging chambermaid, which latter is not always to be had in this northern country, and the next day set off to New Haven where I arrived at four o'clock. Before stopping at the boarding house, I drove to the post office and, as I have before told you, found only one letter.

A gentleman in Washington had given me a letter of introduction to Miss Mary Lives who, he said, kept a very desirable private boarding house here. This letter I had unfortunately lost, but I remembered the name and went to her house. The driver went in to inquire if I could be accommodated, and Miss Lives herself came out, called me by name, said she had been expecting me several weeks, and that the sister of the gentleman who had given me the letter had sent a number of times to inquire if I had arrived.

They talk volumes about you at the Daggetts [presumably cousins through the nearby Milford Bryans], seem to think you a prodigy, and are evidently disappointed that I do not look like you and am not so handsome. Cousin Grace says that when I got into the house, I sat in the very chair that you did the last time you came. Cousin Horace says you used to tell him you know how to cook, and were very much put out when he inquired if you could eat of your own cooking. "She did not like at all," said he, "that I should undervalue her culinary talents."

Give my love to all. Write immediately and direct to Washington. I have thought often this summer how much agony might be saved absent friends, if duplicaty or triplicaty of letters could be written and sent to different places. Make some of your children write me here, as I cannot leave till Brother comes.

P.S. I think my health improving since I wrote last.

The yellow fever epidemic in Augusta continues to cause Maria suspenseful suffering. Maria does not like New Haven, though she has received great hospitality from friends and relatives, and she awaits impatiently her brother's return from Washington, D.C., so that she may start for home.

Maria Bryan Harford to Julia Ann Bryan Cumming

[New Haven, Connecticut]
September 28, 1839 (Saturday)

My dear Julia,

Since writing to you on my arrival here, I have had two of your letters, one of the 1st, which Mr. Forsyth sent on to Boston and which someone dispatched to me here, and another of the 20th, which I have just received. The first one I got after David Smith's information, and did not relieve my mind concerning Mr. Cumming, but the contrary, for besides being written fifteen days before the date of his, the very information you gave me of the state of affairs in the community generally, as well as in your own family, seemed to me a reason why he should be sick. I need not say that you cannot imagine how I have suffered; mine has been of a different kind of suffering from yours, arising from suspense and absence, and the imagination at work with every vague and direct rumour to excite it.

It seems, then, that Mr. Cumming has indeed been sick and David Smith's account was but too true. I am indeed thankful that I can now trust he is out of danger. Mrs. Larned and Mr. Arnold knew that he was sick while I was there, but they would not tell me they had seen the account in the paper. I am most anxious for the rest of you, and can only trust you all to Providence, praying that He may do what is best for us all, and overrule everything to our best good. What you describe of the state of things I can realize, for I have twice been where the raging pestilence was spreading desolation, and where every heart was stricken with horror. I am truly glad that poor Uncle is spared. God grant it may be the occasion of making him a better and a happier man. I can realize what Pa must have suffered during his sickness, and I cannot tell you how I feel in being away from you all while you were so much tried and afflicted. Poor Aunt Wales, too, has been sick. I know Catherine is feeling dreadfully.

I have been here five days, and am most anxious to set off home but I do not know when to expect Brother. The Daggetts are very kind to me. Indeed, I have but one fault to find, they do not leave me enough to myself and I long for retirement and am sick of bustle. The very effort of gratitude for kindness rendered is fatiguing, and suffering as I have been for some time past, it is painful to be in company. Everybody talks of the fever in Augusta. They apply to me for information, and I dread and fear lest someone not knowing me or my relations should suddenly tell of something that would prostrate me to the earth. I have on such occasions been sometimes actually stupefied, and have had questions asked me without either comprehending or replying to them.

Colonel Mosely is a very pleasant man. His wife's niece and his adopted daughter Miss Phelps, our cousin, lives with him; he has urged me so warmly to come and stay with him that I am resolved to go tomorrow, particularly as I am not comfortable here. The house is so crowded that I have a room not ten feet square, and am wearied out during the day in climbing to the third story.

I have been improving in health, I think, ever since I arrived here. I cannot say I like New Haven altogether. I do not feel situated as much to my mind as I have been elsewhere, and I am not at all inclined to prolong my stay. It may be that the state of feeling in which I have been since my arrival has unfitted me to receive favourable impressions. I expect to go to Milford [Pa's birthplace] tomorrow.

Margaret Kelsey has come with her Uncle to see me. She seems perfectly happy. He is an exceedingly pleasant looking man, and seems quite devoted to her. She is sitting for her portrait which he wishes to have, and intends going to school soon. I saw Mrs. Staples and Frances at church today for the first time. They did not know I was here, and reproached me for not sending them word.

I am anxious to see you and yours and all at home, as you express yourself, to see your absent friends. I am sorry that Julien tries you so much. You must let me take him again, and do trust him altogether with us, as the situation is favourable, and being away from so many children is a desirable thing for one of his temper. I hope you have written to Brother. He is very anxious about home. I do hope Mr. Cumming is entirely restored by this time.

While I was feeling so badly about his sickness it was more on your account than on his, for I should have hoped much for him under any circumstances, that all would have been well with him for the sake of His merits who died for us poor sinners, but when I thought of you I could not attain any calmness. For who better than I understands the bitterness of such a loss? It is well for me that *my* memory does not picture the past with the distinctness that it does to some minds, for occasionally when a clear vision comes before me of Mr. Harford, as he looked and acted and spoke to me, I feel as if I could send forth a cry so long and loud and bitter that the very Heaven might ring with the echo of it. But we are all passing away, and if we had faith to see the real nature and value of the present and the future world, we should in sorrow, as well as in joy, act more as if we were pilgrims and steadily advancing onward, whether the way was rough or smooth.

I shall set off for home as soon as I can. I am impatient every day that I lose here, or spend here, perhaps I should say. My best love at home, and to my dear Brother H[enry].

Ever yours most affectionately,
M.H.

In New Haven for more than three weeks, Maria Harford is by now practically out of funds and a thousand miles from home.

Maria Bryan Harford to Julia Ann Bryan Cumming

[New Haven, Connecticut]
October 13, 1839 (Sunday)

My dear Julia,

The sight of a letter directed by you has long and always given me plea-sure, but never, surely, did I feel so much rejoiced as in getting one today. Although your last, and Pa's since yours, informed me that Mr. Cumming was recovering, still I was uneasy about him and anxious about all of you.

The other night a gentleman called here, who has lived in Augusta, and learning that I was from Georgia he inquired if I lived in Augusta. I told him I did not, but my brother-in-law Mr. Cumming did. "Which Mr. Cumming?" said he. "Mr. Henry Cumming," said I. "He is dead," said he. "I saw the account in the papers." I cannot tell you how I felt, and what I have suffered since, though I have tried to comfort myself by thinking that I surely should have heard immediately. I am all the time in a dead gloom and dread of mind, as if I was going to hear something.

I like New Haven less than any place where I have yet been. Though I have been treated with much kindness, still the people and the customs are much less to my liking than any place where I have yet been.

It is now three weeks since I arrived, and I have not had a line from Brother to say when he will be here, and I am almost, or I may say entirely, without funds. He took half my money to pay his expenses back to Washington, thinking he should see me before I had exhausted the rest, and every dollar that I have is United States, and that will not be taken at all in payment of any purchase. So that I am here, more than a thousand miles from home, without a dollar in my purse virtually, and Brother so uncertain that I cannot calculate upon him at all. I have written to him three times since I came, and shall make one more attempt to get an answer from him.

I am really troubled to think how much Pa is disturbed these times in mind and body. Poor Uncle, I had hoped he would get up and enjoy at least his usual health. When I think of how troubled you all have been this Summer, and that I have been away, and still cannot get home, I feel like a bird in a cage, and sometimes I think I must set off. Indeed I am sure I should if I had any money to pay my expenses.

I believe I have not written to you since I have seen Mrs. Staples. She has urged me to stay with her, and I have seen a great deal of her. Frances is very anxious to go home with me, and has urged her mother to allow her, but she will not consent. John Staples lost his wife about six weeks ago. She died very suddenly in child bed, and the family are very much afflicted, for they say she was a very lovely young woman and they were all exceedingly attached to her. Mr. Staples lives in New York, and comes up once a fortnight and spends Saturday and Sunday. They showed me the house they lived in when you were with them, and I have been interested in imagining you there. [The Staples were relatives by marriage of Aunt Wales.]

I have seen one of your schoolmates, who made kind inquiries about you. Her name was Louisa Bishop, and she is now Mrs. Hughes. I think I told you I was staying with Colonel Mosely, and our cousin Miss Phelps. Mrs. Staples wished me to have my baggage carried there, but Colonel Mosely said I might visit as much as I pleased, but he would be exceedingly hurt if I removed my baggage.

I have spent one day in Milford, and visited the graves of Pa's father, and seen the house in which Grandma [Juliana Smith Bryan Buckingham] lived.

[The house still stands.] I have had an invitation from Mrs. Isaac's family to visit them in Norwalk, and Pa, in his last letter, requested that I would do so, but I am uncertain in all my plans and quite perplexed as to what arrangements to make. I shall take pains to make inquiry about the school here. It is taught by a Mr. Skinner, and I hear it highly spoken of. Mrs. Apthorpe I have seen, and her school, too, has a very high reputation. How much Mr. Thomas's family are afflicted. I am truly sorry for them.

I think it must be a gloomy time for poor Sophia, and I do most heartily wish that I was there, to aid and comfort them in some degree. I hope Providence may direct Uncle to a judicious disposition of his property, and that it may be the means of much good to the world.

I quite wished for the command of a fortune last Sunday, in hearing the statements given at a missionary meeting. I heard a discourse from the Rev. Eli Smith, the missionary in Syria, and the next day he called on me. To my utter astonishment, I found he had taught school in Putnam County [Georgia], and been repeatedly at our house, and inquired most earnestly about the family, Pa and you and Brother, etc. etc. I cannot for my life remember about him.

The Daggets are very kind to me but I do not think they altogether like my staying at Colonel Mosely's. I like Mrs. Hunt better than any of them.

My health is improved very considerably since I came here, and I think *would* still more, were my mind but usually composed. Mrs. Staples says she would never have known me, and says the change in my complexion is astonishing since 1832.

You say I have not mentioned Margaret [Kelsey]. I suppose you have received the letter in which I mentioned her.

I have written this letter in great confusion, and hardly knowing what I was saying, for the room has been full all the time and every one talking at once.

If Brother does not write or come for me, and I can borrow money, I must set off for New York in a few days. Write to Washington as soon as you get this.

Give my love to Mr. Cumming and the children, and believe me ever affectionately your Sis.

Maria Harford

While in New Haven, Maria evidently is looking around the town for a likely school to which the Cummings could send their young sons, Julia apparently having attended school in New Haven during her youth. At Yale, Maria met Professor Woolsey — Theodore Dwight Woolsey, who later became Yale's president for twenty-five years. His nephew, William Walton Woolsey, in the late 1880s became the suitor of Julia Hammond, the granddaughter of Julia Bryan Cumming and the great-niece of Maria.

Maria Bryan Harford to Julia Ann Bryan Cumming

[New Haven, Connecticut]
October 20, 1839 (Sunday)

My dear Julia,

I have concluded to write you once more from this place, as I hope to set off in a few days with Mr. Wheeler. I got a letter from Brother yesterday but it leaves me in as much uncertainty as I was before, and through Mr. Wheeler's kind exertions I have been able to borrow money from the bank to be paid at sixty days hence. He found that a check would cost too much.

I have wept much and mourned deeply since I received your letter informing me of the death of Robert [the Cumming servant, not Robert, the Mt. Zion gardener]. I feel as if I had lost myself a humble friend whom I have known and loved from my childhood, and when I consider what will be the regret of yourself and Mr. Cumming, as well as his exceeding loss to you as a servant, my distress is increased. I thought it was rather a singular coincidence; yesterday was a gloomy rainy day, and as I sat in my room alone sewing, I was constantly repeating aloud some lines that had been at some previous time fixed in my memory.

> "Fear no more the heat and the sun,
>   Nor the furious winter's rages.
>   He his earthly task has done,
>   Home has gone and ta'en his wages."

It is indeed a great source of comfort that we can have so much reason to think that he was prepared for the sudden and unexpected summons. Oh, that we, and all we love, may be ready, and watching, for truly "all flesh is grass, and all the glory thereof as the flower of the grass." How many of those whom we have known and associated with have gone, and how constantly we are reminded that "*this* is not our rest."

I am in hopes that the change of weather, which is very great here, will be felt at the South generally. Mobile suffers in every way, and seems as if doomed to destruction. I do not remember whether I have written to you since I saw Mary Teasdale. She is now in this place on a visit to some acquaintances, and has been spending the summer at the North. She has, like myself, suffered a great deal from anxiety about her friends who have been near Mobile during the Season. She tells me Mrs. Casey is dead, though she knows nothing of the particulars of her death.

I am very anxious to be on my journey home, and since this cold weather set in I am still more so.

Mrs. Hickman is expected tonight at Derby, and will go with Mr. Wheeler as far as Richmond, Va. Mrs. Wheeler has been to see me, and I have been to Derby to see her. I *do* think she is one of the most amiable women I ever saw. I think she is very pleasantly situated, and she likes Derby very much, and is exceedingly pleased with the school to which her children go. Mrs. Hall, Mr. Wheeler's sister, sent me an invitation to go and spend the rest of my time in Derby while I remained in Connecticut. I think I should be much better pleased there than I am here, and should like to accept her invitation were I going to stay longer.

Tell Annie I was very glad to get her letter and shall write to her in a day or two. I should have written to her instead of you, had she not insisted upon my writing so long a letter, and I have not the time just at present.

I went today to the college chapel and heard Professor Fitch preach. I saw President Day, Dr. Taylor, and Professors Goodrich and Woolsey, but the most interesting sight was so many youths. The choir is conducted entirely by the students, both the instrumental and vocal part, and the music is very good excepting that they need a treble. There are between four and five hundred students in Yale College this term, more than ever before at one time.

I have made many inquiries about the schools. The one I have heard more uniformly praised than any other is taught by Mr. Skinner, who has twenty five scholars, keeps them in his family, and receives them at the age of eight, or thereabouts. Everything I heard of this school induced me to think you would be better suited with it than any other, and Mrs. Staples who knows him very well, asked permission for me to visit his school. He said I was welcome to do so, but he had no room for more, that he preferred to have his scholars leave him during the vacations, and consequently always preferred those living in New York.

Give my love to Mr. Cumming and the children, and believe me truly your Sister.

Maria Harford

Maria has just reached Washington on her way back home. She expects to be in Mt. Zion in ten days.

Maria Bryan Harford to Julia Ann Bryan Cumming

[Washington, D.C.]
October 30, 1839 (Wednesday)

My dear Julia,

I arrived here tonight and was very much gratified to find a letter from you and one also from Pa. I feel a little uneasy about his fall, of which, of course, you have heard, as I know he makes so light of any of his ailments.

The very day I sent my letter to Annie, Brother arrived in New York. He was in such a hurry to get back to Washington that we left Mr. Wheeler in New York, and I waited for him and Mrs. Hickman in Philadelphia.

Mr. and Mrs. Randall called at the Marshall House [in Philadelphia] and literally almost forced me to go home with them, and there I staid three days. They are a pleasant interesting family, and made me think of yours, two girls and four boys they have, and most remarkably fine children they are. I was treated with as much attention and kindness as if I had been some important personage, and it quite surprised me, but I attribute these things to the overruling kindness of the Providence who watches over those who trust in him. Mr. Randall is a man of middle age, very pleasant and sensible, and a distinguished lawyer in Philadelphia. He knows much of Southern men and Southern politics, and asked me if I was acquainted with "Colonel William Cumming," of whom he said he was a great admirer. When I came away he told me when I saw Colonel Cumming to urge him to visit Philadelphia, and tell him that his house was always open to receive him. I know it is a mere form to tell Colonel Cumming this, but I can only discharge my commission.

I presume you have heard of the death of Colonel [Joseph] White of Florida at St. Louis. He was there with his wife, waiting for the fever to subside in New Orleans before returning there. I saw him at Saratoga in such health and spirits; there is something so awful in witnessing such a man in the vigour of life cut down, amid all his worldly schemes and plans. [Joseph White, Florida delegate in Congress, died in St. Louis on October 19, 1839. It was his wife whose relationship with Richard Henry Wilde caused gossip in Washington.]

I forgot to mention that I saw Miss Mary Telfair in Philadelphia. She desired to be specially remembered to you, and spoke of the pleasure she had had in your society in Savannah, and her regret that your visit was so short. I saw Mr. and Mrs. Ragnet, and if I had been their child they could not have evinced more feeling in seeing me; they wanted me to go and spend some time with them. They appear to be devotedly pious, more than ever confirmed in their Swedenborgian faith, and wished that they had time and opportunity to converse with me on the subject. It seems to make them very happy, and they represent it as a faith capable of affording the most intense happiness—of the entire and perfect reunion of the good who are for a time separated, and of the mutual delight in each other's society they entertain not the smallest doubt, and this seems to be their most comforting doctrine. [The Swedenborgian faith pertains to the religious doctrines of Emanuel Swedenborg (1688–1772), scientist, philosopher, and theologian who claimed to have direct contact with the spiritual world.]

I wish we had sooner known of Mrs. Davis's wish to have the two boys accompany me home. Brother received your letters after my arrival tonight. I shall stay here tomorrow, and Mr. Wheeler proposes to remain several days in Richmond so that if we can devise any plan they may possibly yet join me. Brother is on the lookout now for an opportunity of arranging it. I cannot say when I shall be at home, but hope to sometime in the early part of next week. I have been much improved of late, but am again suffering from the pain in the place where you applied the leeches, and it has troubled me often during the summer.

Pa informs me that Mr. Cumming had sent on funds for me to New Haven.

I take it for granted that it is in the form of a draught, and that there will be no difficulty in arranging it. If it could have come the week before I left, what trouble it would have saved me!

I liked the Miss Bryans very much, and Judge Isaacs and his wife. Norwalk [Connecticut] is a beautiful place. I stood by the grave of Mrs. Rossiter's parents, but have not told them of it at home, meaning to tell her if we meet.

Give my best love to Mr. Cumming and the children — and believe me ever yours

Maria M. Harford

P.S. Brother tells me he has written to Mrs. Henry to send the boys on immediately. You must rub your shoulder with a liniment of equal quantities of hartshorn, lard, sweet oil and spirits of turpentine and wear a piece of India rubber cloth on it. I have bought you a very nice new fashioned pair of India rubber overshoes and if you don't wear them in damp weather I shall take it as a personal affront.

Chapter Ten

PLANTATION LIFE

"I never took such very great pleasure before in reading Madame de Staël, although I have always admired her."

Maria returned to Mt. Zion from her four-month northern trip around November 20 and resumed her tutoring of her nephew Alfred. To carry out this task, she asks Julia to send her the latest advice manuals, including John Abbott's The School-boy.

Maria Bryan Harford to Julia Ann Bryan Cumming

Mt. Zion
December 23, 1839 (Monday)

My dear Julia,

I received your letter Saturday, by Mr. Neal, the first one I have had all in my own right during the month I have been at home. Goode and Alfred are in preparation to go down, and I have concluded to give you a few lines.

If it did any good to complain I could tell you that I had had my hands full for the last week or ten days, and I miss Tom so much, and Caroline is a miserable substitute for even an indifferent manservant, for she is obstinate, self-willed, cross and dirty to a degree.

Catherine's baby has been very sick, dangerously so, and she has suffered very much herself under the apprehension of losing him. I think he appears better today, and her heart is very much lightened in consequence. The expectation of pleasure in the visit has been completely disappointed, and she seems to be extremely wounded and hurt that she has made such an effort to get here, and Sophia would not come this far to meet her. Her own health is miserable but she appears very amiable and interesting, far more so than I ever saw her.

Maria McDonald, and Mary Anne Carter, and Mary Anne McDonald (James McDonald's daughter) have been here for some days, with Alfred, Herbert the engineer, Bonner, Joe Ponce, and Goode, so that the house has been full. They have gone this morning. Herbert is very much in love with Mary Anne Carter and I think him an exceedingly fine young man, not *brilliant* in mind, or handsome, but has very good sense, and an agreeable face, which is indeed a fine one when he smiles.

I do not think Maria is so charmed with her new sister as I expected to find her, though she evidently thinks her a very superior person. She says she is violently opposed to the Baptists, and I thought Maria's eyes filled as she was telling me of the unmeasured terms of dislike in which she spoke of them as a sect. She has sent a polite and pressing invitation to Sophia and I to go down and see her, and told Mary Anne to tell us she should prepare a room for us. Maria is going to Texas the middle of January. Catherine is boarding with little Charles at Mrs. Bozeman's.

I was very glad to get my shawl, and obliged to Mr. Cowes for the trouble he took in getting it, for I feared it was a dead loss. If you have done with the *Confessions of an Opium Eater* [by Thomas De Quincey], please send it, and the volume of Mrs. Smith's poems which Mr. Wheeler gave me. Tell Julien to send the *Parents Assistant* [*or Stories for Children*, by Maria Edgworth (1767–1849)], and if you can conveniently lay hands on them, lend me Sydenham, and Mr. Abot's work. Tell Mr. Cumming he has afforded me a treat in the French books he lent me. I never took such very great pleasure before in reading Madame de Staël, although I have always admired her. Deep sorrows, and the painful experience of a changeful and troubled life, makes our own mind and heart such a commentator and appreciator of one who writes from the deep feeling and thought which her productions manifest.

I am growing a little uneasy about my baggage from New Haven, particularly as there was a dress in it for Catherine and Aunt Wales from Mrs. Staples. Handley, the carriage maker, was to bring the things, and I should like to know what he says about them.

I am glad you have been to see Mrs. Root, and thought you would like her. Give my love to her and tell her I should be very glad to see her and her husband here, and to introduce her to Pa and to other friends, if she has any interim in her school. I fully understand, I think what it is to be a stranger in a strange place, with people and customs and ways entirely different from which I have been used to before.

If I had time and space I could tell you how Pa and I have felt about Mr. Hooker, and how many hard feelings have been excited towards us because we have preferred another's preaching to his. As yet, all things are uncertain, and even if he goes away it is doubtful whether another minister can be procured, for many are prejudiced against Mr. Bonner for no other reason that I know but because Pa likes him. Mr. Ingram has re-engaged himself at Powelton because there was a doubt of Mr. Hooker's staying, and the trustees have procured Mr. Spencer, a northern man, for next year.

I am glad of the prospect of having my little boys here next year. Pa said to my surprise that you intended sending them to the Academy. Of course I wish you to do as you prefer, but of course, too, you know I shall willingly teach them myself if you wish it.

Yours truly,

M.H.

I send you some sausages and wanted to send you some butter but there was not a bit to spare.

M.

Annie Cumming, now thirteen, writes her mother from Mt. Zion, and in an addendum, Maria reports that Sophia is unhappy to discover that Julia does not like Sophia's fiance — Robert Y. Harriss.

Annie M. Cumming to Julia Ann Bryan Cumming
Maria Bryan Harford to Julia Ann Bryan Cumming

Mt. Zion
February 13, 1840 (Thursday)

My dear Mother,

I intended to have written on Tuesday but I did not think of it until it was too late to do it. We got to the Double Wells about eleven but such a place as it was. Miss Train and I had to sleep in a room where there were at least four others. It was such a small as well as dirty room that we could hardly turn round and the bed was no better. The sheets looked as if they had not been washed for a month and checked ones besides. But the breakfast, it was so bad I could not eat at all though Miss Train did and told Mrs. Durden that it was very good.

I have taken one real regular music lesson since I came up. "Poor Bessy Was a Sailor's Wife" is the song; it is very easy and I hope that I can take a new lesson soon. Alf is taking them too. I do believe he is the best natured boy in the world. He don't seem to wish to go home at all, he is very buisy at a garden he is making. Grandpa says he will give him sead to plant and he is fixing his beds to plant some of them.

Miss Train was not very well the first two or three days but she is very well now. She has been to ride three or four times. Mrs. Baxter and Miss Jane and Elizabeth were here yesterday and invited Miss Train and Aunt Sophia there this evening. They are going, and I am going with them I believe.

Miss Train is going on Saturday. Grandpa is going with her to the Double Wells. Pa said as he was going to there to meet her but as Grandpa does not think he will come. Miss Train says that as she has been introduced to Mr. Freeman she does not mind at all going alone if Pa meets her at the Depot.

We all expect you at least by the last of next week.

My dear Julia,

Annie's letter appears to have come to a very sudden conclusion and she has gone to Mrs. Baxter's without leaving any directions about her letter and as Robert wants it to take to the mail, I close and direct it for her. She takes to her music with tolerable willingness, and I give her a lesson in singing daily.

I think if she was willing to exert her energies fully she could make a very agreeable singer in time. I have devised other employment for her too, as I found she was an amazing hindrance to Alfred, besides suffering from the listlessness attendant upon idleness.

I am not able to form an opinion whether Miss Train enjoys her visit or not, but I think her health is better for two days past.

Sophia, I think, suffers a great deal in her feelings, although she makes great efforts to control herself. I think she has been unhappy since Annie told her you did not like H[arriss]. She is more affected by your and Mr. Cumming's opinions and feelings than it is ever well or comfortable for one individual to be affected by others, and since Providence has committed our happiness to ourselves, we must act to the best of our judgment, and of course can do no more. I hope for the best for her, and I earnestly pray that marriage may be the means of correcting her faults and bringing out her best qualities and implanting correct principles of action, so that she may be a useful member of society, and above all fitted for a better world. I feel touched and saddened whenever I think that we had a mother near us at a similar time, and she, the best beloved and the darling of that mother's heart, is deprived of that intense sympathy that would have been hers on the occasion, and I endeavour to make up for it as much as I can.

If you see anybody coming up soon please send us a little carbonate of soda, as Pa suffers greatly from heartburn, and forgot to get some and I need it daily. Ask Mr. Cumming if he will be so kind as to keep his eye out for any box at Hoadleys, for I do want some clothing of which it contains much. Did you forget to send me word about the *Albion*. Love to Mr. Cumming.

Yours affectionately
M.M.H.

Maria Bryan Harford to Julia Ann Bryan Cumming

Mt. Zion
February 20, 1840

My dear Julia,

We have all been disappointed this week that we have heard neither from you or Sophia, and I rather think Jule is of the opinion that his letters are too valuable to be treated with such contempt. He has however given you quite a long epistle for *him* notwithstanding.

We received a letter from Goode a few days ago which has put Pa in very good spirits. He writes that they will make 90 bales of cotton (which they will sell at the advanced prices), and given some other items of intelligence with regard to the sale of lands, collections of debts, etc. which would indicate a favorable prospect for the settlement of affairs. Pa talks of going to Augusta some time next week.

Jule as I mentioned in my last has a cold but he does not mind it much, and has an excellent appetite with all the other proofs of a good state of health.

I had no idea that H. Gaylord Clarke was the author of those lines. I have admired all of his verses that I have seen. I knew then none of those I gave you, for I had them once. Travelling from Hartford to New Haven my only companion part of the way was a very motherly, good natured "person." She had her baggage tied up in a newspaper, upon which I descrest the said poetry. I eagerly requested her to tear them off for me, as we had become very intimate — "I guess," said she, "I cannot till we get down to Noohaven because it will leave my things kinder exposed." I said no more. I forgot about it but when we were in sight of "Noohaven," she tore them off and presented them to me with the air of rewarding me for my patience, but unfortunately I mislaid them afterwards. . . . Give my love to Mr. C. and Annie and the other children and to Mrs. C. and Sarah.

Yours affectionately,

On February 25, 1840, Sophia Bryan married Robert Harriss in Mt. Zion. This letter of Maria's to Julia is filled with news of home and of the Sparta community.

Maria Bryan Harford to Julia Ann Bryan Cumming

Mt. Zion
April 6, 1840 (Monday)

My dear Julia,

I should have answered your letter by the last mail but as Alfred was preparing a letter to send I concluded to wait till another time.

We all feel very much for Miss Anne Wallace and her brother, and would have been very glad if they had come up and spent some days here. What could have occasioned such a total deafness?

As we received no letter from Sophia this morning, we conclude to send for her tomorrow morning agreeable to her last directions. Have you heard anything about my watch? Mr. Corker said he would call and let you know he had left it at Murphy's to be mended. I hope Sophia will bring it up and the Spiritus Vitae from Mr. Wheeler, for besides the pain in my shoulder, I did not know the other day but we would have occasion to use it for Pa. He went to the tanyard Saturday, and John keeps two very severe dogs which Pa had kept off with a stick until he got into the house. Apprehending no danger then, he was coming out of the door, and one of them jumped upon him without the least noise and bit him severely just below the knee. He complained of its being very painful, and I sent to Dr. Rossiter's and got the little [Spiritus Vitae] that was left in the vial and applied it to the bitten part. This eased the pain entirely, but whenever a person is bitten by a dog I feel uneasy lest the dog may be mad. At any rate I thought it would be tantalizing and distressing beyond measure to see one suffering from hydrophobia, and imagining there was a remedy, and no power of procuring it in time to do any good.

As Alfred and I were riding out the other afternoon, we were overtaken by Uncle who rode some way with us. I asked him how his health was. "Oh much better, much better," said he. "I am improving greatly, my colour is very good now, very good, very good indeed." I thought it was strange to call the hue of death itself a good colour. His complexion is wretched still, though otherwise he seems really improved in health. We spoke of Dr. and Mrs. Terrill's afflictions. He said he had thought much of them, but he supposed "they had idolized that child, and 'thou shalt have no other God before Me' *says the commandment*. I have often observed it to be the case, Maria," continued he, "when one sets their heart upon a thing in that way, that some misfortune happens." I wondered to myself, since he repeated Scripture so correctly if he remembered what was called *idolatry* in Scripture besides love of our friends, but so we all go on in life, seeing so clearly for our neighbours and so dimly for ourselves. Or like the picture drawn by the old Satirist of a man walking along under the weight of a bag thrown across his shoulders, his own faults and errors in the hinder part and his neighbours' before him, and full in view.

Mrs. Matthews says she inquired of Mr. Ransome how the Dr. and

Mrs. Terrill bore their misfortune [the loss of their child]. "Ah," said he, "they do not bear it at all. Mrs. Terrill is like one distracted and the Dr. is not very different. They shut up their house and see no one, and the Dr. has not been seen in the streets of Sparta since his return." I sent to Mrs. Bird by Alfred, Saturday, when he and Henry Lawson went in to town, to inquire how they were. Alfred said Mrs. Bird told him to tell me that she went to see them every day, and that "they were as distressed as they could be." I have thought of them increasingly day and night since I have heard of their sore calamity, and would do anything in my power to alleviate and soothe their distress. I can only ask the compassion of the Almighty for them, for when the heart is so bruised and crushed, it is his consolations alone that can be of much avail.

Give my kindest love to Mrs. Campbell. I do hope she will yet revive, and be spared many years, for she will be a great loss indeed to her family and ac-quaintances. Remember me likewise to Miss Train when you see her and tell her if she ever comes to see us again, I hope circumstances will not be so inauspicious for her enjoying her visit.

Pa came home last night apostrophizing and addressing me alternately upon the blessings of "family harmony." He saw some of the neighbours in the afternoon, who advised him to go to Mrs. Duncan's, as they were in trouble there. He found that Duncan had left, but his wife was in great distress of mind. He had come home drunk the night before, and took up a piece of lightwood, saying he would split her head open, and probably would have killed her, but his daughter Julia seized his arm and prevented the blow from reaching its aim. He repeatedly threatened to kill her and Catherine Lightfoot his stepdaughter. Catherine says she would go away and find some place to live, but she don't like to leave her mother entirely in his power.

Mrs. Rossiter is suffering considerably from her eye now, but the Dr. is apparently very well and happy. He has made a very pretty little affair of Annie's Eolian harp, and has hardly thought or talked of anything else for the last few weeks. Do remember to send some strings for it by Isaac Williams who goes down Wednesday.

Pa has been a little surprised that he did not receive any account from the meat, but takes it for granted it must have reached you safely. He went to the mill today, and saw Miss Ingraham; she had made up her mind to leave, but the girls were so earnest in their entreaties that she would not leave them that she had concluded to remain a while longer there. She was boarding at Mr. H.'s. Pa came back with his sympathies greatly excited in behalf of Mr. H. He said he looked so lonely and dejected, and he had a dreadful cough which he had had for seven or eight weeks, and he told Pa he was so very lonely and solitary that he could hardly contain himself.

Give my love to Anne and Sarah and tell them I should be very glad to see them. Ask Mr. [Samuel] Davis [husband of Henry Cumming's sister Mary] if he can't come up and preach for us, and Pa is very desirous to have him do so. Next Sunday we have no preaching, nor the third, nor the first Sabbath in May.

P.S. The travellers arrived about six o'clock—all well. Mary Anne's tongue has not received a Galvanic shock since her abode with you, I find.

Affectionately yours,
M.M.H.

Sophia returned to Mt. Zion accompanied by two of Julia's children, Tommy and Julien. Alfred was already with the Bryans. Maria will devote her mornings to their instruction.

Maria Bryan Harford to Julia Ann Bryan Cumming

Mt. Zion
April 30, 1840 (Thursday)

My dear Julia,

I write a few lines tonight to let you know that the children and Sophia arrived safely last night. They seem to enjoy play and freedom and being with Alf very much, who has had a holiday in honour of their arrival. Pa is, I think, improving, and very much cheered in having them, as well as in Sophia's being at home again. We are all disappointed in hearing that you do not intend coming up to the meeting, as we hoped and somewhat expected. Tommy is quite excited to think he should have just missed a letter to himself, and says I must ask you to send it up. They tell me you wish them to study in the mornings, and I shall arrange their movements tomorrow. Tommy ought not to be kept very closely, for he looks thin and weakly. Robert said tonight at supper, "I like Tommy better than anyone 'um and I bleeve it's cause he's so much like his Mother."

Caroline continues quite sick.

In haste affectionately yours,
M.M.H.

Busy times in Mt. Zion—Maria is cutting out and basting the material for clothes for her father's slaves, and all the while people come and go from the house. In early May, the artist George Cooke had painted in Augusta a portrait of Julia and her daughter Emily. Pa's son-in-law, Henry Cumming, wishes to employ the artist to paint Pa's portrait. Pa objects.

Maria Bryan Harford to Julia Ann Bryan Cumming

Mt. Zion
May 12, 1840 (Tuesday)

My dear Julia,

I did not think it would have been so long before I should have answered your letters, but I have been *very busy about the negroes' clothes,* cutting and basting them, and Mr. Hurlbut, the piano and organ tuner, has been here since Thursday turning the house topsy turvy with noise and litter, and added to that the *meeting,* and Mr. Davis and Mr. Bowman both being here, I could not get a letter ready for Monday's mail as I had intended.

We had no service Saturday, for Mr. Bowman was detained by the high water until late in the afternoon of that day, and had been and was, during his stay, so sick that he could not preach, and Mr. Davis came late Saturday evening. I cannot tell you what an agreeable impression Mr. Davis made upon all by his ministrations, from the hypercritic Mr. Little to Robert Bonner, including all between those extremes, white and black, young and old, everybody was delighted. Sunday afternoon he preached to the blacks, but there were a great many white people present who were among the most attentive of his audience. I do think Mr. Davis is an excellent preacher as well as an excellent man and I don't know when I have been as much pleased and edified by preaching as by his three discourses. He remembered that it was just at the same season twenty years ago that he was present in that house, and he referred to it in a most touching manner, and to those then seated there, whose places were now vacant. Jane Armour and I were sitting together, and we were both overcome, as I suppose at the same moment we thought of our mothers, and indeed everybody was affected, particularly those who had always lived in the place. The poor old Doctor had come tottering to his seat, seeming as if every step he would fall upon his face, and in all probability he will not attend many more times, and Mr. Davis spoke of the *few* remaining, and that they would not be long for this earth. I could not but wish that *I* might not long survive these, for this earth would be desolate if many more of those nearest to me were gone for *I* have not many more to lose. And "there is a rest remaining for the people of God," and I trust that "the Lord will preserve me from all evil, and lead me to his heavenly kingdom." Still I often think of those lines and apply them to myself when disturbed by outward grievances and deep corruption within.

> "But first by many a *stern* and *fiery* blast,
>   The world's rude furnace must thy blood refine,
> And many *a gale of keenest woe* be past,
>   Till every pulse beat time to airs divine."

Mr. Harris arrived this morning to breakfast; he seemed delighted to get back again, and is I think improved by the tanning he has undergone. He does not seem able to give any clear account of Brother or of his movements or intentions, but I hope for Pa's sake he will come home soon.

He says you wished Alfred to come home with him. Alfred was quite willing to stay to the examination and to the picnic, but is equally excited at the prospect of going home. Pa wishes him to stay and meant to take him home, and if you wish to see the latter, I am afraid he will go down on no other terms, for he is or thinks himself very much confined at home by his tanyard, and shop and plantation. Indeed he injures himself by his exertions, and I would be glad if he would go from home a little. The other day, he got in the waggon and drove it to Mr. Harris's mill and back again, and another day, he went in it with John to buy hides. He often says, if ever there was a necessity for bestirring himself it is now when he is so much in debt, and that he never sees Uncle without feeling oppressed and embarrassed.

Mr. Hurlbut has improved my piano very much, which I feared was irremediably ruined. I have gotten him to promise to go by Augusta, and shall give him a letter to you which will furnish him an introduction when he does go. He is a complete Yankee but is good nature embodied, very faithful and very skillful, and I do think will be able to make your piano better than it ever was. He will be there in June or July. I am sure you will enjoy his playing and singing. His execution on the piano and organ is very fine. The children are delighted with him and with his songs, and children so soon find out good natured people. They are round him half the time, and among his tools and at his elbow watching his operations, and I should think were terribly in his way, for when he has to make a move, and change his position they are so thick you might stir them. He plays a comic song for Tommy "The Straw Bonnet," which makes his face glisten with delight.

Tommy is very good and very happy and is at the head of his class in spelling. Spelling is *"being carried"* on now at a large rate, as Pa insisted upon it, that in this day of the diffusion of arts and science, that spelling was thrown too much into the background, and that I must make them spell more.

I suppose you are at the Hill by this time, as Mr. Harris mentioned that you would go out today. He speaks of returning to Augusta the last of this week. If you can conveniently attend to it, I wish you would get me at Cress's a *piece of fine white* cambric, half a doz. prs. of *white stockings,* I do not care about their being very fine, a *piece of bobinet* lace for ruffling night caps, and a yard of some suitable material for making night caps.* If you can arrange for the articles to come up so that the carriage can bring them when it goes to the railroad with Sophia, I shall be glad.

Affectionately yours,

M.M.H.

P.S. Pa desires me to say to Mr. Cumming that he has part of the money from Mr. Kelsey, and thinks he will have the rest to send by Mr. Harris. They will set off from here Monday. Tommy has been riding on horseback with his Grandpa today, and paid a visit to Mrs. Baxter, and he was perfectly delighted. *In addition,* you will find at Carmichael's some small figured cheap calico (or perhaps at Cress's) I wish you would get about *fourteen or fifteen yds.* for a double gown. I prefer the colour blue, but am not very particular.

---

* And the bill with them.

I should be delighted to have Mr. Cook take Pa's portrait and the only difficulty he makes is on the score of the expense to Mr. Cumming. He says these are extraordinarily hard times, and "Mr. Cumming has so much and more than he can manage with." I quote from him. Of course I do not agree with him, and think we should all value a good portrait of Pa's as high as any other possession.

Can [Thomas] Carlyle's works be had in Augusta now? [Maria had, in an earlier letter, inquired into the work *The French Revolution*.] I sent to the North by Frank Thomas for them, and greatly to my disappointment he came home without inquiring for them till he got to Charleston.

In this letter Maria begs Julia to come to Mt. Zion, if only for a few days to comfort her father, who is suffering from "severe mental disquietude."

Maria Bryan Harford to Julia Ann Bryan Cumming

Mt. Zion
May 25, 1840 (Monday)

My dear Julia,

We were a good deal disappointed that we did not get a letter from you yesterday morning, as we had not heard a word since Sophia and Alfred left. I intended to have written, or at any rate meant that Julien or I should have had a letter by Monday's mail, but I was quite unwell from having been caught in a heavy rain Friday afternoon when I was riding out, and Julien was unwell for two days from disordered bowels and stomach, so that he was not willing to undertake the very considerable enterprise of writing a letter.

All of us have been complaining lately. Henry Lawson has been sick, and Robert so very unwell that he has become quite thin, and looks wretchedly. And as to Pa, I do not know where to begin or end my enumeration of troubles on his account. He is very unwell all the time, and makes himself much worse by hard work and exposure. In a rainy day, he is all the time either in the rain out of doors, or sitting in the house with damp clothes and soaked shoes. The next day and perhaps many after it, he has pains in his limbs, walks half bent, and suffering very much from almost constant diarrhea. My remonstrances and prayers are however unavailing. He is restless and disturbed in mind, and he fancies there is an imperative necessity on his part for extraordinary exertion. He does not hear a word from Brother and mail days he is doubly unhappy.

Mr. Bowman's preaching seems to be the principal comfort he has. He left us yesterday morning after having delivered a sermon the day before that some say is "the greatest ever delivered in that house." His text was from Galatians, V chapter and 4th verse. "Christ is become of no effect unto you, whosoever of you are justified by the law, ye are fallen from grace." He did indeed make it appear that the salvation that Christ hath wrought out for us is a *great salvation,* so that they who put their trust in Him shall stand as safe from all condemnation as though they had never sinned, and that we who are the partakers of it through faith, are foolish and ungrateful beyond expression, if we do not strive to devote ourselves to the service of such a benefactor, and exhibit the effects of our faith by a holy and useful and blameless life. Mrs. Bowman expects to be confined in about a fortnight.

We have received the things you sent up by the railroad, and everything suits well. I never saw neater and prettier calico, and indeed am satisfied with the selection throughout.

I suppose you have seen Uncle, as I met him the other day on his way to Augusta. He and Brother may be considered as the spoilers of the peace of one of the best men in this world and one to whom they both owe everything. I pity them both, and pray Heaven to give them a right view of their own behavior. Pa's views with regard to Uncle, or with regard to his debt to him, have become morbid, but I don't know that it is to be wondered at. He said that he was quite sure that if he allowed his portrait to be taken that Uncle would say to himself "he had better employ the money spent in that way in defraying his debt to me."

"Why Pa," said I, "let him know that your children have it taken for their special gratification, and at their own expense."

"Well but," he would then say, "if they are inclined to be so liberal let them give the money to pay his debts."

"And so," said I, "you will then let the worthy suffer for the two most unworthy of the family."

I suppose Sophia is at this time in Columbia. I am at a loss where to direct a letter to her though I suppose she must be getting anxious to hear from home.

Tommy and Julien enjoyed the picnic very much (as would Alf had he been there), and it was reported to me that they were very good boys and behaved with perfect propriety. I put them under the care of Henry Lawson and Mrs. Smith. I was in some hesitation about letting them go, but Pa and Mrs. Rossiter could not endure that the pleasure should be denied them.

By the bye, where are Mr. & Mrs. Cook? Will they not come, and have you really yielded like a dutiful daughter as you are, to your Father's will in the matter. I wish you would come up if only for a few days and try and comfort him. I *believe* in the efficacy of nature's own mode where trouble is concerned, *talking of it to others,* and though I listen willingly whenever Pa is inclined to converse, yet my sympathy is not as *fresh* as yours would be. Now do break off if you can, from what I know are strong claims and duties, and pay a duty where I think sometimes it will not long have to be paid. For though I do not think it right to croak, or communicate in general one's own misgivings when it may occasion pain to another, yet I sometimes think Pa cannot stand long under his severe mental disquietudes, which, I plainly perceive, exercise a most unhappy influence upon all his bodily functions.

Tell Annie I received her letter and shall answer it very soon. Your little boys are well and happy. Tommy studies and reads as much as I wish him to, and Jule is punctual in attending to his music. Give my love to all. Write soon and believe me yours very affectionately till death.

M.M.H.

Julien, in his letter to his mother, sends messages to all the members of his family in Augusta. Maria reports to her sister that Pa had been so sick she thought he would die. Pa, now improved enough, had gone to help conduct a Sunday service for the blacks.

Julien Cumming to Julia Ann Bryan Cumming
Maria Bryan Harford to Julia Ann Bryan Cumming

Mt. Zion
May 30, 1840 (Saturday)

My dear Mother,

I have been waiting a long time for an answer to my letter and I now sit down to write to you again. There are a great many pears up here and they are most all of them ripe. Tell Alf that I have not been a fishing or hunting since I went to Mr. Harris's pond. Tommy and I went to the exhibition with Mr. Bonner and we liked it very much. The two plays were *Miss in her Teens* and *the Irish Widow*. There were a great many people there and the boys acted very well. Tell Sister that I want to see her very much. Tell Alf that I wish he was up here with me. I go to ride with Aunt Maria to the Mineral Springs whenever she goes. Give my love to Pa, Sister, Alf and all the children. Tell Mammy that I want to see her very much. Tell Grandma, Aunt Anne [Anne Cumming married Peter Smith, the brother of Gerrit Smith, philanthropist and abolitionist], Aunt Sarah and Gerrit and Cornelia that I want to see them very much. They all are very well up here except Grandpa and Robert. Grandpa has been sick for two or three days. Tommy is very well and happy. I am reading *Wife and Woman's Reward* and I am most through it.

Your affectionate son,
Julien Cumming

May 31, 1840 (Sunday Night)

My dear Julia,

It has now been more than a fortnight since we have heard a word from you, and we are becoming quite anxious.

Julien has in his communication past over his Grandpa's sickness quite lightly, but in reality it has been a very serious thing. For several days past I should not have been at all surprised had he died—for his diarrheea was unmitigated and wasting him away, so that he had lost his voice and his strength, had a constant fever, and finally began to throw up from sick stomach, and notwithstanding was resolutely opposed to having a physician, or to taking any thing himself. My solicitude, and the sense of responsibility I felt, almost overwhelmed me for I knew that if he did not live, I should hardly be able to exculpate myself from seemingly deserved reproach from his children that he should have died without anything's being done for him.

All the time he seemed to be in that reckless state of feeling that he rather desired death, or at least was not inclined to avert it by his own exertions. The only argument I could use that seemed to influence him was that his pecuniary affairs were in such a state that he was not in that vein prepared to leave the world. He said "*That was true,*" he had always desired to have no debt unpaid, and everything disposed of when that event should take place. He is at present under the care of the Doctor and I am considerably encouraged about him, if he does not take a relapse from imprudence, but after being too sick to be off his bed for several days, today in spite of my prayers and *tears* too, he would go to the church through the hot sun and read and pray in the negroes' meeting—but that indicates at any rate increase of strength. The boys are quite well.

Yours affectionately.
M.M.H.

Joseph Bryan, aged seventy-two, agrees to having his portrait painted for the Cummings. Jane Armour, who was to become Pa's second wife, calls at the house in Mt. Zion to see Mrs. Maria Cooke, who with her artist husband, George, was living with the Bryans while he painted Pa's portrait.

Maria Bryan Harford to Julia Ann Bryan Cumming

Mt. Zion
June 9, 1840 (Tuesday)

My dear Julia,

Your last letter came to hand after a silence of three weeks, and indeed, after we had begun to feel very uneasy about you. Mr. and Mrs. Cook arrived before the letter, and their coming occasioned me much surprise, for I had concluded that you had fairly given up the contest with Pa, and that we should not see them at all. Pa was very much disinclined and almost unamicable about it. However Mr. Cook was very decided, went about all his preparations very quietly, had his easel made, and even got his palette arranged with the colours he needed, and took his seat. Pa at last sat down, and he commenced operations, and has finally become reconciled to the infliction or endurance.

I wish he had been in his best looks when he was taken. I think the likeness is striking, particularly in the upper part of the picture. Indeed, I think Mr. Cook so happy in having caught the resemblance that I have wished very much to have one taken for myself, but Pa positively refuses to sit, which I think very unkind, as I certainly could not spend my money in any way so satisfactory to myself. But he, like a certain Mrs. Juliana Buckingham, [Pa's mother] never thinks his children, however old they may be, are competent to the difficult art of self government. The portrait is taken with one arm over a chair, and the other in his bosom, a very common posture, you know, with him.

Mr. Cook tells me that your portrait is considered a very correct one, and is a very beautiful picture, and indeed, said he, "I consider Mrs. Cumming herself a decidedly handsome woman." Mrs. Smith and Mrs. Ponce and Jane Armour have called to see Mrs. Cook. They both appear to enjoy themselves and we like them very much. Miss Armour says one of the principal reasons of her coming here this summer was the hope of seeing you. I said, "You like Julia as well as ever, I see." "Ah, that I do," said she. She went to see Mrs. Terrill, and tells me she is the thinnest person she ever saw, and though she weeps incessantly and talks about Louisa all the time yet she does not murmur against Providence, but said to her when she left, "Jane, pray for me."

I do wish you would come up if it is only for a day or two, and see Pa. You have no idea how sick he has been. I was afraid he would not live for several days, and I am sure the Doctor thought his symptoms very bad, and Mrs. Rossiter, who knows more of his constitution than any one of the family, was, I am sure, trying to prepare her mind for the worst. She was very much distressed, and said, "We have always thought the Dr. and I could not be buried by anybody else. Oh, when that head is laid low!" and exclamations of that kind. I assure you my heart was as full as I could endure, but Heaven is merciful, and never, I suppose, tasks us beyond our strength.

Mrs. Bowman has a daughter, and is remarkably well. John Rice staid here last night. Jule took the entertainment of him upon his shoulders, and slept with him, and they both appeared to enjoy themselves highly. The boys delight to watch the progress of the painting.

John Mitchell was in here the other day, drunk, and Pa took the portrait and set it out before him and said, "Who is that?" "It's *obliged* to be old Joe Bryan," said he. Everybody that has seen it considers the likeness fine. Dr. Hanes, who was here Saturday, thinks it one of the best he ever saw. But all that is not like one of his own family being satisfied and I do not know how it will strike you. Pa's pleasantest expression is the lighting up of his countenance when he laughs and talks, and of course that can't be painted. However, I wish, such as it is, that Sophia and I had each of us one like it, for in time to come, if we live, it may prove to us all what we may consider as one of our most valuable possessions.

Mr. Cook thinks Jule a prodigy, and I am afraid Jule will find it out. He behaves as well as could be expected, is very pleasant and happy and obedient when he does not forget. Tommy is a [?] boy. The other day at supper, company came in just as we were about sitting down to table. Tommy thinks a great deal of his cup of coffee and when I chance to omit him, always says in a tone that would soften a heart of granite, "Aunt Maria, won't you please, Ma'am, to give me *My* cup of coffee." So I whispered to him, as we were advancing to the table, "Tommy, you must do without your cup of coffee tonight." "Yes, Ma'am," said he, in such a sweet and cheerful, and docile tone and expression of countenance, that my heart was melted. However, I found there was enough for him, and when I gave him his cup, he looked up surprised and pleased but said nothing.

Mr. Sayre has been to see Pa and I think has comforted him about Brother. He says he has business, sees the best company, and is respected, but nothing can excuse his not writing to Pa.

I wish I had my arm around my dear brother Joseph's neck this very minute. He is a man that—but I won't begin to say what I think of him, and I don't suppose either you or him care much what I think of him, so I will keep my thoughts to myself. Pa writes to him by this mail.

Could you get that satin? We are much pleased with the shirts. Julien needs some greatly. Shall I not have him some made, or will you? Write soon.

M.H.

We have just heard today of Mr. Allen Gilbert's death.

Mrs. Cook sends her love to you and Sophia, and Mr. Cook says I must tell you that he is much obliged to you for sending him here. Tell Mr. Harris and Sophy that I am much obliged to them for the Spiritus Vitae. Why does not poor Phil try it? I have the greatest faith in its wonderful efficacy, and white swelling is one of the things the inventor says it will cure.

The artist George Cooke (Maria consistently spelled the painter's name without an e) and his wife after a month-long stay left the Bryans' on June 24, 1840. By June 9, Cooke had finished painting Joseph Bryan's portrait. In the following two weeks, though no mention of it is made in Maria's letters, he painted two more portraits for the family—a second one of Joseph Bryan holding his spectacles in one hand and a Bible in the other, and a portrait of Maria Bryan Harford. The pictures of Julia and her daughter Emily, Pa, and Maria, all painted in 1840 by George Cooke, appear in this book.

Julien Cumming to Julia Ann Bryan Cumming
Maria Bryan Harford to Julia Ann Bryan Cumming

Mt. Zion

June 25, 1840 (Thursday)

My dear Mother,

I was very glad to receive your letter Monday and I now sit down to write you an answer. I have had a very bad cold for five or six days but it is getting better now. I thought you would say something about comeing up here in your letter. I wish you would come up. I read to Aunt Rosseter every day that she can hear me. They are all very well up here. Mr. and Mrs. Cook left here in the morning yesterday. Tommy told me to tell you that he wanted you to write to him. Mat and Bird are making a house for a dry well which Mr. Hannah is going to dig. Give my love to Mammy and tell her that I want to see her very much. Today Tommy, Edward and me. Ed. told me to tell you that he wanted you to come up here soon. Tell Joesy and Emmy that Tommy found a birds nest that had three little white eggs in it and that Edward and me found a nest that had two little bluebirds in it.

Your affectionate son

Julien Cumming

My dear Julia,

Jule wants to tell you that Tommy, Ed and himself pulled and collected the blue plums for drying (in which by the bye they took great delights) but whether his mind went off in a pleasing reminiscence, or what happened neither he nor anyone can tell, but his sentence is unfinished as you will perceive and much to his mortification.

Mr. & Mrs. Cook went away yesterday morning. Pa sent them to Greensborough, and they have sent word that they now expect to leave there Friday morning. I think they are both devotedly pious and consistent Christians, "adorning the doctrine of God their Saviour in all things."

Pa wishes you, if Uncle Jacob has not left before this reaches you, to procure at Barrett's a pound of Carbonate of Soda, as he occasionally suffers very seriously from heart burn.

Jule has had a cold lately, but Tommy is perfectly well, and quite delighted with the *Swiss Family Robinson* which he is very intently reading for some time past. Mr. Cook has told them divers narratives, most of them *true,* and they almost expected one every night while he staid. There is a little packet here for you from Mrs. Cook which I shall send the first opportunity.

Mrs. Rossiter still continues unwell, and can neither read or work. Julien reads to her most of the time, when she is well enough to listen to him.

My love to Mr. Cumming.

Affectionately,
M.H.

Maria recounts to Julia how fond the personal servants at Mt. Zion are of Tommy and Julien. The boys, who have heard so much talk on the presidential election of 1840, have become strong political supporters of William Henry Harrison in the Harrison–Martin Van Buren contest. "Van Buren has been in long enough," said Tommy.

Maria Bryan Harford to Julia Ann Bryan Cumming

Mt. Zion
July 2, 1840 (Thursday)

My dear Julia,

We were very glad to hear from you, as it had been a long time since we had had a line from any of you. Sophia has only written once since she left.

I often think if Pa's absent children could be with him and see him as I do daily and hourly, and observe his varying moods, his frequent despondency and indisposition, they would make great and continued efforts to contribute what they can to the comfort and solace of his declining years. But when I see him watching the mails, and returning sad and slowly home, "no letter," I am sorry that those whose silence I know is not occasioned by want of affection or reverence did not know as I do how necessary unfailing and frequently expressed sympathy seems to be to his unbraced spirits and growing infirmities, and angry almost beyond endurance at that "ingratitude keener than a serpent's fang" that is discolouring all his days, and disturbing his quiet, from one whom no charity could call by any other than the terms of "unkind and undutiful."

He *has* been a great deal better, but he is so restless in mind, and so anxious about his crop that he has again turned in to hard work, and looks wretchedly. The other day he went out with the reapers, and followed them up all day, drinking their molasses and water, and eating their coarse fare for his dinner, and did not get home until some time after supper. Mr. Johnson has been taken sick, and he now has to do duty as overseer, and is so much in the grass that Ed has gone over to assist, and so we have no waiters, but Martha and little George. The latter, however, furnishes unfailing amusement to Tommy and Jule, and as soon as everybody rises from the table goes up and begs them for what is left on their plate.

I was much amused today in listening to a conversation which took place between Tommy and Jule. They hear so much politics talked over the street at Williams's that they have caught the mania, and discuss the respective merits and demerits of Harrison and Van Buren, and are both of them strong partizans of the former. Tommy says "Van Buren has been *in* long enough." But for the conversation:

"Tommy," says Jule, "*you* ever seen a Governor?"

"Yes," said Tommy, "I *have so.*"

"What Governor you *seen?*"

"I *seen* Governor *MacDonil*. I seen him *at* Knoxville when he come to see Grandpa." [Chester J. McDonald was governor of Georgia from 1839 to 1843.]

"*I* seen him once when he was a *Judge,*" said Jule.

Tommy, too, had seen him when he was but a Judge, but not willing to relinquish his reflected honours, he very adroitly changed the subject.

Julien has had a boil and a cold which has given him some fever, and made him quite unwell for several days, and Pa has given him some medicine. Tommy [nearly nine years old] is very well and his Grandpa calls him "little forty eight and a quarter." "Grandpa," says Tommy, "how do you know anything about the quarter, I never weighed but just 48." "Yes, but you have had time to gain the other quarter *since.*"

Uncle has arrived but we have not seen him. I wish you would come up soon before anybody else comes here. I got a letter the other day from Mrs. Iverson saying that Julia would be here when her Father came, which would be about the first of August or the last of July.

I wish you could have overheard some remarks of Robert to Julien the other day, whom he had been reproving for climbing on some place where he was in danger. "Naow, Julin, you think because anybody scolds at you and tells you things, that it's cause they don't think nawing *on* you, but that's jest the reason that I due tell you when you go wrong. I don't go and tell every boy in the street haow he must due, cause it's nawing at all to me haow he does, but I think a great deal of you children, a *great* deal on you, and it hurts me to see you going on wrong. And naow Jule if you'd a fell daown from thatar place you'd jest a sure a broke *your* back, or one of your legs as ever you come into this world, and I guess I'd a felt bad enough abaout it tue — and I would tue." Jule listened very intently all the time with great apparent respect, giving Robert one of his earnest, unwinking looks, and I cooperated with Robert in all he said.

But Tommy is one of the "little birds" that stands highest in Robert's opinion of the whole nest; indeed, Tommy is exceedingly esteemed by everybody, and from Jenny, who is very good in every way to both of them, Tommy can get away the last egg she possesses, or get her to leave her work when most pressed to rid him of a flea, or tie a string to his whip, or fix his popgun, or perform any operation upon the toy which is the reigning favorite of the time.

Popguns are lords of the ascendant here at present, and as chinaberries don't seem to fail, notwithstanding the immense number they have shot off, I am afraid it will be a lasting passion. They had had such keen and vivid delight in the amusement that I have not had the heart to cross them, though hoping the excess of the pursuit and the pleasure would produce satiety in time, but there is no prospect as yet of that kind, and my nerves and my noonday rest are sorely disturbed by the popping.

Pa says the mails are so very uncertain that he wishes you would let him know some time before that he may know when to send. Give my love to Mr. Cumming and Annie and Alfred.

Very affectionately yours,
M.

Sophia and Robert Harriss, married since February, are boarding in Augusta. Julia wrote Maria in early June 1840 that she wished Sophia and Robert to remain with them, "but Mr. Harris was in a perfect fever all the time he was here to get to some place where he could feel he was paying his way." In this letter, Sophia has been visiting in Mt. Zion and is sick. Alfred Iverson has married again, and his new wife, Julia Frances Forsyth Iverson, daughter of John Forsyth, the United States secretary of state and a Georgia politician from Augusta, has written Maria that Julia Maria will not be coming to visit her cousins in Mt. Zion.

Maria Bryan Harford to Julia Ann Bryan Cumming

Mt. Zion
August 16, 1840 (Sunday night)

My dear Julia,

I have been confined to my room all day and most of the time to my bed, but must write you a few lines, as I presume from what Mr. Harris told you, you must feel considerable anxiety about Sophia. She goes down stairs and sits up most of the time, but, besides suffering from what the French call "mal au coeur" to a most painful degree, she has a regular chill and fever every other day, and looks most wretchedly sick and altered. She, however, "keeps up a good heart" as old Mr. Wiley used to say, and laughs and talks with great glee during her intervals of suffering.

Pa's heart is actually melting within him. He is not only father and mother both in his sympathies, but all the fathers and mothers in the world in one in the excess and degree of his interest and feeling towards her. If I were not so sorry for her, I might be tempted to feel a little jealous and neglected as I lie hour after hour in my room pitying my poor side, and listening to my unparticipated and unechoed groans, but, thank God, I have learned I trust to repose upon myself, and especially upon Him. I feel like a solitary leaf floating down the stream of time, soon to reach the great ocean, and to change the figure, I hope I am learning to die when my time comes, willingly and joyfully, and without a fear or a pang in quitting the world.

> "Afraid to die? afraid to bear
> The pang that but a moment tries,
> And on the sway of pain and care,
> Ascend the mansions in the skies?"

I could not but have a little hope that you would come with Mr. Harris, though I presume you could not well leave your children; though could not your boys stay a while with their Grandmother, and let you run up and see us for a few days? As to Annie's coming, you know we are always glad to have any of the children, but I cannot take upon me to advise or recommend at this season of the year. As yet it is quite healthy, and I don't know of a single case of fever excepting Frank Ponce. So if you are willing to send her, you know that I shall take good care of her in sickness and in health.

Julia Iverson is not coming, her mother writes that Mr. I., yielding to J.M.'s [Julia Maria's] wishes, who imagines Mt. Zion a dull place, has consented to let her remain in the convent.

We are delighted that you are pleased with the portrait [of Pa] to the degree which you express. Your criticisms are precisely mine — I always thought that the expression of the mouth was caught and could not be changed during his first reluctant sittings.

If you were not quizzing me, I am very proud that you should have discovered any indications of genius in my late unpretending epistle, but the *manner* in which it was praised surpasses the thing by far. It reminds me of some talented reviewer who takes a humble and obscure volume as the heading and text of his own eloquent effusions on the same subject. Mine was but the nucleus—yours the rich and juicy pulp formed upon it. But a truce to compliments and badinage. Robert is in a fever for me to finish my letter and scrapes his foot so impatiently as he walks that it makes me nervous.

In haste your sister,

M.

"Your letter shall be burned as you wish, and of course you will see the propriety of doing the same with this," writes Maria.

Maria Bryan Harford to Julia Ann Bryan Cumming

Mt. Zion
September 3, 1840

My dear Julia,

I have been waiting with some impatience to receive a letter from you since your last, and this bright and sweet looking morning has brought it, pleasant in itself, and pleasant in its contents. I am inexpressibly pleased that your feelings are what you express, and unfeignedly thankful to you for expressing them, for I know protestations are not in your line, and that it is something of an effort for you to make them. In this case though they are appropriate and useful and welcome.

The expression of your opinion with regard to our friend ["our friend" probably is a reference to Julia Frances Forsyth, the new Mrs. Iverson, and is Julia's response, paraphrased by Maria, to the news contained in Maria's letter of August 16] and the impression she leaves and the influence she produces, is in a style worthy of any diplomat who ever lived, from Richelieu to John Forsyth, but it is so thoroughly understood by me that it is a proof that this sort of language, much as it has been abused, is extremely to be approved, since it conveys the idea clearly enough to the initiated and veils it from all others. Yes, truly, "her words are arrows and her tongue a pointed spear, on whose sharp point peace bleeds and hope expires," and the unity of brethren and of family, so sweet and lovely and desirable that even the pen of inspiration has sketched its lineaments in a glowing picture, must be and is sacrificed to the unconquerable desire to *lower,* and to *blacken* and to *misrepresent.* Your letter shall be burned as you wish, and of course you will see the propriety of doing the same with this.

I have been afraid you will all be troubled by hearing Pa's plans and schemes for selling his house, etc. They are numerous, and disturb me more than I can tell you. Sometimes it is to take Aunt Wales's house, and her with him, and live there, sometimes to move over to the plantation and fit up the red kitchen!!! But never mind, so far as my influence will go, he shall continue in that position which alone is suitable for his own respectability and that of his family, and that is to continue here. If there is a nominal change about which he talks so much, I desire it to be only nominal until his deranged notions on one subject can be done away by some arrangement with Uncle which can set him at ease. You, my dear Julia, will never, I hope, distrust me. I have no mercenary or ambitious views, and I say it not with Pharasaic boasting, "*my* treasure is in heaven," and all I desire in relation to Pa or his possessions is to contribute to the happiness and comfort of the one, and to act as a good steward in relation to the other. He must and will have his way, and let that take its course, for the strength of his will will never be subdued this side the grave.

By the bye how I have wished that you could have heard Mr. Waddel when he gave (in a sermon) one of the finest sketches of the character of David I ever heard, for in many points it so resembled Pa's, not in the circumstances of its history, but its leading traits, his susceptibility, his liability to depression, and to an after glow of happiness, and gratitude to God, one in whom the Almighty saw so much to rebuke, and so much to comment, for after all there was ardour and sincerity in love to Him. But I do no *justice* I am aware to the paraphrase, or to my own comparisons.

I should be very glad indeed to see the books of which you speak. I have seen some extracts from Miss Sedgwick's work [Catherine Maria Sedgwick (1789–1867), author of American fiction, whose works included *Redwood*, *Hope*, *Leslie*, and *Amy Cranstoun*], which makes me very desirous to read the whole. I heard the details of one of her letters when I was in Boston, which Mrs. Minot had just received. She had just been dining at Lord Dunham's (I think) and remarked that the people in this country misapprehended in supposing the English never unbent from the stiffness and formality of their manners, for "they did talk across the table then," just as we do.

As to your "conversing gracefully of books," I will never own a maternity to any offspring I never brought forth, and must be permitted to say en passant what I might never other-wise have said, that I have always held quite the contrary opinion, and the proof of it is that I never heard you speak of a book that it did not make such an impression upon my mind that I was anxious until I got it, and read it from the force of the recommendation. That our opinions and tastes about books are not invariably in harmony, we have both often said, and mutually wondered and laughed about, as in the instance of Charles Lamb [1775–1834, poet, playwright, essayist, critic, and author of books for children] and others.

Mrs. Alston and her daughter are now staying at Mr. Bonner's; Robert was here the other morning, and I asked him if his Aunt Alston did not feel very badly that Willis [Alston] had killed Reid.

"Feel badly," said he, "why, she rejoiced at it."

"Why, then," said I, "she is not religious as I thought."

"Religious," said he again repeating my words, "why, she does not make any pretensions to it."

Jane Baxter professes to have been a convert at the camp meeting, and has joined the Church.

I am very sorry your visit here has been delayed, and it seems there is always something to keep you away.

When I told the Dr. [Rossiter] that Julien had cut himself badly, he says, "Now why didn't July bring him up and let me treat him?" He seems, as his mind has become enfeebled, to have the greatest idea of his skill imaginable, and was almost angry that Dr. Burt did not employ him.

Tell Annie I saw the Miss Merriwethers yesterday, and they asked me when she was coming up, and said they intended to call when she came.

I would send you more of my hair, but it has come out until it is very thin. If you knew how to straiten hair, I could give you a bunch which would make a bracelet ten yards long.

Your Sister,

M.

Annie Cumming, aged fourteen, writes her mother from Mt. Zion. Maria also writes and says that she was shocked to hear of the death of Mr. Fitzsimons, "though [she] did not know him." Paul Fitzsimons died at the age of forty in Augusta on September 26, 1840. His nephew, Harry Hammond, married Emily, Annie Cumming's younger sister, in 1859.

Annie M. Cumming to Julia Ann Bryan Cumming
Maria Bryan Harford to Julia Ann Bryan Cumming

Mt. Zion
October 3, 1840 (Saturday)

My dear Mother,

I was very much surprised that I received no letter from you. Tho' you did not say positively you would write I thought you intended to. I did not keep my promise of writing twice a week. But, really, I had nothing to say nor have I much to say now.

Grandpa has had a very severe cold since he came from Augusta and has now a cough. I think it is better tho' than it was. He is going to Presbytery next Thursday week and as he will be there until the Monday following I expect I shall come down Monday night in the cars. Though that is nearly a week later than I intended, I thought you had rather I should wait a few days longer and come with Grandpa than come at the appointed time, without him. He has not said he will act in this way, but as I asked him to go as soon as he could I am in hopes he will do so. When I write again I can probably tell you positively when I shall come.

I have finished one night cap this week at a great expense of labor and pulling out. I am very proud of it and I shall do the next in much less time.

I am almost afraid to tell you what is proposed for you, for fear you might wish for them too much when you can't get them for two weeks yet. But we have the greatest number of chesnuts and chinquepins. Aunt Maria has six hundred on the table by her as well as four or five hundred upstairs. They are so fresh and big and would last such a long time. I do wish you had them now. I intend to get as many as I can carry up/down to you. Tell Emmy that Aunt Maria gave me five hundred chinquepins and I put two hundred by to string for her. I expect I can get some more and it will make a long string tho they will be so old and dry she can't eat them. Tell the boys I haven't heard Robert say anything about there squirrel lately except he wants to get one for all the children. Robert does little else now but talk politicks.

I believe Aunt Maria will write before my letter goes tho as she has been very unwell all day I don't know whether she will do it today or not. Give my love to Pa, Mammy and the children.

Your affectionate daughter,
A.M. Cumming

My dear Julia,

Annie appears to enjoy herself quite well, and indeed, very much part of the time. She took a ride on horseback today with her Grandpa, and as she has informed you, has worked most diligently on the cap. She has never been here before under just such circumstances, no routine of employment and so small a family as there is here now, so that the first night or two she had the blues horribly. Since then she has got along quite well, is reading *Discipline* [: *A Novel*, by Mary Bruton (1778–1818), published in 1814] in her leisure hours, eats chinkepins [neither pupil nor tutor spell *chinquapin* or *chestnut* correctly] and chestnuts in all hours, and has had her dullness enlivened by one or two calls from the girls about, and a visit of some length from Mr. Francis Ponce and Dewitt Wilcox, with both of whom she got on very well, particularly while I was out of the room.

Pa has had one of the worst colds that I ever knew him to have, and a very bad cough with it. He exposes himself in the daytime and is, as usual when sick, very low spirited. Annie and I try to cheer him up all we can but there is not much use in trying until he gets well, as I hope he will soon, though now he looks worse than since his attack in the Spring.

Mrs. Matthews will do your quilt as soon as you send it up, and any other work that you wish, for, as she tells Mrs. Rossiter, Heaven only knows what is to become of her, for she can get nothing to do. She must incur some expenses, and does not make on an average two dollars a month. I pity her with all my heart.

Don't forget the lining and thread for we cannot get those things on near as good terms as in Augusta.

I was shocked to hear of the death of Mr. Fitzsimmons—though I did not know him. How true are the words of Scripture that death cometh as a snare upon the sons of men. Oh, to live ever ready for our summons, and oh, for that faith which may illumine the dark and dreary path of life, and make the eternal towers of our future home shine so brightly before us as to cause us to rejoice in every step however rough and painful which is bringing us nearer to it. Faith can do all this, I am sure. I feel that my reasoning faculties have gone through the process which convinces me of its wondrous power even to demonstration, but I cannot always exercise it so as to feel its strengthening and cheering influence but it is promised in answer to prayer and pray I will.

I have been a great deal better lately, felt quite like returning health—but was taken with a severe headache yesterday from tasting pickles that I was making. Best love to Mr. Cumming and believe me ever yours,

M.H.

Chapter Eleven

REMARRIAGE

"Sophy reproaches me that 'I long so much for love and affection.'"

Annie Cumming is still in Mt. Zion, and Maria tutors her niece, looks after an ailing father, and works on making the slaves' clothing.

Maria writes that their wealthy friend Nathan Sayre, a Sparta lawyer, publicly acknowledged at a recent revival that he had "gotten religion." What Sayre did not publicly reveal to friends and neighbors was that he had fathered three children by Susan Hunt, a free African American. "Pomegranate Hall," Sayre's large house in town, contained, in effect, a secret suite of rooms in which Sayre hid his family of color while he presented himself to the community as a bachelor.

Maria Bryan Harford to Julia Ann Bryan Cumming

Mt. Zion
October 8, 1840 (Thursday)

My dear Julia,

We have been hoping to hear from you or Sophia during the past week, but no letter has been received from either. Annie looked yesterday morning when the mail came in as if she felt rather neglected, but she soon got over it. She is pleasant and cheerful, and notwithstanding the foibles of her age, and the faults of her peculiar temperament is, in my humble opinion, a fine and interesting child.

Pa heard from Goode a few days since, and he wishes him to come out to Alabama, as he says a tract of land can be immediately sold and payment received, and if he is not there Mr. Lawson will send it on to [Brother in] Washington. Whether this is a mere crude suspicion of Goode, without any certain knowledge, I can't say, but at any rate it has made Pa very anxious to set off to Alabama, though he says his business here would suffer without him exceedingly.

He was wishing the other day that he had a buggy, and I begged him to procure one for himself as I disliked to see him want anything at his time of life, and I did not see why he should be so afraid of spending money for his own comfort. He replied, "It's very easy to *talk*. I am afraid to spend money because I am directed to owe no man anything, and until that debt of Isaac's is paid I cannot be easy."

Oh, that unfortunate loan! It is my firm belief, made up upon constant observation, that that affair has made Pa in mind and body a ten years older man. He hardly knows peace by night or day, works incessantly, and exposes himself, and all with the reason he assigns to himself that he must make every effort to save and to accumulate, to discharge that debt. Sometimes when I think on the subject, of how little Uncle needs (for his own necessities or the claims upon him from others), this wretched sum, every dollar of which seems to be a dagger to wound the peace and destroy the happiness and the life of the man he is most indebted to, it does seem to me that if I cannot "pull his ears," or tell him by word or deed the odiousness of his conduct in my view, to act as a sort of safety valve to my opprest and irritated feelings, I shall explode. "But the *weapons of our warfare are not carnal.*"

Pa's health is not better but worse, and his cough from exposure continues violent, and sometimes it seems as if he would break a blood vessel. Imagine then, how I feel seeing him as I can from the window, toiling up that hill from the tan yard, repeatedly during the day, and sometimes with a large roll of leather on his shoulders, assisting to carry it for the man who has bought it, when I know he is so weak and feeble that he requires the most entire repose. You ask me to go and stay with you, my dear Julia—but if my inclinations led me to leave home, my duty would forbid it, for Pa is no more fitted now to be without someone with him to watch over and take care of him than his own little namesake [four-year-old Joseph Bryan Cumming]. As it is I can't do much, for my influence in these matters is small, but I am sure if he had no society in the house he would never come in, and should never do one thing to cure himself when he got sick, if it was not urged upon him by others. [Pa is seventy-two years old.]

Besides I am now busily engaged with the negroes' clothes, and you know our sewers are slow and unskillful. Thinking I should not be well enough to undertake them, I proposed to him to give the job to some of these numerous poor women in the neighbourhood, but he would not listen to it, and, perceiving it would disquiet him very considerably if it were not carried on at home, I have undertaken it myself.

I hope you will be able to send up your quilt before long. Uncle Jacob goes down the last of this week or the first of next. I intend sending you a few of pickles if they are good enough, but I have been very unfortunate this season either from the dampness affecting the juices or something in the vinegar or some other cause. Every peach is spoiled, and most of the mangoes so soft I shall have to throw them away. Would you like to have me put you up a jar of crabapples? Do tell me if you would.

Larned has lost his wife. She died the last day of August after an illness of some months. I believe poor Larned is no great favourite of yours, and yet I am sure you will feel for him when you picture his situation at that sickly climate of Fort Gibson, with his poverty and three little *motherless* children, the youngest about five months old. May God help the creatures He has made, for truly sometimes do the trials sent upon them seem greater than human nature can endure.

How is Sophia? in health and spirits? [Sophia is pregnant.] I hope the best for her, as her constitution is good, and I know your kindness will be unremitting. Mr. Harris too—I never saw a man more unwearying in his attentions to a sick friend.

Mrs. Terrill has sent a most earnest request for me to visit her and I should go immediately, but I do not like to leave Annie alone and I would not take her, as I am sure the Doctor and herself would be greatly affected by the company of a young girl of Annie's age. She is said to be still very much determined to "get religion," as the Methodists term it, has subscribed for a religious newspaper, and sent for some catechisms to instruct her negroes.

There is a great state of excitement now in all the churches about. At the "Piney Woods meetinghouse" there has been a revival. The meeting continues and has been held for nearly a fortnight. Likewise at Powelton and Sparta. I understand that Nathan Sayre is very serious, and at some meeting lately some minister, I forgot who, conversed with him, and he wept very much, said he was "a praying man," and he felt deeply the importance of Christianity, that other things "were but as a bubble compared in importance to the interests of the Soul."

Pa wishes Mr. Cumming to write to him as soon as he hears from Brother. I wish, if you have an opportunity, you would send up a bottle of Jayne's Expectorant, for I am very uneasy about Pa's cough. My love to all.

Affectionately yours,
M.

Julia Cumming had been on a brief visit to Mt. Zion and had now returned to Augusta accompanied by her daughter Annie. Maria misses Julia and describes her visit to Sparta. One family she found on the eve of a wedding and another on the eve of a funeral.

Maria Bryan Harford to Julia Ann Bryan Cumming

Mt. Zion
October 29, 1840 (Thursday)

My dear Julia,

Your communication respecting the organ must be addrest to "Henry Platt Esq. organ builder, Winchester, New Hampshire." That will take a letter right plump into Deacon Platt's front door, from whence it will doubtless be conveyed by the back way into his workshop, and will in due time produce you an instrument "right down *complete*," as they say down East. If you wish me to write for you, I will willingly do so, and perhaps having obtained one from him may make some little difference in price, and in his efforts to please.

Would you not prefer its being set upon castors or rollers? I have always considered it a defect in mine as regarded facility in moving it. Pa forgot until last night to tell me the request for his address, and I begin with complying with it for fear I might forget it myself.

I am quite unlucky about my presents of late though, of course, not the less indebted to the donors. The apples Mr. Cumming was so kind as to send me, Pa left upon Durden's table, and your oranges were all soft and good for nothing, but three of them. I have sent you jars today, and there is one of Sophia's in it which you will please send to her with the contents, as I could not get it in her box. That is the only jar belonging to her as I did not put your preserves in her jars as I intended and told you I should.

I miss you very much, and am constantly thinking of something I wanted to say to you. Miss Camfield also felt your absence very much, I soon perceived, and as I "so much need discipline" (thanks for the information), and cannot hold out against a tear, which is a complete battering ram to the strongest of my bulwarks of severity and dislike, I set about treating her with the utmost attention and kindness, which I own she had not obtained from me before. And now, for the proof: Finding that she dreaded making her first appearance in Sparta, *toute seule,* what do I do, but puts on my cloak and bonnet, and goes along *with* her (as Pa could not!!!). Mrs. Bird came out to the carriage as I did not go in, and Rosier, and Mary Berrien.

Mrs. Crawford [Sarah Ruffin Rhodes] is not expecting to live from hour to hour, and her sister [W. Eliza Rhodes Terrell] does not stir from her room day or night. Miss Eliza Crawford whom I saw tells me that Mrs. [William] Terrill's interest for her sister is so aroused, and she is so desirous to impart comfort and ease to her if but for a moment, that it seems to have drawn off her thoughts from her loss [of her daughter Louisa] almost completely, and that she is actually improving in health. What a comment upon the Apostle's injunction, "Bear ye one another's burdens." I have no doubt but it could be philosophically demonstrated (as it is daily *practically* demonstrated) that the more we feel for others' woes, the less we suffer from the weight of our own.

There was a contrast between the two houses, the bustle and gayety of a preparation for one of life's gayest and most joyful scenes in the one, and in the other a human being sinking slowly and surely to the tomb, in spite of the exertions and prayers of physicians and friends, thus showing that holy writ is ever true, and of the lives of human creatures, "none of us can redeem his brother or give to God a ransom for him." If I were excited to envy or desire *even,* by seeing or hearing of such things, as every one was talking of them, P.'s carriage & four, and the bridegroom-elect's barouche & two, and their white servants, these feelings would have been moderated by the reflections which arose in my mind, as I remembered the *short time before,* that she who lay there preaching the sad lesson of the vanity of human hopes was herself the object of envy and admiration etc., but these sort of things move me not for a moment; they have forever & aye lost all association in my mind with happiness. True, domestic peace and love always seem to be desirable, and as Cowper says they are "the only bliss of paradise that has survived the fall," but *greatness* and *ambition,* and *notoriety* are words of folly for the creatures of a day.

Mr. Dean was at Mr. Little's when you went away and was very sorry he did not see you again, and repeated his regrets frequently. Your kindness, I perceived, had won its way to his heart. He is gone to Milledgeville but I think will be back to spend Sunday. Tell Annie her rings are safely deposited in her Grandpa's desk. I forgot, Julia, one thing I meant to ask you for, viz., for the remaining Cologne in your bottle. I did not see any bottle, but I smelt some delightful perfume from your handkerchiefs. Will you be so kind as to send me by Uncle Jacob, some of a similar kind? Dr. Connel's bill is $8.00 — a dollar for each visit, and the rest for medicine. I suppose it is not worth while to send it. Shall I pay it for you?

Give my best love to Mr. Cumming, and to my dear little Annie, and to all my little boys. Bless their hearts. How did you find Sophia? I hope I shall hear from you tomorrow. I neglected sending a message to Miss McDowell that she would come and see us, but after the one to Mrs. Read we went off into a digression about New Haven kin and your modesty etc. I must stop for I have been hard at work all day, as Uncle Jacob brought in some cloth to make clothes for "Phonse," and they must be done today, the way he always serves me.

Affectionately your Sister,

M.

P.S. Since finishing this Miss Camfield has been here. She came out with P. Simonton and will go to Greensborough tomorrow.

How is your dyspepsia? Take the soda after each meal for sometime, and *don't* work or read for half an hour after eating, and above all take regular exercise upon foot. This with a moderate use of the Roman Kalydor will restore far more than your fair *proportion* of the charms of your set, for you have not like a French woman is frequently said to do, to make her beauty from the very foundation — "the *King's* daughters" are (said to be) "all glorious *within*." This King, the beauty of whose family is so radiant, is said to value the ornament of a meek and quiet spirit beyond all other things, and pronounces them to be "*blessed*" who are poor in spirit. Of course this poverty of spirit leads to freedom from that restless desire of notice and admiration which takes away all quiet and content of mind, and enables one to acquiesce in all the trying conditions of humanity because it is His will that it should be so.

And while on this subject I will quote the exact passage from [German essayist and novelist John Paul Frederick] Richter [1763–1825], of which I gave you the spirit and meaning as near as I could remember, and I have since found it: "I hold the constant regard we pay in all our actions to the judgements of others, as the poison of our *peace*, our *reason* and our *virtue*. At this slave chain I have long filed and I scarcely hope ever to break it entirely asunder. I wish to accustom myself to the censure of others, and be willing to appear a fool that I may learn to endure the comments and disapprobation of fools."

Pa is well and cheerful and seems to cluck with pleasure on the recollection of your visit. I hope you will come again soon. You must commence your lessons on the organ soon, and not let it arrive without being in some measure familiarized to its use. I shall charge you cheaply for your lessons as I expect an apt scholar, and will take your company for part pay.

Pa will go, he says, to Alabama as soon as he gets the papers from Washington. I don't often apologize for my letters even when they are such scrawls as the present, but this looks dreadfully. My pen is poor. I have no knife, and have written it, with constant interruption and persons passing and talking. If you can not read it, then throw it in the fire, do.

                                                                              M.

Though this letter lacks a year to date it, it plainly belongs here. In the previous letter Julia Cumming owed Dr. Connell eight dollars. In this letter Maria pays Julia's medical bill. Maria makes a strong plea to Julia to turn her son Julien, considered by his parents a rebellious child, over to her and Pa to feed, clothe, educate, and raise. She tells Julia it would revive Pa also to have a nominal claim on one of his grandchildren.

Maria Bryan Harford to Julia Ann Bryan Cumming

Mt. Zion

November [1840]

My dear Julia,

I am much obliged to you for the solicitude you felt about my health, and am happy to assure you there was no cause for it, as I am perfectly well and have been ever since you left. I am, as you imagine, very busy about the negroes' pantaloons, jackets, etc., but should have replied to your letter received Friday, by the next mail, but we had company all the time of the meeting, which commenced Friday morning, and to begin to write Sunday evening, or any mail evening, the very look of Robert's impatient countenance is enough to deter one from the undertaking.

I hope you have gotten over your cold, for I know yours are not ordinary things of the kind. Your way of exposing yourself, I suppose, will always be the same; it *used* to give me an immense deal of dissatisfaction; or to see *any* friend injuring so invaluable a blessing as health, particularly those whose lives were very important to a number of others, but I find anxiety affords no remedy, and I have therefore (in regard to those who I hope have a better portion than earth), fallen back upon the consolation that Mr. Newton made use of for a friend whose house had been destroyed by fire. "I rejoice, my friend, that you *have so much* that cannot be injured by calamity, or accident." I do, indeed, believe that I have this degree of faith for my friends as well as for myself, to desire for them not any thing which this world can give, of fame or pleasure or wealth, but God's "covenant blessings"; the light of his countenance shining upon them while making this rapid journey on earth, and unfailing treasures in Heaven. I know and lament that I have not enough faith to enable me to appreciate or comprehend how great is "God's goodness which he has laid up" for those who confide in him, and how unspeakable the bliss that will in so short a time be the possession of his children, bliss so great as to make a Parent of such tenderness regard with unmoved firmness the earthly condition of his most dutiful children even though want and sorrow may be their daily portion; I feel like a child to whom is pointed out the rich possessions of a father, and told that he is *heir* to them, but who has not yet had experience enough of life, or sufficient expansion of intellect to realize his advantages or his destiny, and yet feels it is something valuable and to be envied. Still for them and myself I can use the sentiments of the lines

"I will not pray for pomp and might
Lest I be sinful in thy sight;
For *earthly pride,* and worldly power
Are but the *trifles of an hour.*

Whate're I ask, I dare not raise
A single thought for human praise,
For that though grateful it *may be,*
Would only draw my heart *from thee.*

Whate'er the treasures I behold
Yet I will never pray for gold,
Why should I in its glitter trust,
Since it and I, are *only dust.*

Hear thou my prayer, for thou canst give
Thy grace and show me *how to live;*
Hear thou my prayer; thou canst supply
My wants, and *teach me how to die.*

Maria McDonald requests me to say to you and Mr. Cumming that she would have written, but has been confined to her bed with the toothache, and cold taken in her jaw. She will write when Charles Couling's services will be required, but as Mrs. McDonald has had several very severe attacks lately, she is now in doubt whether she will be able to undertake the charge of a party at all. She thinks of going to Texas in January. *She,* third person singular number, feminine gender referring back to *Maria* McDonald.

It makes *me feel* much to see Dr. Gilbert and of course it must you *more*, for I do think the emotion and gratitude with which one regards a physician who has rendered them great and especial service, and relieved them from excruciating pain and hopeless sickness, is a strong and peculiar feeling. Thus it is that our poor sex so subject to bitter bodily trials and sufferings, and inclined constitutionally to a devotional spirit, often regard their physician and their clergyman as a sort of demigod because the one is the instrument of giving health to the body and the other to the soul.

I know something of the "sad remembrances of merry hours," the "tristos pensamientos de allegras memorias," in the beautiful Spanish tongue, for I felt them the other day when I went to see Mrs. Abner Cook, and sat by the old fireplace whose familiar aspect recalled crowds of thoughts of pleasant and sorrowful scenes and conversations, now (to quote from you) "receded into the gloomy past." But why should we feel so? That past too was cheered and blessed by the care of the Almighty, its very sorrows and troubles acting as the parent of future wisdom and all but as a part of an interminable existence which cannot be expended, and whose rich crowding joys of unutterable delights will make all that we now enjoy seem poor in the comparison. Yes, I am one to whom "life and immortality has been brought to light by the gospel," and I do believe that

> "Heaven's immortal spring shall yet arrive,
> And man's majestic beauty bloom again
> Bright through the eternal year
> Of love's triumphant reign."

Pa has today received the papers, and a respectful letter from Brother, and is in fine spirits. He will set off for Alabama after Synod. I want him to go immediately and not lose this fine weather—but he will not consent. It will, therefore, be a fortnight before Julien can come up with him, so that, he says, if you had rather not wait and will have him brought up to Durden's any day, that you will let him know and he will send for him. By sending Jule's clothes in a bag, Ed can go for him on horseback, and Jule can ride Essex or the poney. Tell Jule I have had an offer lately of some elegant hickory nuts and walnuts, diced and hulled, for "thrip a hundred," and I'll buy some for *him,* and he can pay me back the money when he comes up. I shant charge him interest for advancing for him, though this seems to be customary in our family towards one another [a thrust by Maria at Uncle Isaac].

Do let Jule come for good and all. If you could read my heart and see in it the feelings to him and to all of your children, you would not be so reluctant to let him stay here and *visit* at home at least for some years to come. You get discouraged because he falls back into old faults upon his return to the same scenes in Augusta but he is too young as yet for habit to restrain impulse which, after a course of discipline, and freedom from temptation will, I hope, be the case. I think it would revive Pa's youth if you would just give him a *nominal claim* upon one of your children and let him feel that he had again a son to clothe and educate and take care of. [Julien comes to Mt. Zion in early December and apparently stays with the Bryans until May.] Do, Julie, think of this, and teach Mr. Cumming to consider me as his *own own* Sister, and not to feel proud in receiving what he may think is obligation from me. Talk of renewing Pa's age, I think I have never seen another mortal to whom sympathy is so essential. He has interrupted me, I was going to say, a hundred times since commencing this letter. I have been asking him for some time to trim the trees in the front yard, and when he commenced he said, "Come now, Maria, you must come and encourage me and show me what to do."

Love to all.

Your Sister,

M.

Mrs. Rossiter has been very sick, and hardly expected that she would live. I shall be glad to get the brandy for her. I think the bitters would do her much good if she could be quiet, but she works herself almost to death. I got a letter from Mrs. Carter the other day, and speaking of you she says, "How I love and admire her. I have now seen her in all the relations of life and she is admirable in all." She will spend the winter in Cherokee. Mrs. Dean does not consent to come. I have sent the letter. Did I, or not, tell you in my last that I had paid your bill to Dr. Connell which I did immediately upon the reception of your last letter.

Truly yours,

M.

2nd P.S. Mrs Matthews has finished the quilt, and I have paid her what she asked $5.00. She wants you to let her know how you wish the other quilted.

Mr. Dean writes Pa that he is truly obliged to Mrs. Cumming for speaking a good word to him to the Florida gentleman, but his wife is a timid woman and would not like to go so near the Florida Indians.

Maria, ill with a cold, decides to spend a quiet day alone in her room reading, but one social interruption follows after another with the result that the sun goes down without her having any rest or solitude. Maria's sorrowful reference to Colonel Foster cannot be explained, since he had just been reelected to Congress.

Maria Bryan Harford to Julia Ann Bryan Cumming

Mt. Zion
November 18, 1840 (Wednesday)

My dear Julia,

Pa is quite excited at my report of a portion of your letter that Sophia even *spoke* of coming up, and has resolved to write immediately to her, urging her to make up her mind and let him know. I shall, if she chooses to come, do my best to make her comfortable, and so, I doubt not, will every member of the family. I trust Providence will overrule and direct us to what is best. For myself I am wholly incompetent to determine upon the best plan.

I have been able to sympathise with you in good earnest lately as it regards your cold, for I have had a very severe one for the last few days attended with cough, stricture of the heart, etc. I live in only a little less bustle and hurry than you describe, and yesterday I resolved to stay in my room and keep close quarters, and take good care of myself if perchance thereby I might get rid of my troublesome companion. So I had my sofa carried in my room and stretched myself upon it, and as I drew feet up, I thought "Well now for a good comfortable day all to myself, with nothing to do but to read and to think; it's really almost worth the pain of being a little sick for the bare prospect of the *dolce far niente* that is before me."

But I had not more than fairly gotten into Joshua's wars which I was reading than Martha came and said, "Miss Maria, there's a red faced gentleman downstairs that asked if he could see Mrs. Harford." It proved to be a German named Otto, a piano tuner. Then came Eliza Thomas and, finding my room very warm and comfortable, consumed *two* of my dedicated hours. Then, as Pa had "*norated* it about" (as old Mr. Battle used to say) that I was sick, came Mrs. Allen and staid two more. "Now for it," said I, not even yet heartless, though my own experience and that of Seged of Ethiopia was before me, but "Miss Margaret Shivers" came in bringing her work, and so ended the day.

I cast a rueful glance at the setting sun when I saw him declining, as I could not, like the before named General, compel him to delay his movements, or say with any effect, "Sun, stand thou still in Mount Zion." Indeed, I think from that time to this, he has been endeavouring to make up for his delay in Gibeon, by a double quick time movement. At any rate I am always taken by surprise when he bids my side of the world adieu till next day. Heaven grant it may not be so when my day of life is to end, but that I may be found to have worked so well in the allotted hours that "when the night comes" I may be in no hurry or confusion, but ready for the rest prepared for the dutiful servant.

Really poor Anne [Julia's sister-in-law] must have suffered a great deal. Who but the Searcher of hearts can tell how much of gloom and irritability of temper, and apparent indolence might have originated in this [gynecological] disease long preying upon the vitality of health and cheerfulness and comfort. I truly hope she may be thoroughly restored. Who was her physician? I have heard of the instrument which was made use of, I think it is called a speculum, but most ladies have an unconquerable aversion to its use on their own persons. But Old Satan for *once*, after the battle which plunged him forever and aye into Pandemonium, told the truth; it was when he said "Skin for skin, all that a man hath will he give for his life," and what is health but the *soul of life*. Existence without it is as a hateful and odious carcass, useless and offensive.

Your "aspected Father" is at this time busier, if possible, than ever, killing hogs, selling leather, settling accounts, doctoring sick negroes, and hurrying his blacksmiths and working for a wager with his tanners. I do not think, however, that he looks so well as he did, for he *over*works himself. The other night, he could not be gotten in to his supper, but staid out until eight or nine o'clock helping to unload a waggon of corn.

I think I was worse frightened last night than I have been in a long long time, and it led me to think of the price of that passion of *fear* in the human mind, and how, if we were all under the government of a malevolent being who delighted in tormenting us, it might be used as an instrument of unspeakable misery to us. I was sick and feverish and nervous, or I should not have been so alarmed, and now to my tale. It was not a *ghost,* but an ear wig! I was alone in my room, and just before getting into bed, I put in a piece of light wood which made a brilliant illumination, and its cheerful light thrown upon my bed and curtains, etc. made me think what a pleasant thing it was to have a comfortable place to repose upon, and how pleasant the prospect of sleep in *sickness* as well as in health. So I lay with my face to the wall, and my eyes wide open for about ten minutes perhaps, when slowly emerging in sight and crawling along the back curtain I beheld a long black monster of the length of my finger. I did not know what it could be at first, and even after I had, with the desperate energy of fear and horror, crushed the creature, I lay trembling and agitated and half believing that I had beheld an incarnation of the Evil one, and was only comforted upon the strength of the argument that Satan when he wants to communicate with, or tempt we poor mortal creatures has sagacity enough to assume a lovely and enticing form, and not prevent all *parley* even, by clothing himself in a hideous and disgusting one.

I am sorry for Colonel Foster, how tantalizing the cup of happiness has ever been to him. Long, long withheld, and when at last grasped in ecstacy and delight, snatched away or so mingled that its very contents seem changed. Poor fellow, according to the old proverb he ought to have been for life a prodigiously happy man, that beauty and ill luck go hand in hand. Surely one would suppose that the very concentration of all that he ought to have borne was in his bodily appearance.

I must close my letter or Robert will be after me. "Point de nouvelles" as the French say, excepting that we have made some sausages, which idea by the bye might be gleaned from another passage of this epistle. But truce to your hopes—they are neither for you nor for me but Pa destines them for Sophia. Has himself given orders to have them made, and has superintended the manufactory thereof. Love to all.

Your affectionate Sister,

M.

Maria writes Julia on Christmas Eve, and Julien adds a few lines. Although Christmas is not celebrated by the Bryans, Julien, described by his Aunt Maria as "a charming little boy," has his poppers (firecrackers) ready to set off that day, according to southern custom. It is a holiday, however, for the slaves at Mt. Zion, and Maria reports they had been coming in for their "passes"—written permission from their owner to be out on the public roads after dark.

Maria Bryan Harford to Julia Ann Bryan Cumming

Mt. Zion
December 24, 1840 (Thursday)

My dear Julia,

Pa arrived safely and in good health yesterday about four o'clock, and I very soon perceived what good care you had all taken of him by the very great amendment indicated in his appearance. I think indeed he looks better than before his illness; and he has a marvelous good appetite.

Julien is very well, though for a day or two he was quite sick. Saturday he was so unwell and had so high a fever that I became uneasy and sent for Connell, but he, after examining his pulse and his tongue and felt his skin, advised me to give him no medicine at all, as that might disorder his stomach, and he felt sure he would be well in a few days. He looked at his poppers last night very longingly and calculated the probable price, and then spoke of Augusta, and seemed as if he did not know what to determine upon. At last he said, "Well, I won't say whether I'll go or not until tomorrow." He is now quite reconciled to staying, and indeed I think from some plans he has made he would leave with considerable reluctance.

He has been a charming little boy during the visit; I do not speak unadvisedly, but repeat with emphasis he has been a *charming little* boy, so gentle, and affectionate, and obliging, and obedient that his society has been pleasant indeed, without any drawback. I am honouring your request that he should attend to his music, so far as to be teaching him the rules which can never be too thoroughly learned, and I have moved the piano in this room, that I may hear him practice, and that he may not acquire a disgust to the thing by having to take his lessons and play in that cold and cheerless parlour, and indeed his poor little hands are now as rough as a nutmeg grater, they are so chapped.

Tell Emmy I thank her very much for the oranges she sent to me, and every time I look at them or taste them, I think of her. I am very much obliged to you for what *you* sent to me; the Cologne must have come from "the Delectable mountains," at least it almost transports me there when I inhale it. I should like to have it in my power to send you something, or do something for you too; not that I feel your kindness, or the gratitude for it, at all onerous. On the contrary, I think I do not deceive myself when I say that the delights inspired by sentiment, or the assurance of interest and affection which my gift from a friend indicates, is the predominant feeling ever. And you may therefore imagine, if more sentiment can outrun the ecstasy which my olfactories enjoy when they are suitably administered to, it must be a very pleasurable emotion.

Sophy has made it a sort of reproach to me many a time and oft: that I "*long* so much for *love* and *affection*." But if it is my nature, how can I help it? "Give to the flower the dew drop," and things which are constituted for a certain element must be indulged with that element or they die. And yet for myself I must be the Amphibia, for I do not enjoy much of it and still I subsist. None of the nearest and tenderest ties of life are mine. To be sure, I have, as Isaiah said, "a father, an old man," but he is today so engaged in his tan yard, and in settling his various accounts, that I have to exhaust myself tonight in writing metaphysics to you.

I sent Mrs. Cunningham the oranges. Mrs. Matthews said to me the other day laughingly, "I had a great mind to ask Mrs. Cumming when she came up, where was my cape." What cape is it? As well as I understood it, it was one which you have worn at some previous time, and she asked you to give it to her after you were done with it. I said to her, "I told Julia, Mrs. Matthews, that you would take anything from her before you would from anybody else."

"It is true," said she, "that there is nobody that I do more admire and respect than Mrs. Cumming. And I do think (she added) that I don't know of anybody in all my acquaintance who is what I would call so improving a character as Mrs. Cumming. Whenever I see her again I perceive advancement in moral excellence from the previous time I saw her."

This is exactly what she said and a great deal more—but she is a clear-sighted woman, and judges correctly, where prejudice does not distort the medium through which she looks. And here have I without meaning it affixed my seal to her remark. Not that I do *not* mean it, but I did not wish to appear to flatter, or did not particularly care about expressing my opinion at all on the present occasion.

Mrs. C. continues very ill, and is alarmed and agitated, and wretched.

Pa says you would like to have my "Piano a vent" if it was in order. I would send it to you, but I do not think it would answer your expectations, for besides being a very frail thing, and as uncertain and capricious as a woman's temper, the smallness of the keyboard makes it difficult and inconvenient to play upon. I do not disparage it to keep you from desiring it, but to moderate your expectation about it. It gives no sound at all now, but I hope Mr. Hurlbut [the northern piano tuner] will come here before long. He has a brother in Greenesborough, and goes there occasionally, and I have some agents there appointed to carry my wishes to him about coming here.

I hardly know what I have been writing about, Julia, for I have been quite sick today, and my head is so confused this evening that I have not a clear idea in it, and the negroes have been coming in for passes, and Robert who is just back from his Eatonton trip talks so long and so much, that I have written this in pain of nerves beyond expression. He does not wish to go *now* to Augusta, but when he can get "gaardin seeds," which will be in February, he says. He was speaking of his last visit there, and recalling its incidents with much pleasure — "Colonel Cummins," says he, "was very polite to me, just as polite as though I'd a been a king," and with that he laughed as loud and long as if he *had* been a king. Indeed, I don't think the crowned heads of these days of our world enjoy such heart-felt mirth and self gratulation often.

Tell Sophy I should be glad if she will keep Jenny strictly and closely engaged and make her sleep in the house. She will do just as much as she is required to, and go as far the other way as she is permitted. My best love to my best beloved brother, and Annie and the other children — and to Sophia.

Yours Truly,

My dear Mother,

I would have writen to you before but I thought that I was going down so soon. I have been sick but am quite well again. I hope I shall see you before long. Aunt Maria is teaching me how to play Chess and I like it very much.

Your affectionate son,

J. Cumming

Maria gives Julia a long, heartrending account of their father — a pitiful old figure harassed by a debt to his own brother, Isaac. Maria is indignant at her uncle.

Maria Bryan Harford to Julia Ann Bryan Cumming

Mt. Zion

January 16, 1841 (Saturday)

My dear Julia,

I wrote you a short letter soon after receiving Mr. Cumming's comforting intelligence that Harford [Julia's seventh child, now two years old] was better. It relieved us all considerably though we still feel anxious, particularly as the weather has been and continues so unfavourable. I hope we shall hear by the next mail.

Mr. & Mrs. Deane are still here, and the former terribly out of health and spirits from the gloomy weather. He thinks if he cannot get into business immediately that he will not return to the North at this season and has, therefore, engaged board at Mr. Neal's as one of the most convenient houses in this vicinity.

Indeed, we have been almost as gloomy within as without, for some time past, for Pa has received a visit from his loving relative Mr. I. Bryan, which has put him into a state of mind anxious and wretched beyond description. He again presses for a "*settlement*," and wishes Pa, if he cannot pay him the money, to give him notes (of which he has a number upon his neighbours for blacksmith's work, leather, etc. etc.). Pa says he does not like to subject neighbours and friends to the unpleasantness of being sued or pressed beyond measure for money in these hard times, and will only give him such notes in case he cannot make an arrangement in Alabama.

Uncle threatens to sue Mrs. Carrington, now lying on her sick bed and but just rescued from the grave apparently, for the sum of thirty dollars, and upon Pa's urging him not to do this, he says, "Well, you must give me *your* note for the sum." Pa replied, "She now owes me more than twenty times that sum and I dislike to increase the debt." He returned another day, and says, "Well, if you don't wish to have Mrs. C. sued, you must give me some other person's note from whom I can get the money." Pa's own expression is, "He *is* my tormentor," and that I have heard him say as many as three times within a day or two. He is almost sick, and looks wan and haggard of mornings, and his temper as well as his spirits are affected beyond what I have known them to be, or the *former* certainly.

Yesterday morning he said to me, "I had a most distressing dream. I thought Isaac came to me and said, 'I *must* sue you,' and I replied, 'Well, go on then.' Such," said he, "was my agitation and distress that I awoke and my first idea then was, 'Oh, that *I was dead,* that I might be out of his power,' but I reflected that it did not become me to feel so, but rather to pray for strength to support me under the trial."

One might be almost inclined to wonder how Pa can be affected to the degree in which he is, when he knows he means to pay him and has the means of doing so, but then it must be considered that he cannot have the strength of endurance that he possessed when a younger man, and he is proud and sensitive and such treatment harasses and worries him and is exceedingly mortifying, and more than all *he is alone* now, and *I* know the meaning of those words, though, thank God, *you* do not, for though *I* try to console him and reason him into indifference and cheerfulness in the matter during the day and evenings, yet at night during which I think he passes many sleepless hours, he has no one to sympathise with him, but his imagination aggravates the evils of the case fourfold.

And I do think his imagination is diseased on this point, and if the matter is pending much longer, he will be almost as afraid of expense as Mr. Isaac himself. He will not buy a chicken, or a dozen eggs, or a box of blacking, or pay out a dollar for a little sewing by some poor woman. On the contrary every such thing I am compelled to do myself. And I do not mention this in a spirit of *complaint* but with pity and regret, and as a painful evidence of the pain suffered before such effects could be produced, and because I know you will feel about it in the same way. I will not trust myself to make any comment upon the author of all this, nor "fret myself in any wise to say or do evil," but the burning feeling of indignation and contempt with which I regard the man, and the deep shame I feel in a relationship with him is not, I am aware, a suitable feeling for a fallen creature, "compassed with infirmity" as I know myself to be.

Last night Pa was sitting by the fire, gloomily descanting on the subject, Robert and I listening, and saying whatever we could suggest to soothe him, and after a long fit of musing, his heart seemed to grow lighter and he commenced singing one of those old songs that I reckon he learned in Mr. Cunningham's time,

> "How happy every child of grace
> Who knows his sins forgiven.
> This earth he cries is not my place
> I seek a home in heaven."

But I fear that he will actually set off to Alabama on horseback, as I find my remonstrances have not the slightest effect in changing his plan. Mr. Howell has to take his mother to visit her daughter in Harris County, and he has asked him to continue with him to Tallapoosa, and this is my only hope that he will not go alone and in that way, but even then he says he will go on horseback being he cannot afford to buy him a buggy. But I will change this subject after begging you to burn this as soon as you have read it.

If you find anybody coming up soon (Mrs. Booth is going tomorrow) please send me a quarter of a pound of sewing silk from Cress's or Carmichael's.

Have you an old carpet that you have laid aside that you could give Mrs. Rossiter? Next to begging for one's self it is humiliating to beg for another, but I know you will grant or refuse in this case as suits your convenience. I hear her saying that the Dr. so constantly trips up upon her old patched carpet, and she is entirely disappointed in getting the money for [their servant] Ellen's hire, and she said the other day, "Well, I must get me

some kind of a carpet, even if we go without comforts to buy it." I shall hope
to hear tomorrow.

Your Sister,

M.

Julien Cumming writes his mother two letters without coaching or correction by
Maria. Julien concludes both his letters with an affectionate message to his nurse-
maid, "Mammy." Maria complains in her second letter to Julia of being sick and
is glad Pa is with her.

Julien Cumming to Julia Ann Bryan Cumming
Maria Bryan Harford to Julia Ann Bryan Cumming

Mt. Zion

January 28, 1841

My dear Mother,

I now sit down to write you a letter and I hope you will answer it very
soon. I study French and say two lessons every day. Aunt Maria is teaching
me how to pronounce it and I like it very much. When Aunt Maria is teaching
me of nights Robert sits by and laughs and says he thinks it would strain
our nerves dreadfully. I went up to Mr. Hanells last night and spent a very
pleasant evening with Tom, Lily and Jef Hunt. I like staying up here very
much indeed. Tell Tommy and Alf that they must come up here for I think
they will like to stay here.

I read aloud every day to Aunt Maria in Stephens Travels in Egypt and
Arabia and I think it is a very interesting book. The last chapter I read
contained a description of the great pyramid in the neighborhood of Cairo.

Mr. Benson is painting the inside of the church and I think it is very much
improved. Give my love to Grandma and Aunt Sarah and to Pa and to Mammy
and to the children.

Your affectionate son,

Julien Cumming

My dear Julia,

. . . I have just received a letter from Aunt Wales. Catherine [Wales Erwin] had a son on the fifteenth which she has called Joseph Bryan. Aunt Wales seems dreadfully hurt that you should not have thought enough of her letter to answer it.

Jule is a very good boy and appears very happy; as he says Robert is always exceedingly amused at the French lessons, and says well don't it strain your "narries."

I hope to hear from you soon.

Your sister,

M.

P.S. He is faithful in his music.

Mt. Zion

March 2, 1841 (Tuesday)

My dear Mother,

I received your letter which you sent to me by Miss Norton this morning, and was very glad to get it. I went up and read it to Aunt Rosseter and she was very much pleased with it, and told me to give her love to you when I wrote. I am very sorry to hear that Harford is so unwell but I hope he will get better soon. Tell Alf that I will expect a letter from him this week and tell him that if he writes I will answer him directly I get it. I wrote a letter to Tommy intending to have sent it by Grandpa yesterday, but forgot, but I sent it this morning by Mr. Williams to put it in the office at Sparta. I [hope] you can come up with Grandpa and fetch Harford and Emmy and Josy [Joseph] and sister and stay two or three weeks for I wan to see you very much indeed. I had a great deal rather you would come up yoursef than answer this letter if you had time. I wish you would let Tommy come up with Grandpa and stay a little while with me and then go back again. Mr. Marchant is still staying here with Grandpa working in the Tan yard and he seems very well contented with staying here, and Grandpa says that he is a very industrious young man and that he is an excellent tanner. Give my love to Pa, Aunt Sophia and all the children. Aunt Maria received your and sister's and Pa's letters yesterday. I cannot write you as long a letter as you wrote to me. Give my love to Grandma and Aunt Sarah. Tell Mammy that I want to see her very much.

Your affectionate son,
Julien Cumming

My dear Julia,

Your son has just handed me his letter to fold and direct which I have not seen since it left the room in a white sheet. Sometimes I suggest a few ideas, but today I have not given him the least assistance, and I have concluded of late that I would not correct his letters but let you see just his position as it regards writing, spelling and composing. I perceive he always takes occasion to mention Mr. Marchant who stands high in his favour, from possessing that greatest of attractions, a good-natured obliging disposition, and being always ready to talk, or to listen, both of which qualifications Jule duly appreciates.

I never saw a fellow more pleased and more agreeably surprised than when I returned from a walk this morning (having called a moment to say howday to Harriet N.) and asked him what he would give me for something which I had for him. Its not being mail day, he never thought of a letter, until I pulled out that which is certainly, associations et cetera considered, the most beautiful of objects next to the "human face divine." I knew Mrs. Rossiter would be interested in hearing of the unfortunate man of whom you wrote, and sent him up to read it to her, as she was sick and low spirited. I suppose, as he indicates, she was very much pleased with it, and succeeded in persuading *him* that it was a gem of its kind of the first water, for he returned in a fine flow of pleasurable feeling, in being the owner of so valuable a morceau, for you know that vanity, in any or all its varieties, may be considered as the moral "vin du Champagne" of our nature. Surely the effects being so exhilarating and delightful no one could object to a glass of its being occasionally taken, but for the unfortunate consequence of its becoming in a measure *essential* after a few indulgences, which is true in both cases.

Tell Pa, Marchant is [working] as factotum to the full extent of his wishes, to the shop with his slate, and then committing that to the books, then off to the tan yard as though he had the profits of all. As for me I shall be obliged to say "Othello's occupation's gone," unless somebody or other will come along that owes him, and let me settle accounts, and thus have an opportunity of showing off my "larning," as I did to Mr. Tommy Jackson's great admiration some few weeks ago. I entirely forgot reminding him of Margaret Kelsey's order, and will, therefore, thank him to purchase 2 doz. of Brown's Catechism at the Depository and have them charged to me. Ask him to get us a loaf of sugar, and a box of composition or spermacetti [whale oil] candles, as we are out, as he will be pained to remember. It is always like a sudden thunder clap in a clear day to me when I hear the announcement that "the candles are gone."

I have been quite sick today, and lying down most of the time, and I don't find indisposition so easy to bear since I have been pampered upon the exquisite enjoyment of good health for three or four months past. I have got cold upon cold which has made me feel uncomfortable in every way, and I believe if Uncle was here tonight, I would set aside the Lobelia [an herbal remedy], I'd "go through a camass" to get the cold out of my bones, and the "*canker*" out of my system.

Your affectionate Sister,
M.

P.S. Query — which is the best — "a short short letter," or no letter at all? "Answer expected next week"?

Julien Cumming writes his mother of Dr. Connell, Maria's future husband. Julien has been in Mt. Zion since early December, and Maria seems to be serving again as tutor for Julien and Annie.

Julien Cumming to Julia Ann Bryan Cumming
Maria Bryan Harford to Julia Ann Bryan Cumming

Mt. Zion
March 27, 1841 (Saturday)

My dear Mother,

I thought that I would wait until another letter came but as no letter has come yet I thought I would write to let you know that they are all well up here. Today Sister [Annie Cumming] has gone out with Grandpa to spend the day at Dr. Whitten's [a transplanted South Carolinian family who lived near Mt. Zion], with the Miss Meriwethers who have just come from South Carolina. Aunt Maria got a letter from Aunt Sophia saying that she was going to Columbia to stay a few days and then would come up here but she has not come yet. Last Saturday I went out with Dr. Connel to see Mrs. Griggs the woman who had her leg cut off, and I had a very pleasant evening. Tell Tommy that I have not got a letter from him yet but I shall expect one from him, though Grandpa says he is going down very soon to buy something to go to Alabama in. I do want to see you and Harford up here as soon as you can come. Give my love to Tommy and Alf and Pa and all the children. I am still studying French and I like it very much indeed. I am going to learn "the old English Gentleman" [a ballad arranged with chorus and accompaniment for the piano by Henry Russell (1812–1900)]. Your affectionate son,

Julien Cumming

My dear Julia,

It has been several days over a fortnight since we have had a line from you and I do not know how to account for your silence. The children, particularly Annie, have been very impatient indeed. She is pretty well and keeps herself constantly employed, either in practising or studying or at her sewing and nitting. She seems violently opposed to studying French, and as she quotes your permission that she need not be *compelled* to study anything, I have concluded not to force her on the point.

Pa went to Sparta yesterday and saw Mr. Nesbit just from Washington City. He told him that he had seen Brother frequently, but could give no account of his employments or intentions, and Pa returned home sadly out of spirits and complaining of feeling sick.

I presume you have seen Mr. Sparrow, and become acquainted with him before now. We were all very much pleased with him indeed. I presume he gave you my watch. Please send it to me by the first safe conveyance, as I miss it extremely, and you know you say it is my idol.

We have expected you until we have almost ceased to look for you, and indeed are in total ignorance of all your movements. Jule is a good boy and is improving in his music, and progressing well in his other studies. He is in excellent health, is a universal favourite "up here" as he calls it, and studies so well that he has ample time to play and ride, both of which he delights in, the latter especially when he can be permitted to mount Ellis. My love to all.

Affectionately your Sister,
M.

Maria Bryan Harford married Dr. Alva Connell on April 11, 1841, while her father was in Alabama. The why and wherefore of this union can only be surmised. Alva Connell lived and practiced medicine in the Mt. Zion community, where Maria was a lonely widow of thirty-four. Her earlier letters reveal not the slightest interest, sentimental or intellectual, in Dr. Connell, and her subsequent ones provide no clue to her real feelings. She certainly was not in love with him in the way she was with her first husband, Harford. She and the "Dr.," as she called him, established a separate household from Pa after their marriage, and her focus of interest shifts abruptly away from her father and the Bryan home. Maria rarely comments on her new husband but sometimes includes him in her affectionate messages to her Cumming kin. One guess is that Maria's marriage to Dr. Connell was due less to romantic feelings and more to loneliness and propinquity.

In this letter Pa Bryan and his grandson Julien have just returned from a trip to the Bryan lands in Alabama. Pa went there to sell his property but was unsuccessful.

Julien Cumming to Julia Ann Bryan Cumming
Maria Bryan Connell to Julia Ann Bryan Cumming

Mt. Zion
May 8, 1841 (Saturday)

My dear Mother,

We arrived here yesterday evening about sundown and Grandpa was very well only he was very tierd and had the backache very bad from not haveing anything to lean against in the little carriage that we went in. I wrote to you while I was in Alabama but I do not know whether you received it or not for the mails are very uncertain. I hope you and Aunt Sophia will come up next week. We had very comfortable houses to stay at every night as we were on the way home. Uncle Goode [operating a plantation in Alabama] wanted to come with us very much but he said he could not come till June. Yesterday we crossed over a water course called little river, three miles the other side of Eatonton and the water came into our little buggy and wet our clothes very much. Tell Pa that Uncle Goode is going to send him a white deerskin after Mr. Marchant has dressed it he is haveing it dressed with the hairs on and it looks very pretty. He says he would have [sent] you and Aunt Sophy some venison hams of his own killing and cureing but he had no way to send it. Give my love to all. Tell Aunt Sophy I wish I could see her and her little boy [Joseph Bryan Harriss].

Your affectionate son,
Julien Cumming

May 9, 1841 (Sunday)

My dear Julia,

I had been riding out Friday afternoon, and when I returned and entered the room, to my surprise I found Pa lying on the sofa. I did not expect him until next week, for he said very certainly that he would not be back to the meeting. He has not accomplished anything as it regards the sale of land, but has had the titles made to himself of several valuable tracts by Mr. Lawson. He looks quite well, but was very much fatigued.

Julien has had a delightful time according to his own account; is in perfect health; very much sunburnt. Pa says he only had to reprove him once while he was gone, and that was for keeping one Sabbath (or being disposed to) in Alabama style; he was with the young Lawsons who hunt, fish, etc., *especially* on that day.

Mr. Bowman preached a most excellent sermon today. I wish you could have heard it, "If Christ is not risen, then is your faith vain, ye are yet in your sins."

Pa thinks of going to Augusta some time soon, either this week or the next. Give my love to Annie and Emily, and Mr. Cumming and Sophia. I was quite sorry when I remembered that I had not sent any message back in my last in reply to Emmy's.

Pa is waiting for the pen to write a few lines to Uncle so I conclude.

Affectionately yours,

Uncle Isaac is still pressing Pa to settle his debt. Pa dislikes the idea of selling his
slaves out of the family, but Isaac continues to pressure him.

Maria Bryan Connell to Julia Ann Bryan Cumming

Mt. Zion

May 10, 1841 (Monday)

My dear Julia,

Uncle brought your letter this evening and I drop you a few lines by the
mail tonight to inform you of Pa's intention of setting off to Augusta on
Monday of next week. He will take Julien with him according to your request.
Jule commenced his studies again the beginning of this week without even
being directed to do so, and learns well, and behaves as he did before he left
with perfect propriety.

Pa had but a few minutes' conversation with Uncle, but that seemed to
have left him in a most unhappy state of feeling. He told him that he was determined to sell property to pay him, and would sell anything that he owned.
He said *he* thought of offering his plantation for sale, to which, said Uncle,
"I think you *had* better sell it." Pa said he disliked selling his negroes out of
the family, but would part with Cuffee. "I reckon," said he, "Cuff *would sell*,"
without saying one soothing or consoling word, or "You may take your time,"
or "Do not incommode yourself." Pa has been remarkably cheerful since he
came home until this interview, pleased with Goode, pleased with the meeting, with the appearance of Mr. Johnson's crop, and especially so with some
accounts of Brother from a gentleman just from Washington, which perfectly
harmonizes with the information of Mr. Alfred Cumming, contained in your
letter.

I am really disturbed, my dear Julia, to find that you suffer so much from
your toothache. What a thousand pities that you will not wear thick solid
shoes when you walk out. Have you tried Ma's remedy yet for the toothache,
the cherry bark tea? I have often heard her say that in her younger days
she was almost a martyr to the toothache, and the habitual use of this cold
[mixture] made her teeth and gums healthy. She never suffered with either
afterwards, and you remember how remarkably sweet was her breath.

Mrs. Ponce has been up several weeks. She is well, and amiable and pleasant as ever, and seems to be delighted with her daughter-in-law. I suppose Miss Jane Armour will hardly be up this summer. Mrs. Rossiter suffers much now, and is, I think, failing greatly. She often inquires affectionately after you and inquires when I have heard. Jule sends his love.

Affectionately yours,

Chapter Twelve

MRS. MARIA BRYAN CONNELL

"How much of a slave a woman finds herself when she comes to act out of her usual routine."

In this letter Maria has just returned from a visit to Augusta, where she had gone shopping for furniture and china.

Maria Bryan Connell to Julia Ann Bryan Cumming

Mt. Zion
February 23, 1842 (Wednesday)

My dear Julia,

I have been intending ever since I came home to write to you, but have been almost sick from my night's exposure at the railroad depot. We arrived there about midnight, and the rain was pouring down, the water was ankle deep so that my indian rubber shoes were no protection at all, and my stockings and the skirts of my clothes got wet. And when we entered that most comfortable of inns, there was no fire and no other convenience. I could not get my trunk to get anything dry, nor could get any night clothes, so that I had to sleep in my damp frock. And to add to everything else, when I got into bed, I found that it rained upon me. Betsy (who had taken possession of one half the bed, and waked up when I entered the room, telling me that her mother had directed her to sleep there, as I might be afraid to sleep in a room by myself) proposed very good-naturedly that I should change places with her and take the dry side of the bed. I thought that the precept to "bear one another's burdens" implied a sort of obligation to permit them to be borne by those willing to do so, and so accepted Betsy's offer, as it seemed to me anyhow that I was wet and jaded enough to feel the effects to my cost.

It rained so hard during the night that we heard in the morning that the river was so full that it was over the bridge. We thus had no other prospect than that of spending the day and perhaps the following night. But about nine o'clock William Sayre came, on his way from Petersburg where he had been to carry Mr. & Mrs. Patton, and a baggage waggon with him. He offered us a conveyance to the river where we found George waiting on the other side. We remained about three hours on the bank waiting for it to fall, and arrived home about night.

Goode has come. He is well and cheerful, and talks of going to Augusta soon. He and Julien staid here last night, and took breakfast with us this morning. Jule is very well, and gets along well, was very much pleased with his Grandma's present, and has taken but a small pinch as yet, and is greatly interested in reading Charles O'Malley. He took the disappointment about Tommy better than I expected, and seems now perfectly happy in being with his Uncle Goode and listening to his Alabama stories.

I am afraid all the plants you gave me excepting the Japan honeysuckle will die. We are now enjoying comforts of your providing, as our fire is reposing upon the andirons, *your* gift, and the rocking chair affords even a pleasanter seat here than in the furniture store. I am mortified indeed about the chairs. When I parted from you to go to Dunlap's and the hardware store, I meant to pay them, and Parson's too, but finding my funds were not sufficient, I concluded I had better leave the bill for the chairs unpaid, as I knew that Pa had spoken to them there. How could Pa— — — —but no matter! I am truly obliged to Mr. Cumming for settling the business, and for this addition to his many other kindnesses. Dr. Connell has the money ready now, and will send it down the first safe opportunity to Mr. Cumming and get him to have the bill receipted. I presume Miss Draper has not done the work as Uncle Jacob has given me no account of it. Tell Emmy that when I opened my trunk after I got home it was just as she said, sure enough there was the neck ribbon.

Will you have the kindness to look at the Bookstores and inquire for two books for me, *The House Book* by Miss [Eliza] Leslie [1787–1858, Philadelphia author, editor, and moralist], published by Carey & Hart, and the *American Flower Garden Directory* by Robert Buist. If they are not in Augusta please inform me for the Dr. has a friend in Philadelphia, who will be here in April and can get him to procure them for me. If there, you can send them by Uncle.

Dr. Rossiter is much better. Mrs. Bailey is still in the neighbourhood. She seemed very much gratified at your message. My pen is wretched and I write in great haste. Tell Celia I am much obliged to her for sending my night clothes. I did not know I had left them until I untied the bundle. Write soon. My love to all.

Your affectionate Sister,

M.

Maria Connell feels in part responsible for her sister Julia's bad cold because she took her out in rainy weather during her recent shopping trip in Augusta. It is clear from this letter and other correspondence that Julien again is on an extended visit to Mt. Zion. His father wrote his son on December 26, 1841, that he hopes Jule understands "that they do not love him the less because they think it best for him to be away from home at present."

Maria Bryan Connell to Julia Ann Bryan Cumming

Mt. Zion
February 26, 1842 (Saturday)

My dear Julia,

I received your and Annie's letter today, and though I wrote you yesterday, yet I cannot forbear a few lines again to express my regret at your indisposition. I felt, too, some considerable misgivings, and did even before hearing from you, lest I may have occasioned an aggravation of your cold, from dragging you out with me in that unpleasant weather. I perceived that you were drooping very much the last day I was with you, but supposed that, in addition to feeling uncomfortable from your cold, you were a little out of spirits too. I fear lest I have in my nature too much of one of our good father's least-to-be-admired traits, and that is to become so absorbed in some scheme or business deemed at the moment of paramount importance as to lose proper consideration for others who may be useful in forwarding it, as well as for myself. If you and your friends have laid the blame of your increased indisposition on me I fear that I must plead guilty in act, though not in intention. For truly I had myself much rather *be* sick than to hear that *you* are so, for I consider your life as of so much more importance than mine that illness upon myself does not seem to me to portend such evil as yours does.

Again I must declare my mortification and regret at the difficulty about the chairs, though I was fully under the impression that you *understood* all about it. As I said before, I thought it best to leave *them* unpaid for, thinking that the owners of the establishment would be satisfied from Pa's having spoken to them, and I paid away everything I had in other places excepting twelve & a half cents. I suppose Pa was as good as his threat, and never returned to explain to them that they would be paid in due time. I am much obliged to Mr. Cumming for advancing the money, though Uncle Jacob said nothing about the receipt.

Did not you suppose there were *a dozen and a half* of cups and saucers belonging to that set of china I bought at Mustin's. I am sure that you gave as one reason why I should take *them* in preference to the white set at Dunlap's that in addition to their being prettier, there were half a dozen more of them. But to my surprise and chagrin, upon opening them I found only a dozen, and I should like much to know whether it is *my mistake* or their dishonesty, and were it not so disagreeable an agency, should request you to inquire into it.

Adeline Thomas was here yesterday; she is in great trouble at present, and great as is her usual reserve and reticence of manner and character, she wept much as she recounted her father's pecuniary embarrassments, and the many mortifications they had been subjected to since their mother's death, and indeed *besides* that, actual privations of comforts to which they had always been accustomed. Mr. Thomas is now near Carllodinsville where he has rented a farm and some of his negroes have been levied on and his land which he had lately sold here. Adeline did not know from what quarter the thing came, but was greatly distrest when the sheriff put the paper in her hands, and sent in great haste and agitation for Dr. Connell to go to Sparta and inquire into the matter, and if possible stop the proceedings, which he did.

Saturday Evening.

Jule took supper with us tonight, and is well, and in every respect as usual. I do wish you'd let Alfred come up in April, as he wishes to, and spend a few weeks with me. I don't think it would be altogether lost time to him, for besides the exercise and recreation there are some things I could assist him in that boys of his age are apt to be negligent about, as writing, spelling, and music, etc. If he comes let it be understood it is to pay me a visit, that is if you are willing to trust him with me. Give my love to Annie and tell her I was very glad to get her letter, and shall answer it before long. I am surprised she should think she could not interest me.

Write soon. Remember me kindly to all, and believe

Affectionately yours,

M.

An upset Maria writes Julia that she cannot come to Augusta because no one at home ever thinks she needs "any recreation or pleasure, more than a door post."

Maria Bryan Connell to Julia Ann Bryan Cumming

Mt. Zion

April 30, 1842 (Saturday)

My dear Julia,

I have just heard since I wrote to Annie that the [Georgia Railroad] cars go by Durden's at midnight. As I have no one to go with me down, I shall feel too bad to enter the cars among a number of strange men at that hour of the night. I have tried my best to persuade Uncle to go with me but he will not consent. The Dr. cannot leave home now, for he has several sick patients upon whom he is in constant attendance, and cannot even go with me to the railroad. For some reason or other Pa has never approved of my going, and consequently gives me no encouragement or assistance in any way. I beg you will not blame me, I have been straining every nerve for a week past to go, and really wished to very much, but no one here ever thinks I need any recreation or pleasure, more than a door post. I cannot think of any future time that I can go, for the difficulties will be no less hereafter than now that I see.

Your affectionate Sister

Maria's relationship with her father, which had been strained again by her recent marriage, appears to be better, and news of him appears in this letter to Julia.

Maria Bryan Connell to Julia Ann Bryan Cumming

Annadale

June 27, 1842

[Postmark: Mt. Zion]

My dear Julia,

Annie is so much engaged in her tapestry that I think you stand but a poor chance of receiving a communication from that quarter — and I have a fancy that you will be somewhat disappointed if you do not hear by the next mail. I forewarn you of a stupid letter, though for my ideas do not flow freely today. During the tremendous storm last night, I got up and put my arm out of the window to unfasten the shutters that I might draw them together, and got my arm so wet that I have today a crick in my neck and a pain in my shoulder, and I am sure that the nervous fluid does not pass freely to and from the brain. Happy are they who can give so philosophical a reason for being dull and stupid!

I am glad that the boys arrived in safety. Poor little Emmy, I am concerned to think she should continue so much indisposed. It seems to disturb Pa so much that last night as we were there spending the evening he said, "I do think it would do Emily a great deal of good to come here and stay a while, and if her mother would consent, I would go down myself and fetch her."

Pa is quite lonesome now, though he is very cheerful whenever I see him. He has been very much engaged of late about his negro clothes. We have been assisting him up here some, and I had him eleven garments made which helps somewhat. I do really wish you would come up yourself now and pay him a visit. I think he would particularly enjoy it at this time. Sophia does not write to him, or at least he has not received a letter from her since she left Augusta. He got a letter from Goode, Monday. He writes that he has a fine crop and a most excellent overseer, but does not think he will be in until August. *Do* write to Goode and try to persuade him to come home without any delay. I cannot account for it myself.

Pa expects Mr. & Mrs. Bowman this week. The former is to marry Tom Grimes to Fanny Merriwether on Thursday next. I believe they are going to assemble a great many on the occasion. But there's to be a blow out tonight at the Baxter's. The two girls are quite excited about going. I thought that the Dr. or I would one of us go with them, but Pa says we ought both to go, so that is determined on unless it should rain very hard. The Miss Baxters spent one day here since they came, and called yesterday to invite them there. I suppose everybody who visits them from this place and from Sparta will be present.

If you were like Mrs. Baxter I might, with the anticipation of pleasing you, tell you that everybody admires your daughter [Annie] very much, but alas, unnatural mother that you are, no such thing as this pleases you, because of the association with which this said admission produces. I can almost fancy you saying with Judge Frank in *The Home*, "I don't wish my worst enemies the pain of having grown up daughters. When one has educated them, and just when one begins to have real pleasure in them, one must lose them." No doubt, all those things must produce pain, but such is our destiny, struggle, efforts, self-denial, and out of it all gracious good for others as well as ourselves. To perform the various duties, and submit to the manifold trials of the several stages of our brief existence, so as but to please Him who is by these very means fitting us for a better and unending life, is indeed desirable. Apropos of Judge Frank have you read *The Home?* It is a most excellent book. Life in those northern regions of Sweden and Russia and Norway must be very pleasant.

Mrs. [Carlisle] Beman has been in the neighbourhood for a week or more. She has been staying at the Baxter's though she was on the Hill during the days of the examination. She took tea with Pa one evening. I asked her to spend a day here, and she seemed to wish to do so, but Mrs. Baxter said she was going to have company that day and would not consent to her coming. Mrs. B. says her sister Catherine is in wretched health, and she expects constantly to hear of her death—her husband has separated from her, and has sent her to live at Mrs. Witherspoon's (Mary Jane Casey). She does not assign any reason for it. Now don't there seem to be a curse attached to that family? And sometimes I think it is because of their exceeding ridiculous and wicked family pride, and think of the words of Hannah, "Talk no more so exceeding proudly; let not arrogancy come out of your mouth; for the Lord maketh poor and he maketh rich, He bringeth low, and lifteth up."

I hope I shall hear from you again before long. Give my love to all. Tell Emmy if I had thought of it I would have sent her the "Parents' Assistant" by the boys.

Affectionately yours,

Here is one of the rare complaints from Maria about the hot weather of a Georgia midsummer. Annie Cumming, almost sixteen years old, is still visiting her Aunt Maria and is easy to entertain and easy to feed. Not so is a woman friend of Goode's, whom Maria finds strains her hospitality. Maria makes an anti-Semitic remark about this guest and asks her sister Julia to forgive her for "violating the duties of hospitality in speaking of it."

Maria Bryan Connell to Julia Ann Bryan Cumming

Annadale
July 15, 1842

My dear Julia,

The change in the arrangement of mails throws me out of all routine about hearing from or writing to you. Your letter which was dated the previous Monday I did not receive until last Monday, a week after it was written, and was wondering why we did not hear from you, and was really beginning to feel quite uneasy. I should have answered it by the next mail, but had not a scrap of paper in the house and indeed have had to borrow this.

I think I know how fully to appreciate your sufferings about hot weather. Indeed, it seems as if I should melt completely away. You appear to have blamed Annie for her remissness in writing, but she was waiting day after day to hear. She seemed quite distrest to find that you complained of being lonesome and low spirited without her; I assure you her engagements do not make her forget you. She often speaks of your wishes and commands as something she must attend to, and if I am not mistaken, is greatly improved in all her ways. She certainly is the easiest person to entertain that I ever saw. She requires no cares or attentions whatever, and as it regards her food, I do not think she would even complain if you set nothing but cold water and a piece of cornbread before her.

I find it entirely a different matter with the Chosen Seed. I did not at all comprehend the trouble occasioned by their notions of unclean and forbidden food until I had a daughter of Abraham under the roof. She will not eat one mouthful of the finest fresh pork or the most delicate ham or, indeed, any but beef and mutton and chickens, and where this is the case, and no market convenient, it keeps me upon the Stretch — to contrive something for her to eat, for it is very perceptible that it is not an unimportant consideration with her. Pray let this be entre nous, for I feel as if I am in some respect violating the duties of hospitality in speaking of it. Pray, my dear, what has made you serve me so about my carpet? I have been expecting constantly each mail to hear from you that it had been sent up to the railroad. I believe I told you the exact quantity I wanted, 30 yds. If you will send it immediately, and let me know, I shall have an opportunity of sending for it soon to the Depot. Those crimson table cloths, what are the price of them, one about 2 yards & a quarter in length? Please charge your memory with it, and let me know the price in your next.

The Dr. is amazingly afraid about troubling you concerning the shirts. He is now in the room, and says, "I am very much afraid it will trouble Mrs. Cumming too much. I really do not like to trouble Mrs. Cumming so much, Maria" — but I tell him if you felt it too much so, you would not have offered. He has them open before, two wide plaits on each side, and two buttonholes in the collar, through which he passes a gold button, his sleeves require to be very long, and the wrist-band about four inches wide. He does not possess gold sleeve buttons so that you may put but one buttonhole there. Please get half a piece of shirting at Carmichael's from which you can make them.

How are you interested in *George IV?* [*Memoirs of His Life and Reign* by

Hannibal Evans Lloyd had first been published in London in 1830.] I shall send you the other volume the first opportunity.

Pa is well but works very hard. I go to see him as often as I can. He never comes here. He is quite hurt that Sophia does not write.

The Dr. waits impatiently to take this to Sparta. He has a patient there with the palsy, on whom he is trying the influence of electromagnetism. This has been scratched off in great haste, you know how impatient men can look.

                                                Affectionately yours,

P.S. Do come up soon and see your poor father.

The Connells are about to build a brick house, and Pa, now more friendly toward his daughter and son-in-law, is keeping an expert eye on the brick burning.

Maria Bryan Connell to Julia Ann Bryan Cumming

                                                Annadale
                                                July 19, 1842 (Tuesday)
                                                [Postmark: Mt. Zion]

My dear Julia,

I was very much in hopes that I should have received a letter from you by the last mail. Indeed, had exertion on my part have been of avail, I should have been with you before now. But I have proved since this effort what has been demonstrated to me many hundred times before — how much of a slave a woman finds herself when she comes to act out of her usual routine. Friday evening I was spending with Pa. Uncle, too, was there, and I inquired when he was going to Augusta.

"In the morning," said he.

"Well," said I, "I wish I could go with you."

Pa spoke, and said, "I can send you to the railroad so that you can go down with him tomorrow night."

He made a faint sort of offer to see me down, but gave so much indication that he did not want my company (perhaps fearing that he should have to pay my expenses) that Pa and I both concluded that I had better not force myself upon him.

I suppose you have heard that Dr. [James] Ponce has committed suicide in Charleston. What a shocking thing it is! His father and mother are greatly distrest, although they have not told Mrs. Ponce that he died by his own hand, and she is under the impression that he had fever. I think this is an injudicious course, for when she finds it out, as she inevitably will sooner or later, her grief will be renewed. They sent for Pa, and he went there yesterday afternoon. They say they knew of nothing that disturbed him, and cannot imagine what could have induced him to commit the act. Mr. Gildersleeve wrote to Mr. Ponce, and said he had arrived there the evening before, and delivered some letters of introduction, and told his friends that he should leave in the morning for Savannah. His door was found locked in the inside in the morning. They broke it open and he was discovered lying in bed, his throat cut from ear to ear, and a razor by him. The blood was stiff so that of course he must have killed himself as soon as he retired to his room. Mrs. Ponce says that he left the key of his office in Sparta with her, and of that she thought strangely at the time, as he had so many acquaintances in the place. He took leave of them all with much affection, and said perhaps he might go to the West Indies before he returned home. [The *Charleston Courier* of July 16, 1842, reported Ponce's suicide.]

Pa is expecting Sophia the last of this week. Indeed, I do not know but he would have gone to Augusta himself at this time had it not been for that. We have not heard from Sophia but once since she left.

Manty has arrived and is staying in the kitchen at home. I do not know what they intend doing with her.

I see Pa once or twice every day, for he passes by here and calls in frequently. The Dr. is having his bricks burned [for a new house at a local kiln], and Pa goes often to see how they are getting on.

Give my love to Mr. Cumming, Annie and the children and write soon.

Your affectionate Sister

Satterlee from Sparta, who had haunted Maria's early letters, has been taken in by the Connells and put to bed as a very sick man. Maria feels pity and horror for this "most wretched human being."

Maria Bryan Connell to Julia Ann Bryan Cumming

Annadale

[Undated; probably July 1842]

My dear Julia,

I cannot let the opportunity by Mr. Harwell pass without dropping you a few lines. I was very much disappointed that Uncle Jacob went away without the bag I sent down to him the morning that he was to leave, but he had been gone more than half an hour.

When will you come up? The weather is delightful now, and I shall be glad to see you here once more.

Satterlee is again here, the most wretched human being in mind and body that I ever saw. He had set his heart upon coming again, though he is not able to move out of bed but from the exertion he makes. Oh, how wretched he makes me feel! Indeed, I am unhappy all the time day and night, and my very dreams are affected by the mingled feelings of pity and horror that I all the time feel. The Dr. is away a great deal of the time, and late at night, so that I am much alone with him. And such a disposition! He finds fault with me, scolds outright at the Dr., and storms at the servants though we are all doing the best we can for him. Indeed, I feel as though it were a fiend about to be disembodied and I know not how soon — for I do not think he can stand it long.

I was very much obliged to you for the oranges, they came most timeously, just as I was sweating over the quilts. All are well at home. Love to all, *do* write soon.

Yours affectionately,

Satterlee is still staying with the Connells and is now submitting to the ministrations of the doctor. Maria doubts he will recover.

Maria Bryan Connell to Julia Ann Bryan Cumming

July 25, 1842 (Monday Morning)
[Postmark: Sparta]

My dear Julia,

It does seem as if there were something always to oppose my visit to you. I had prepared myself, my mind, and my clothing, to go with Mr. Bowman to Greensborough today, and take the cars there for Augusta, but received a note from Julia Maria [Iverson], saying she was in Sparta, and wished me to send for her as she had come to pay me a visit. Of course there was no help but for me to stay at home. Her [younger] brother Alfred is now with Pa, and will go to school [at Mt. Zion]. He appears to be a very pleasant and well behaved boy and Pa seems to like to have him there.

I went with Mr. Bowman yesterday afternoon to see Mrs. Ponce. The family are in great affliction, though they bear it like real Christians. When we got in Mr. Ponce was sitting by his wife reading to her Baxter's *Saints* [*Everlasting*] *Rest* [written by the Reverend Richard Baxter (1615–91) and published in the 1830s by the American Tract Society]. They have now told her every particular and she seems more composed since she heard it, for before she was constantly suspecting something, she now persuades herself that he was insane or he would never have committed the act. It has not yet been found out what occasioned his distress of mind, whether it was merely indisposition or what, and perhaps it never will be known, for poor Joe was singularly incommunicative, *always*.

We have heard nothing from Sophia, but by your letter. Indeed, she has written only once since she left here. Pa seems to be in very good spirits and is in good health, looks remarkably well even for him. Satterlee is still staying here. Dr. Connell is prescribing for him, and he is most docile in submitting to everything. At this time the Dr. applies leeches to his heart and throat every day and sometimes twice in the day. He does not cough as much, and says he feels better than he has in many a long day but whether the improvement will continue and be permanent I have my fears. Poor fellow, he is so irreligious. If I could see a change in that respect I should hail it with still more pleasure. There is very little sickness in the neighbourhood, nor has there been much. Maria Carrington has been dangerously ill but is now amending. Dr. & Mrs. R. are uncommonly well particularly the latter.

I wish you could have heard Mr. Bowman's sermon yesterday. It was better than usual even, from this text, "I know in whom I have believed, and am persuaded that He is able to keep what I have committed with Him until that day."

But I must conclude as my time is hurried and I wish this to go by the mail today.

Yours affectionately.

At last, after three and a half months, Maria has her plans set to go to Augusta to visit her sister and her family.

Maria Bryan Connell to Julia Ann Bryan Cumming

Mt. Zion
August 14, 1842 (Sunday)

My dear Julia,

I set off tomorrow morning with Mr. Bowman to Greensborough, on my way to Augusta. I was very sick last week, and did not feel able to write, and in addition to that, I did not care about writing until I could tell you something definite about my visit. I shall be too much fatigued after tomorrow's journey to go any further, and besides it would be impolite and unkind to Mr. & Mrs. Bowman after he has had the trouble of carrying me over, not to spend any time with them. I shall accordingly wait until Tuesday night.

I am extremely obliged to Mr. Cumming for offering to meet me at Durden's but it will be useless for him to take the trouble of coming (unless he wishes the jaunt) for Mr. & Mrs. Gilmer go down Tuesday night and will leave from Mr. Bowman's house, I believe. And indeed, if he will just send Moses with the carriage to the [Augusta] depot, I had rather that than to keep him up at night. I shall thus have the pleasure, I hope, of breakfasting with you Wednesday morning.

In great haste, your affectionate Sister,
M.

Maria has arrived in Greensboro on her way to Augusta. The Georgia Railroad had reached Greensboro in 1838 and by 1842 was well past Madison on its way to Atlanta. Goode Bryan had long since left the railroad's employ to become a planter in Alabama.

Maria Bryan Connell to Julia Ann Bryan Cumming

Greensborough, Ga.
August 15, 1842 (Monday)

My dear Julia,

I wrote to you last night, but sent the letter so late (having forgotten it) that I am uneasy lest it might not have been put in the mail. I therefore repeat what I then said, that I shall go down tomorrow night, and shall hope to meet Moses at the depot, as it is quite unnecessary for Mr. Cumming to be kept up. I shall go down in company with Mr. & Mrs. Gilmer. They tell me that the mail is nearly ready to close so I will conclude, hoping to see you all soon. If you know how much effort it has cost me to make the visit, you would, I am sure, give me credit for a reasonable desire to see you.

Yours affectionately,
M.

The Connell house is nearly completed, and Maria complains of the "dirt and noise and confusion, from carpenters, painters and masons." She suffers also from an "unnamed pain."

Maria Bryan Connell to Julia Ann Bryan Cumming

Mt. Zion
November 8, 1842 (Tuesday)

My dear Julia,

I had been sympathising with you in your sufferings from rheumatism before I had received your letter, for this longtime unnamed pain of mine enables me fully to realize the agony caused by anything akin to it. I have been suffering very much lately, and partly that, and partly because I was expecting each mail day that I would get a letter from you induced me to postpone writing—and *not* ceremony.

Added to this the whole house is constantly such a scene of bustle and dirt and noise and confusion, from carpenters, painters and masons, that I rarely have a quiet minute to myself. But I do not the less think of you, and many a kindly thought and wish is each and every day expended upon you and yours. I wish you would take blue pills again for that pain of yours, and rub it with Spiritus Vitae or Jewetts Ointment, and three times a day take as much of the carbonate of iron as may lie upon the point of a fruit knife. This course has done me more good than anything else. I am sure we both suffer alike, and that it is a species of neuralgia, and iron in moderate quantities is always so beneficial in restoring a healthy tone to the nerves. Besides the carbonate of iron is extremely pleasant to the palate, as much so as the white kind. But what am I expending all this time and paper for in writing what you will just set down as quackery, and not do after all.

Annie is sitting on one side of me knitting away on a new pair of socks that she has commenced for Julien. She says her grandpa says if you have a longing to have her go home, he has a longing to keep her. She was very mindful of your wishes, and staid all the time with him after Sophia left until Aunt Wales arrived—and seemed to be a great comfort to him. I used to go down every evening, and Julia [Maria Iverson] and the Dr., so that he used to have quite a large circle round his fireside with the addition of Alfred [Iverson] and Jule and Robert.

We all went in to Sparta last Friday to attend the agricultural fair, and heard Judge Andrews deliver an address with which we were very much pleased. We saw some home made silk dresses, and divers other articles of female workmanship, and some very pretty horses, and most remarkable hogs— at least so far as size was concerned. We dined at Mrs. Bird's with a large party consisting of Mrs. Baxter and her daughter and niece, Dr. Casey and Dr. Mackey, and two Mr. Bonners, and Pa and the two girls.

Julia received a letter from her mother yesterday saying that the carriage would be here in the course of a week or so to take her and Alfred to Columbus. I had until then expected that Julia would remain here during the winter.

I hope that you will find when you go into town [move back into the downtown Augusta house] that you can pay us a visit. I have a very great desire to see you, and Emmy in particular, and I think you ought to try and be with Pa every opportunity that you can, for it is such a great satisfaction to him. Annie and I still talk of going to Scottsborough, although she appears to be so well satisfied that she is not as anxious about this visit as I thought she would be.

The Dr. has been looking out for horses, every drove that has come along, but has not yet found any that suit him. He desired Uncle Jacob to bring up the carriage when he comes, and he has promised to do so if he has not too heavy a load up. Dr. send[s] the little dog by Uncle Jacob.

I am most sad and melancholy since my visit to Sparta, and it is that I cannot cease to think of Satterlee. It would agonize your heart to see him now. I don't speak figuratively, for really I never saw any one for whom I felt a more profound interest and commiseration. He said that he thought at one time he would be able to get to Augusta, but it was impossible now, he was so weak. He can hardly speak without great effort, and pants all the time, and is so shrunk that he looks like a skeleton with clothes hung on him. He intends coming out, he says, and I think if he does it will be to die, but I will most willingly render him every service in my power unto the last, that he may require from a mortal. And oh, if I could see that he had any prospect or hope in the future I should not be so inexpressibly distrest in seeing him and thinking of him. His lips quiver whenever he speaks; he is evidently aware that his time is short. He looked at Annie with great interest as she was sitting conversing with someone in the room, said she was very pretty, but not at all like you.

Don't let it be so long again before you write. Remember me most affectionately to Mr. Cumming and the children, and to Mrs. C. and Anne and Sarah.

I remain very truly yours,

The Connell house is completed, except for some final painting. In the middle of Maria's letter to Julia she quotes James Thomson's The Seasons *from memory, and except for lines out of order, she was remarkably accurate. James Thomson (1700–1748) was a poet and a writer of hymns, odes, and songs.*

Maria Bryan Connell to Julia Ann Bryan Cumming

Mt. Zion
November 24, 1842 (Thursday)

My dear Julia,

I was under the impression, until I received yours, that you had received several letters since the [school] exhibition, informing you of Jule's performances etc. etc. I saw none of them myself for the weather was very inclement, and I had no conveyance, not even the protection of my indian rubber shoes, so that I was not out at all. And that reminds me to ask you if you have seen anything of them at your house since I left. They must be either there or were left in the car, for I have not seen them since my return, and they are rather hard to procure at present. So I am pretty much confined to the house in this bad weather, of which we have an abundance.

I heard, however, abundance of commendation as a number staid with us who were there. Indeed, I am afraid that Johnston and Pa between them will spoil Jule by considering him such a prodigy, and he is quite cute enough to find out what any one thinks of him, even though Pa were better skilled than he is in hiding his emotions. I really did not like Johnston's putting Jule last in his speech [the finale], as there were boys so much older than himself, and some very smart ones too. He probably meant it to produce effect, his speaking so agreeably while such a little boy comparatively, but then that is always the situation of honour at a literary display like this, and was calculated to produce some conceit in the one thus distinguished. From all I can learn Mr. Johnston the elder and Pa have tacitly agreed to flatter and bepraise their two descendants to each other in words and looks and manner ad infinitum.

I was amused at a speech made by Ned Rudisell who staid here the night of the exhibition (you remember seeing him in Powelton).

"Well," said he, "I don't think I ever did see such a dead match, as three men that sat together there tonight."

"Who were they?" said I.

"Why, Pa and Mr. Bryan and Mr. Johnston, and I don't know which was the best pleased."

Jule has been here since the exhibition and was horribly ennuied after so much excitement. I gave him a ghost story to read, for that will excite me when everything else fails. And then got him to read aloud to me the history of Mrs. Brownrigg, thinking nothing but dose after dose of the horrible would suffice to produce a reaction of mind. I believe he went off pretty cheerful, and at present meditates a visit to Mr. Bonner's.

Annie has been effectually relieved from all such feelings by the grand panacea employment, though the weather has been enough to conjure up gloom. "First joyless rains obscure, drive through the mingling skies with vapour foul; And shadows vast, deep tinged and damp, and congregated clouds, and all the turbulence of heavens involve the face of things. The soul of man dies in him, loathing life, and black with more than melancholy views," (see James Thomson's *Seasons*—"Winter"). Yet she has been all life and energy and cheerfulness.

What a strange thing she is. You know how little she cares about dress, less than any one of her age I ever saw. Well, she has taken it into her head lately that she wanted a black dress, and spoke of it so often that I at last put in a petition to Pa to get her one. That was "no go," so as the desire was often exprest, I bethought me of an old satin of mine, and told her she might have that if she would. She picked it to pieces, and I had it brushed over and ironed out, and nothing can exceed the earnestness with which she is working away to make it wearable. I have not been as much amused lately, for I am sure I have never seen her as proud of any dress as she is of the black satin—though she will probably not wear it more than once or twice before she will throw it aside.

I am trying to make the inside covers for the carriage, as I find it very much motheaten, and it is rather the most unpleasant business to fit it that I have undertaken lately. I was in hopes that Uncle Jacob would go down soon, and bring up what was left of the harness. I asked Pa if we had not better try and get the missing parts made up here, but he advised to send for them, as there is not harness-maker about, and I will trouble you to get Moses to put them in a box, and either send them to the railroad, or by some waggoner that may know us. If they could come up to Mr. Durden's care, so as to be there when Pa goes down with Annie. And will you likewise, my dear Julia, get Alfred or Tommy to go to D'Antignac's and ask for a quart of blue grass seed (charging it to Dr. Connell) and send it up by the same conveyance.

Annie is quite reconciled not to go to Scottsborough, though I got a letter from Maria McDonald the other day urging me to come. Pa says nothing about going to Texas, and says Mrs. Franklin is still there and does not like the prospects of her adopted country and would be glad to abandon it if her husband was willing. Poor Mrs. Matthews, I feel for her, and join most earnestly in your prayers on her behalf. I have thought much of the Clays, and remember hearing when I was to Boston that Miss Anne Clay was in bad health, though I have heard nothing special about her since. I rejoice in any happy circumstances of Tom Clay's lot. He is a worthy man whom I greatly esteem, and who deserves to be happy if anybody does.

I have not written to you since Mrs. Brown was here. She came with her son Sidney, who joined the Church at the last communion. She staid with me, and I think is as happy a mother as I ever saw. She thinks she is a witness of the efficacy of prayer, for she says many a time when she has prayed she has felt that it was an omen, for she had so little to base a hope upon but upon the omnipotence and mercy of God.

We are now in a situation quite tantalizing with regard to our house. It is all done and could soon be occupied, but for about three or four days of painting. The painter is a drunken fellow, and has gone away because we had no oil at the time, and we cannot get him back, and there is no other one in the county to be obtained. We are thus in a situation in which we cannot move, either to clean up or do anything but sit there and wait his pleasure.

Give my best love to Mr. C., to your mother, Anne and Sarah, and to your children. Kiss Emmy for me. The Dr. specially desires that I send his best regards to you. It is late and I am cold so good night.

Maria has just returned from a visit to Julia and has a bad cold and cough. As usual, she spent a miserable night's lodging at Durden's, slept fully clothed to keep from freezing, and concluded that the discomforts of the accommodations "caused a great gulf" between herself and Julia.

Maria Bryan Connell to Julia Ann Bryan Cumming

Mt. Zion

January 2, 1843 (Monday)

My dear Julia,

If it were not for my recollection of your request and my promise, I would not write to you by this mail, as I am so sick that I can hardly hold up my head. My cold has been greatly increased since I left you, and my cough is so violent and constant that it does seem as if I should break a blood vessel.

We were sufficiently comfortable in the cars, but in getting out found it intensely cold, and had to stand knocking some time at Durden's before we could waken any one, and then there seemed to be no place ready for me to sleep. After some time, Nancy vacated her place by her sister, and I was directed to sleep there. I kept on all my clothes, and believe if I had not, I should have frozen in the open room and under the scanty covering. Johnston said in the morning that he never slept upon such miserable little soft pillows, and that he was tempted to steal one and give it to somebody for a cradle pillow. I suggested that it would have been a good thing if he has concluded on the theft to have presented it to some lady friend for a *"torneo."* All this going to prove *that* [Durden's] is in all its departments the most miserable establishment ever kept, *professedly* for the accommodation of the way worn traveller. It seems to me after one of my times there that I shall never go to Augusta again, and that that place causes a great gulf between you and me; it is, however, possible that as in times past the distant object, (like heaven to the weary pilgrim), may seem so attractive as to make the intervening difficulties overlooked.

We set off at daybreak the next morning and took breakfast at Mr. Rudisell's. Then I parted from my companion and went home alone. George was waiting for me, and told me that the Dr. could not come as he had several very sick patients. One of them I find is Jane Baxter who has a severe attack of pleurisy. The Dr., so far from looking sour about the loss of the money, seemed disposed to be my comforter, and the serenity of his countenance was not for a moment disturbed, as he said, "You couldn't help it." But I know it will cause him very great inconvenience, as he finds it extremely difficult to make collections, indeed in some cases apparently impossible without sueing which he is very unwilling to do.

Tell Annie Mr. Lewis has been spending the afternoon here and taking supper with us, and made many kind inquiries of her, and says he wishes he could see her, and wants to know when she is coming up again. By the bye, Wm. Lewis was a classmate of Wm. Henry Cumming [at Princeton] and upon my giving him the latest information of him, he says, "Well, is not that singular."

One day he said, in a meeting of one of their literary societies (the Phi Kappa) Wm. appeared with a manuscript under his arm of some size, and in due time, rose to read it. It was an imaginative thing altogether, supposing himself as having been a physician in the celestial empire, meeting with great success, and finally being called upon to attend the emperor who had broken his leg. The leg had healed and was crooked. He described the first interview at some length, and then gave a description of his method of procedure. He first broke the leg, and then reset it. Lewis says it gave him an opportunity to express his opinion of a troublesome young man who was constantly getting up, without any formality, and interrupting others, and who attempted to bring Wm.'s composition into ridicule. "He hoped," said this other fellow, "if Brother Cumming (the fraternal appellation used in these societies) was so skilful a physician that he would call at his room and prescribe for him as he felt himself very unwell." Lewis says he ran up and begged that Brother Cumming if he prescribed in this case should proceed with the patient's head as he had with the emperor's leg, and break it.

I went down last night and staid two or three hours with Pa. I had not seen him as I past, as he had been summoned to Mrs. Samson's to divide the property. He talked a good deal about it, and seemed quite excited at the state of things between the daughter and her husband. He says there is no prospect of any happiness, for she never speaks to him, and never looks at him. That she has consented to live with him solely on account of the property. They have come to the terms, and the writings have been drawn, that if she leaves him he is to have half of the property, and if he leaves her she is to have all.

Pa seems to be much gratified at the expectation of Julien's coming back. I told him what you said about his coming down, and he made no explicit answer. His leg is much better, and Robert is also better.

Dr. Brown is dead, but was never married; that is an entire mistake.

It seems to be much colder here than in Augusta. The ground around the house is as stiff and rigid from the frost as a mesmerized limb. I planted out my cutting in good rich earth as soon as I arrived home, though my hopes were feeble when I remembered your and Emmy's prophecy that not one of them would live.

The Dr. is highly pleased with his guard chain, and shows his valuation of it by having immediately fastened it to his watch, and occasionally casting some loving and protecting glances to his bosom which it adorns. In opening my trunk I was disappointed in not finding a little bundle that I was sure was in it. It contained some ribbon, and a yard of pure white linen. I did put several bundles between the bed and mattress in the room over the parlour where my trunk was, because it was so difficult to lock and unlock my trunk, but I was sure I had removed it. Will you ask Cynthia to look there, and if it can be found, send it to me the first opportunity.

Give my love to all. Write soon and believe me ever truly and affectionately yours.

Julien and Thomas Cumming have just arrived from Augusta, Tommy to stay with the Connells, Julien with his Grandfather Bryan. The Connell household is "sad and gloomy" because Satterlee is back and in bed dying of tuberculosis.

Maria Bryan Connell to Julia Ann Bryan Cumming

Mt. Zion
January 26, 1843 (Thursday Evening)

My dear Julia,

I have but one moment to spare to write you a few lines by the mail which leaves tonight. The boys have arrived in safety, and are both here now. They are well and cheerful, and Jule appears to be perfectly happy and contented. The Dr. and I are more pleased than we can express that you have let Tommy stay with us; and we renew our promise to take precious care of him. So far from his having less influence over Jule by his being here, I think the effect will be this—instead of wanting to go elsewhere, he will be much here to see

Tommy, and when Tommy goes to his Grandpa's he will feel more inclined to stay with him.

We have a sad and gloomy house here now, and mine is a sad and heavy heart, night & day. Satterlee does not leave his bed, and we think each night will be his last. The Dr. has not undressed for three nights past, but lies across a chair or anywhere that he can snatch some sleep; for he cannot bear to have him leave him a moment. He asked me this morning when you were coming up, and says he should like to see you, and to see Joe [Brother], and his eyes filled with tears. But I should almost hate to have you see him, for the shock would be too great, unless you could do him some good by seeing him. Pa has conversed daily with him, and told him there was no hope, and begged him to look to the Saviour, and place his reliance upon him. I don't know what he thinks about it, but his soul's concerns are apparently in as hopeless a state as his bodily ones. I could not begin to express what my feelings are, to see that I can do him no good, and sometimes when I am out of the room he sends for me, and looks me in the eyes so earnestly and pitifully, and his countenance is now so ghastly that it is dreadful.

The Dr. examined him yesterday with a stethescope, and says one side is perfectly hollow, the lung entirely decayed, and the other wasting rapidly away. At times he coughs an hour without ceasing, and seems as if he would choke, and has to be fanned, and every window and door closed. The neighbours are very kind to him, and some one comes every night to sit up with him. He has sent for the Sayres today.

Write soon, and believe me affectionately yours.

Mesmerism has become the current rage of the community. How much better, Maria muses, were the old days of Queen Anne "than the stir and excitement and bustle of the unquiet Nineteenth Century." Aunt Wales, staying with her brother Pa Bryan, has had a stroke.

Maria Bryan Connell to Julia Ann Bryan Cumming

Annadale
April 1, 1843 (Saturday)

My dear Julia,

I was just doing up a few "little chores" being Saturday, and intending to go down home and see Pa, when he came stepping in. I am very much obliged to you for the oranges; nothing between this and "furthest Ind" could affect my palate so delightfully. I am sure if the fruit in Eden had been oranges, I should have "plucked and ate" without old Satan to egg me on. I fear me so at least.

As you say, Pa is very much excited on the subject of animal magnetism. He has been talking incessantly on the subject since his return. What are we to think? What are we to believe? I have always felt convinced that the time would come when all the powers of wonder and astonishment of which our natures are capable would be drawn upon, but I thought it was after we should have crossed the cold stream that we must all pass before reaching the other world. And poor you! If it were not that I am too selfish to be willing to part company with you even in idea, I could wish you the dame of some quiet old fashioned manor house in the times of good Queen Anne with your tapestry frame ever before you, delving away upon some Scripture piece, Deborah sitting under the oak giving laws to Israel and a multitude of tents seen in the distance worked in white floss silk, or Judith and Holofernes embroidered in flaming crimson and gold, done in cross stitch, or Solomon riding into Jerusalem upon the most symmetrically shaped ass that ever strode from under a lady's needle. How much better this than the stir and excitement and bustle of the unquiet Nineteenth Century with the lights streaming in so strangely upon all points as to dazzle the eyes with excess of brilliance.

What a truly distressing circumstance is that of Harding and Platt. Not knowing either of them I have felt terribly shocked. How much more so those who were in the spot where the occurrence took place. [Platt shot and killed Harding in Augusta, allegedly over a social rebuff. The jury later returned a verdict of not guilty.]

I have seen Aunt Wales within the hour past. She appears more like living than she did Sunday and Monday, but it is exceedingly painful to see her now—both arms in a degree parylized, and not able to articulate a single syllable. She tries hard to talk, and seems very impatient when she cannot be understood, and I do not think you can have an idea, without being present, of how it makes me feel to see her struggling to say something and every one exerting himself to catch what she says but in vain, and then asking her to repeat what she said, and after doing this a second and a third time you are forced to give up the effort to know what she means. And her own despair, and impatience, and her fretful, puling stories like a sick child. What a world we live in! Ah my God, in looking above, beneath, around, I see no refuge or peace for frail and helpless mortals but to hang upon Thy arm, to rely with humble childlike submission and confidence on Thy love and power and goodness.

I received yesterday a long letter from Mrs. Carter in which she expresses great regret that you could not come to see her when you were here. Her two sisters are at Macon. They had just heard of the arrival of Eliza Brantley and her husband at Galveston. She intends going soon to Cosawattee for the summer, and urges me very much to pay them a visit. I feel half inclined to go, but hate to leave poor Aunt Wales in such a condition.

Pa tells me that you wish to have D'Aubigne's work, not having read it yourself. He had sent the first volume to me and I have read a hundred and fifty pages with much interest, but we will watch for an opportunity of sending you this volume as you requested whether I have finished it or not, hoping to have the pleasure of reading, perhaps owning it at some future day. It is written with much eloquence, and the author has a fervour of piety that produces a feeling of almost enthusiasm in the reader. I have always been interested in everything connected with the Reformation as one of the greatest events recorded in history, and in Luther as one of the most wonderful men of all time, but this book has strengthened these impressions greatly. [Volume one of D'Aubigne's work is *History of the Great Reformation in Germany and Switzerland*.]

We have your little darling Tommy as you say with us, and we find him a most pleasant companion. Jule and him [*sic*] are both with us at the moment and very much amused at the Dr.'s mesmeric experiments. We have just returned from Sparta, where he has had a good deal of conversation with a lecturer there, and seen some exhibitions of his power, and seems literally crazy on the subject. Tommy took up his dumbbells this morning, and says, "Well, I will try my very best to get straight [improve a bad posture], I know how it would please Pa if I was to," and with that he flourished away at them until he was tired, and then ran off to hunt rabbits. He is looking very well. There is a mutual and very tender friendship subsisting between the Dr. and him that it is refreshing to behold. Tommy is a remarkable child, guileless, almost faultless, and so reasonable. Well, the ways of Providence are strange, you with so many bairns, each one of whom is enough to interest and engross the affections, and occupy the time and talents of a body to bring up rightly. I am reading aloud to the two, *Tom Burke of ours*, and they are greatly interested in it, and it is amusing to observe the profound silence with which they listen — ears and mouth and eyes wide open.

I feel very anxious to read [George] Borrow's *Bible in Spain* of which I have read some extracts in the [magazine] *Albion*. Have you seen it? Do get it — I see it is published at the North.

Give my love to Mr. Cumming, Annie and the children. Jule and Tommy, seeing that I am writing to you, say "Give my love to Ma." I don't think you have any great reason to complain of me for not writing. You are not very good in this way yourself of late. The Dr. desires his kind regards to you.

Your affectionate Sister

P.S. Jule is in a very credulous state about this said thing of mesmerism. He is sitting at my right side reading, and watching the Doctor's operations [mesmeric experiments] upon [their servant] Annette and every now and then leans over to me and says in a whisper, "Do you think Annette is in a common kind of sleep?"

Maria had been to Augusta and now returns on the train with her nephew Alfred and a Mr. Jones, who is some sort of medical quack with a machine to heal Aunt Wales's paralysis. Three of Julia's sons are now in Mt. Zion: Alfred, fourteen; Julien, twelve; and Thomas, eleven.

Maria Bryan Connell to Julia Ann Bryan Cumming

Annadale
May 18, 1843 (Thursday)

My dear Julia,

We arrived at Durden's about 1/2 after eleven and found the carriage in waiting. The moon was shining so beautifully and the air so balmy and pleasant that Alfred and Mr. Jones were still more intent than myself on making the rest of the journey. You remember I told you that I had not slept well the night previous, and I was so perfectly overcome with drowsiness that I could not keep wide awake for a moment at a time. But Mr. Jones was in full possession of his faculties and talked incessantly, every moment making inquiries of me as to the nature of the soil through which we were passing, and what was growing in the fields near the road, and I so sleepy that I would rather have slept even if we had been passing through the valley of Golconda than to have staid awake to look at the diamonds. Once, said he, "How still everything is; not a leaf stirring." But there's a tongue stirring, thought I.

However, we got home just as day was dawning. I put Alfred in one room and Mr. Jones in another all ready prepared, for there was no one up, and we soon were all, I suppose, in a profound slumber till breakfast.

Mr. Jones praised the coffee and rolls and ham by deeds as well as words, and immediately after commenced fitting up his machine. He found it a good deal rubbed and marred by the friction of travelling, but he took it philosophically as he appears to do all other things, and after getting it in order, the Dr. shouldered it, and he and Alf, Mr. Jones and I started off home. We saw Pa when we got half way, riding up to make him a call, but seeing us he turned back, and putting up his horse, came to meet us just as we approached the church fence. He was in his coat, and was looking his best, and received Mr. Jones with great dignity and courtesy. I had taken the precaution to call Mr. J. *Professor* Jones in my letter, and I saw that the effect had been favourable, Pa having all the Connecticut veneration for learning and science, and having been brought up near enough to Old Yale to consider the title of Professor as a most sonorous and imposing one.

I found Aunt Wales in a state of high expectation, laughing and crying by turns; and in the course of fifteen minutes, Mr. Jones was introduced and commenced his operations. She has a great deal of faith that it is going to benefit her, and she can now move her arm with the assistance of the other, higher than she could. He has been at work again today and thinks there is some prospect of success. He is going by request to deliver a lecture tonight, and again tomorrow night. Some of the Sparta people are coming out to hear him; now let Mount Zion alone for entertaining a guest.

Pa, from his own account, has had a time of it since I left, Aunt Wales fretting and crying, he says, so that she could be heard to the store. One morning, he said, he heard her screaming so that he got up and went to her, and said, "What is the matter, Julia?"

"Why, here I am, sick and helpless. I have worked until I have brought myself to this state, and no money, nor not a friend in the world."

"And have you brought yourself to think that," said he, "Julie, not a friend?"

"No, I have no friend in the world."

Pa says he never sees anything [in Aunt Wales] which seems like a Christian spirit either in conduct or language, though Mrs. Rossiter thinks it is the buffetings of Satan, and he would fain hope it was, without its being anything worse. He thinks of trying to get her off by the first of June [to her stepdaughter, Catherine Erwin, in Clarkesville], though he says that, anxious as she is to go, it does not seem right to put her upon Catherine, limited as are her circumstances. It does seem as though Uncle and himself ought to support her. He is in hopes that Uncle will come to go with her, agreeable to his promise, for, said he, "I cannot conveniently leave home now on account of the little boys, and my harvest is coming on." Do tell Mr. Cumming that I hope he will try and make Uncle see the obligation he is under to come and relieve Pa from this undertaking. I believe he can do more with him than anyone else.

The boys are well, and were delighted with their present. They have borrowed my board for the present, and are going to get Mat to make them one. Alfred seems to be enjoying himself finely. He came up today to borrow Essie to take a ride with Mr. Jones.

Mr. Bowman did not come last Sabbath, but sent on a servant to say there was such a state of things in his church that he could not leave, but the Sacrament will be here on the fourth Sabbath.

Pa seems to be very anxious to have you come up and pay him a visit. He was pleased with his gloves, and particularly the elastic fixment at the wrist, and when I gave him D'Aubigne he said, "Well, well, this is a present indeed."

I hope you will write soon. It seemed really strange to me the next morning to be sitting down to breakfast here, when just at night before I had been with you.

The Dr. is so pleased with his coat that he cannot leave it off for a minute, although there is a change of twenty degrees in the thermometer since yesterday.

Tommy and Jule came up to see Alf, and went to his room, and waked him up the morning he arrived. A letter has just been received from Eliza Beman. She is very sick, thought to be in a consumption, but intends, if she can travel, to set off for Georgia the first of June. Tell Annie, Cornelia has come home.

Give my love to Emmy and tell her I want to see her so bad, I don't know what to do. Love to Mr. Cumming and Annie.

Yours most affectionately.

P.S. Robert has lost his contract, was under bid by Duncan. Poor fellow, he takes it sorely to heart, but bears it better than was expected. Pa is in some stir of mind at present, having heard that William Lewis says that Brother has a situation in the Post Office. He was very anxious to know something of Sophia's movements, not having received a letter. Is she still with you?

Tell Col. C. [William Cumming] that the Tobacco Seed I have brought up has produced so great an excitement that even Pa talks of going largely into the business next year. Ask him if any more can be procured.

I have found a singular inmate here, a well digger, an Irish man whose name is Diamond. He is a perfect monomaniac. The subject on which he wanders is the loss of some property, and it is amusing and strange to hear his vagaries. The Dr., who is a living Democritus and finds entertainment in everything, draws him out to talk until he looks like an inspired prophet. The former had just returned from a visit to a man who was bitten this morning with a moccasin snake and Diamond is just assuring him that not only will snakes not live in Ireland, but upon his word of honour if you will bring a little bit of Irish earth and throw upon an American snake it will die instanter. A thorough blessing that of Saint Patrick.

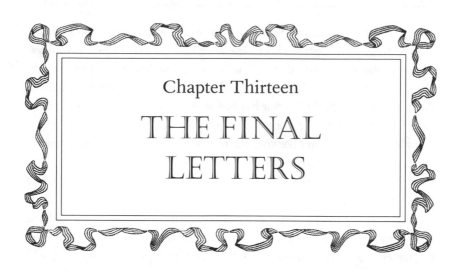

Chapter Thirteen
THE FINAL LETTERS

"*Uncle Isaac said, 'Your father says things are gone too far for him to retract now, even if he wished to.'*"

The subject of a second marriage by Pa, though not specifically named here as such, comes up for the first time between his daughters Maria and Julia. Ma has been dead six years and Pa is seventy-five years old at this writing. Sophia, her husband Robert Y. Harriss, and their son, Joseph Bryan, are now living nearby, and Maria wishes aloud that "Goode will marry some nice girl" and live at home with their father.

Maria Bryan Connell to Julia Ann Bryan Cumming

Annadale

August 11, 1843 (Friday)

My dear Julia,

I received your letter this morning in which you make some little complaint of my tardiness in writing before, and as everybody has gone to church and left me alone, I concluded to spend the time in writing to you. I am very far from being well, and not able to walk to church tonight, but Annie and the Dr. are the representatives from here. Mr. Bowman and Mr. Talmage are the only ministers we have, and today (Friday) there have not been many in attendance.

I am truly concerned to hear that you continue so unwell. [Julia is two months pregnant.] Sophia, whose sympathies are greatly enlisted in your behalf, says she is sure you do not take the pills punctually, or *often* enough. She expresses the utmost confidence in their efficacy, and I have never known them to fail, though the Doctor has had some very uncommon cases of the suffering for which he prescribes them. I do feel very much for you, but know not what consolation to offer you, but to exhort you to that patience which I have no doubt you strive to exercise. It is a comfort to think that "our times are in God's hands," and as Romaine says, "Our crosses are all appointed by Him, their *number*, their *weight*, their *continuance*." And then to know from the declaration of His word that He is not ignorant or unconscious of our trials, "for the eyes of the Lord are upon the righteous and His ears are *open* to their cry." And lest, in that self tormenting spirit prompted by a sense of our own unworthiness, or the malice of Satan ever willing to snatch every comfort from us, we should doubt our right to rank ourselves among the righteous, Scripture tells us that "*Blessed* is the man whose iniquities are *forgiven*, whose sin is *covered*," covered by the righteousness of Christ imputed to the guilty soul that is enabled to trust in Him. And "Like as a Father pitieth his children so the Lord pitieth them that fear Him, for He knoweth our frame, He remembreth that we are but dust."

My own spirit has of late often sunk within me as I thought upon the multitude of evils and sorrows of our mortal state, and I have literally longed for that state where the wicked cease from troubling and the weary are at rest. But let us not despond too much, but trust ourselves as St. Peter says, into the hands of a "faithful *Creator*," who from *that* relationship to us *is* pledged to care for us in all those various circumstances of joy and trial in which His own righteous Providence sees fit to place us. Let us at least endeavour to do our part even though that part be to suffer much, let us live

> "A life that shall send
> A challenge to its end,
> And when *it* comes —
> Says '*Welcome friend.*' "

Sophy's baby continues very sick with the [w]hooping cough. She says she was very much alarmed about it last night. I think, with Annie, that Mr. Harris's manner is too rough, and that in habituating himself to it he violates good taste and propriety, but I have come strongly to the conclusion of late, that in his way he is very much attached to her and is really proud of her, and much more indulgent than I once thought him. She has got the house (at least the lower rooms) fixed up quite nicely, and has had the piano tuned, and all looks comfortable and pleasant at home. Pa has today received a letter from Goode, in which he tells him he is much moved by you and Annie's representations of his loneliness, and that he will certainly come home between the fifteenth and twentieth of the month if he is not sick. It has comforted Pa greatly, though he is almost sick with a cold.

As to the matter to which you refer I hardly know what to say about it, and have felt an unwillingness to enter upon the subject in a letter. But it is my opinion that he would never have seriously thought of the matter but for the constant urging of some officious persons, the principal one of whom is the eloquent Mrs. Beman, for you know she *has* the gift of speech in great perfection. I have my notion too (and in my own mind feel pretty confident of it) that Mr. & Mrs. Bowman have advised him to it.

The other day the two Johnstons were coming out from Sparta, on their way to their Father's marriage, and he [Pa] was with his negroes at work upon the road. He sent by them his special congratulations to the older Mr. Johnston, saying he highly approved of his course, and was much inclined "to follow suit." I have had some feelings about it and have shed bitter tears in the solitude of my own chamber, for all his previous language and feelings have rendered us unprepared for such a step. I have never heard one single person named. How I wish Goode will marry some nice girl and live with him. I find it is commonly talked of in the neighbourhood as a probable event, the former I mean.

We have heard from Catherine. She gave birth to a son two months before the expected time, on the eighteenth of June. It is still living, she says.

I am sorry to send you such a blotted letter, but my pen is wretched and I have no knife to mend it. Your letter is in ashes agreeable to direction. Annie was quite struck by my *literal* fulfillment of your request. Give my love to all. Sophy says she wrote to you last week.

> Give my love to all.
> Your affectionate Sister

Pa is about to marry Jane Armour, thirty years his junior. Over the years, as re-corded in Maria's letters to Julia, Jane has been a visitor at Mt. Zion and a friend of the family. This "unpleasant business" is disapproved of by the entire Bryan family.

Maria Bryan Connell to Julia Ann Bryan Cumming

Annadale

November 14, 1843 (Tuesday)

My dear Julia,

Annie says it is your request that I would write oftener. It seems to me as if my letters were much more frequent than yours, as this is the third certainly since I received one from you. But truly, I am very willing to write if my letters could afford one half of the pleasure I receive when I get them, for it seems to me of late that I am separated from all intercourse, directly or indirectly, with my nearest of kin and that at a time when I would most wish to communicate with them, particularly on some subjects upon which we cannot but feel in common.

I have been for part of the last week and two days of this confined to my room and almost to my bed by one of the worst colds and coughs I almost ever remember to have had, indeed, I have been very sick, with high fevers, and great oppression of breathing etc., and entirely missed the meeting, though Mr. Bowman was here and preached three days in succession.

Uncle is in the neighbourhood at present, and has been several times to see me, and recommending the "composition," some of which I have taken. He came up this morning, and again introduced this unpleasant business, and though he seems greatly to have disapproved of the step Pa has taken, yet he counsels me again and again to make the best of it and be reconciled etc. He says that Pa got a letter from Brother this morning, and read it to him, and he says he never heard such a letter, "It was like a lawyer pleading." Uncle did not give me a very distinct account, so I can only quote his words. He says Pa was affected by it, for, said he, "Joseph brought up his mother, and spoke of things that occurred at the grave, and said a great deal." "But," says he [Isaac], "your father says things are gone too far for him to retract now, even if he wished to." Pa told the Dr. [Connell], for he has had no conversation with me (because I have resolutely avoided it), that Jane Armour inquired particularly if it would be agreeable to his children, for she would not like to enter a family where they were not willing. I do not know what he could have said to this, and been honest, and yet for him to persevere. He says he showed her your letter. He has made very much of that letter, and I suppose has spoken of it hundreds of times. Certain it is that they have very little idea of our feelings, for Mrs. Baxter overtook Dr. C. one day as he was going to Sparta, and put her head out of the carriage and commenced talking with him about it, and says, "How are his children pleased?" "Why, I presume," said the Doctor, "that they had *rather* such a thing would not take place." "Ah," said she, "why, I am surprised for Frank Ponce had told us it was *very agreeable* to the family."

Pa spends much of his time at Dr. Rossiter's. I presume he gets more comfort there than anywhere else, for Mrs. Smith, who prides herself on being very familiar and sociable with him now, and Mrs. R. are, I understand, both pleased with it. Never did I think I should have such feelings to Mrs. Rossiter as I now have; indeed, as you may readily infer both directly and indirectly from what I say, I have been and am in a great struggle of feeling, between the desire to avoid doing or saying or feeling worry, and the sore trials I am constantly undergoing. The preparations that they are making down there, plastering this week, Dr. & Pa's talking of his journey, and constantly speaking to the Doctor for *his* horses to be sent to Londersville when he returns for them — all these things which seem trifles work upon me sometimes until I am almost crazy. Indeed, the whole world seems to me out of joint, and I can find no pleasant thought in human affairs or connexions or prospects, for though Holy Writ warns us, and experience would deter us from it, yet if we do not have some mortal hold we are in despair.

A most dreadful occurrence took place in the neighbourhood night before last. The Dr. was summoned about midnight, every other man in the place in turn, to act as a jury of inquest upon the bodies of two men who had been killed at sunset the same evening. You have heard of this difficulty between Jane Lawson and her husband, Enoch Jackson. It arose out of that, and though she was living with her mother, Jackson, in company with Ob. Culver (as he is called), went to Mrs. Lawson's and entered her house and attacked her son John, attempting to whip him. He made his escape out of the house taking with him a gun, but they pursued him and Culver fired a pistol at him. John Lawson turned round and shot them both dead [his brother-in-law Enoch Jackson and Ob Culver]. The bodies lay there all night, and the Doctor says he never saw such a scene, and he really felt horribly while he was cutting them to see where the shot and bullets had lodged. Lawson has given security for his appearance at the next court in a bond of ten thousand dollars.

I am sorry to find from Annie's letter that you, too, have been suffering from this cold. How much I wish I could see you and be with you now. I presume you will go into town soon. I hope I shall hear from you in a day or two. I write a postscript to Mr. Cumming which please hand him.

Yours,
M.

My dear Mr. Cumming,

Will you do me the favor to procure for me, either at Hanes's or Service's, four quarts of blue grass seed? Have it enclosed in a box and send up to Durden's to meet the first waggon going there from this place. Now is the time for sowing it, and I will be glad if you will get this year's crop of seed in preference to the last if it has arrived. I hope this little matter you can attend to without its interfering with your more important business and thus oblige your sincere friend and affectionate Sister,

M.

Maria fills this letter to Julia's daughter Annie with the news of young people in the Mt. Zion community whom Annie knows. In fact, Maria's letter is so full of bright gossip that it sounds much like those she used to write Annie's mother almost twenty years earlier.

Maria Bryan Connell to Annie M. Cumming

Annadale
November 23, 1843 (Thursday)

My dear Annie,

I have been intending every mail since I received your letter that I would answer it, but the days are so short, and I always have so much to do that I have put it off longer than I expected. I suppose you have got to town by this time [the Cummings' annual move back to Augusta after summering on the Hill], though it does not look much like winter yet; indeed, it is very extraordinary weather for the season. I often wish you were here, or some of the children now, as it is so pleasant.

I was sitting in my room yesterday, when Annette called me down to see Mrs. Wiley and Elizabeth. As soon as I entered the room I saw that something was the matter with E. as she looked like she had been crying. Upon inquiry I found she was suffering very much from the tooth ache, and had come for the Dr. to pull it out. He had been about all night, and did not return in several hours so she had to lay on the couch and suffer.

Mrs. Wiley and Mrs. Smith went to spend the day at Mrs. Knowles's, and after a while Cornelia came here. The two girls were amusing each other and me, talking of the Janes at "Cornucopia" [the Eli Baxter house, built in Mt. Zion in 1823], where they had both been visiting. Sally Baxter [probably Sallie Baxter of Athens, Georgia, who married Edgeworth Bird of Granite Farm in 1848] is still there, and they say they never heard or saw such romping and loud laughing as she and Blandina keep up, and spend most of their time in the elegant amusement called "horseplay," punching each other, and taking up pieces of light wood or the shovel and chasing each other.

The young men about seem greatly pleased with Miss S. Baxter, and praise her much for her talents and sprightliness. For her part she is delighted, and says she likes every thing and every body she has seen in Hancock. Cornelia wanted much to go home with Elizabeth, but Mrs. Smith always has so much for her to do, and is now so crazy in her preparations for going to house-keeping that poor Cornelia does nothing but work and quilt etc. and has no time for visiting or reading or music or anything else. Mrs. Rossiter, from the great delight she takes in Mrs. Smith, has made her a bed quilt with her own hands, and this of a very elaborate kind in stars, and last week they spent at her house quilting it.

Dr. Mackie staid here Sunday. I don't think he has been in the house before since you left; indeed, he has been so engaged in his professional duties that he has not left Sparta at all. He has had a great deal of business, and has been very successful, I understand, and is very much liked. He inquired very specially after you and when you were coming up again, and says he intends going to Augusta the first of January, as among other things, he feels very anxious to see the many ladies who have returned from their European tour. He says he understands that "Miss Annie says he would fall in love with Lizzy Moore now, if he could see her, she is come back looking so well," etc.

There was a great Methodist meeting here for three days last week, and Sunday the Dr. brought home quite a crowd of gentlemen to dine with him. Mr. Baugh and Mr. Benjamin Harris and Mr. Rudisel, and Mr. Johnston, and Dr. Mackie and Frank Ponce. Frank is all devotion now to Miss Sally Baxter, though I presume there is nothing serious in his attentions. Osborne Smith is to be married between now and Christmas to Amanda Lawrence. She was at the meeting and staid with Mrs. Harwell.

I do not know whether I mentioned to you the death of poor Mary Hunt. She suffered very little comparatively, but gradually became weaker. She never returned home, but died in Sparta at Mrs. Alfriends'. She had had her shroud made before her death, and spoke of dying with much calmness. Mr. & Mrs. Harwell went to the burying which took place at her father's, and Mrs. Harwell said the servants had put the house in the neatest order as if she had been living to direct, and her own room looked just as it used to when she was alive and at home.

I received a letter from Maria McDonald lately in which she urged me to come on to the Commencement, and bring you. She says her brother James and his wife are there now, and will remain until their house in Clinton is finished, which will not be until January. Mrs. Carter and her daughter are not coming home this winter I believe, and she says Catherine Eliza says that she and her mother suffer from homesickness.

I am expecting Alfred every week now, although I do not hear what his movements are to be. Remember me affectionately to your Father & Mother and the children and believe me every yours truly.

P.S. I send you a violet, or, as Ophelia said, a pansy and that's for thoughts. There are thousands of them now, and I often wish I could send you a bunch.

Maria Connell died suddenly at the age of thirty-six, before the grass sprouted in the spring, on January 15, 1844. Julia would name her third daughter and eighth and final child, born in Augusta on March 7, 1844, Maria Bryan Cumming, in memory of her dearly loved sister.

her husband would "give it if needed." That November, Annie accidentally overturned an oil lamp at the rectory of their small parish church on John's Island near Charleston, and she and her maid died of severe burns. Of Julia and Henry's three daughters only Emily Cumming had a long life. She married Harry Hammond, the eldest son of the South Carolina plantation owner James Henry Hammond, in 1859. She moved to Redcliffe on the eve of the war, and after her mother's death, in 1879, Emily brought to Redcliffe the bundles of letters written by her Aunt Maria to her mother, Julia. Emily and Harry Hammond had five children. The first child, born August 20, 1860, was named Julia in honor of Emily's mother. Their daughter Katharine, named for Harry's mother, was born two years after the war. Katharine married John Sedgwick Billings at Redcliffe in 1897, and at Redcliffe in 1898, their son, John Shaw Billings II, was born. Emily died in 1911 at the age of seventy-seven.

As for Maria Bryan's siblings in Mt. Zion, Joseph Bryan became a lawyer, farmed in Alabama, and later moved to Washington, D.C., and became an agent for Indian claims. He never married. A failure in the eyes of his family, Brother died in the capital on August 21, 1863. Maria's younger brother, George Goode Bryan, served in the Mexican War and during the Civil War held the rank of brigadier general of the Sixteenth Georgia Regiment. After a long courtship he married Frances Maria Myers of Savannah in July 1849. She died two months later. He subsequently married Anna Twiggs of Augusta, the daughter of General David E. Twiggs. They had a son and three daughters. After the war he returned to planting. He died in Augusta in 1885, a Confederate war hero. Maria's sister Sophia married Robert Y. Harriss of Appling, Georgia, and bore her husband two sons. Isaac Bryan, the bachelor uncle from Augusta, described by Maria as a miser, bequeathed at his death in 1853, at the age of seventy-three, $100,000 of his estate to his niece Julia and $40,000 to his niece Sophia.

The ailing Aunt Wales of Maria's letters also outlived her niece and died after a stroke in March 1846 at the age of seventy. She was buried in the Mt. Zion cemetery. Close by are the graves of the New England Rossiters. Deborah Rossiter died on April 28, 1845, at the age of eighty, and almost four months later to the day of her death, on August 27, 1845, Timothy, her husband, died at the age of ninety-two.

Long lost in the mists of time to Maria's family, Maria's second husband,

Alva Connell, a physician whom she felt had neglected her during their brief marriage, remarried in 1845, a year after her death. His new wife, Jane Baxter, was the daughter of the wealthy and prominent Judge Eli Baxter of Cornucopia Plantation near Mt. Zion. Maria, in her letters to Julia, had mentioned Jane Baxter as the doctor's patient. Jane and Alva became the parents of two sons and one daughter. During the Civil War the doctor served in Company B of Terrell's Light Artillery, named for Dr. William Terrell of Sparta, Georgia. After the war Dr. Connell and his family considered moving to Texas, to land his father-in-law owned. However, in the fall of 1866 he was still in Georgia, where on a foxhunt he was described with awe by someone much younger than he as shouting "gleefully" and, in fact, quite electrifying "the party by his vivacious ardor."

That spark of life that lasted so long in Dr. Connell, which Maria described as finding "entertainment in everything," had also burned in self-confident, vigorous, and independent young Maria. However, by the time of her marriage to Connell in 1841, it had all but disappeared. Illness, fatigue, crumbled dreams, an unfortunate second marriage, and a breaking of the family ties with her father evidently shattered her orderly world. Several weeks before she died, Maria wrote her niece Annie, "I have been very ill."

Meanwhile, beyond the tiny domestic world Maria wrote about, the storm clouds of war were gathering momentum.

Maria's letters are our best record of the once vital life in Mt. Zion. The cotton plantations and farms are long gone, the homes are reduced to scattered foundations overgrown with scrub, the Mt. Zion Academy is but a few foundation stones far off the paved roads and never observed even by the seven present-day inhabitants of the region, lifelong residents all. The cultivated fields disappeared finally with the advent of the boll weevil in the early part of this century. The limited agriculture consists of fields of hay and tree farming. The Presbyterian Church still stands, but is no longer used, on the west side of Highway 77, about seven miles north of Sparta. Behind it, overgrown and protected from casual human incursions by ticks and snakes, lie the gravestones of Maria and her family. Maria's letters to Julia, however, endure. They shine through a century and a half not only as a memorial to a life cut short but also as a rich description of antebellum southern society in all its complexity and vibrancy.

BIBLIOGRAPHY

MANUSCRIPTS

Billings, John Shaw. Diaries, 1910–72. South Caroliniana Library, University of South Carolina, Columbia, S.C. (hereafter cited as SCL).
————. Papers. SCL.
Bird Family. Papers. Manuscript Room, University of Georgia, Athens, Ga.
"The Central Register of Convicts," 1834. Georgia Department of Archives and History.
Cumming Family. Letters, 1794–1954. Reece Library, Augusta College, Augusta, Ga.
"The Diary of Dolly Lunt Burge, 1848–1879." Edited by Christine Jacobson. Atlanta, Ga. Manuscript.
Halterman, Bryan M. "An Example of Civic Virtue in Augusta: Henry H. and Joseph B. Cumming." Augusta, Ga. Manuscript.
Hammond, James Henry. Papers. SCL.
Hammond-Bryan-Cumming Family. Papers. SCL.
"The Letters of Julien Cumming: Glimpses into the Antebellum South." Edited by Mary Ann Cashin, with an introduction by Edward J. Cashin. Augusta, Ga. Manuscript.

NEWSPAPERS

Augusta Chronicle
Charleston Courier
New York Morning Herald

INTERVIEWS

Cashin, Edward J. Telephone interview by editor, March 9, 1993.
Cashin, Mary Ann. Telephone interview by editor, April 8, 1993.

Connolly, Nancy Cumming. Telephone interviews by editor, March 10, 1993, and
    April 12, 1993.
Davis, Joseph S., Jr. Interview by editor. Sparta, Ga., October 16, 1992.
Halterman, Bryan M. Interview by editor. Edgefield, S.C., May 5, 1992.
Rainsford, Bettis. Interview by editor. Edgefield, S.C., May 5, 1992.
Walsh, Patrick. Telephone interview by editor, July 13, 1995.

ARTICLES

Bleser, Carol K. "Southern Plantation Wives and Slavery." In *The Meaning of South
    Carolina History,* edited by David Chesnutt and Clyde N. Wilson, 104–20. Colum-
    bia: University of South Carolina Press, 1991.
Bonner, James C. "Genesis of Agriculture Reform in the Cotton Belt." *Journal of
    Southern History* 9 (November 1943): 475–500.
————. "Profile of a Late Ante-Bellum Community." *American Historical Review* 4
    (July 1944): 663–80.
Fox-Genovese, Elizabeth. "Family and Female Identity in the Antebellum South:
    Sarah Gayle and Her Family." In *In Joy and in Sorrow,* edited by Carol Bleser, 15–31.
    New York: Oxford University Press, 1991.
Genovese, Eugene. " 'Our Family White and Black': Family and Household in the
    Southern Slaveholders' World View." In *In Joy and in Sorrow,* edited by Carol
    Bleser, 69–87. New York: Oxford University Press, 1991.
Painter, Nell Irvin. "Of Lily, Linda Brent, and Freud: A Non-Exceptionalist Approach
    to Race, Class, and Gender in the Slave South." *Georgia Historical Quarterly* 76
    (Summer 1992): 241–59.
Roark, James L. "Hidden Lives: Georgia's Free Women of Color." *Georgia Historical
    Quarterly* 76 (Summer 1992): 410–19.
Rudulph, Marilou Alston. "George Cooke and His Paintings." *Georgia Historical
    Quarterly* 43 (June 1960): 117–53.

GRAVESTONES

Gravestones in Beech Island Cemetery. Beech Island, S.C.
Gravestones in Milford Cemetery. Milford, Conn.
Gravestones in Mt. Zion Cemetery. Mt. Zion (Sparta), Ga.
Gravestones in Summerville Cemetery. Augusta, Ga.

SELECTED BOOKS AND PAMPHLETS

Standard reference books and many biographical directories on nineteenth-century Georgia and South Carolina have been consulted to compile the data needed by the reader to identify the people, places, and events mentioned in Maria Bryan's letters. They are included in the following bibliography:

Abbott, Morris W. *Milford Tombstone Inscriptions.* Milford, Conn.: By the author, 1967.

————. "The Bridge on the Wepawaug." Milford, Conn.: By the author, 1972.

————, comp. *Milford Cemetery: Index to Chart of Oldest Part.* Milford, Conn.: By the author, n.d.

Abbott, Susan Woodruff. *First Families of Milford, Conn.* Vol. 1. By the author, 1976.

Alden Associates, comp. *Hancock County, Georgia: Early Records.* Albany, Ga.: Alden Associates, 1965.

Alexander, Adele Logan. *Ambiguous Lives: Free Women of Color in Rural Georgia, 1789–1879.* Fayetteville: University of Arkansas Press, 1991.

Augusta Genealogical Society, comp. *Summerville Cemetery.* Augusta, Ga.: McGowan Printing Co., 1990.

Auser, Cortland P. *Nathaniel P. Willis.* New York: Twayne Publishers, 1969.

Baldwin, C. C. "Alexander Bryan of Milford, Connecticut, His Ancestors, and His Descendents." Cleveland, Ohio, 1889.

Bell, Malcolm, Jr. *Major Butler's Legacy: Five Generations of a Slaveholding Family.* Athens: University of Georgia Press, 1987.

Blassingame, John W. *The Slave Community: Plantation Life in the Antebellum South.* New York: Oxford University Press, 1979.

Bleser, Carol, ed. *The Hammonds of Redcliffe.* New York: Oxford University Press, 1981.

————. *Secret and Sacred: The Diaries of James Henry Hammond, a Southern Slaveholder.* New York: Oxford University Press, 1988.

Bonner, James C. *A History of Georgia Agriculture, 1732–1860.* Athens: University of Georgia Press, 1964.

Bright, Marion C., comp. *Early Georgia Portraits, 1715–1870.* Athens: University of Georgia Press, 1975.

Brockett, Rutheva Baldwin. *A Walking Tour of Historic Milford Connecticut, Founded 1639.* Milford, Conn.: N.p., 1991.

Burton, Orville Vernon. *In My Father's House Are Many Mansions: Family and Community in Edgefield, South Carolina.* Chapel Hill: University of North Carolina Press, 1985.

Bynum, Victoria E. *Unruly Women: The Politics of Social and Sexual Control in the Old South*. Chapel Hill: University of North Carolina Press, 1992.

Cashin, Edward J. *The Story of Augusta*. Augusta, Ga.: Richmond County Board of Education, 1980.

Cashin, Edward J., and Heard Robertson. *Augusta and the American Revolution: Events in the Georgia Back Country*. Darien, Ga.: Ashantilly Press, 1975.

Cashin, Joan E. *A Family Venture: Men and Women on the Southern Frontier*. New York: Oxford University Press, 1991.

Censer, Jane Turner. *North Carolina Planters and Their Children, 1800–1860*. Baton Rouge: Louisiana State University Press, 1984.

Chapman, Rev. F. W. *The Buckingham Family: Or the Descendants of Thomas Buckingham One of the First Settlers of Milford, Connecticut*. Hartford, Conn., 1872.

Clinton, Catherine. *The Plantation Mistress: Women's World in the Old South*. New York: Pantheon Books, 1982.

Cochran, Hamilton. *Noted American Duels and Hostile Encounters*. Philadelphia: Chilton Books, 1963.

Coleman, Kenneth, gen. ed. *A History of Georgia*. Athens: University of Georgia Press, 1977.

Cott, Nancy F. *The Bonds of Womanhood: "Women's Sphere" in New England, 1780–1835*. New Haven: Yale University Press, 1977.

Coulter, E. Merton. *John Jacobus Flournoy: Champion of the Common Man in the Antebellum South*. Savannah: Georgia Historical Society, 1942.

Davis, Mary E., ed. *The Neglected Thread: A Journal from the Calhoun Community, 1836–1842*. Columbia: University of South Carolina Press, 1951.

Farnham, Christie Anne. *The Education of the Southern Belle: Higher Education and Student Socialization in the Antebellum South*. New York: New York University Press, 1994.

Forrest, Mary. *Women of the South Distinguished in Literature*. New York, 1861.

Fox-Genovese, Elizabeth. *Within the Plantation Household: Black and White Women of the Old South*. Chapel Hill: University of North Carolina Press, 1988.

Franklin, John Hope. *A Southern Odyssey: Travelers in the Antebellum North*. Baton Rouge: Louisiana State University Press, 1976.

Friedman, Jean E. *The Enchanted Garden: Women and Community in the Evangelical South, 1830–1900*. Chapel Hill: University of North Carolina Press, 1985.

Gelles, Edith Belle. *Portia: The World of Abigail Adams*. Bloomington: Indiana University Press, 1992.

Genovese, Eugene D. *The World the Slaveholders Made: Two Essays in Interpretation*. New York: Pantheon Books, 1969.

———. *Roll, Jordan, Roll: The World the Slaves Made*. New York: Pantheon Books, 1974.

———. *The Slaveholders' Dilemma: Freedom and Progress in Southern Conservative Thought, 1820–1860*. Columbia: University of South Carolina Press, 1992.

Gutman, Herbert George. *The Black Family in Slavery and Freedom, 1750–1925*. New York: Pantheon Books, 1976.

Halttunen, Karen. *Confidence Men and Painted Women: A Study of Middle Class Culture in America, 1830–1870*. New Haven: Yale University Press, 1982.

Harris, William J. *Plain Folk and Gentry in a Slave Society: White Liberty and Black Slavery in Augusta's Hinterlands*. Hanover, N.H.: University Press of New England, 1985.

Hennig, Helen Kohn. *Great South Carolinians: From Colonial Days to the Confederate War*. Chapel Hill: University of North Carolina Press, 1940.

Herzstein, Robert E. *Great South Carolinians of a Later Date*. Chapel Hill: University of North Carolina Press, 1949.

———. *Henry Luce: A Political Portrait of the Man Who Created the American Century*. New York: Charles Scribner's Sons, 1994.

Houston, Martha Lou. *Marriages of Hancock County, Georgia, 1806 to 1850*. Baltimore: Genealogical Publishing Co., 1977.

Humphreys, Margaret. *Yellow Fever and the South*. New Brunswick, N.J.: Rutgers University Press, 1992.

Jones, Charles C., Jr. *The Dead Towns of Georgia*. Savannah, 1878.

Jones, Charles C., Jr., and Salem Dutcher. *Memorial History of Augusta, Georgia*. Spartanburg, S.C.: Reprint Co., 1966.

Kelley, Mary, ed. *The Power of Her Sympathy: The Autobiography and Journal of Catherine Maria Sedgwick*. Boston: Massachusetts Historical Society, 1993.

Kenzer, Robert C. *Kinship and Neighborhood in a Southern Community: Orange County, North Carolina, 1849–1881*. Knoxville: University of Tennessee Press, 1987.

Knight, Lucian Lamar. *Georgia's Landmarks, Memorials, and Legends*. Vol. 2. Atlanta: Byrd Printing Co., 1914.

Lebsock, Suzanne. *The Free Women of Petersburg: Status and Culture in a Southern Town, 1784–1860*. New York: W. W. Norton, 1984.

Lewis, Jan. *The Pursuit of Happiness: Family and Values in Jefferson's Virginia*. New York: Cambridge University Press, 1983.

Lippy, Charles H., and Peter W. Williams, eds. *Encyclopedia of the American Religious Experience: Studies of Traditions and Movements*. 3 vols. New York: Charles Scribner's Sons, 1988. Vol. 3: *The South*, by Samuel S. Hill.

Lytton, the Earl of. *The Life of Edward Bulwer: First Lord Lytton*. 2 vols. London: Macmillan and Co., 1913.

MacKethan, Lucinda H. *Daughters of Time: Creating Woman's Voice in Southern Story*. Athens: University of Georgia Press, 1990.

Matthews, Donald G. *Religion in the Old South*. Chicago: University of Chicago Press, 1977.

McMillen, Sally G. *Motherhood in the Old South: Pregnancy, Childbirth, and Infant Rearing*. Baton Rouge: Louisiana State University Press, 1990.

Meyers, Robert Manson, ed. *The Children of Pride: A True Story of Georgia and the Civil War*. New Haven: Yale University Press, 1972.

Milford Bicentennial Observance Commission. *Tour Guide Book of the Colonial Homes of Milford, Connecticut*. Milford, Conn.: Milford Bicentennial Observance Commission, n.d.

Miller, Stephen F. *The Bench and Bar of Georgia: Memoirs and Sketches*. Vols. 1, 2. Philadelphia, 1858.

Northen, William J. *Men of Mark in Georgia*. 7 vols. Spartanburg, S.C.: Reprint Co., 1974.

Orr, Dorothy. *A History of Education in Georgia*. Chapel Hill: University of North Carolina Press, 1950.

Otto, Rhea Cumming, comp. *1850 Census of Georgia (Hancock County)*. Savannah: N.p., 1980.

Peterson, Owen. *A Divine Discontent: The Life of Nathan S. S. Beman*. Macon, Ga.: Mercer University Press, 1986.

Reidy, Joseph P. *From Slavery to Agrarian Capitalism in the Cotton Plantation South*. Chapel Hill: University of North Carolina Press, 1992.

Rosenberg, Charles E. *The Cholera Years: The United States in 1832, 1849, and 1866*. Chicago: University of Chicago Press, 1987.

Rowland, A. Ray, and Helen Callahan. *Yesterday's Augusta*. Miami, Fla.: E. A. Seemann Publishing, 1976.

Rozier, John. *Black Boss: Political Revolution in a Georgia County*. Athens: University of Georgia Press, 1982.

———, ed. *The Granite Farm Letters: The Civil War Correspondence of Edgeworth and Sallie Bird*. Athens: University of Georgia Press, 1988.

Rubin, Louis D., Jr. *The Edge of the Swamp: A Study in the Literature and Society of the Old South*. Baton Rouge: Louisiana State University Press, 1989.

Scott, Anne Firor. *The Southern Lady: From Pedestal to Politics, 1830–1930*. Chicago: University of Chicago Press, 1970.

Shivers, Forrest. *The Land Between: A History of Hancock County, Georgia, to 1940.* Spartanburg, S.C.: Reprint Co., 1990.

Smith, Daniel Blake. *Inside the Great House: Planter Family Life in Eighteenth Century Chesapeake Society.* Ithaca, N.Y.: Cornell University Press, 1980.

Smith, Elizabeth Wiley. *The History of Hancock County, Georgia.* 2 vols. Washington, Ga.: Wilkes Publishing Co., 1974.

Smith, Robin Bolton, and Dale T. Johnson. *Tokens of Affection: The Portrait Miniature in America.* Washington, D.C.: National Museum of American Art, 1990.

Smith, Roy McBee. *Vardry McBee, 1775–1864: Man of Reason in an Age of Extremes.* Columbia, S.C.: R. L. Bryan Co., 1992.

Smith-Rosenberg, Carroll. *Disorderly Conduct: Visions of Gender in Victorian America.* New York: Oxford University Press, 1986.

Stowe, Steven M. *Intimacy and Power in the Old South: Ritual in the Lives of the Planters.* Baltimore: Johns Hopkins University Press, 1987.

Tebeau, Charlton W. *A History of Florida.* Coral Gables, Fla.: University of Miami Press, 1971.

Tucker, Edward. *Richard Henry Wilde: His Life and Selected Poems.* Athens: University of Georgia Press, 1966.

Ulrich, Laurel Thatcher. *A Midwife's Tale: The Life of Martha Ballard, Based on Her Diary, 1785–1812.* New York: Alfred A. Knopf, 1991.

Utley, Francis Lee, and Marion R. Hemperley. *Placenames of Georgia: Essays of John H. Goff.* Athens: University of Georgia Press, 1975.

Wainwright, Loudon. *The Great American Magazine: An Inside History of* Life. New York: Alfred A. Knopf, 1986.

Wakelyn, John L. *Biographical Directory of the Confederacy.* Westport, Conn.: Greenwood Press, 1977.

Wood, W. Kirk, ed. *A Northern Daughter and a Southern Wife: The Civil War Reminiscences and Letters of Katharine H. Cumming, 1860–1865.* Augusta, Ga.: Richmond County Historical Society, 1976.

Woodward, C. Vann, ed. *Mary Chesnut's Civil War.* New Haven: Yale University Press, 1981.

Woodward, C. Vann, and Elisabeth Muhlenfeld, eds. *The Private Mary Chesnut: The Unpublished Civil War Diaries.* New York: Oxford University Press, 1981.

WPA. *History of Milford Connecticut 1639–1939.* Bridgeport, Conn.: Braumworth and Co., 1939.

Wyatt-Brown, Bertram. *Southern Honor: Ethics and Behavior in the Old South.* New York: Oxford University Press, 1982.

————. *Honor and Violence in the Old South.* New York: Oxford University Press, 1986.

Yardley, Jonathan. *Our Kind of People: The Story of an American Family.* New York: Weidenfeld and Nicholson, 1989.

INDEX

Abolitionism, xxiv, xxvi; in England, 237

Abott, John, 275, 276

Alabama: Joseph Bryan's new plantation in, 184, 204; travel to, 205, 331–32

Albion (magazine), 92, 93, 279, 361

Alexander, Adele Logan, xxxiv

Alf. *See* Cumming, Alfred

Allen, Capt., 142, 146, 155

Allen, Ina, 64, 198, 211, 318

Alston, Mr., 40, 41, 79, 80, 86, 105

Alston, Mrs., 18, 40, 41, 80, 84, 105, 121, 302

Alston, Anne, 41, 84, 105, 108

Alston, Augustus, 66, 80

Alston, Caroline, 126

Alston, Gideon, 109–10

Alston, Henrietta, 12, 18, 30, 41, 48, 59, 64, 66, 72, 77, 78, 79, 80, 98

Alston, Joseph, 209

Alston, Mrs. Joseph, 209

Alston, Willis, 69, 302

Alston family, xxxii, 12, 13, 75, 76, 98, 105, 107

Ambiguous Lives (Alexander), xxxiv

American Flower Garden Directory (Buist), 337

American Hotel, New York, 256–57

American Tract Society, 347

Amy Cranstoun (Sedgwick), 301

Annadale, letters from, 340–46, 359–73

Annette (Connell servant), 361, 371

Anti-Semitism, 342

Apling, Anne, 92, 95, 98, 146

Armour, Jane, xxxii, 76, 100, 165, 206, 246, 248, 285, 291, 292, 334, 368, 369, 375

Athens, Tenn., letter from, 81–82

Atticus (Plumer), 241

Augusta, Ga.: Maria's visits to, 8, 125, 335, 348–49, 361; fire in, 91, 93, 186; Sand Hills near, 101; yellow fever in, 261, 264, 265, 266; development of, 376

Augusta Canal, 375

Aunt Wales. *See* Wales, Julia Bryan

Bailey, Mr. (teacher), 15–16

Bailey, Mrs. (widow), xxxii, 24, 51, 55, 65, 72, 74, 77, 170, 221, 222, 337

Bailey, Alexander, 55

Bailey, Elizabeth, xxxii, 156, 222

Bailey, John, 65

Bailey, Margaret, xxxii, 24, 45, 50, 54, 55, 65, 72, 88, 108, 109, 170, 219